Navigating the Souring Seas

Navigating the Souring Seas explores how ocean acidification (OA) – a significant yet under-governed environmental threat – is being addressed on the global stage. Bridging science, law, and international policy, this interdisciplinary book introduces global experimentalist governance as an innovative and adaptable framework for tackling complex and uncertain issues like OA. It provides a clear overview of the scientific background of OA and maps the international governance landscape, identifying it as a regime complex. Through detailed interview-based case studies of the OA Alliance and the International Maritime Organization, this book evaluates real world efforts to govern OA and highlights how experimentalist features, such as flexibility, learning, and multilevel collaboration, can enhance their effectiveness. Accessible and timely, this book is essential reading for scholars, students, policymakers, and environmental practitioners seeking practical, forward-looking governance strategies for ocean and climate challenges. It offers both theoretical insights and concrete recommendations for improving global environmental governance.

Annika Frosch is a research fellow at University College London (UCL) and a DAAD-funded PhD graduate from the European University Institute. This book is based on funded research stays at University of California, Davis, National University of Singapore, and UCL. She is an emerging leader in ocean acidification governance, advising governments on climate–ocean policy and shaping negotiations at the International Maritime Organization.

Transnational Environmental Law

TEL

SERIES EDITORS

Thijs Etty, Amsterdam University College, University of Amsterdam, The Netherlands
Josephine van Zeben, European University Institute, Italy

Transnational Environmental Law (TEL) is a series of books for the study of environmental law and governance beyond the state. It approaches legal and regulatory developments with an interest in the contribution of non-state actors and an awareness of the multi-level governance context in which contemporary environmental law unfolds. TEL has a broad disciplinary focus open to scholarly contributions covering a wide range of environmental issues and the evolving dynamics between environmental law and other legal disciplines. TEL strives for a new generation of environmental scholarship that will bridge geographical boundaries, scholarly styles and generations.

BOOKS IN THE SERIES

Jessika Eichler and Mario G. Aguilera, *Indigenous Environmental Rights: Towards a Holistic Regime*
Roger Merino, *Governing International Commons: From Polycentric to Plurinational Governance in the Amazon*
Annika Frosch, *Navigating the Souring Seas: The Global Experimentalist Governance of Ocean Acidification*
Agung Wardana, *Turning Defenders into Defendants: The Use of Lawfare against Environmental Activists in Southeast Asia*

Navigating the Souring Seas

The Global Experimentalist Governance of Ocean Acidification

Annika Frosch
University College London

TEL

CAMBRIDGE
UNIVERSITY PRESS

CAMBRIDGE
UNIVERSITY PRESS

Shaftesbury Road, Cambridge CB2 8EA, United Kingdom

One Liberty Plaza, 20th Floor, New York, NY 10006, USA

477 Williamstown Road, Port Melbourne, VIC 3207, Australia

314–321, 3rd Floor, Plot 3, Splendor Forum, Jasola District Centre, New Delhi – 110025, India

103 Penang Road, #05–06/07, Visioncrest Commercial, Singapore 238467

Cambridge University Press is part of Cambridge University Press & Assessment, a department of the University of Cambridge.

We share the University's mission to contribute to society through the pursuit of education, learning and research at the highest international levels of excellence.

www.cambridge.org
Information on this title: www.cambridge.org/9781009689113

DOI: 10.1017/9781009689083

When citing this work, please include a reference to the DOI 10.1017/9781009689083

First published 2026

A catalogue record for this publication is available from the British Library

Library of Congress Cataloging-in-Publication Data
Names: Frosch, Annika author
Title: Navigating the souring seas : the global experimentalist governance of ocean acidification / Annika Frosch.
Description: Cambridge, United Kingdom ; New York, NY : Cambridge University Press, 2026. | Series: Transnational environmental law | Includes bibliographical references and index.
Identifiers: LCCN 2025034312 (print) | LCCN 2025034313 (ebook) | ISBN 9781009689113 hardback | ISBN 9781009689083 ebook
Subjects: LCSH: Ocean acidification – Law and legislation | Marine pollution – Law and legislation | Law of the sea | Environmental law, International
Classification: LCC K3590.4 .F76 2026 (print) | LCC K3590.4 (ebook) | DDC 341.4/5–dc23/eng/20250730
LC record available at https://lccn.loc.gov/2025034312
LC ebook record available at https://lccn.loc.gov/2025034313

ISBN 978-1-009-68911-3 Hardback

I saw with regret, (and all scientific men have shared this feeling) that whilst the number of accurate instruments was daily increasing, we were still ignorant

—Alexander von Humboldt, *Personal Narrative of Travels to the Equinoctial Regions of America, During the Years 1799–1804 – Volume 1*

CONTENTS

FIGURES

TABLES

PREFACE BY THE SERIES EDITORS

The oceans cover more than 70 per cent of our planet, sustaining ecosystems, economies, and human societies alike. Yet, beneath the waves, a silent transformation is underway. Ocean acidification (OA), driven primarily by the absorption of anthropogenic carbon dioxide emissions, is altering the chemical composition of seawater. The consequences of this process are profound: the weakening of coral reefs, the disruption of marine food chains, and the destabilisation of livelihoods that depend on healthy marine ecosystems. Although the scientific community has documented these changes with growing precision, the governance of OA has lagged significantly behind the science. Legal frameworks remain fragmentary, institutional responses piecemeal, and global awareness of the issue strikingly limited.

In *Navigating the Souring Seas: The Global Experimentalist Governance of Ocean Acidification*, Annika Frosch addresses this governance deficit with analytical depth and conceptual innovation. By combining insights from environmental science, international law, and transnational governance, this book brings long overdue attention to a global challenge that too often remains overshadowed by broader debates on climate change. While OA is intimately linked to climate dynamics, its governance requires distinct approaches. As Frosch demonstrates, the fragmented and uncertain nature of OA demands governance frameworks that are adaptive, inclusive, and capable of responding to rapidly evolving scientific knowledge.

At the heart of this book is the proposal of global experimentalist governance as a promising pathway for tackling OA. This approach emphasises flexibility, multilevel engagement, and iterative learning. Rather than relying on rigid, top-down legal regimes, experimentalist governance invites diverse actors – states, international organisations, alliances, and civil society networks – to contribute to a shared problem-solving process. Crucially, it allows for recalibration in light of new evidence, an essential feature given the scientific uncertainties and cross-sectoral implications of OA.

By articulating a model of global experimentalist governance, this book provides a conceptual framework with resonance well beyond OA. It offers lessons for addressing other complex, transboundary environmental challenges marked by uncertainty and institutional fragmentation, from biodiversity loss to plastic pollution. At the same time, it delivers actionable policy insights, bridging the gap between scholarly theorising and practical governance solutions.

In line with the aims of the *Transnational Environmental Law* (*TEL*) book series, *Navigating the Souring Seas* exemplifies interdisciplinary engagement, theoretical originality, and policy relevance. It contributes to emerging debates on how best to govern global environmental commons under conditions of scientific complexity and institutional pluralism. In doing so, it underscores the importance of adaptive and inclusive governance in the Anthropocene.

We are delighted to include this timely and important work in the *TEL* series as an essential resource for those who share the urgent task of ensuring that the world's oceans remain a foundation of life for generations to come.

Thijs Etty and Josephine van Zeben

ACKNOWLEDGEMENTS

This book began as a PhD dissertation written between 2019 and 2024 at the European University Institute (EUI) – a period shaped by personal growth, global upheaval, and academic exploration. What started as a scholarly inquiry soon transformed into a journey across disciplines, institutions, and continents: from the hills of Tuscany to the cliffs of California, the museums of London, and the hawker centres of Singapore. I remain deeply grateful for the people and places that helped shape both this work and the person behind it.

First and foremost, I owe immense thanks to **Professor Joanne Scott** for her unwavering patience and belief in me. She challenged me intellectually, supported me personally, and never recoiled when I ventured into the thorniest scientific puzzles. Her guidance – always thoughtful and kind – taught me that even the smallest details matter, a lesson I sorely needed as someone who naturally gravitates towards the big picture. I am equally grateful to my dissertation committee – **Professors Jolene Lin, Gráinne de Búrca, and Karen Scott**. Your constructive critiques sharpened my arguments and broadened my thinking in ways that shaped this book. Many of the questions you posed have stayed with me, sparking continued reflection long after our discussions ended.

This project would not be what it is without the generous support of several institutions. I am particularly thankful to the **University of California, Davis**, and especially to the **Center for Environmental Policy and Behavior** and the **Bodega Marine Laboratory** for welcoming me into a community of natural scientists. Special thanks to **Professor Tessa Hill** for inviting me to join her research group, to **Meghan Zulian** for her invaluable conversations (both scientific and otherwise), and to **Professor Tyler Scott** for showing me the ropes. To **Manny, Jacquie, Keira, Sam, Claire, Lily, Audrey, Alisha, and Emily** – thank you for sharing your knowledge, your fieldwork adventures, and your favourite local creatures. You made science both accessible and fun.

At **University College London's Shipping and Oceans Research Group**, I was introduced to diplomacy and shipping decarbonisation. Here, I learnt that no matter how well you prepare for an interview, it often takes its own direction – more like improvisational theatre than scripted dialogue. I am grateful to **Professor Tristan Smith** and **Dr Nishatabbas Rehmatulla** for including me in their group and facilitating access to the **International Maritime Organization**. Their insights and openness helped me navigate the complexities of this highly technical and political space. Thanks also to **Marie, James, and Domagoj** for the many lunches, conversations, and shared laughter along the way.

My visit to the **Asia-Pacific Centre for Environmental Law** at the **National University of Singapore** provided yet another perspective. I thank **Professor**

Jolene Lin for transforming what was intended to be a brief conference trip into a profoundly enriching academic stay. I also appreciate **Shirley Mak** and **Elicia Chia** for their logistical expertise. **Sroyon, Kwang, and Kanika** – thank you for the unforgettable explorations of Singapore's food, forests, and photography spots.

I am indebted to the team at the **OA Alliance**, whose tireless work continues to inspire. **Jessie Turner**, thank you for your energy, insight, and unwavering support – you've been both a sounding board and a cheerleader, and I'm fortunate to have you in my corner. I am also grateful to **Inken and Jula** for their thoughtful perspectives and patience as I navigated the turbulent waters where science, policy, and law collide.

Special thanks go to **Professor Igor Tkalec** for his technical assistance and to **Professor Jochen von Bernstorff** and **Professor Andreas Kulick** – thank you for encouraging me to apply to the EUI in the first place. I am also grateful to **Professor Helen Findlay** for addressing those tough scientific questions that most would prefer to avoid.

To those who opened their homes to me during fieldwork and research trips – **Mary Lou and Tim**, **Tessa and Peter**, and **Birgit og Sven** – thank you for your generosity, good company, and excellent meals. *Tak for at forkæle mig og følge mig rundt om søen efter middagen.*

To my friends and loved ones: thank you for the grounding, the joy, and the necessary distractions. **Nikita, Natalia, Niklas, and Chester** – your legendary brunches and garden parties provided much-needed levity. **Isaure, Marc, and Chris** – thank you for the bike rides, board games, spontaneous performances, and occasional chaos. **Daniel and Laura**, your calm wit and loyal friendship offered balance and clarity when I needed it most. **Miguel**, thank you for reminding me to laugh, for your impeccable taste in food, and for helping me enjoy even the things I thought I hated (including mussels). **Davide**, thank you for the time 'we all lived in Florence together', and for cheering on my unexpected minigolf glory. **Órlaith and Mira**, thank you for tolerating my ocean monologues and providing refreshing counterpoints to the intensity of academic life. Lastly, I want to thank **Anne** – my flatmate, travel companion, intellectual sparring partner, and dear friend. Your fierce intellect and honest feedback shaped this work more than you know. Your loyalty, humour, and sheer presence made the ups and downs of writing and living abroad not only bearable but often joyful. I could not have asked for a better companion for this long and strange adventure.

Ich möchte mich auch bei meiner Familie bedanken: **Ursula, Walter, Markus und Sabrina**. Eure unerschöpfliche Neugier hat mich von klein auf begleitet und durch diese Jahre getragen. Danke, dass ihr mich immer unterstützt habt – auch auf einem Weg, der euch nicht immer vertraut war.

ABBREVIATIONS

AALCO	Asian African Legal Consultative Organization
BBNJ	Biodiversity beyond national jurisdiction
BIOACID	Biological Impacts of Ocean Acidification Program
BROA	Brazil Ocean Acidification Research Network
Ca^{2+}	Calcium
$CaCO_3$	Calcium carbonate
CARICOM	Caribbean Community
CBD	Convention on Biological Diversity
CCS	Carbon capture and storage
CO_2	Carbon dioxide
CO_3^{2-}	Carbonate
EAA	European Economic Area
EEZ	Exclusive economic zone
EPOCA	European Project on Ocean Acidification
EU ETS	European Union Emissions Trading System
GESAMP	Joint Group of Experts on the Scientific Aspects of Marine Environmental Protection
GGC	Global governance complexes
GOA-ON	Global Ocean Acidification Observing Network
H	Hydrogen
H_2CO_3	Carbonic acid
H^+	Hydrogen ions
H_2O	Water
H_2SO_4	Sulphuric acid
High Seas Treaty	Agreement under the United Nations Convention on the Law of the Sea for the conservation and sustainable use of marine biological diversity of areas beyond national jurisdiction
HNO_3	Nitric acid
ICAO	International Civil Aviation Organization
IMCO	Inter-Governmental Maritime Consultative Organization
IMO	International Maritime Organization
INTERTANKO	International Association of Independent Tanker Owners
IOC–UNESCO	Intergovernmental Oceanographic Commission
IPCC	Intergovernmental Panel on Climate Change
ISWG-GHG	Intersessional Working Group on Reduction of Greenhouse Gas Emissions from Ships
mCDR	Marine carbon dioxide removal
MEPC	Marine Environment Protection Committee

MPA	Marine protected areas
NAP	National action plans
NDC	Nationally determined contribution
NO_x	Nitrogen oxides
OA	Ocean acidification
OA Alliance/OAA	Ocean Acidification Alliance
OAiRUG	Ocean Acidification International Reference User Group
OARS	Ocean Acidification Research for Sustainability
OECD	Organization for Economic Co-operation and Development
P	Potential
PCC	Pacific Coast Collaborative
PPM	Parts per million
SO_3	Sulphur trioxide
SO_x	Sulphur oxides
The Convention	Convention on the International Maritime Organization
UKOA	United Kingdom's Ocean Acidification Research Programme
UN	United Nations
UNCLOS	United Nations Convention on the Law of the Sea
UNEP	United Nations Environment Programme
UNFCCC	United Nations Framework Convention on Climate Change

CHAPTER 1
Introduction

One of the most, if not the most, daunting problems humankind is currently facing is climate change. The issue is ubiquitous. Constant reminders that climate change is progressing are provided daily when watching, reading, or listening to the news. The impacts of climate change, including storms, heat, and drought, are well known and frequently mentioned.[1] However, not all effects of climate change have received equal attention. Those impacts that are not immediately visible have particularly been flying under the radar. One such impact is ocean acidification (OA).[2] The oceans have long served as an enormous carbon sink. In fact, they have absorbed up to 39 per cent of the carbon dioxide (CO_2) produced since the Industrial Revolution.[3] Although this uptake has limited the amount of CO_2 in the atmosphere and thereby mitigated impacts on land, it has come at a high price.[4] Ocean chemistry is undergoing substantial changes, including a 30–40 per cent decrease in ocean pH compared to pre-industrial levels.[5] These changes are referred

[1] See, for example, Mark Poynting and Esme Stallard, 'How Climate Change Worsens Heatwaves, Droughts, Wildfires and Floods' (*BBC News*, 9 August 2021) www.bbc.com/news/science-environment-58073295 accessed 8 December 2023; Rachel Ramirez, 'Without Climate Change, These Extreme Weather Events Would Not Have Happened' (*CNN*, 15 June 2023) www.cnn.com/2023/06/15/world/extreme-weather-events-climate-change/index.html accessed 8 December 2023; Dawn Liu and Denise Chow, 'China's Summer of Extremes Has Farmers Worried' (*NBC News*, 8 August 2023) www.nbcnews.com/news/world/china-floods-drought-farming-wheat-climate-change-rcna96111 accessed 8 December 2023.

[2] Cf. Sandra L. Cooke and Sojung C. Kim, 'Exploring the "Evil Twin of Global Warming": Public Understanding of Ocean Acidification in the United States' (2019) 41 *Science Communication* 66, 67.

[3] Galen A. McKinley and Others, 'External Forcing Explains Recent Decadal Variability of the Ocean Carbon Sink' (2020) 1 *AGU Advances* 1, 1.

[4] Cf. Megumi O. Chikamoto, Pedro DiNezio and Nicole Lovenduski, 'Long-Term Slowdown of Ocean Carbon Uptake by Alkalinity Dynamics' (2023) 50 *Geophysical Research Letters* 1, 1; Hilal Elver and Nilufer Oral, 'Food Security, Fisheries and Ocean Acidification: A Human Rights Based Approach' in David L. VanderZwaag, Nilufer Oral and Tim Stephens (eds), *Research Handbook on Ocean Acidification Law and Policy* (Edward Elgar Publishing 2021) 75.

[5] Helen S. Findlay and others, 'Ocean Acidification around the UK and Ireland' (2022) *MCCIP Rolling Evidence Updates* 1, 3.

to as OA. However, OA is more complex than it initially appears, as it is not solely related to CO_2 emissions. For instance, processes in the coastal zone can also create OA hotspots in coastal waters.[6] Whether in the open ocean or coastal areas, OA negatively impacts many marine organisms and ecosystems.[7]

Once CO_2 reaches the seawater, a series of chemical reactions follows, causing the water to become more acidic.[8] This rise in acidity makes carbon ions less available as building blocks for shells, corals, and other marine organisms. Therefore, building and maintaining structures such as shells becomes difficult for these so-called calcifying organisms, including oysters, sea urchins, and some types of plankton.[9] However, non-calcifying species can also be affected by these changes in ocean chemistry. For example, certain fish may experience behavioural changes and become unable to detect predators.[10] Thus, more acidic waters pose a risk to the entire food web as well as to the people relying on it. Many individuals and economies depend on fish and shellfish for their daily calorie intake.[11] Chapter 2 will provide the non-scientist reader with a detailed overview of what the problem is and its repercussions.

While OA has become a topic of intense discussion in the scientific literature,[12] in the international social science literature, the problem has received much less attention (see below). Indeed, policy changes to address this issue at the international or regional level are scarce, and no laws have been passed at the international level to address OA. To increase understanding of OA and the governance landscape surrounding this issue, this book will explain OA for non-scientists and investigate the problem from a governance perspective. More specifically, this book will explore how OA is and should be governed in light of the nature of the problem it presents.

When examining how OA is and should be governed, the focus is on identifying the forms of governance applied to OA rather than providing exhaustive details of the governance landscape. In addressing the 'should' question, the focus is on assessing the suitability of a global experimentalist governance framework for OA. That said, a brief appraisal of the current governance landscape is included in Chapters 3 and 5 (for a longer explanation, see Annex B).

[6] Ryan Kelly and others, 'Mitigating Local Causes of Ocean Acidification with Existing Laws' (2011) 332 *Science (New York, N.Y.)* 1036, 1036.

[7] See, for example, Scott C. Doney and others, 'Ocean Acidification: The Other CO_2 Problem' (2009) 1 *Annual Review of Marine Science* 169.

[8] Ibid., 172.

[9] Steeve Comeau and others, 'Pacific-Wide Contrast Highlights Resistance of Reef Calcifiers to Ocean Acidification' (2014) 281 *Proceedings: Biological Sciences/The Royal Society* 1, 1; Secretariat of the Convention on Biological Diversity and others, *An Updated Synthesis of the Impacts of Ocean Acidification on Marine Biodiversity* (2014) 7, 13, 14.

[10] Arctic Monitoring and Assessment Programme and others, *AMAP Assessment 2013: Arctic Ocean Acidification* (2013) 50; Secretariat of the Convention on Biological Diversity and others (n 9) 8, 46, 70.

[11] Secretariat of the Convention on Biological Diversity and others (n 9) 82.

[12] Cf. Dan Laffoley and others (eds), *An Introduction to Ocean Acidification: What It Is, What We Know, and What May Happen* (International Union for Conservation of Nature and Natural Resources IUCN 2017) 8.

Before starting to explore the question posed above in the following chapters, this introduction will provide an overview of the relevant social science literature regarding OA (Section 1.1), the methods used (Section 1.2), and the argumentation employed (Section 1.3).

1.1 The Relevant Social Science Literature

Before delving into the question of how OA is and should be governed, it is imperative to understand the literature. As OA is an environmental problem that can be scientifically explained, the state of the natural science literature also needs to be consulted in addition to the law and governance literature. Without a firm understanding of the science behind OA – including, for example, the problem's causes – it is difficult to find governance solutions that can tackle OA. OA, by its nature, is a very complex and creeping problem that will endanger ecosystems and humans alike. Unsurprisingly, OA science and scientific literature have grown rapidly over the years to gain a better grasp of the issue.[13] In fact, research on OA has become one of the fastest-developing fields in the marine sciences.[14] This rich body of literature explains not just the causes of OA but also engages in many more important questions surrounding OA. For instance, researchers attempt, through different experiments, to understand the reaction and resilience of various species in the face of changing ocean chemistry.[15] Researchers are also working to understand how OA and other ocean stressors, including fishing and ocean warming, interact.[16] Thus, the body of scientific literature contains many highly specific and technical papers, which makes it difficult for the non-scientific reader to understand. Nevertheless, a sound understanding of OA is necessary to answer the research question and, specifically, to investigate how OA should be governed. Therefore, Chapter 2 of this book will provide the non-scientist reader with an overview of what OA entails.

While the scientific literature is quickly growing, the topic has only recently entered the social science literature as a point of discussion. This review will provide an overview of the development of two strands of literature relevant to this book: the law and global governance literature. First, it will examine how these two bodies of literature understand and frame OA. Second, it will explore how they currently classify the governance landscape of OA. Finally, it will summarise both the

[13] Cf. ibid.

[14] Ulf Riebesell and Jean-Pierre Gattuso, 'Lessons Learned from Ocean Acidification Research' (2015) 5 *Nature Climate Change* 12, 12.

[15] Daniel S. Swezey and others, 'Evolved Differences in Energy Metabolism and Growth Dictate the Impacts of Ocean Acidification on Abalone Aquaculture' (2020) 117 *Proceedings of the National Academy of Sciences* 26513; Kristy Kroeker and others, 'Kroeker K. J., Kordas R. L., Crim R. N. & Singh G. G. – Meta-Analysis Reveals Negative yet Variable Effects of Ocean Acidification on Marine Organisms', (2010) 13 *Ecology Letters* 1419.

[16] Isabelle M. Côté, Emily S. Darling and Christopher J. Brown, 'Interactions among Ecosystem Stressors and Their Importance in Conservation' (2016) 283 *Proceedings of the Royal Society B: Biological Sciences* 20152592.

legal and governance literatures. This book positions itself within and builds on these literatures, including their shared understanding, framing, and description of the governance landscape concerning OA. Therefore, this literature review will closely analyse how both law and governance literature understand and frame OA (Section 1.1.1) and describe the existing governance landscape of OA (Section 1.1.2). After this, the discussions of OA law and governance will be examined separately (Section 1.1.3). This is because, despite their common debates regarding understanding, framing, and governance landscape, they focus on different questions and constitute separate bodies of literature.

1.1.1 Understanding and Framing of Ocean Acidification

The understanding of how OA can be framed and presented as an issue has rapidly evolved in the international law and governance literature. Originally, many authors, such as Simons and Stephens,[17] Baird and colleagues,[18] Downing,[19] Stephens,[20] and Kim,[21] focused their discussions on OA primarily on mitigation, specifically the reduction of CO_2 emissions. At most, geoengineering activities were considered alongside emission reductions.[22] This narrow perspective on OA restricts the initial discussions regarding law and governance to the mitigation of these emissions. The only outlier at the time appears to be Billé and colleagues,[23] who considered, among other topics, 'Local Factors of Ocean Acidification' and 'Strengthening Ecosystem Resilience to Ocean Acidification'.[24] Otherwise, Simons and Stephens' thoughts on OA reflect the characteristics of the early OA literature: '[i]n contrast to climate change, where there is the possibility of mitigation, adaptation and even geoengineering solutions (…) ocean acidification can only be effectively addressed by mitigating CO_2 emissions or drawing them down into terrestrial biomass. With ocean acidification there is limited capacity to adapt'.[25]

[17] Meridith Simons and Tim Stephens, 'Ocean Acidification: Addressing the Other CO_2 Problem' (2009) 12 *Asia Pacific Journal of Environmental Law* 1.

[18] Rachel Baird, Meredith Simons and Tim Stephens, 'Ocean Acidification: A Litmus Test for International Law' (2009) 3 *Carbon & Climate Law Review* 459.

[19] Yangmay Downing, 'Ocean Acidification and Protection under International Law from Negative Effects: A Burning Issue amongst a Sea of Regimes?' (2013) 2 *Cambridge Journal of International and Comparative Law* 242.

[20] Tim Stephens, 'Warming Waters and Souring Seas: Climate Change and Ocean Acidification' in Donald Rothwell and others (eds), *The Oxford Handbook of the Law of the Sea* (1st ed., Oxford University Press 2016) https://academic.oup.com/edited-volume/42608/chapter/357548970 accessed 12 November 2023.

[21] Rakhyun E. Kim, 'Is a New Multilateral Environmental Agreement on Ocean Acidification Necessary?: Is a New Agreement on Ocean Acidification Necessary?' (2012) 21 *Review of European Community & International Environmental Law* 243.

[22] Ibid., 249, 250; Downing (n 19) 261; Simons and Stephens (n 17) 10, 11; Baird, Simons and Stephens (n 18) 464, 465.

[23] Raphaël Billé and others, 'Taking Action against Ocean Acidification: A Review of Management and Policy Options' (2013) *Environmental Management* 761.

[24] Ibid., 767, 768.

[25] Simons and Stephens (n 17) 5.

Simons and Stephens, as was typical for the literature at the time, only focus on and understand the need to discuss the mitigation of CO_2 emissions when tackling OA. They do not see any potential for adaptation, for example, which is a widely discussed aspect of OA today. However, this perception of OA has changed, and authors are increasingly moving away from this narrow understanding of the problem. Over the years, authors have painted a more holistic picture of OA, in line with the continuously evolving scientific literature. For example, thanks to authors such as Harrould-Kolieb and Hoegh-Guldberg,[26] Harrould-Kolieb,[27] Makomere and McDonald,[28] Scott,[29] Jagers and colleagues,[30] and Gordon,[31] non-climate drivers of OA, as well as considerations related to resilience and adaptation, redress, and restoration, have entered the discussions apart from mitigation. Thus, the law and governance literature has developed in accordance with the scientific literature, broadening its understanding of OA, including the aspects that are necessary to consider when tackling the issue in a holistic manner.

In the same vein, the framing or presentation of OA as an issue has been discussed. A frequently raised question in both the law and governance literatures is whether OA can be considered a concurrent problem to climate change or an effect of it. In other words, the question is whether OA is a parallel but distinct issue to climate change or an effect of it. Downing, for instance, suggests that '[o]cean acidification is a problem concurrent to climate change, sharing the same root cause of anthropogenic CO_2 emissions'.[32] Other authors express similar opinions.[33] In contrast to these authors, Harrould-Kolieb[34] recently relied on definitions of climate change elaborated by the Intergovernmental Panel on Climate Change (IPCC) to show that OA is an (adverse) effect of, rather than a concurrent problem with, climate change.[35]

[26] Ellycia R. Harrould-Kolieb and Ove Hoegh-Guldberg, 'A Governing Framework for International Ocean Acidification Policy' (2019) 102 *Marine Policy* 10.

[27] Ellycia R. Harrould-Kolieb, 'Framing Ocean Acidification to Mobilise Action under Multilateral Environmental Agreements' (2020) 104 *Environmental Science & Policy* 129.

[28] Reuben Makomere and Jan McDonald, 'Responding to Ocean Acidification beyond Climate Governance' in Jan McDonald, Jeffrey McGee and Richard Barnes (eds), *Research Handbook on Climate Change, Oceans and Coasts* (Edward Elgar Publishing 2020) https://china.elgaronline.com/view/edcoll/9781788112222/9781788112222.00026.xml accessed 12 November 2023.

[29] Karen N. Scott, 'Ocean Acidification: A Due Diligence Obligation under the LOSC' (2020) 35 *The International Journal of Marine and Coastal Law* 382.

[30] Sverker C. Jagers and others, 'Societal Causes of, and Responses to, Ocean Acidification' (2019) 48 *Ambio* 816.

[31] Jennicca Gordon, 'The Legal Implications of Ocean Acidification' in Paul G. Harris (ed), *Routledge Handbook of Marine Governance and Global Environmental Change* (Routledge 2022).

[32] Downing (n 19) 250.

[33] Scott, 'Ocean Acidification' (n 29) 383; Kim (n 21) 247, 254, 257; cf. Dan Laffoley and others, 'Ocean Acidification: Scientific Understanding and Challenges' in David L. VanderZwaag, Nilufer Oral and Tim Stephens (eds), *Research Handbook on Ocean Acidification Law and Policy* (Edward Elgar Publishing 2021) 12; Dorothee Herr and others, *Ocean Acidification: International Policy and Governance Options* (2014) 11.

[34] Ellycia R. Harrould-Kolieb, '(Re)Framing Ocean Acidification in the Context of the United Nations Framework Convention on Climate Change (UNFCCC) and Paris Agreement' (2019) 19 *Climate Policy* 1225.

[35] Ibid., 1229.

Harrould-Kolieb identifies that, according to article 1(2) of the United Nations Framework Convention on Climate Change (UNFCCC), climate change is 'change in climate which is attributed directly or indirectly to human activity that alters the composition of the global atmosphere'.[36] According to the author, who relies on the IPCC for her argumentation, one interpretation of the word 'climate' within this definition includes the state of the climate system.[37] Therefore, climate change is a change in the state of the climate system.[38] As the climate system also encompasses the ocean and not just the atmosphere, put simply, this interpretation of climate change also includes changes to the ocean resulting from an altered composition of the atmosphere caused by human activity.[39] Hence, Harrould-Kolieb argues that: '[g]iven that ocean acidification is a result of the absorption of anthropogenic CO_2 into the ocean from the atmosphere it can therefore justifiably be understood as being an adverse effect of climate change under the Convention'.[40]

Although Harrould-Kolieb makes an important point – namely, that framing OA as a concurrent problem to climate change has led to several shortcomings regarding OA governance (see below) and needs to be reconsidered – the author's argument is difficult to follow. For example, it is unclear why OA is considered an effect of climate change and not part of climate change itself. If the word 'climate' in the definition of 'climate change' refers to the climate system, which includes the ocean and its changes, why is OA only viewed as an effect of climate change and not as part of this change of the climate system itself? Especially since OA can be attributed indirectly to human activity and alters the composition of the global atmosphere by absorbing CO_2 and maintaining a balance of the levels of CO_2 between the atmosphere and ocean (see Chapter 2). Even though some steps in the argument seem to be omitted, the importance of Harrould-Kolieb's point remains unchanged: OA should not be treated separately from climate change (but rather as an effect of climate change). This connection between the issues is, as Harrould-Kolieb also mentions, aligned with the 2010 Cancun Agreements, in which OA is included in a footnote as an example of a slow-onset event.[41] These slow-onset events fall under the adverse effects of climate change.[42] The author provides two valid reasons why this artificial split between the two issues is problematic.

Harrould-Kolieb criticises the framing of OA as a concurrent problem at the international level, as it has led to two problems regarding OA governance.[43] First, the UNFCCC has been interpreted as having no obligation to address OA because, being a 'concurrent' problem to climate change, it is considered distinct from the UNFCCC's general competences regarding climate change. Second, this

[36] Ibid., 1228, 1229. [37] Ibid., 1229. [38] Ibid. [39] Cf. ibid. [40] Ibid.

[41] United Nations, 'FCCC/CP/2010/7/Add.1 – Report of the Conference of the Parties on Its Sixteenth Session, Held in Cancun from 29 November to 10 December 2010' 6 https://unfccc.int/resource/docs/2010/cop16/eng/07a01.pdf accessed 13 January 2024.

[42] Ibid.

[43] Harrould-Kolieb, 'Framing Ocean Acidification to Mobilise Action under Multilateral Environmental Agreements' (n 27) 130.

exclusive focus on the reduction of CO_2 as the sole global approach to combat OA has removed the possibility of responses from other regimes, such as those related to ocean and biodiversity.[44] In Harrould-Kolieb's words: '[T]he international level has focused heavily upon mitigation and the need for rapid and substantial reductions in CO_2 emissions. Far less attention has been paid to the role of adaptation and redress activities'.[45]

Thus, because the literature has focused primarily on the mitigation of CO_2 emissions and the UNFCCC as the relevant instrument, little attention has been given to what other regimes could achieve, particularly concerning resilience and adaptation, redress, or restoration. In other words, Harrould-Kolieb argues that the epistemic community's framing of OA as a parallel problem to climate change has led to a lack of action on the international stage. Specifically, although the literature has strongly emphasised the climate change regime in its discussions, this framing of OA as a concurrent issue has distanced the problem from ongoing discussions within the regime. Simultaneously, the potential to address OA through other multilateral environmental agreements has been overlooked, as these agreements have not received adequate attention.[46]

Therefore, this book will continue the trend already present in the literature and provide a holistic understanding of OA based on rapidly developing scientific knowledge. Consequently, answering the question posed above will be anchored in a scientific understanding of the problem of OA. Additionally, this book will frame OA as an effect of climate change, while also acknowledging other causes and interactions with additional ocean stressors such as warming, fishing, and pollution. Thus, this book aligns with the framework outlined by Harrould-Kolieb and will present OA as a complex issue with various causes, stressors, and adaptation options. Therefore, it will focus on the multifarious instruments and actors that can address these causes, stressors, and adaptation strategies relevant to this complex problem and its governance. Consequently, while recognising the significance of discussions surrounding the climate change regime (which will also be briefly addressed in the forthcoming discussions), this book will refrain from engaging in the already crowded legal debates at the international level.

1.1.2 The Already Existing Governance Landscape of OA

Along with debating the understanding and framing of OA as a problem, and before diving into discussions of either the legal or governance literatures, many authors explain that OA has not yet been properly addressed on the international plane.[47] Some authors point out that the problem exists within an 'international

[44] Ibid. [45] Ibid. [46] Ibid.

[47] Cf. Harrould-Kolieb and Hoegh-Guldberg (n 26) 10; Gordon (n 31) 39; Simons and Stephens (n 17) 2; Kim (n 21) 243; Nilufer Oral, 'Ocean Acidification: Falling between the Legal Cracks of UNCLOS and the UNFCCC?' (2018) 45 *Ecology Law Quarterly* 9, 11; Charles Galdies, Rachel Tiller and Beatriz Martinez

legal twilight zone'.[48] For instance, Makomere and McDonald state that 'responses to date have been piecemeal, governed by an uncoordinated assortment of environmental laws and policies'.[49] Meanwhile, Downing explains that '[e]xisting international regimes only tangentially address the issue'[50] and that '[t]he current international legal machinery in place (...), consists of an uncoordinated array of multilateral and regional regimes'.[51] In addition, OA is considered a complex problem that is unlikely to be resolved by one unifying treaty but instead is governed by an array of regimes.[52] Therefore, many authors classify OA as a 'regime complex'.[53]

While the literature indicates that OA is a complex problem likely governed by multiple existing regimes rather than a single treaty, none of the authors actually maps out the governance landscape for OA or tests it against regime complex theory. Therefore, it remains unclear what the regime complex for OA looks like or whether it even exists. Although many relevant legal instruments have been mentioned by authors over the years,[54] which actors are involved in OA governance remains largely unexplored. Thus, in contrast to certain other authors, this book will not assume that the OA governance landscape can be characterised as a regime complex. Instead, it will map out the OA governance landscape and test it against regime complex theory as defined by Raustiala and Victor.[55] This identification as a regime complex, along with the scientific background mentioned above, will be essential for understanding what type of governance approach is suitable and can build on the characteristics of OA as a problem and a regime complex.

1.1.3 Discussions of Ocean Acidification Law and Governance

Sections 1.1.1 and 1.1.2 elaborated on common themes between the law and governance literature. However, these two bodies of literature remain distinct from each other due to their different approaches to discussing OA. First, the stream of

Romera, 'Global Ocean Governance and Ocean Acidification' in Walter Leal Filho and others (eds), *Life Below Water* (Springer International Publishing 2021) 6 http://link.springer.com/10.1007/978-3-319-71064-8_109-1 accessed 12 November 2023; Katja Fennel and David L. VanderZwaag, 'Ocean Acidification: Scientific Surges, Lagging Law and Policy Responses' in Robin Warner and Stuart B Kaye (eds), *Routledge Handbook of Maritime Regulation and Enforcement* (Routledge 2016) 342; Herr and others (n 33) 5.

[48] Baird, Simons and Stephens (n 18) 460; Oral (n 47) 11; Kim (n 21) 243; Gordon (n 31) 440.

[49] Makomere and McDonald (n 28) 330. [50] Downing (n 19) 242. [51] Ibid., 249.

[52] Fennel and VanderZwaag (n 47) 342; Scott, 'Ocean Acidification' (n 29) 389; Ellycia Harrould-Kolieb and Tim Stephens, 'Ocean Acidification' in Rosemary Rayfuse, Aline Jaeckel and Natalie Klein (eds), *Research Handbook on International Marine Environmental Law* (Edward Elgar Publishing 2023) 264, 265 www.elgaronline.com/view/book/9781789909081/book-part-9781789909081-20.xml accessed 12 November 2023; Harrould-Kolieb and Hoegh-Guldberg (n 26) 10; Makomere and McDonald (n 28) 346.

[53] Scott, 'Ocean Acidification' (n 29) 390; Gordon (n 31) 39; Simons and Stephens (n 17) 1; Harrould-Kolieb and Stephens (n 52) 265; Baird, Simons and Stephens (n 18) 459; Kim (n 21) 247.

[54] See, for example, Stephens (n 20); Kim (n 21); Baird, Simons and Stephens (n 18); Scott, 'Ocean Acidification' (n 29).

[55] Kal Raustiala and David G. Victor, 'The Regime Complex for Plant Genetic Resources' (2004) 58 *International Organization* 277.

literature that explores a governance and policy approach to OA aims to provide a general overview of the problem and responses to it through governance options.[56] This stream debates the necessary steps, evaluated from a scientific perspective, to combat OA, such as by implementing mitigation, adaptation, or resilience-strengthening measures. Second, the other stream of literature addresses how OA can be handled through international law.[57] More specifically, it enquires which legal instruments and treaty regimes may be relevant and to what extent they are equipped to address the problem. In the following discussion, the latter stream will be addressed first, followed by a return to the first stream.

1.1.3.1 The Legal Literature

To understand whether states have legal obligations to address OA, all of the papers examine instruments that may be relevant to OA, primarily treaties such as the UNFCCC and the entire climate change regime, the United Nations Convention on the Law of the Sea (UNCLOS), and the Convention on Biological Diversity (CBD), among others.[58] However, as noted earlier, the discussion often centres on the climate change regime and UNCLOS.[59] The emphasis on these regimes is easily explained: OA manifests its effects in the ocean and is triggered by CO_2, a greenhouse gas governed by the climate change regime. Thus, these treaties – particularly the climate change regime – attract the most interest and debate. The most common

[56] Jagers and others (n 30); Harrould-Kolieb and Hoegh-Guldberg (n 26); Makomere and McDonald (n 28); Harrould-Kolieb, 'Framing Ocean Acidification to Mobilise Action under Multilateral Environmental Agreements' (n 27); Billé and others (n 23); Galdies, Tiller and Martinez Romera (n 47).

[57] Cf. Heidi R. Lamirande, 'From Sea to Carbon Cesspool: Preventing the World's Marine Ecosystems from Falling Victim to Ocean Acidification' (2011) 34 *Suffolk Transnational Law Review* 183; Ellycia R Harrould-Kolieb, 'Ocean Acidification and the UNFCCC: Finding Legal Clarity in the Twilight Zone' (2016) *Washington Journal of Environmental Law & Policy* 612; Baird, Simons and Stephens (n 18); Cecilia Engler, David L. VanderZwaag and Katja Fennel, 'Ocean Acidification Post-Paris: Gauging Law and Policy Responses in Light of Evolving Scientific Knowledge' (2019) 33 *Ocean Yearbook Online* 207; Gordon (n 31); Downing (n 19); Simons and Stephens (n 17); Scott, 'Ocean Acidification' (n 29); Kim (n 21); Ellycia R. Harrould-Kolieb, 'The UN Convention on the Law of the Sea: A Governing Framework for Ocean Acidification?' (2020) 29 *Review of European, Comparative & International Environmental Law* 257; Stephens (n 20); Oral (n 47); Fennel and VanderZwaag (n 47); Ellycia Harrould-Kolieb and Dorothee Herr, 'Ocean Acidification and Climate Change: Synergies and Challenges of Addressing Both under the UNFCCC' (2012) 12 *Climate Policy* 378; Harrould-Kolieb, '(Re)Framing Ocean Acidification in the Context of the United Nations Framework Convention on Climate Change (UNFCCC) and Paris Agreement' (n 34); Harrould-Kolieb and Stephens (n 52); Ellycia R. Harrould-Kolieb, 'Implications of the Paris Agreement for Action on Ocean Acidification within the UNFCCC' in David L VanderZwaag, Nilufer Oral and Tim Stephens (eds), *Research Handbook on Ocean Acidification Law and Policy* (Edward Elgar Publishing 2021); Naporn Popattanachai and Elizabeth A. Kirk, 'Ocean Acidification and Multilateral Environmental Agreements' in David L. VanderZwaag, Nilufer Oral and Tim Stephens (eds), *Research Handbook on Ocean Acidification Law and Policy* (Edward Elgar Publishing 2021).

[58] Gordon (n 31); Downing (n 19); Simons and Stephens (n 17); Kim (n 21); Harrould-Kolieb (n 57); Scott, 'Ocean Acidification' (n 29); Oral (n 47); Stephens (n 20); Baird, Simons and Stephens (n 18).

[59] Harrould-Kolieb (n 57); Scott, 'Ocean Acidification' (n 29); Oral (n 47); Harrould-Kolieb, '(Re)Framing Ocean Acidification in the Context of the United Nations Framework Convention on Climate Change (UNFCCC) and Paris Agreement' (n 34); Harrould-Kolieb, 'Ocean Acidification and the UNFCCC: Finding Legal Clarity in the Twilight Zone' (n 57).

approach the authors of this stream use for their analysis is to identify the relevant treaties applicable to the problem and discuss rules or related reports that may be useful.[60] All of them arrive at the same conclusion: existing legal obligations are insufficient to address the issue of OA to the extent necessary to prevent negative consequences for humans and ecosystems.[61] A variety of solutions are proposed to tackle this problem. There are several lines of discussion and arguments in the literature that have been debated more extensively. An example will be provided to illustrate the types of issues that the authors have considered thus far.

As indicated above, authors seem to look towards the climate change regime to find solutions to OA. Particularly lively are the discussions surrounding the question of whether the problem of OA fits within the regime's mandate.[62] More specifically, there is a debate related to the application of the UNFCCC to OA, which includes discussions about the focus of the treaty and the entire climate change regime. The authors raise the question of whether the regime is concentrated on the atmosphere/temperature.[63] This focus is significant because a regime that deals solely with the atmosphere/temperature is unlikely to adequately address the issue of acidification, which is related to ocean chemistry. Consequently, the parties would have no specific obligations to prevent OA.[64] Article 2 UNFCCC is a key component of the debate and is relevant to the question of the applicability of the convention to a specific problem, as it establishes the objective of the entire climate change regime.[65] Authors discuss whether OA can fall under the objective of the convention, which, according to article 2 UNFCCC, is to stabilise 'greenhouse gas concentrations in the atmosphere at a level that would prevent dangerous anthropogenic interference with the climate system'.[66] For instance, one group of authors (Baird et al.,[67] Simons and

[60] Baird, Simons and Stephens (n 18); Simons and Stephens (n 17); Kim (n 21); Gordon (n 31); Harrould-Kolieb and Herr (n 57).

[61] Gordon (n 31) 48; Downing (n 19) 272, 273; Harrould-Kolieb, '(Re)Framing Ocean Acidification in the Context of the United Nations Framework Convention on Climate Change (UNFCCC) and Paris Agreement' (n 34) 1235; Harrould-Kolieb and Herr (n 57) 5; Fennel and VanderZwaag (n 47) 354; Oral (n 47) 28, 29; Stephens (n 20) 797, 798; Baird, Simons and Stephens (n 18) 471; Kim (n 21) 257, 258; Scott, 'Ocean Acidification' (n 29) 406–408.

[62] Baird, Simons and Stephens (n 18) 463, 464; Downing (n 19) 250–254; Fennel and VanderZwaag (n 47) 350–351; Kim (n 21) 245, 246; Harrould-Kolieb, 'Framing Ocean Acidification to Mobilise Action under Multilateral Environmental Agreements' (n 27) 131.

[63] Harrould-Kolieb and Stephens (n 52) 273; Baird, Simons and Stephens (n 18) 463; Kim (n 21) 246; Gordon (n 31) 41; cf. Downing (n 19) 250–253; Simons and Stephens (n 17) 7; Oral (n 47) 13; Fennel and VanderZwaag (n 47) 39; Harrould-Kolieb, 'Implications of the Paris Agreement for Action on Ocean Acidification within the UNFCCC' (n 57) 25.

[64] Harrould-Kolieb, '(Re)Framing Ocean Acidification in the Context of the United Nations Framework Convention on Climate Change (UNFCCC) and Paris Agreement' (n 34) 1228.

[65] Downing (n 19) 251; Gordon (n 31) 41; Simons and Stephens (n 17) 7; Baird, Simons and Stephens (n 18) 464; Oral (n 47) 13.

[66] Downing (n 19) 251; Gordon (n 31) 41; Simons and Stephens (n 17) 7; Baird, Simons and Stephens (n 18) 464; Oral (n 47) 13.

[67] Baird, Simons and Stephens (n 18) 463, 464.

Stephens,[68] Downing,[69] Kim[70] and cf. also Oral[71] and Engler et al.[72]) problematise that 'dangerous anthropogenic interference' in the climate system is meant to be a threshold, and they question whether, due to the atmospheric focus they ascribe to article 2 UNFCCC, even though OA is mentioned by the IPCC, dangerous interference can be defined by referring to dangerous ocean pH thresholds. Harrould-Kolieb criticises the notion of an exclusively atmospheric focus of the regime, arguing that such an interpretation would misrepresent the ordinary meaning or purpose of the UNFCCC text.[73] Concerning the question of whether OA can be considered dangerous interference, the author presents the argument that article 2 UNFCCC 'does not focus on the atmosphere to the exclusion of other elements of the climate system'.[74]

From this brief overview of the legal literature, it is evident that legal instruments – particularly the climate change regime and UNCLOS – have garnered attention. Given that this area is relatively well explored, rather than contributing to this already rich discussion, this book will primarily focus on which other instruments and actors are pertinent to the governance of OA.

1.1.3.2 The Governance Literature

The governance literature is quite broad and challenging to categorise, making the identification of common themes difficult. However, most texts share a common focus on how these frameworks can or should address OA at large.[75] More specifically, authors pinpoint the areas where action is needed regarding OA, such as mitigation, including local causes of OA, adaptation, and resilience. For example, Makomere and McDonald[76] and Billé and colleagues[77] identify and examine four different categories of responses to address OA: mitigation, resilience, adaptation, and reparation (Billé et al.)/reverse or reduce local OA (Makomere and McDonald). Although they use similar response categories for OA, the papers adopt distinct approaches to governance. Makomere and McDonald do not discuss how OA should be governed but rather state 'that response strategies to ocean acidification provide an important foundation for governance of the problem'.[78] Contrarily, Billé and colleagues categorise the feasibility and potential of governance tools within the four categories mentioned above[79] and identify that more coordination among relevant international frameworks is needed to effectively govern OA.[80] Yet another

[68] Simons and Stephens (n 17) 7, 8. [69] Downing (n 19) 250–253. [70] Kim (n 21) 246.

[71] Oral (n 47) 14, 15. [72] Engler, VanderZwaag and Fennel (n 57) 216, 222.

[73] Harrould-Kolieb, 'Ocean Acidification and the UNFCCC: Finding Legal Clarity in the Twilight Zone' (n 57) 614.

[74] Ibid., *624*.

[75] Makomere and McDonald (n 28); Billé and others (n 23); Jagers and others (n 30); Harrould-Kolieb and Hoegh-Guldberg (n 26); cf. Harrould-Kolieb, 'Framing Ocean Acidification to Mobilise Action under Multilateral Environmental Agreements' (n 27).

[76] Makomere and McDonald (n 28) 333, 334. [77] Billé and others (n 23) 762.

[78] Makomere and McDonald (n 28) 346. [79] Billé and others (n 23) 773. [80] Ibid., 775.

approach to discussing OA governance is presented by Galdies et al.[81] The authors provide an overview of the scientific background of OA and then review the legal literature, presenting some of the legal instruments that currently govern OA, such as the UNFCCC, the CBD, and the Marine Strategy Framework Directive at the EU level.[82] All of these papers offer a contextual overview of significant aspects of OA governance, categorising different response areas and reporting on the current governance framework surrounding the issue. Nevertheless, a more systematic exploration of OA governance would be beneficial, as none of them thoroughly investigates suitable methods for governing OA.

A more systematic approach to OA governance is offered by Harrould-Kolieb and Hoegh-Guldberg.[83] Drawing on natural science literature, the authors provide a 'science-based governing framework' to tackle OA.[84] The paper created an '(…) analytical framework through [which] existing governance structures can be explored for their capabilities to respond to OA'.[85] In other words, the authors organise the possible responses to OA systematically and establish a framework that is meant to be used to 'guide future actions or assess the capabilities and gaps in existing governance structures'.[86] In addition, Harrould-Kolieb and Hoegh-Guldberg foresee, for instance, that multiple actors could work on OA simultaneously but in accordance with their respective mandates and restrictions.[87] This is consistent with the arguments put forward in this book.

Inspired by Harrould-Kolieb and Hoegh-Guldberg, this book adopts a science-based approach to governance and identifies areas where responses to OA are necessary, including mitigation, stressors, and adaptation. Furthermore, this book will build upon these responses to outline the governance landscape, recognise global experimentalist governance as an appropriate governance form, and examine its presence in case studies.

Overall, several points can be made regarding the reviewed literature. First, in terms of understanding and framing, there is an increased comprehension of the scientific background of OA in the literature. Recent studies portray the issue more holistically, considering not only the mitigation of CO_2 emissions but also local sources of acidification and adaptation. Nevertheless, as Harrould-Kolieb outlines, despite intense discussions of OA and the climate change regime – due to framing OA as a concurrent problem to climate change – the issue has yet to be properly addressed within this framework. Furthermore, there is a lack of engagement with other multilateral environmental agreements and their potential role in OA adaptation and similar efforts. Second, while the literature has identified that the issue of OA is governed by a regime complex, none of the authors have actually mapped the OA governance landscape or tested it against the theory of regime complexity. Consequently, the appearance of the regime complex for OA remains unexplored.

[81] Galdies, Tiller and Martinez Romera (n 47). [82] Ibid., 6–8.
[83] Harrould-Kolieb and Hoegh-Guldberg (n 26). [84] Ibid., 10. [85] Ibid. [86] Ibid., 11.
[87] Ibid., 15.

Although many relevant instruments have been discussed by authors, the roles of various actors in the governance of the issue remain under-explored. Third, regarding the literature addressing the law and governance of OA, it has been noted that while different responses to OA and even a framework to guide future actions or assess the capabilities of governance structures have been discussed, suitable governance options have neither been debated nor evaluated by the authors.

Section 1.2 will provide an overview of the methodological choices made to investigate the question posed above, which aims to address these shortcomings in the literature.

1.2 Overview of Methods

Throughout this book, several methodological choices have been made, which will be explained chapter by chapter in the following sections, starting with Chapter 2. While the methods used will be discussed in detail in the separate chapters, a brief overview is provided here as an introduction.

Chapter 2 reviews the scientific literature and provides the non-scientist reader with an overview of what OA entails, including an explanation of its causes, other ocean stressors, and adaptation options. To navigate through the technical and intricate natural science literature, the social science literature was first consulted to investigate how these authors describe the problem, as this literature tends to keep scientific explanations relatively simple. Thus, the social science literature could help gather a fundamental understanding of the issue. Subsequently, with the help of references from the social science literature, scientific papers were consulted to answer open questions and gain a deeper understanding of the chemical underpinnings of OA, for instance. This deeper understanding of OA is necessary, on one hand, to explain OA in simple language in this chapter and, on the other, to explore in this book which governance options should be applied to OA. Later, references (this time from the scientific literature) were again consulted to find additional sources to clarify the remaining questions. As a final step, during a research stay at the UC Davis-Bodega Marine Laboratory (Ocean Climate Lab), the chapter was revised based on what had been learned during discussions with scientists and feedback on the chapter provided by a scientist at the lab.[88]

In Chapter 3, a map of the OA-relevant legal instruments and actors is provided to create an overview of the OA governance landscape. The map includes legal instruments and actors that were either considered relevant by the legal and scientific literature or discovered through an internet search. Thus, the map aims to give the reader an idea of the number of actors and instruments that could potentially

[88] Comments provided by Meghan Zulian, PhD candidate in the Ocean Climate Lab at UC Davis and Bodega Marine Lab.

be relevant for OA governance, without claiming to be exhaustive. Regarding the internet research, Google was used as the primary search engine.

The internet search was conducted in two rounds. First, to create an initial overview of institutions capable of tackling OA, keywords such as 'ocean acidification', 'ocean acidification governance', and 'CO_2 governance' were used, among others (see Chapter 3). Second, following the initial search, each institution was examined individually to determine whether it had the potential to address aspects of OA (causes, stressors, adaptation) and could therefore be included in the map, as further explained in the chapter. Once all the institutions were selected, they were compiled in an Excel sheet, which was then transformed into a map using JMP, a program that links data to graphical representations. After creating the map, it was tested against the various governance options to see which ones were present (ranging from integrated regime to fragmentation). Lastly, employing what the theory refers to as 'forces' – namely, uncertainty, interests, and linkages – the governance landscape can be identified as a regime complex. Additionally, the forces were utilised to enhance the understanding of why OA, as an issue area, yields a regime complex.

Chapter 4 builds on the lessons learnt from the science (Chapter 2) and the current governance landscape (Chapter 3) to identify a suitable governance approach. Multiple governance options were considered, including orchestration, regime interaction, and global experimentalist governance. Ultimately, global experimentalist governance was chosen as the focus of the analysis, as this governance approach is well-suited to address the problem of OA and can leverage the existing governance landscape. This will be detailed in Chapter 4. To evaluate whether OA as a problem and global experimentalist governance as a theory are a good match, the characteristics defining OA were identified and compared to the characteristics of the problems that global experimentalist governance can effectively address. Additionally, the chapter draws on the literature to explain the foundations of global experimentalist governance. Based on this theory, a framework consisting of five steps describing the ideal type of global experimentalist governance was created. Grounded in this ideal type, Chapters 5, 6, and 7 conduct a case selection and two case studies to determine if global experimentalist governance is currently being pursued by two actors included in the map.

Chapter 5 selects two actors for case studies in Chapters 6 and 7. Following this case selection, Chapters 6 and 7 each engage in a case study of the OA Alliance and the International Maritime Organization (IMO), respectively. While the work of the OA Alliance allows for a strict comparison of its work procedures to global experimentalist governance, the IMO requires a different approach. As the IMO does not directly deal with OA (as opposed to the OA Alliance), as will become apparent in the chapter, the chapter first identifies the areas of the IMO's work relevant to OA and where OA could be embedded within those efforts. Afterwards, the working procedures within one area through which the IMO indirectly addresses OA are examined to evaluate the presence of features of global experimentalist governance. The case selection rests on six criteria: suitability, significant potential, variation in targeted organisations, focus on CO_2, differences in legalisation, and access. Therefore, a table based on the map of institutions was created to facilitate the selection. The table encompasses institutions that could be suitable as case studies. The chapter distinguishes between instruments and actors that are merely suitable to address OA and those with significant potential to tackle it. This distinction is founded on the science behind OA. It was found that the majority of the actors and instruments included in the table have significant potential to address OA. Due to space and time constraints, not all of these potentially interesting case studies could be examined, so the focus was ultimately narrowed to two actors. Thus, to arrive at the case selection, five different actors and their related instruments from the map that show significant potential were selected and analysed in greater detail. For example, institutions that operate solely at the regional level were excluded.

Following this, institutions were chosen that can specifically tackle CO2, as science indicates that CO_2 is the leading cause of OA. Therefore, this book initially focuses on the OA Alliance, a relatively new and growing institution dedicated solely to OA, which nonetheless engages in numerous activities, including addressing CO_2 emissions. Second, it examines the IMO as a case study because transportation (and as part of that, the shipping sector) is a continually increasing contributor to CO_2 emissions. Moreover, the IMO also regulates other aspects of shipping relevant to OA. Methodologically, these cases can be considered to have intrinsic importance for this topic of study, as they highlight key players in addressing OA. Furthermore, since the issues identified in their governance approaches are symptomatic of employing global experimentalist governance to OA, it can be argued that other actors would also encounter the same challenges as these institutions in institutionalising global experimentalist governance.[89]

Additionally, these two actors differ from one another and are characterised by varying degrees of legalisation, as will be shown in the chapter. This difference in degrees of legalisation also renders the two cases independent of each other, meaning they do not overlap or directly influence each other's work.[90] By choosing different cases, more diverse challenges that institutions might face when using this governance form to tackle OA can be uncovered.

Finally, individuals working with these two actors were available for interviews with the author, enabling a deeper analysis of the actors. This access ensured not only that empirical material could be obtained but also that information not accessible to the general public was provided to the author, both crucial aspects of a case study.[91] This unpublished empirical material facilitates an in-depth analysis that can illuminate the governance procedures within each of the actors.

[89] John Gerring, *Case Study Research: Principles and Practices* (2nd edn, Cambridge University Press 2017) 42, 43, 45, 46.

[90] Ibid., 43. [91] Ibid., 43, 44, 45.

Therefore, interviews are used alongside documents and websites as empirical sources in the case studies. While the documents and websites provided by the two actors contain information about their respective work, the websites are often created solely to inform the general public. As a result, these websites and attached documents do not provide in-depth information about, for example, procedures within the actor, and the information provided often lacks the detail necessary to assess whether or to what extent global experimentalist governance is present. Thus, some dynamics of the governance procedures of these institutions cannot be captured by their websites and documents alone, necessitating further information gathering. Hence, this book also employs interviews to collect additional information.

The objective of the interviews is to gather information; thus, they were unstructured – an approach that allows for the discovery of new dimensions in the use of governance and for knowledge gained from previous interviews to inform questions in later ones. The choice of unstructured interviews partly rests on their informational nature and partly on the fact that the purpose of the case design is not to directly compare the two cases but to understand how and to what extent global experimentalist governance exists and functions in these different contexts.[92] This approach allowed the author to ask about specific aspects of the interview in detail, creating a more nuanced understanding of any interesting or pertinent aspects.[93] An interview guide was therefore not created; however, questions were asked concerning, for example, working procedures, stakeholder involvement, and communication with other states.

Interviews were conducted with personnel from the OA Alliance and experts and delegates of the IMO. All interviews were carried out under the premise of anonymity; therefore, each interviewee will only be identified by their organisation and position, designated by numbers (e.g., IMO Delegate Interview #1) to distinguish between the various interviewees. For the OA Alliance, interviews and information exchanges occurred over the course of over a year after introduction to the actors' personnel. This ongoing dialogue facilitated numerous questions (including follow-ups) and insights into internal documentation that informed the case study. The interviews with IMO delegates and experts took place either during the Marine Environmental Protection Committee's meetings (MEPC 79), including those of the Intersessional Working Group on Reduction of GHG Emissions from Ships (ISWG-GHG 13), or afterwards online. Unlike the interviews with the OA Alliance, these interviews were time-constrained and did not permit follow-up questions, but they did allow for a broader spectrum of interviewees. In addition to the interviews themselves, attending the meetings enabled valuable observations regarding the dynamics within the organisation. Therefore, the interviews conducted for both

[92] Felice D. Billups, *Qualitative Data Collection Tools: Design, Development, and Applications* (SAGE Publications, Inc 2021) 37 https://methods.sagepub.com/book/qualitative-data-collection-tools accessed 19 November 2023.

[93] Svend Brinkmann and Steinar Kvale, *Doing Interviews* (SAGE Publications Ltd 2018) 42, 48 https://methods.sagepub.com/book/doing-interviews-2e accessed 19 November 2023.

case studies provided invaluable material for gaining insights into the procedures of these two organisations.

Before delving into the science of OA in Chapter 2, an overview of the book's argumentation will be provided.

1.3 Overview of Argumentation

In Chapter 2, this book will, similar to recent literature, present the scientific background of OA in accordance with rapidly advancing scientific knowledge. This scientific knowledge will be crucial for the argumentation throughout the entire book. Thus, answering the research question will be rooted in the scientific understanding of the problem of OA. Regarding the framing of OA as an issue, it is understood as an effect of climate change, while additional causes and stressors stem from other sources. Consequently, OA is presented in the science section and throughout the entire book as a complex problem with various causes, stressors, and adaptation options. Though this work acknowledges the importance of discussions surrounding the UNFCCC and the climate change regime, these discussions will not be elaborated upon in the following chapters. As noted in the literature review above, these legal discussions are extensive, and this book will primarily focus on other instruments and actors relevant to the governance of OA. Therefore, in Chapter 3, similarly to the literature discussed above, this work also identifies the governance landscape for OA as a regime complex.

However, before determining that this is the case, the international and transnational governance landscape for OA will be mapped out and tested against regime complex theory. For the purpose of this book, the main distinction between international and transnational is that whereas the former focuses on interactions between the governments of nations within the framework of international organisations,[94] the latter emphasises the processes that occur at non-state levels as well.[95] Thus, the term international assumes the primacy of nation-states and the interactions among them, while transnational encompasses anything that transcends or extends across national border.[96] Transnational is therefore understood as 'referring to the scope of political action and power structures beyond the nation'.[97] Therefore, international solely deals with public international institutions, whereas transnational includes non-state actor institutions.[98]

[94] Jolene Lin and Joanne Scott, 'Looking beyond the International: Key Themes and Approaches of Transnational Environmental Law' (2012) 1 *Transnational Environmental Law* 23, 23.

[95] Ibid., cf. Joseph S. Nye and Robert O. Keohane, 'Transnational Relations and World Politics: An Introduction' (1971) 25 *International Organization* 329, 331.

[96] Ingo Richter, Sabine Berking and Ralf Müller-Schmid (eds), 'Introduction', *Building a Transnational Civil Society: Global Issues and Global Actors* (Palgrave Macmillan 2006) 9.

[97] Ibid.

[98] Alvina Hoffmann, 'The Transnational and the International: From Critique of Statism to Transversal Lines' (2022) 35 *Cambridge Review of International Affairs* 796, 798; Lin and Scott (n 94) 23.

This book will consider both the international and transnational levels. Therefore, the chapter discussing regime complex theory will provide insights into OA's current governance landscape, including an overview of relevant legal instruments and actors. This overview of the governance landscape, as well as the identification of that landscape as a regime complex, can, along with the scientific background, help determine suitable governance approaches to OA. In other words, this identification as a regime complex will, together with the scientific background mentioned above, be essential for understanding what type of governance approach is suitable and can build upon the characteristics of OA as a problem and a regime complex. Accordingly, in Chapter 4, global experimentalist governance is identified as a suitable governance approach. In addition to this identification, the chapter outlines and explains the five steps of the ideal type of global experimentalist governance. These five steps can be utilised to assess the extent to which global experimentalist governance is present in an actor. Therefore, to examine the presence of global experimentalist governance, Chapter 5 chooses two case studies based on several criteria (see methodological choices): the OA Alliance (Chapter 6) and the IMO (Chapter 7).

Overall, this book will argue that global experimentalist governance is a suitable governance approach for addressing OA. Although these two cases provide promising examples of actors who, according to their mandates and objectives, could engage with OA, global experimentalist governance is currently observed only to a limited extent within the tested cases, as will be seen and discussed in the case studies and conclusion.

CHAPTER 2

Understanding Ocean Acidification

OA is an environmental phenomenon that has recently started to gain more attention. It has implications for ecosystems and humans alike if left unaddressed. Nevertheless, since the academic community's initial engagement with the problem in 2005,[99] little seems to have changed on the international plane regarding addressing this issue. To remedy this shortcoming and identify the possibilities law and policy offer to tackle this newly arising issue, one must understand what OA is and, most importantly, where it originates. Without a profound knowledge of the causes and repercussions of OA, it would be challenging to identify the relevant fields of law and address the problem at its roots. Therefore, this chapter will thoroughly explain what OA is. However, this question is not easily answered and requires comprehension of complicated scientific evidence. Understanding the necessary scientific knowledge and translating it into a language that can facilitate the tractability of the issue for lawyers and policymakers is no simple task. This is especially true because science and law are, as Sulyok has described, two 'distinct cultures'[100] with often diverse understandings of seemingly the same concepts. Among others, concepts such as cause and causation differ in scope in the two disciplines, which can lead to misunderstandings between lawyers and scientists.[101] Therefore, working with science and law becomes an interdisciplinary exercise during which it is essential to have a sound knowledge of both disciplines and acknowledge their differences.[102]

Before engaging further with the scientific literature, it is important to keep a few things in mind. More often than not, science is associated with terms such as

[99] Royal Society (Great Britain), *Ocean Acidification Due to Increasing Atmospheric Carbon Dioxide.* (Royal Society 2005); Harrould-Kolieb and Hoegh-Guldberg (n 26) 11.

[100] Katalin Sulyok, *Science and Judicial Reasoning: The Legitimacy of International Environmental Adjudication* (Cambridge University Press 2021) 4.

[101] Cf. ibid., 28.

[102] Ibid., *20*.

objectivity, truth, or certainty.[103] These terms suggest that science will provide the perfect answer to all questions raised. Concerning OA, answers will be needed, for instance, regarding the causes or development of problems and their influence on the world over time. However, like every other area of research, science is not flawless, as it is produced by human beings, and it can be biased, value-laden, or uncertain.[104] When it comes to OA, a problem that has only recently started to gain more attention and is insufficiently understood, a substantial lack of clarity and uncertainty can be expected and has to be acknowledged.

In relation to OA, science and scientific literature have grown over the years, and more profound results and information have come to light.[105] In fact, research around OA has become one of the fastest-developing fields in the marine sciences.[106] However, much remains unknown, and long-term experiments are particularly lacking. The scientific literature focuses on explaining OA and its associated chemical and biological reactions, with particular attention given to the consequences of the problem (to the extent they are understood). It often investigates specific questions, such as OA in relation to shipping or particular species of calcifiers, such as corals.[107] This concentration of various experiments on highly specific scenarios has been described by Dupont and Pörtner as 'stamp collecting', leading to the issue that little is genuinely known or researched about the realistic, complex circumstances surrounding OA.[108] Future research needs to shift from examining individual stress-inducing factors to considering multiple factors, and from focusing on single species to communities and ecosystems. Additionally, OA research must expand to further encompass adaptation.[109] Accordingly, what is logically rather difficult to find in the literature are papers that compile results and analyse or describe all the different actions and their consequences that can cause or exacerbate the problem of OA. Instead, this information must be gathered from a variety of sources that focus on diverse particularities regarding OA. Admittedly, one of the reasons for the lack of more holistic perspectives on these matters is likely due to the high complexity of OA and its surrounding circumstances, which are still not completely understood.

Nevertheless, this chapter aims to provide an overview for non-scientist readers about what OA entails. In the process, a special focus will be on causes, so-called

[103] Ibid., *3*. [104] Ibid., *24, 25*. [105] Cf. Laffoley and others (n 12) 8.

[106] Riebesell and Gattuso (n 14) 12.

[107] Tyler Cyronak and others, 'Enhanced Acidification of Global Coral Reefs Driven by Regional Biogeochemical Feedbacks' (2014) 41 *Geophysical Research Letters* 5538; Kenneth RN Anthony, 'Coral Reefs under Climate Change and Ocean Acidification: Challenges and Opportunities for Management and Policy' (2016) 41 *Annual Review of Environment and Resources* 59; Keith A. Hunter and others, 'Impacts of Anthropogenic SO_x, NO_x and NH_3 on Acidification of Coastal Waters and Shipping Lanes: Acidification of Coastal Waters' (2011) 38 *Geophysical Research Letters* 54; Ida-Maja Hassellöv and others, 'Shipping Contributes to Ocean Acidification' (2013) 40 *Geophysical Research Letters* 2731.

[108] Sam Dupont and Hans-O Pörtner, 'A Snapshot of Ocean Acidification Research' (2013) 160 *Marine Biology* 1765, 1767.

[109] Riebesell and Gattuso (n 14) 13.

stressors, and adaptation options related to the problem. Understanding these causes, stressors, and adaptation options is essential for following the forthcoming chapters of this book. For example, mapping the international and transnational landscape for OA (Chapter 3) and selecting actors for case studies (Chapter 5) will require knowledge of causes, stressors, and adaptation. In addition to these three points, the repercussions of OA will be briefly explained in this chapter so that the reader can get an idea of the potential consequences of OA. The description of the problem of OA provided here seeks to reflect the current state of research in an accessible manner so that it can be easily understood and utilised by lawyers and policymakers. This, in turn, will hopefully provide a foundation for further research on law and governance concerning OA.

Therefore, in what follows, the causes of OA will be examined first (Section 2.1). An overview of other ocean stressors will then be provided (Section 2.2) in order to explain afterwards some of the repercussions of OA (Section 2.3). Adaptation options will be described (Section 2.4) before the chapter reviews how scientific information can assist in tackling the problem (Section 2.5).

2.1 The Reasons behind Acidifying Oceans

The problem of OA and its complex processes is still not well understood. Nonetheless, understanding the science behind this problem is essential for identifying the causes of OA. This knowledge is crucial to addressing the issue. Hence, this chapter will first explain how acidity is measured (Section 2.1.1), then evaluate the chemical background of OA (Section 2.1.2), and finally describe the pathways of compounds that trigger acidification in ocean water (Section 2.1.3). In addition, the regional variability of the problem will be discussed (Section 2.1.4). To conclude the causes section of this chapter, the most important information will be summarised (Section 2.1.5) before other ocean stressors exacerbating OA are examined in Section 2.2.

2.1.1 Measuring Acidity

The first step in understanding acidity is comprehending how it is measured. Acidity is quantifiable, and while the scale is straightforward and leads to a clear measurement, certain characteristics of acidification should be considered when interpreting the results. In the following, both the scale and these characteristics will be examined.

Acidity is measured on a pH scale that specifies how acidic (sour) or alkaline water is. The pH scale ranges from 0 to 14; water is highly alkaline or basic if it reaches 14 and highly acidic if it remains at 0, while 7 is neutral. Thus, a decrease in pH means an increase in acidity.[110] However, what the pH scale actually shows is

[110] European Project on Ocean Acidification (EPOCA), D. Laffoley and JM Baxter, 'Ocean Acidification: Questions Answered' 7 https://portals.iucn.org/library/node/9721 accessed 15 November 2019.

the potential (P) to produce hydrogen (H) atoms/ions, and therefore the relative amount of these ions in the water. Furthermore, the scale is logarithmic, meaning each step is a factor of ten (e.g., a step from 6 to 5 represents a tenfold increase in acidity, whereas from 6 to 4, the increase is 100-fold).[111]

For example, up to the year 2000, the ocean's pH – or more specifically, the average pH for the surface of the open ocean – had changed from 8.2 in pre-industrial times to 8.1.[112] Even though this sounds like a minor change, it actually translates into a change rate of 30 per cent.[113] However, during the past decade, ocean surface pH has continued to decrease to the extent that in 2020, the ocean surface was around 40 per cent more acidic compared to pre-industrial levels.[114]

There are two particularities of acidification that should be taken into consideration when measuring and interpreting pH measurements to avoid drawing hasty conclusions. First, by nature, the acidity of seawater varies according to different factors. Changes in acidity occur due to diurnal and seasonal cycles, geographic variations, and also depending on water depth.[115] Therefore, a measurement taken, for example, in one particular location near a coastline on one day could differ significantly if taken another day during a different cycle. Hence, these natural variations can make it difficult to draw clear-cut conclusions and to be certain about how acidification has affected or will affect the oceans and the organisms within. This observation shows that OA is a relatively young area of science, and to achieve a fuller understanding of the impacts on the oceanic ecosystem, only long-term experiments can provide answers.[116] Hence, water pH and related natural or anthropogenically induced changes vary on local and global levels and even within the local context.

Second, the ocean's reaction to acidification is delayed, particularly concerning the discharge of anthropogenic emissions into the atmosphere.[117] This delay means that ocean chemistry will not change immediately after the release of, for example, CO_2. Thus, there are no instant negative effects. It follows that even if humanity were to stop emitting all CO_2 today, acidification would continue for some years to come.[118] Therefore, the true damage to the ocean, caused by emissions that have already been generated, will only become apparent on the pH scale in the future.

2.1.2 The Chemical Background

In addition to measuring OA, it is essential to understand which diverse compounds can trigger acidification. Later in this book (particularly in Chapters 3 and 5), actors and legal instruments will be mapped and evaluated based on their

[111] Arctic Monitoring and Assessment Programme and others (n 10) 1.
[112] European Project on Ocean Acidification (EPOCA), Laffoley and Baxter (n 110) 14; Findlay and others (n 5) 3.
[113] Findlay and others (n 5) 3. [114] Ibid.
[115] Secretariat of the Convention on Biological Diversity and others (n 9) 7.
[116] Dupont and Pörtner (n 108) 1766. [117] Laffoley and others (n 12) 14. [118] Ibid., 14.

ability to address these compounds. The three groups of compounds (CO_2, NO_x, SO_x) that can form acids causing acidification in the ocean will be discussed. The material below describes what occurs when these compounds come into contact with water, thereby explaining the chemical process behind OA.

The first, and according to the latest scientific knowledge,[119] the major driver of OA is CO_2. When CO_2 enters water (H_2O), these elements combine to form carbonic acid (H_2CO_3). More precisely, when CO_2 dissolves in H_2O, the molecules react to produce H_2CO_3. However, the issue is that the carbonic acid can break down (ionise) and release hydrogen ions (H^+), which then disperse in the water. This increase in hydrogen ions contributes to rising acidity in the oceans, as previously explained, which is reflected on the pH scale.[120]

The other two groups of compounds that have the potential to cause the ocean to acidify are sulphur oxides (SO_x) and nitrogen oxides (NO_x).[121] These two groups of compounds are often referred to jointly because the chemical reactions through which they form acids are similar, and they partially derive from the same sources.[122] Sulphur and nitrogen oxides can form acids such as H_2SO_4 (sulphuric acid) and HNO_3 (nitric acid) under various circumstances, typically involving a series of chemical reactions.[123] As an example, sulphur oxides (SO_2, SO_3) react to form acids when they come into contact with water molecules. In the case of sulphur trioxide (SO_3), the reaction is as follows: sulphur trioxide (SO_3) + water (H_2O) → sulphuric acid (H_2SO_4). Similar reactions occur during the formation of nitric acid.[124] In essence, this means that if NO_x and SO_x (either directly or after reactions with other materials) come in contact with water molecules, they can generate strong acids. These strong acids decrease the pH of the water because, similar to carbonic acids, they dissolve (ionise) in aqueous solutions and release hydrogen ions, which are then reflected on the pH scale.[125]

However, there is a difference between strong acids, such as sulphuric or nitric acid, and weak acids, like carbonic acid, regarding how much they influence water pH. While strong acids ionise completely – meaning all the acid particles dissociate to release hydrogen ions and lower pH – weak acids do not behave the same way because they do not fully dissociate. This is because, in contrast to weak acids, the

119 For example, cf. Brian Gaylord and others, 'Ocean Acidification through the Lens of Ecological Theory' (2016) 6 *Washington Journal of Environmental Law and Policy* 253; Swezey and others (n 15); Harrould-Kolieb and Hoegh-Guldberg (n 26).

120 Doney and others (n 7) 172.

121 David R. Turner and others, 'The Potential Future Contribution of Shipping to Acidification of the Baltic Sea' (2018) 47 *Ambio* 368, 368.

122 See Turner and others (n 121); Hassellöv and others (n 107); Hunter and others (n 107).

123 Monica Butnariu, 'Consequences of Acid Rain' (2014) 04 *Journal of Ecosystem & Ecography* 1 www.omicsonline.org/open-access/consequences-of-acid-rain-2157-7625.1000e119.php?aid=32697 accessed 17 February 2021; Anita Singh and Madhoolika Agrawal, 'Acid Rain and Its Ecological Consequences' (2008) 29 *Journal of Environmental Biology / Academy of Environmental Biology, India* 15, 16.

124 Singh and Agrawal (n 123) 16.

125 Turner and others (n 121) 368; Todd Silverstein, 'Weak vs Strong Acids and Bases: The Football Analogy' (2000) 77 *Journal of Chemical Education* 849.

ionisation of strong acids is not reversible.[126] In summary, this means that strong acids, which release more hydrogen ions, have a more severe effect on water pH that is not easily reversible.

Though NO_x and SO_x create strong acids that significantly impact seawater pH, their emissions are released in far lower quantities than carbon dioxide.[127] Thus, they have a much smaller effect on OA. Nevertheless, strong acids can reduce the pH of ocean water. Scientists focused on OA have largely concentrated on the impacts of CO_2, while the effects of NO_x and SO_x on OA have not received as much attention.[128] It remains to be seen whether this lack of research on strong acids has led to an underestimation of the relevance of these compounds to OA.

Having gained a firmer grasp of what OA entails, the question that arises is how these compounds end up in the ocean. There are two different ways through which these substances can reach ocean water. First, compounds can enter the ocean due to an activity. Second, compounds can be produced in the ocean when an activity leads to the release of a different compound that eventually causes the formation of one of the acidification-triggering compounds (namely NO_x, SO_x, and CO_2) in the water. The upcoming section will shed light on the ways in which the compounds NO_x, SO_x, and CO_2 find their way into the ocean. Understanding the activities that can contribute to OA is crucial to grasping the acidification problem at its roots. Later in this book (particularly the case selection in Chapter 5), the question of which actors and legal instruments address activities that can lead to OA will be raised.

2.1.3 The Compounds' Pathways into the Ocean

As foreshadowed in Section 2.1.2, this part will focus on how the compounds triggering acidification end up in the ocean (Table 2.1). More precisely, on one hand, attention will be paid to the various activities that directly carry these triggers into the water. On the other hand, it will examine how activities can introduce materials into the ocean, leading to the formation of compounds that trigger OA in the water. It is important to keep in mind that pathways for compounds to reach or be formed in the ocean may multiply in the future. However, the list of options introduced below, while not comprehensive, does examine the pathways currently endangering the ocean the most. Therefore, the following first describes how CO_2 makes its way into the water, as shown in Figure 2.1 (Section 2.1.3.1), and then explores SO_x and NO_x, as shown in Figure 2.2 (Section 2.1.3.2). Within each section, the significance of the different actions and consequences for OA will be explained. In the same vein, the timeframe (short/long-term) for addressing these compounds and

[126] Turner and others (n 121) 368; Silverstein (n 125) 849.

[127] See OECD, 'Air and GHG Emissions' www.oecd-ilibrary.org/environment/air-and-ghg-emissions/indicator/english_93d10cf7-en accessed 9 February 2023.

[128] Turner and others (n 121) 369.

Table 2.1 The activities through which OA triggers can reach the ocean.

<table>
<tr><th colspan="2"></th><th colspan="2">Activity</th><th>Consequences</th></tr>
<tr><td rowspan="16">Compounds triggering OA</td><td rowspan="11">CO_2</td><td rowspan="3">Anthropogenic CO_2 emissions</td><td>Electricity</td><td rowspan="3">CO_2 absorption</td></tr>
<tr><td>Transportation</td></tr>
<tr><td>Industry</td></tr>
<tr><td rowspan="3">Geoengineering and CCS</td><td>Direct injections</td><td>Injection of CO_2</td></tr>
<tr><td>Nutrient fertilisation</td><td>Enhanced primary production</td></tr>
<tr><td>CCS</td><td>Possible leakage</td></tr>
<tr><td rowspan="5">Coastal activities</td><td>Suboptimal coastal planning</td><td rowspan="5">Soil erosion, runoff, pollution supply nutrients and organic material that lead to enhanced primary production</td></tr>
<tr><td>Land-based pollution</td></tr>
<tr><td>Land-use change</td></tr>
<tr><td>Land use</td></tr>
<tr><td>Deforestation</td></tr>
<tr><td rowspan="5">NO_x and SO_x</td><td rowspan="4">Anthropogenic emissions</td><td>Energy transformation</td><td rowspan="4">Precipitation</td></tr>
<tr><td>Energy consumption</td></tr>
<tr><td>Industry processes</td></tr>
<tr><td>Shipping</td></tr>
<tr><td>Scrubber</td><td>Scrubbing</td><td>Acidic wash water</td></tr>
</table>

Source: Compiled by the author.

the levels (local, regional, global) from which they derive and have the most substantial effects will also be discussed.

2.1.3.1 Carbon Dioxide (CO_2)

According to the latest scientific research, CO_2 enters or is formed in the ocean due to three different types of activities, which will be looked at below. These activities are anthropogenic CO_2 emissions, geoengineering and carbon capture and storage (CCS), and coastal activities.

2.1.3.1.1 Anthropogenic CO_2 Emissions Anthropogenic CO_2 emissions are the best-researched and, according to today's knowledge, the largest contributor to CO_2 in OA. In fact, the very definition of OA has been determined by many as a chemical process caused by the increasing level of CO_2 in the atmosphere.[129] Even though

[129] Doney and others (n 7); Royal Society (Great Britain) (n 99); Secretariat of the Convention on Biological Diversity and others (n 9) 11.

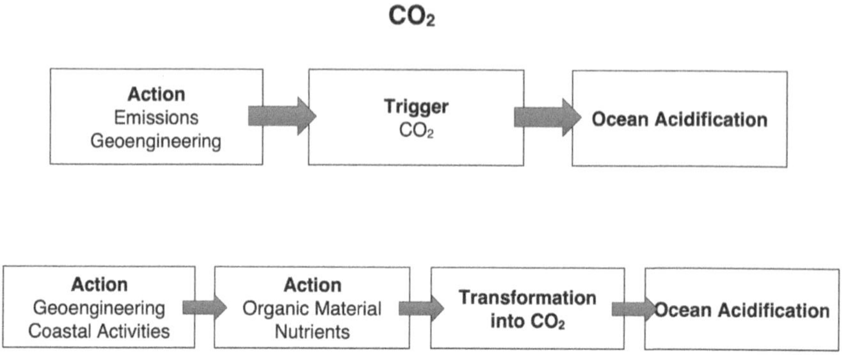

Figure 2.1 Pathways of CO_2 into the ocean.
Source: Compiled by the author

this chapter demonstrates that compounds, including CO_2, can contribute to the acidification of the oceans through different pathways, the generation of CO_2 emissions, indeed, plays the most significant role. The emission of CO_2 due to, for instance, the burning of fossil fuels over the last 200 years – particularly in the last 30 years – has led to a release of more than 500 billion metric tons of CO_2 into the atmosphere.[130] The ocean has absorbed 39 per cent of what has been produced since the Industrial Revolution.[131] Since the level of emissions is rising, the ocean has taken in greater amounts of CO_2 over time.[132]

Anthropogenic carbon dioxide emissions come from a variety of sources. Globally, the sectors with the largest contributions to these emissions include electricity generation (~41 per cent), transportation (~23 per cent), and industry (~20 per cent).[133] However, there is geographic variation, and the extent to which each activity contributes to OA depends on the location. While burning fossil fuels is a crucial factor in some areas, in others, it could be shipping, such as in the Baltic Sea.[134]

After CO_2 emissions are generated into the atmosphere, the ocean water absorbs the gas. This initiates the chemical process of acidification described above. The absorption occurs because the surface water attempts to match its CO_2 level with that of the atmosphere, thus achieving balance. Therefore, the greater the concentration of this gas in the atmosphere, the more the ocean must absorb it to maintain

[130] Laffoley and others (n 12) 6; Tobias Friedrich and others, 'Detecting Regional Anthropogenic Trends in Ocean Acidification against Natural Variability' (2012) 2 *Nature Climate Change* 1, 1.

[131] McKinley and others (n 3) 1.

[132] Laffoley and others (n 12) 6; Friedrich and others (n 130) 1.

[133] Elizabeth Kocs, 'The Global Carbon Nation: Status of CO_2 Capture, Storage and Utilization' (2017) 148 *EPJ Web of Conferences* 1, 3.

[134] Jagers and others (n 30) 818.

equilibrium.[135] Thus, due to an increased release of anthropogenic CO_2 emissions, the problem of OA has also grown.[136]

In summary, regarding the importance of OA, it has been noted that anthropogenic emissions of CO_2 are the primary cause of OA. These emissions are generated globally and have far-reaching consequences. Furthermore, reducing these emissions requires cooperation across many sectors.[137] Thus, concerning the anticipated timeframe, it can be concluded that a complete shift away from CO_2 emissions is unlikely to occur quickly in the short term.

2.1.3.1.2 Geoengineering and CCS Another set of activities that can lead to consequences causing acidification in the ocean is geoengineering, particularly CCS in geological formations. Both CCS and the other geoengineering techniques presented here are designed to ameliorate climate change.[138] CCS, for example, is viewed as a tool enabling emissions reduction during the desired transition to a 'carbon-free world'.[139] Geoengineering is an umbrella term encompassing various techniques to manipulate and intervene in the earth's climate system, including the oceanic environment, to moderate global warming.[140] These activities only pose a danger to the oceans when actively in use, and CCS, in particular, is still in its infancy. Nevertheless, they should not be omitted.[141] Overall, the contribution of these techniques to OA is minor compared to emissions or coastal activities as described below. However, experts in the field note that interest in geoengineering, including techniques such as alkalinisation, macroalgae cultivation, and marine cloud brightening, has increasingly attracted attention from policymakers in recent years.[142] Within the realm of geoengineering, several of these techniques could trigger OA, particularly the following three: injection, fertilisation, and CCS.

First, one way to remove CO_2 from the atmosphere is by directly injecting carbon dioxide into ocean water. Just as in the case of natural absorption of the gas by the water, this leads to the described chemical reactions in the sea and hence to OA.[143] Another, more complicated technique to lower the amount of CO_2 in the atmosphere is ocean fertilisation.[144] Fertilisation, in contrast to injections, relies on

[135] Arctic Monitoring and Assessment Programme and others (n 10) 1.

[136] Harrould-Kolieb and Hoegh-Guldberg (n 26) 10.

[137] Cf. Aditi Mukherji and others, 'Synthesis Report of the IPCC Sixth Assessment Report (AR6)' https://report.ipcc.ch/ar6syr/pdf/IPCC_AR6_SYR_SPM.pdf.

[138] Kocs (n 133) 4. [139] Ibid., 4, 6, 8.

[140] Intergovernmental Oceanographic Commission (IOC) and others, 'Marine Climate Engineering "Ocean Fertilization: A Scientific Summary for Policy Makers"' (International Maritime Organization 2011) IMO Report LC/SG 34/INF.3 1.

[141] Kocs (n 133) 4, 5, 6, 13.

[142] Interview with Internal IMO Expert #1, 'Internal IMO Expert Interview #1' (January 2023).

[143] Herr and others (n 33) 8.

[144] For example, cf. Long Cao and Ken Caldeira, 'Can Ocean Iron Fertilization Mitigate Ocean Acidification?' (2010) 99 *Climatic Change* 303; Intergovernmental Oceanographic Commission (IOC) and others (n 140).

natural processes in the ocean. Nutrients are either directly added to the ocean water or the nutrient supply from deep water is boosted, which enhances the growth of planktonic (drifting) microorganisms.[145] These planktonic organisms, then among other things, require CO_2 taken from the atmosphere to conduct photosynthesis. Hence, these natural processes can fix carbon in the ocean, and the higher the number of these organisms, the more gas is taken up. Therefore, this deliberate increase in primary production is enhanced to a great enough degree to noticeably increase the absorption of CO_2.[146] Studies have shown that while fertilisation might have minor beneficial effects on surface water pH, it will boost acidification, in line with the chemical reactions described above, in lower and especially deep water levels.[147] This occurs because atmospheric CO_2 can reach these water levels following the natural processes it undergoes after photosynthesis.[148] However, predicting the exact repercussions for the ocean and the acidification resulting from a larger fertilisation undertaking in the open ocean (and not under experimental circumstances) is difficult.[149]

Last, CCS is a geoengineering technique that has gained more attention in recent years. Before the goal of long-term storage in, for instance, sub-seabed geological formations can be reached, there are different steps the CO_2 must undergo. First, the gas is captured from power plants or industrial sites and then transported through pipelines to the location where it can be injected into a geological formation.[150] The risk that arises from this geoengineering technique is that if the storage is done improperly, there may be leakage of CO_2 into the ocean water.[151] Releasing the gas into the water would then lead to the chemical reactions that trigger OA.

In sum, geoengineering activities are currently a minor contributor to OA. However, should these techniques gain more traction in the coming years, they will lead to additional acidification, though the extent is unclear. The risk of acidification from geoengineering can be prevented or at least limited immediately. Since extensive geoengineering activities have not yet begun, solutions and alternatives can be found and implemented in the short term. Additionally, the impact of geoengineering activities is very localised, affecting only the areas where, for instance, nutrients have been released. Nevertheless, if not prevented, the effects remain harmful to the local or regional area where the activity occurs.

[145] Intergovernmental Oceanographic Commission (IOC) and others (n 140) 1, 2, 3.

[146] Herr and others (n 33) 8, 27; Intergovernmental Oceanographic Commission (IOC) and others (n 140) 1, 2, 3; Cao and Caldeira (n 144) 304.

[147] Cao and Caldeira (n 144) 307–309; Intergovernmental Oceanographic Commission (IOC) and others (n 140) 10, 11.

[148] Joseph Street, 'Iron, Phytoplankton Growth, and the Carbon Cycle' (2005) 43 *Metal Ions in Biological Systems* 153, 183, 184.

[149] Intergovernmental Oceanographic Commission (IOC) and others (n 140) 1.

[150] Arshad Raza and others, 'Significant Aspects of Carbon Capture and Storage – A Review' (2019) 5 *Petroleum* 335, 336.

[151] Herr and others (n 33) 27.

2.1.3.1.3 Coastal Activities Another group of activities that can cause acidification in the ocean is coastal activities. This group includes activities that occur on land but negatively impact the ocean, such as suboptimal coastal planning, land-based pollution, land use or land-use change, and deforestation.[152]

Even though the problem of negative influences from such activities is indicated within the relevant literature, the actual processes, causal links, and the aquatic range affected by these activities are not explained thoroughly. It often remains unclear which activities lead to what consequences and how and where they contribute to OA.[153]

Nevertheless, the literature indicates that for waters near a coastline, these actions could lead to harmful acidification effects. These biogeochemical perturbations may be as significant as anthropogenic CO_2 in contributing to changes and rising acidity levels near coastal areas.[154] Therefore, coastal waters experiencing consequences from coastal activities, which will be explained below, are referred to as hot spots. Kelly defines these hot spots as 'patches of ocean water with significantly depressed pH levels relative to historical baselines occurring at spatial scales of tens to hundreds of square kilometers'.[155]

Coastal hot spots arise because the aforementioned coastal activities have various repercussions that negatively impact the ocean. The consequences of these actions – such as soil erosion, runoff, and pollution – can introduce organic matter and nutrients into the water.[156] For instance, industry or farmland near estuaries, surrounded by poorly planned infrastructure, serves as sources of these materials.[157]

These terrestrial anthropogenic disturbances lead to changes in ocean metabolism close to the coast. The detrimental consequences of an excess of nutrients have been seen above in relation to geoengineering. However, more precisely, with the enhancement of the entire metabolism, including primary production, the issue is that when plankton dies, it sinks as organic matter towards the sea bottom. In addition to organic matter from coastal activities, this organic matter is decomposed by bacteria. In this process, the bacteria dissolve the organic matter into inorganic substances, one of which is CO_2. Consequently, OA occurs at lower water levels.[158]

However, measuring the exact impact of nutrients and organic matter in coastal waters is a difficult exercise. One particularity, already addressed above in relation

[152] Kelly and others (n 6) 1036, 1037; Structured Expert Dialogue (SED), 'FCCC/SB/2015/INF.1' 159 https://unfccc.int/resource/docs/2015/sb/eng/inf01.pdf accessed 22 October 2020; Jagers and others (n 30) 818, 822; Laffoley and others (n 12) 15; cf. Joseph Salisbury and others, 'Coastal Acidification by Rivers: A Threat to Shellfish?' (2008) 89 *Eos, Transactions American Geophysical Union* 513, 513.

[153] Cf. Kelly and others (n 6); Billé and others (n 23); Cyronak and others (n 107); Structured Expert Dialogue (SED) (n 152); Jagers and others (n 30).

[154] Cyronak and others (n 107) 5544; Kelly and others (n 6) 1036.

[155] Kelly and others (n 6) 1036.

[156] Jagers and others (n 30) 818; Kelly and others (n 6) 1036, 1037.

[157] Cf. image by Kelly and others (n 6) 1037.

[158] Arctic Monitoring and Assessment Programme (AMAP), *AMAP Arctic Ocean Acidification Assessment: Summary for Policy-Makers* (2013) 4; Cyronak and others (n 107) 5543, 5544; Wei-Jun Cai and others, 'Acidification of Subsurface Coastal Waters Enhanced by Eutrophication' (2011) 4 *Nature Geoscience* 766, 766.

to pH measurements, that makes identifying changes in waters near the coastline challenging is the greater natural variability due to diel (daily) and seasonal geochemical, physical, and biological processes in these waters.[159] Thus, the exact significance of coastal activities for OA is not yet understood, but it is expected to be considerable.

In summary, coastal activities, although not as significant as anthropogenic CO_2 emissions, are an important cause of OA at both local and regional levels. Similar to geoengineering, the effects of coastal activities are localised, yet the impacted areas can be extensive, especially in regions with substantial farmland or urbanisation. Nonetheless, solutions can be implemented within a relatively short timeframe, such as by improving coastal planning or filtering wastewater.

2.1.3.2 Nitrogen Oxides (NO_x) and Sulphur Oxides (SO_x)

Nitrogen and Sulphur oxides enter the ocean as a result of two types of activities, which are described below (also see Figure 2.2). Similar to CO_2, the first type of activity involves the generation of emissions, while the second type pertains to the release of scrubber effluents.

2.1.3.2.1 Anthropogenic NO_x and SO_x Emissions As noted above, anthropogenic emissions of NO_x and SO_x and their relevance to OA have received comparatively little attention relative to CO_2 emissions. However, what is known, and what will be discussed further, is that these emissions may contribute to OA, at least in certain ocean areas.

According to a publication by the Organization for Economic Co-operation and Development (OECD), the leading sources of NO_x and SO_x are 'atmospheric pollutants from energy transformation, energy consumption and industrial processes'.[160] Such sources include, more specifically, road traffic and combustion in industry for nitrogen dioxide and burning fossil fuels for sulphur dioxide.[161] Beyond that, both of these gases are emitted by the shipping industry.[162] Shipping likely has the greatest influence on NO_x and SO_x emissions that contribute to OA.[163] The reason the shipping industry is so important is the behaviour of the gases in the atmosphere. Once released into the atmosphere, these gases exhibit a different behaviour than CO_2. Unlike CO_2, these gases have a short atmospheric residence time, meaning they do not travel as far from the source as CO_2. Thus, the concentration of NO_x and SO_x is linked to the amount and proximity of sources of these gases.[164] As a result, heavily trafficked shipping lanes,

[159] Secretariat of the Convention on Biological Diversity and others (n 9) 7; Cyronak and others (n 107) 5538.

[160] OECD, *Environment at a Glance 2020* (OECD 2020) 26 www.oecd-ilibrary.org/environment/environment-at-a-glance/volume-/issue-_4ea7d35f-en accessed 4 March 2021.

[161] Ibid., *27*.

[162] Turner and others (n 121); Hassellöv and others (n 107); Hunter and others (n 107).

[163] Hassellöv and others (n 107) 2731; Turner and others (n 121) 369.

[164] Turner and others (n 121) 369; R Delmas, Dominique Serça and Corinne Jambert, 'Global Inventory of NOx Sources' (1997) 48 *Nutrient Cycling in Agroecosystems* 51, 1, 2.

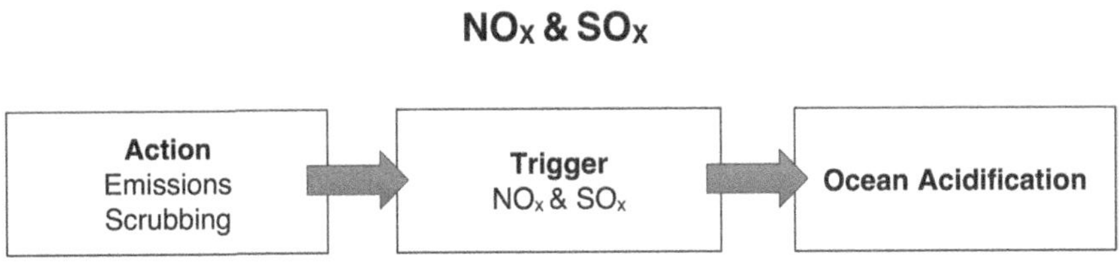

Figure 2.2 NO_x and SO_x pathways into the ocean.
Source: Compiled by the author

harbours, and coastal areas close to sources of these gases are particularly affected by acidification. Research in these areas indicates that regional pH decreases of similar magnitude to CO_2-driven acidification can arise within these heavily trafficked areas.[165]

After being emitted, sulphur dioxide (SO_2) undergoes chemical reactions that produce sulphur trioxide (SO_3). This SO_3 then dissolves in water molecules, such as cloud droplets, to form sulphuric acid (H_2SO_4), which is subsequently removed from the atmosphere and ends up in ocean water through rain-out or wash-out if absorbed by raindrops. Similar processes occur concerning other SO_X or NO_X.[166] In line with what has been seen in the chemical background part, once these strong acids enter the ocean, the pH of the water decreases.

In summary, anthropogenic emissions of NO_X and SO_X and their relevance for OA are not well understood. However, research indicates that heavily trafficked shipping lanes and harbours, among others, located near sources of these gases, are particularly affected by OA. Therefore, regarding geoengineering and coastal activities, the effects of this cause of OA are also local or regional. Attempts to regulate such emissions are already underway, as seen below. However, alternatives for reducing these emissions, such as scrubbers, are equally harmful. It remains to be seen whether functional solutions can be found in the short term.

2.1.3.2.2 Scrubber Effluents The issue of scrubber effluents is relatively recent and has begun to manifest as emissions from shipping, particularly NO_X and SO_X, have gained increased attention. Regulations were drafted to address the emissions problem through guidelines and restrictions;[167] and as a result, exhaust gas cleaning systems like scrubber technology have become more popular.[168]

[165] Hasselöv and others (n 107) 2731; Turner and others (n 121) 369.

[166] Singh and Agrawal (n 123) 16; Butnariu (n 123) 1; Heinz Rennenberg and Arthur Gessler, 'Acid Rain' (2001) 1.

[167] *International Convention for the Prevention of Pollution from Ships, 1973, as Modified by the Protocol of 1978* (MARPOL 73/78) 1973 (UNTS 1340 (p61), 1341 (p3)) annex VI, Reg. 13, Reg. 14.

[168] Turner and others (n 121) 369, 370; Sonja Endres and others, 'A New Perspective at the Ship-Air-Sea-Interface: The Environmental Impacts of Exhaust Gas Scrubber Discharge' (2018) 5 *Frontiers in Marine Science* 139, 1, 2.

Scrubber technology is a tool designed to remove mainly SO_x and also NO_x from exhaust gases released into the atmosphere and to dispose of it as acid wash in the ocean. Three types of wet scrubbers exist: open, closed, and hybrid.[169] Open-loop scrubbers are frequently used because they are the cheapest option, but also the most harmful, so they will be the focus here. The concept of this type of scrubber is to use seawater as a medium to eliminate SO_x from exhaust gases since the alkaline water is meant to neutralise the acids that form during this process, as explained in the chemical background section. However, after the process, the water released back into the ocean has a very low pH.[170]

A significant reduction in seawater pH is expected due to this technology, particularly in heavily trafficked areas of the sea. A 2020 study on SO_x conducted by Dulière et al. concerning the southern North Sea predicted a pH decrease because of open-loop scrubbers 'equivalent to 2 to 4 years of climate change acidification on average over the whole domain, and to 10 to 50 years, in more local areas'.[171] Scrubber techniques can cause such harmful consequences, as the scrubber effluents directly transport detrimental materials into the water. Thus, introducing effluents through scrubbers is more damaging than gas from a smokestack, which releases gases over a wider area since the acid wash directly enters the water.[172]

In summary, the impact of scrubber effluents on OA is similar to that described above for NO_x and SO_x emissions. The impact is localised to the area where the effluents are released. Additionally, it remains uncertain whether NO_x and SO_x can be reduced in a short time through technologies that do not contribute to OA. However, stricter regulations regarding scrubbers (particularly open-loop scrubbers) appear to be a short-term solution. Less harmful alternatives – such as closed-loop scrubbers, which have a more limited discharge of acidic water compared to open-loop ones – are already available.[173] Nevertheless, open-loop scrubbers remain dominant in the market.[174]

2.1.4 Regionality and Ocean Acidification

OA is a global phenomenon that is, however, characterised by geographic diversity, as indicated in part a. above. Water pH and its natural or anthropogenically induced changes vary at local levels (in the vicinity of the coast) and global levels (open ocean), and even between different localities (various coastlines).

[169] Endres and others (n 168) 5, 6; Turner and others (n 121) 370.

[170] Endres and others (n 168) 6; Turner and others (n 121) 370; Valérie Dulière, Katrijn Baetens and Geneviève Lacroix, *Potential Impact of Wash Water Effluents from Scrubbers on Water Acidification in the Southern North Sea* (2020) 9.

[171] Dulière, Baetens and Lacroix (n 170) 8.

[172] Turner and others (n 121) 372.

[173] Cf. ibid., 370.

[174] Johannes Teuchies and others, 'The Impact of Scrubber Discharge on the Water Quality in Estuaries and Ports' (In Review 2020) preprint 2 www.researchsquare.com/article/rs-23441/v2 accessed 12 July 2023.

In addition to this variety between and within levels, it is observed that some areas are more vulnerable to environmental changes (including the effects of OA) than others.

The literature identifies the Arctic, Antarctic, and other ice-covered areas as especially sensitive.[175] There are several reasons for this, and one simple explanation is that ice-covered waters are typically characterised by low biodiversity and a simple food web.[176] Thus, if there is a disturbance in the system, the repercussions will be evident at all levels of the food web immediately. Furthermore, organisms in these areas are already challenged by extreme conditions, so OA constitutes an additional stressor on these ecosystems.[177] Another reason why impacts will appear first in ice-covered areas is that colder waters naturally absorb more CO_2 than warmer waters. Additionally, the melting sea ice uncovers more ocean surface, which increases the area that can absorb CO_2 from the air.[178] Hence, there are oceans that are more prone to OA and will show effects sooner than others. Therefore, depending on the location, ecosystems are affected to varying degrees, and their ability to adapt (see also Section 2.4) to or cope with changes is contingent on their area.

Other regions that might be more vulnerable to OA are areas with coastal upwelling. Simply phrased, coastal upwelling describes a phenomenon where winds blow from the coast and cause surface water to move offshore. In the process, water from the deep ocean rises (upwells) towards the surface and replaces the surface water. The water that surfaces from the deep is colder, nutrient-rich, and has a different chemical composition.[179] This bottom water fuels productive food webs.[180] However, among other things, the bottom water is more acidic than the surface water that was previously in its place.[181] Hence, ecosystems and organisms that experience upwelling have been exposed to higher acidity than those that do not experience upwelling events. This difference might mean that ecosystems and populations of organisms from those regions have developed a higher or lower tolerance to changes in acidity. The question remains whether those populations will be more or less prepared for OA. Thus far, acidification experiments with red abalone populations seem to indicate that abalone from areas with upwelling are tolerant to OA compared to populations raised in captivity and sourced from a lower upwelling region, albeit with possible trade-offs in, for instance, growth.[182]

175 Arctic Monitoring and Assessment Programme (AMAP), *AMAP Assessment 2018: Arctic Ocean Acidification*. (2018) 1.

176 Arctic Monitoring and Assessment Programme and others (n 10) 4, 39, 62.

177 Ibid., 3, 4, 32.

178 Michiyo Yamamoto-Kawai and others, 'Aragonite Undersaturation in the Arctic Ocean: Effects of Ocean Acidification and Sea Ice Melt' (2009) 326 *Science (New York, N.Y.)* 1098, 1099.

179 Oregon State University and others, 'The Dynamics and Impact of Ocean Acidification and Hypoxia: Insights from Sustained Investigations in the Northern California Current Large Marine Ecosystem' (2019) 32 *Oceanography* 62, 67.

180 Ibid., 63.

181 Ibid., 67.

182 Cf. Swezey and others (n 15).

2.1.5 Understanding the Causes of OA

As shown above, OA is a problem that scientists are only slowly beginning to comprehend. One reason understanding OA is challenging is that the pH and both natural and anthropogenically induced changes vary on local and global levels, as well as within local areas. Additionally, OA is a creeping process, with repercussions gradually becoming more visible. Nevertheless, having understood which compounds trigger OA and how these acidification triggers enter the ocean, we can conclude that the oceans do not acidify solely due to anthropogenic emissions of CO_2, as is commonly believed. In fact, the compounds and actions that cause acidification in the oceans, are manifold and often difficult to comprehend, especially for non-scientists. It is evident that OA results from the interplay between the ocean, atmosphere, and land. Furthermore, the effects of these compounds and actions on the ocean vary, impacting significance and levels at local, regional, and global levels.

Additionally, some compounds and actions can be addressed sooner than others. For instance, while tackling anthropogenic CO_2 emissions is a long-term project, addressing coastal activities can be accomplished in a shorter timeframe. Coastal activities can be resolved more quickly since these local and regional contributors to OA can even be managed by individual states or regions and do not necessarily require coordinated action from the entire community of states. Properly understanding the outlined procedures regarding OA is essential for mitigating the problem and will be discussed in Chapters 3, 5, 6, and 7.

However, in addition to these causes of OA, there are also activities that can impose consequences putting the oceans and associated ecosystems under additional stress, making them more vulnerable to the adverse effects of OA. This vulnerability makes it more challenging, for instance, for species to adapt to further stressors such as OA. To afford the ocean a better opportunity to adapt to OA, now and in the future, it will be essential to minimise these other ocean stressors as much as possible.[183] Therefore, Section 2.2 will provide an overview of some of the main stressors that threaten the ocean's ability to adapt to acidification before discussing adaptation itself (in Section 2.3). Information about ocean stressors will be referenced in Chapters 3 and 5 of the book, where actors and legal instruments will be mapped and considered for one of the case studies (Chapters 6 and 7).

2.2 Activities Leading to Additional Ocean Stressors

As indicated at the end of Section 2.1.5, some activities have consequences that stress the ocean and its organisms, making it less able to respond to additional changes such as OA. Hitherto, little is known about the interaction of OA with other

[183] Dupont and Pörtner (n 108) 1766, 1770; Anthony (n 107) 61, 67, 68; Secretariat of the Convention on Biological Diversity and others (n 9) 9.

environmental hazards, as only a few experiments – let alone under completely realistic circumstances – have been conducted.[184] It is known that ecosystems and the species living within them can naturally adapt to changes they are exposed to.[185] However, if an ecosystem has to adapt to and combat a variety of changes at the same time, this task becomes more difficult as the level of stress increases. Thus, every influence that challenges an ecosystem makes it harder for it and its species to adjust to the next one.[186] Stress induced by different sources compounds, eventually leading to cumulative impacts and impaired resilience.[187]

Harmful activities and their consequences can exacerbate the effects of OA on the ecosystem. To comprehensively address OA and activities that contribute to other ocean stressors, it must be understood and tackled as well. Activities that create additional stressors, which will be discussed in the following sections, partially overlap with those already analysed. These activities include anthropogenic emissions (Section 2.2.1) and geoengineering, coastal activities, and shipping, which will be discussed as a group here due to their similar repercussions and stress (Section 2.2.2). Additionally, fishing (Section 2.2.3) will be considered another activity causing ocean stress before this part can be summarised (Section 2.2.4). Also, the stressors, their source levels and adverse effects, and the timeframe for addressing them will be briefly mentioned.

2.2.1 Anthropogenic Greenhouse Gas Emissions

The release of greenhouse gas emissions into the atmosphere drives climate change and global warming. This climatic change leads to a chain of other well-known problems; for example, sea-level rise, coral bleaching, deoxygenation, and ultraviolet radiation. All of these repercussions of climate change increase stress on the oceanic ecosystem, and they are all accelerating at an alarming rate.[188]

Sea-level rise serves as an example of how ecosystems suffer from and are overwhelmed by compound and cumulative stress. The primary cause of rising sea levels is the thermal expansion of ocean water and water flowing into the sea from melting ice sheets and glaciers due to increasing temperatures.[189] It is likely that, for instance, coral reefs will struggle to keep up with the rapidly rising water levels, especially where multiple stressors are present simultaneously, such as acidification, pollution, or overfishing. This impact on coral reefs can, in turn, alter

[184] Laffoley and others (n 12) 15; Secretariat of the Convention on Biological Diversity and others (n 9) 9; Dupont and Pörtner (n 108) 1767.
[185] Laffoley and others (n 12) 10.
[186] Herr and others (n 33) 8, 39; Structured Expert Dialogue (SED) (n 152) 153.
[187] Anthony (n 107) 61.
[188] Structured Expert Dialogue (SED) (n 152) 159; Laffoley and others (n 12) 12, 13, 14.
[189] Anny Cazenave and Gonéri Le Cozannet, 'Sea Level Rise and Its Coastal Impacts' (2014) 2 *Earth's Future* 15, 15, 19; S Jeffress Williams, 'Sea-Level Rise Implications for Coastal Regions' (2013) 63 *Journal of Coastal Research* 184, 185.

hydrodynamic and ecological conditions in coastal areas in certain parts of the world since coral reefs in healthy ocean conditions act as a barrier against incoming waves. Changing water conditions will lead to further repercussions for ecosystems related to and dependent on coral reefs. Hence, this could have a domino effect, potentially endangering many species.[190] When these already burdened ecosystems must additionally adapt to acidification, managing both sea-level rise and acidification concurrently becomes impossible.

Furthermore, sea-level rise and other repercussions of climate change can both contribute to and exacerbate the consequences of anthropogenic activities that lead to OA, as described earlier in this chapter. For example, potential implications of sea-level rise include shoreline erosion, which is often caused by anthropogenic coastal activities but is occurring more frequently due to rising sea levels.[191] As previously mentioned, erosion carries nutrients into the water, which leads to increased acidification. Therefore, the ocean is simultaneously exposed to a variety of changes due to the release of anthropogenic emissions and the consequential impacts of climate change, making it difficult for the ocean to adapt properly to any of these, including OA.

Similar to anthropogenic emissions of CO_2, the cause and effect of GHG emissions and resulting climate change are also global. Like the reduction of CO_2, the reduction of GHG emissions is a collective task requiring the involvement and commitment of many sectors. Therefore, the timeframe for addressing these issues is also long-term.

2.2.2 Geoengineering, Coastal Activities, and Shipping

Geoengineering, coastal activities, and shipping together represent a group of actions that, despite their differences, produce similar consequences and stress. However, as with causes, geoengineering currently poses only a minor threat in terms of stressors. The three activities can release nutrients, and in the case of coastal activities and shipping, other pollutants into the ocean, as explained in Section 1.3. In addition to scrubber effluents (which, apart from acids, also contain other harmful substances), shipping further endangers the marine environment through, for instance, oil spills, dumping, and the release of ballast water into the ocean.[192]

An excess of nutrients, apart from eventually leading to OA, can also induce stress on the ocean and its ecosystems since it may cause eutrophication. Eutrophication, the process of over-enriching aquatic ecosystems with nutrients,

[190] L. Keyzer and others, 'The Potential of Coastal Ecosystems to Mitigate the Impact of Sea-Level Rise in Shallow Tropical Bays' (2020) 246 *Estuarine Coastal and Shelf Science* 1, 1, 2, 8, 9; Ilsa Kuffner, 'Coral Reefs Could Drown as Sea Levels Rise' (2018) 558 *Nature* 378.

[191] Cazenave and Cozannet (n 189) 15; Williams (n 189) 191.

[192] M. Vikas and GS Dwarakish, 'Coastal Pollution: A Review' (2015) 4 *Aquatic Procedia* 381, 384.

increases the growth of plant biomass such as plankton and has a series of repercussions, the most well-known being hypoxia.[193] The state of hypoxia – or, in other words, oxygen depletion – arises when this excessive amount of biomass dies and decomposes with the help of bacteria, a process that consumes available oxygen. Since stratification, due to discrepancies in temperature and salinity, limits the exchange of oxygen from surface waters, this oxygen depletion can eventually lead to so-called dead zones.[194] Other consequences of excessive algal bloom include the disappearance of subaquatic vegetation due to light blockage and the change and loss of bottom-dwelling (benthic) aquatic species.[195] Apart from eutrophication being another stress factor for the oceans, it might also increase the general susceptibility to OA in some areas. However, there is generally a poor understanding of the interactions between eutrophication and OA or other repercussions of climate change.[196]

There are many different types of pollution that affect the ocean. For instance, oil pollution from ships can be used to understand how pollution negatively influences and stresses oceanic ecosystems. Oil pollution from ships serves as an example. Daily, oil is released into the oceans due to shipping, which has detrimental effects on the ecosystem. Oil does not dissolve in water; instead, it builds up as oil sludge.[197] This build-up adversely affects fish, birds, and mammals, as well as the entire ecosystem that comes into contact with the oil. Among fish, oil can lead to mortality and endanger fish eggs and larvae. Birds and marine mammals can suffer from hypothermia, as the oil interferes with the protection fur and feathers normally provide against the cold water.[198] Hence, in cases of oil spills or other types of pollution, the ecosystem struggles to function and must combat these dangers, leading to stress.

This group of activities is likely to cause a significant and increasing amount of stress on the oceans, especially in coastal areas. The cause and effect of geoengineering, coastal activities, and shipping align with what has been explained (see Section 2.1.3), which is more local or regional. More specifically, cause and effect will occur in the same area of the ocean. For coastal activities, this refers to the water in the vicinity of a coastline. The timeframe within which these stressors could be addressed is short term. For example, larger geoengineering activities have yet to start and could be prevented before they even begin, as already discussed in Section 2.1.3.

193 Mindy Selman and others, 'Eutrophication and Hypoxia in Coastal Areas: A Global Assessment of the State of Knowledge' (2008) WRI Policy Note 1, 1; Samuli Korpinen and Erik Bonsdorff, 'Eutrophication and Hypoxia: Impacts of Nutrient and Organic Enrichment' (2015) 202; Cai and others (n 158) 766.

194 Selman and others (n 193) 2; Andrew H. Altieri and Keryn B. Gedan, 'Climate Change and Dead Zones' (2015) 21 *Global Change Biology* 1395, 1.

195 Selman and others (n 193) 2.

196 Cai and others (n 158) 766, 768, 769.

197 Vikas and Dwarakish (n 192) 384.

198 Deng Yuewen and Linda Adzigbli, 'Assessing the Impact of Oil Spills on Marine Organisms' (2018) 06 *Journal of Oceanography and Marine Research* 2, 3 www.omicsonline.org/open-access/assessing-the-impact-of-oil-spills-on-marine-organisms-2572-3103-1000179-102276.html accessed 18 March 2021.

2.2.3 Fishing

Lastly, an activity that has not been mentioned before is fishing. Overfishing – and, even more so, dangerous or disruptive fishing practices – are additional activities that induce stress on fish stocks, their habitats, and ecosystems in general.[199]

An example of a dangerous and disruptive fishing technique is the use of trawlers. A trawler is a mechanised fishing boat that uses nets to collect every organism in its path without selection.[200] This fishing method has a wide range of negative impacts on the ocean, its ecosystems, and particularly biodiversity. Due to its lack of selectivity, trawling catches and kills non-targeted species, including endangered ones. Trawling techniques also harm and damage the sea bottom and the bottom-dwelling species found there.[201] Therefore, these and other disturbances from fishing pose stress factors for oceanic ecosystems and species, disrupting their ability to prepare and maintain balance necessary to cope with and adapt to new challenges such as OA.

Fishing as an activity that causes ocean stress could be addressed more quickly through better fisheries management (see also adaptation). The stress caused by fishing is felt at the local or regional level where the activity occurs. However, its effects can be global. If fish stocks, especially those that migrate between different sea areas or jurisdictions (for instance, while travelling between living and spawning grounds), are overfished, the impact could be considered global.

2.2.4 Understanding Additional Ocean Stress

The aforementioned activities cause some of the most significant stress on oceans (Table 2.2). However, new and additional sources of ocean stress are continually emerging, while older ones are increasing in significance. For instance, deep-sea mining is a recent activity that will contribute to additional stress in the near future.[202] It is likely that this activity cannot occur without inducing ocean stress due to the environmental damage it inflicts, such as biodiversity loss.[203] For the ocean to react and adapt to OA, it will be crucial to minimise factors that induce stress. The extent and interplay of ocean stressors remain poorly understood, but interaction between various stressors is likely.[204] More research under real life

[199] Arctic Monitoring and Assessment Programme (AMAP) (n 158) 8; Laffoley and others (n 12) 14; Secretariat of the Convention on Biological Diversity and others (n 9) 17.

[200] Biju Kumar and G. Deepthi, 'Trawling and By-Catch: Implications on Marine Ecosystem' (2006) 90(7) *Current Science* 922.

[201] Ibid., *924*.

[202] Cf. Bernd Christiansen, Anneke Denda and Sabine Christiansen, 'Potential Effects of Deep Seabed Mining on Pelagic and Benthopelagic Biota' (2020) 114 *Marine Policy* 103442; cf. Marlene Pinheiro and others, 'Stressors of Emerging Concern in Deep-Sea Environments: Microplastics, Pharmaceuticals, Personal Care Products and Deep-Sea Mining' (2023) 876 *Science of the Total Environment* 162557.

[203] Cf. Christiansen, Denda and Christiansen (n 202).

[204] Cf. Cai and others (n 158); Altieri and Gedan (n 194).

Table 2.2 Activities causing additional ocean stress.

	Activity		Consequences
Activities leading to ocean stress	Anthropogenic emissions	Electricity	Climate change, global warming lead to sea-level rise, coral bleaching, deoxygenation, ultraviolet radiation
		Transportation	
		Industry	
	Geoengineering, coastal activities, shipping	Nutrient release	Eutrophication/Low-oxygen, hypoxia
		Pollution	Adverse effects on taxa due to pollution
	Fishing	Dangerous and Disruptive Fishing	Disruption and destruction of fish stocks and ecosystem
		Overfishing	

Source: Compiled by the author.

conditions is essential to gain a comprehensive understanding of how the ocean will respond to increasing OA as an additional stressor. Furthermore, similar to the causes, stressors can be examined across different timeframes and can affect various scales, from local to global.

Section 2.3 will provide an overview of some repercussions of OA for the environment and humanity. Research in this area is still limited and sometimes even points in opposite directions. Nonetheless, this overview hopefully underscores the pressing need to address OA.

2.3 Repercussions of Ocean Acidification

Scientists use geological history alongside experiments to better understand what to expect from the increasing acidification of the oceans.[205] The Paleogene included a period, the Palaeocene–Eocene Thermal Maximum, ca. fifty-six million years ago, characterised by high temperatures and atmospheric CO_2 levels.[206]

During that period, the problem of acidification emerged similarly to what is observed at the moment.[207] At that time, ocean warming and acidification together led to mass extinctions. Therefore, due to the similarity of past and current events, we can expect that biodiversity will be threatened if acidity increases. However, a concerning difference between now and the Palaeocene–Eocene boundary is that

[205] Secretariat of the Convention on Biological Diversity and others (n 9) 36, 37. [206] Ibid., 37.

[207] Tali L. Babila and others, 'Capturing the Global Signature of Surface Ocean Acidification during the Palaeocene–Eocene Thermal Maximum' (2018) 376 *Philosophical Transactions of the Royal Society A: Mathematical, Physical and Engineering Sciences* 1, 2.

OA occurred at a much slower pace during that time.[208] Furthermore, according to geological history, the recuperation of ocean waters happens very slowly. From the Palaeocene–Eocene boundary, we learn that ocean recovery will probably take thousands of years. Previously, no less than 100,000 years was needed for the ocean to recuperate.[209]

However, while useful, the context of geological history is insufficient to clearly predict the impacts of OA. Despite the support of geological history, the consequences of OA cannot be accurately predicted for the time being. This limitation is partly due to considerable uncertainty regarding human behaviour and ecosystem reactions.[210] Therefore, the science surrounding OA is based on varying levels of reliability. The scale describing confidence in OA research ranges from low to very high confidence.[211]

A 'very high level' of confidence means high agreement and robust evidence. Scientists have, for instance, very high confidence that ocean waters will be impaired in serving as a carbon sink. Very high confidence is also present regarding the fact that the reduction of CO_2 emissions would slow down OA.[212] The second highest level is 'high confidence', which is present when there is high/medium agreement and medium/robust evidence. High confidence is at hand for the fact that different stressors together compound the effects of OA or that molluscs are one of the groups of species most sensitive to OA.[213] 'Medium confidence' is present when there is high/medium/low agreement with limited/medium/robust evidence accordingly. Scientists have medium confidence about the fact that OA may have direct adverse effects on, for instance, fish behaviour or fitness.[214] Last, 'low' is the lowest level of confidence. 'Low confidence' is at hand if there is medium or low agreement paired with limited or medium evidence accordingly.[215] It is, for example, unclear, and there is little agreement and limited evidence as to what effects OA will have on top predators or fisheries.[216]

Overall, scientists agree that there is a high probability that OA will contribute to the degradation of the marine environment, which will eventually impact human beings. Nevertheless, there is considerable variability within and between species, and OA will likely transform marine life, producing winners and losers.[217] This difference in responses could suggest the ability of ecosystems, or at least

[208] Jelle Bijma and others, 'Climate Change and the Oceans – What Does the Future Hold?' (2013) 74 *Marine Pollution Bulletin* 495, 502.

[209] Secretariat of the Convention on Biological Diversity and others (n 9) 37–40; Babila and others (n 207) 1, 2; cf. James C. Zachos and others, 'Rapid Acidification of the Ocean during the Paleocene-Eocene Thermal Maximum' (2005) 308 *Science* 1611.

[210] Laffoley and others (n 12) 10.

[211] Wendy Broadgate and others, *Ocean Acidification, Summary for Policymakers, Third Symposium on the Ocean in a High-CO2 World* (2013) 12–22; Laffoley and others (n 12) 6.

[212] Laffoley and others (n 12) 6; Broadgate and others (n 211) 13. [213] Ibid. [214] Ibid.

[215] Broadgate and others (n 211) 13. [216] Ibid., 13; Laffoley and others (n 12) 6.

[217] Laffoley and others (n 12) 10; Kroeker and others (n 15) 1419, 1431; Secretariat of the Convention on Biological Diversity and others (n 9) 9, 15, 16; Arctic Monitoring and Assessment Programme and others (n 10) 50.

individual species, to adapt to changes. However, more research needs to be conducted to better understand these possibilities while also considering, for instance, the emergence of other stressors concurrently.[218] The influence of OA on coastal zones (see also regionality and OA above) is especially poorly understood, and it may be assumed that these areas are less susceptible to OA since they are naturally exposed to pH fluctuations, as explained above. It is, however, essential to consider shifts in the potential range and fluctuations instead of only the absolute pH value in this context. Furthermore, due to the variability, coastal areas may reach harmful levels more rapidly than, for example, the open sea.[219] Hence, diverse reactions and the complexity of the interactions within oceanic ecosystems render thorough analysis and prediction challenging.[220] Below are possible repercussions of OA on the environment (Section 2.3.1), including the resulting effects on humans (Section 2.3.2), followed by a brief summary of the repercussions (Section 2.3.3).

2.3.1 Impacts on the Environment

The repercussions of OA on the environment are manifold and affect various species, known as taxa, that inhabit oceanic ecosystems, as well as the biogeochemistry of the ocean itself. These taxa can be directly impaired by the acidification of the ocean or indirectly affected due to changes in habitats and marine food webs.[221] The following will examine the impacts on particularly vulnerable species and life stages (Section 2.3.1.1), the frequent physiological repercussions that may be expected to arise (Section 2.3.1.2), the effects of OA on species concerning their habitats (Section 2.3.1.3), and the biogeochemical consequences of OA (Section 2.3.1.4)

2.3.1.1 Particularly Vulnerable Species and Life Stages

Particularly at risk and most likely the first group of species affected by OA are those animals and plants with skeletons or shells made of calcium carbonate.[222] Scientists anticipate negative repercussions for these calcifying organisms, such as corals and molluscs, since they require calcium carbonate ($CaCO_3$) to build their skeletons. Calcium carbonate forms from a chemical reaction between calcium (Ca^{2+}) and carbonate (CO_3^{2-}), which is dissolved in seawater. Since carbonate also reacts with the increasing hydrogen ions in the water, this reduces the availability of carbonate that organisms need as a building material. Consequently, the amount of carbonate dissolved in the water is insufficient for calcifying organisms to build and maintain strong skeletons. As a result, these organisms require additional

[218] Secretariat of the Convention on Biological Diversity and others (n 9) 9. [219] Ibid., *15, 27*.
[220] Ibid., *16*. [221] Laffoley and others (n 12) 10.
[222] Ibid; Kristy J. Kroeker and others, 'Impacts of Ocean Acidification on Marine Organisms: Quantifying Sensitivities and Interaction with Warming' (2013) 19 *Global Change Biology* 1884, 1890; Secretariat of the Convention on Biological Diversity and others (n 9) 7.

energy to create shells, leaving them in an overall weaker state or even at risk of dissolving completely.[223]

There are uncertainties and high variability even within a single species regarding fertilisation and early life stages.[224] Uncertainty is particularly salient concerning the influence of OA on the fertilisation success of invertebrates, which often inhabit different marine environments during their life cycles and developmental stages. Furthermore, OA can adversely affect calcifying larvae, as indicated before.[225]

2.3.1.2 Frequent Physiological Repercussions

Many different taxa – including organisms that do not rely on calcium carbonate, such as fish, invertebrates, and sediment fauna – may suffer from a variety of direct impacts of acidity on various functions, including negative effects on cellular functions, fertilisation and life, behaviour or immune reaction.[226]

For example, impairment at the cellular level, such as acid-base regulation, can lead to possibly detrimental metabolic suppression, reduced protein synthesis, and long-term fitness impacts. Nevertheless, a few species might be able to adjust their energy allocation to compensate for the increasing energy costs required to manage OA.[227]

Another physiological reaction of fish and some invertebrates to OA may be the alteration of sensory systems and behaviour, such as a loss of discrimination ability between chemical cues or bold, risky behaviour of larvae as they move to the reef, which makes them easier catches for predators, thus leading to high mortality.[228] Last, regarding immune response and disease, more research is needed. However, it seems that OA could impair immune functions and enable the survival of pathogens.[229]

2.3.1.3 Effects on Species in Relation to Their Habitat

Species that dwell on the bottom and are part of the benthic communities (for instance, corals) will experience lower survival and growth rates.[230] There is, though, a variability among species (particularly seaweed and seagrass) that may be able to tolerate or even benefit from future pH values. Calcifying macroalgae, however, may be affected by OA, as indicated above.[231]

Species that inhabit the water column – the so-called pelagic zone – also exhibit differences among taxa. While silica-based phytoplankton, like diatoms, may thrive under more acidic conditions, the responses of calcifying phytoplankton

[223] Comeau and others (n 9) 1; Secretariat of the Convention on Biological Diversity and others (n 9) 7, 13, 14.

[224] Secretariat of the Convention on Biological Diversity and others (n 9) 9, 44, 45.

[225] Ibid., 9, 44.

[226] Cf. also Laffoley and others (n 12) 10.

[227] Secretariat of the Convention on Biological Diversity and others (n 9) 8, 42; Arctic Monitoring and Assessment Programme and others (n 10) 49.

[228] Arctic Monitoring and Assessment Programme and others (n 10) 50; Secretariat of the Convention on Biological Diversity and others (n 9) 8, 46, 70.

[229] Secretariat of the Convention on Biological Diversity and others (n 9) 47.

[230] Ibid., 54.

[231] Ibid., *8, 54*.

species, such as coccolithophores, are more varied among both inter and intraspecies.[232] Many of these single-celled planktonic calcifying organisms (foraminifera, coccolithophores) will be threatened by OA, making the situation even more precarious. Since single-celled organisms are close to the base of the food web, their endangered status may also jeopardise every organism that follows in the food chain. Furthermore, this could impact the efficiency of carbon transport between water layers.[233]

2.3.1.4 Biogeochemical Consequences

Lastly, it is anticipated that there will be changes in aspects of ocean biogeochemistry, including the disruption of climatic feedback. This disturbance will likely affect, among other things, carbon cycling processes such as primary production, as well as possibly reducing the ocean's ability to store carbon.[234]

2.3.2 Impacts on Human Beings

The effects of OA will show in human society.[235] When human well-being and economic wealth are at risk because the necessary components of nature can no longer guarantee these qualities, there is a peril to ecosystem services.[236] The concept of ecosystem services can create a link between the 'functioning of ecosystems and human welfare'.[237] More concretely, one definition was provided through the Millennium Ecosystem Assessment, which describes these services as 'the benefits people obtain from ecosystems'.[238] Furthermore, these services can be divided into four different groups: provisioning, regulating, cultural and supporting services.[239] In all of these groups, problems can be anticipated. In the following, examples of how OA can interfere with the four types of services will be given.

Supporting services form the foundation for all other services; thus, disturbances will impact the entire range of ecosystem services. Examples of supporting services include processes such as ecosystem resilience, nutrient cycling, and primary production.[240] As mentioned earlier, ecosystem resilience will be weakened due to OA. Calcifying organisms like corals, for example, provide habitat for various organisms. However, increasing acidity levels will hinder their ability to build and maintain structures.[241] As a result, the ecosystem's ability to respond to challenges

[232] Laffoley and others (n 12) 10; Secretariat of the Convention on Biological Diversity and others (n 9) 9.
[233] Kroeker and others (n 15).
[234] Secretariat of the Convention on Biological Diversity and others (n 9). [235] Ibid., 78, 81.
[236] Ibid., 81; cf. Brendan Fisher, R. Kerry Turner and Paul Morling, 'Defining and Classifying Ecosystem Services for Decision Making' (2009) 68 *Ecological Economics* 643.
[237] Fisher, Turner and Morling (n 236) 643.
[238] Millennium Ecosystem Assessment (Program) (ed), *Ecosystems and Human Well-Being: Synthesis* (Island Press 2005) 40.
[239] Ibid., 39. [240] Ibid., *40*.
[241] Secretariat of the Convention on Biological Diversity and others (n 9) 82.

will be compromised, resulting in decreased ecosystem resilience. Although these disturbances may not directly impact humans, they do affect them indirectly due to the disruptions they cause within other ecosystem services.

Products harvested from the sea, such as food, can be categorised under provisioning services.[242] When it comes to this type of service, the impacts of OA are already evident. The oyster industry, a multi-million-dollar sector in the United States, has experienced financial losses due to increasing mortality rates of oysters linked to acidification.[243] Another example is the deterioration of coral reefs as a habitat for organisms, which poses a corresponding threat to food security. Currently, around 400 million people's livelihoods are connected to these habitats.[244]

Regulating services encompass all benefits derived from the management of ecosystem processes. This includes coastal defence regulation, which is increasingly vital as coral reefs face destruction and will no longer be able to buffer waves or storms.[245] The final category is cultural services, which are educational, recreational, or inspirational in nature and represent nonmaterial benefits.[246] This category spans everything from the relationship of indigenous peoples with nature to the decline in tourism due to environmental degradation.[247]

Having identified the different types of ecosystem services, it is evident that there will be adverse effects extending from ecosystems to human society. Naturally, this comes with economic costs that have not been studied sufficiently up to this point. However, it is predicted that unmitigated OA will cause a loss to the world economy of more than US$ 1 trillion annually by 2100.[248]

2.3.3 Understanding the Repercussions of OA

As seen in this part, research concerning the effects of OA on the environment and human beings is far from comprehensive. Despite these gaps in understanding, it has been shown that repercussions will be severe not just for the oceans but also for humans. In addition to the adverse effects of OA, there are interactions with other ocean stressors and their cumulative consequences, which are poorly researched and understood. Nonetheless, knowledge about the consequences of the problem is essential for addressing adaptation to the growing issue, which will be discussed in Section 2.4. Overall, it becomes obvious that research at all levels is necessary to tackle OA.

[242] Millennium Ecosystem Assessment (Program) (n 238) 40.
[243] European Project on Ocean Acidification (EPOCA), 'Ocean Acidification: The Facts – A Special Introductory Guide for Policy Advisers and Decision Makers' 3; Laffoley and others (n 12) 10.
[244] Laffoley and others (n 12) 11; Secretariat of the Convention on Biological Diversity and others (n 9) 9.
[245] Secretariat of the Convention on Biological Diversity and others (n 9) 83.
[246] Millennium Ecosystem Assessment (Program) (n 238) 40.
[247] Secretariat of the Convention on Biological Diversity and others (n 9) 83.
[248] Ibid., *78, 83*.

2.4 Adaptation Options

Different forms of adaptation to OA are gaining increased attention. Similarly, methods for mitigation beyond merely reducing CO_2 emissions are also under consideration. In particular, when it comes to blue carbon, adaptation and alternative mitigation strategies overlap.[249] Therefore, in addition to serving as a tool to facilitate adaptation, blue carbon can also be leveraged for mitigation, as will be explained below. However, in this field of OA research, more work is needed. In the following, three frequently mentioned examples of adaptation will be discussed,[250] namely, blue carbon, marine protected areas, and fisheries management. Accordingly, blue carbon will be covered first (Section 2.4.1), followed by an explanation of marine protected areas (Section 2.4.2). Afterwards, fisheries (Section 2.4.3) will be discussed before summarising the adaptation options (Section 2.4.4). These adaptation options and alternative mitigation strategies are essential for addressing OA. Adaptation will guide the selection of actors and legal instruments included in the mapping (Chapter 3) as well as influence the case study selection and the case study itself in Chapters 5, 6, and 7.

2.4.1 Blue Carbon

Previously, natural carbon storage often comprised mainly terrestrial ecosystems, which can be referred to as 'green carbon'.[251] The term 'blue carbon' refers to carbon fluxes, capture and storage in marine systems such as marine and coastal ecosystems and species.[252] With the help of blue carbon ecosystems, carbon from both the atmosphere and ocean can be sequestered and stored.[253] For example, coastal blue carbon comprises the capture and storage by rooted vegetation like mangroves, seagrass, or salt marshes in coastal zones.[254] These types of vegetation have mitigation potential through rapid sequestration and storage along with adaptation potential by, for instance, protecting coasts and enhancing fisheries.[255]

[249] Anne B. Christianson and others, 'The Promise of Blue Carbon Climate Solutions: Where the Science Supports Ocean–Climate Policy' (2022) 9 *Frontiers in Marine Science* 851448, 2.

[250] For example, cf. Christianson and others (n 249); Dorte Krause-Jensen and others, 'Sequestration of Macroalgal Carbon: The Elephant in the Blue Carbon Room' (2018) 14 *Biology Letters* 20180236; Peter I Macreadie and others, 'Blue Carbon as a Natural Climate Solution' (2021) 2 *Nature Reviews Earth & Environment* 826; University of California, Santa Cruz and others, 'Planning for Change: Assessing the Potential Role of Marine Protected Areas and Fisheries Management Approaches for Resilience Management in a Changing Ocean' (2019) 32 *Oceanography* 116; George Hoppit and others, 'Are Marine Protected Areas an Adaptation Measure against Climate Change Impacts on Coastal Ecosystems? A UK Case Study' (2022) 2 *Nature-Based Solutions* 100030.

[251] C. Nellemann and GRID–Arendal (eds), *Blue Carbon: The Role of Healthy Oceans in Binding Carbon: A Rapid Response Assessment* (GRID–Arendal 2009) 8, 15.

[252] Christianson and others (n 249) 2, 3.

[253] Dorothée Herr and others, 'Pathways for Implementation of Blue Carbon Initiatives' (2017) 27 *Aquatic Conservation: Marine and Freshwater Ecosystems* 116, 116.

[254] Christianson and others (n 249) 5.

[255] Macreadie and others (n 250) 5, 6.

Regarding mitigation more specifically, this type of vegetation can sequester and store carbon in its biomass and in the sediments beneath it. Three main reasons lead to the high carbon sequestration capacity of these blue carbon ecosystems, namely their ability to produce, capture, and preserve carbon through, for example, photosynthesis or respiration. Their high carbon trapping ability allows these ecosystems to accrete sediment and accumulate carbon produced by other ecosystems. This carbon is then stored in forms that can resist microbial attack (so it is not released again), mainly because of the ecosystems' saturated and saline conditions that limit decomposition.[256] For example, the biomass productivity of mangroves is comparable to that of tropical forests. Thus, mangroves are a large carbon sink.[257]

In addition to three groups of rooted vegetation, macroalgae and kelp, in particular, are also discussed under the umbrella of nature-based solutions and blue carbon.[258] Kelp forests can help the ocean mitigate and adapt to OA. Macroalgae, which are rootless (as opposed to the vegetation described above), have the potential to be carbon sinks due to their high productivity. However, the presence of macroalgae results in less on-site carbon burial compared to other blue-carbon ecosystems. Instead, because macroalgae are rootless, they can transport carbon away from their area of origin. Macroalgae are gaining more attention as they can, for instance, grow rapidly and capture significant amounts of carbon in their biomass.[259]

Generally, blue carbon is regarded as a so-called nature-based solution to climate change.[260] Especially recently, blue carbon has garnered more interest in discussions surrounding these nature-based solutions.[261] The concept of nature-based solutions is relatively new and still being elaborated.[262] The International Union for Conservation of Nature (IUCN) defines nature-based solutions as 'actions to protect, sustainably manage and restore (...) ecosystems, which address societal challenges (e.g. climate change) (...) while simultaneously providing human well-being and biodiversity benefits'.[263] In other words, these nature-based solutions have developed to rely on ecosystems rather than reverting to engineering choices to mitigate and adapt to, for example, climate change effects. Simultaneously, the protection of natural ecosystems and biodiversity should be enhanced.[264] Thus, nature-based solutions aim to incorporate natural systems in addressing societal problems such as climate change.

[256] Ibid., 6; cf. also Lydia Kapsenberg and Tyler Cyronak, 'Ocean Acidification Refugia in Variable Environments' (2019) 25 *Global Change Biology* 3201, 3204.

[257] Christianson and others (n 249) 5.

[258] Ibid., 5, 6; cf. Krause-Jensen and others (n 250).

[259] Christianson and others (n 249) 5, 6.

[260] Cf. Christianson and others (n 249).

[261] Macreadie and others (n 250) 5; Nellemann and GRID–Arendal (n 251) 8, 15.

[262] E. Cohen-Shacham and others (eds), *Nature-Based Solutions to Address Global Societal Challenges* (IUCN International Union for Conservation of Nature 2016) xii https://portals.iucn.org/library/node/46191 accessed 2 June 2023.

[263] Ibid.

[264] Ibid.

In summary, both rooted vegetation and macroalgae must be conserved, restored, and protected to ensure their mitigation and adaptation potential. Coastal degradation and the annual GHG emissions resulting from losses are comparable to up to 19 per cent of annual GHG emissions from global deforestation.[265]

2.4.2 Marine Protected Areas

Marine Protected Areas (MPAs) have become the subject of discussion regarding ecosystem-based management. More specifically, the question is whether and how they can be part of resilience management against ocean change.[266] Resilience management can be defined as 'promoting factors that increase the resistance of an organism, population, or ecosystem to disturbances, as well as those that increase the rate of recovery to its predisturbance state'.[267] Thus, MPAs could serve as tools to create more resilient organisms, populations, or ecosystems. Resilience is especially needed in the face of ocean changes such as OA. MPAs are areas of the ocean where explicit protections from human uses and activities exist. Among many other effects, this non-disturbance promotes larger populations of species.[268] These larger populations, for instance, have greater genetic variation that enhances the probability of adaptive capacity.[269] It is likely that larger populations also improve the likelihood of more resistant genotypes within a population.[270] Another example of the positive effects of MPAs is the increased richness of species or diversity within a community that can develop when there is no human disturbance.[271] This can elevate the ecosystem's resistance. Even if one species is, for example, lost due to a disturbance, the chance that another more tolerant species with the same or a similar function can take over rises with richness in species.[272] Apart from fishing, the reduction of other local stressors in MPAs can also foster greater resistance against ocean change.[273] As an example, land-based pollution can lead to increased vulnerability to coral bleaching in coral species.[274] Hence, preventing these additional stressors could also result in greater resilience in MPAs. These are just some instances of how MPAs can facilitate resilience. MPAs can, of course,

[265] Herr and others (n 253) 117.
[266] University of California, Santa Cruz and others (n 250) 117.
[267] Ibid.
[268] Cf. SE Lester and others, 'Biological Effects within No-Take Marine Reserves: A Global Synthesis' (2009) 384 *Marine Ecology Progress Series* 33; Hoppit and others (n 250) 1.
[269] Cf. Morgan Kelly, 'Adaptation to Climate Change through Genetic Accommodation and Assimilation of Plastic Phenotypes' (2019) 374 *Philosophical Transactions of the Royal Society B: Biological Sciences* 20180176.
[270] University of California, Santa Cruz and others (n 250) 119.
[271] Cf. Lester and others (n 268).
[272] Cf. Shigeo Yachi and Michel Loreau, 'Biodiversity and Ecosystem Productivity in a Fluctuating Environment: The Insurance Hypothesis' (1999) 96 *Proceedings of the National Academy of Sciences* 1463; University of California, Santa Cruz and others (n 250) 119.
[273] Cf. Kira A. Krumhansl and others, 'Global Patterns of Kelp Forest Change over the Past Half-Century' (2016) 113 *Proceedings of the National Academy of Sciences* 13785.
[274] Cf. Jessica E. Carilli and others, 'Century-Scale Records of Coral Growth Rates Indicate That Local Stressors Reduce Coral Thermal Tolerance Threshold' (2010) 16 *Global Change Biology* 1247.

also encompass blue carbon ecosystems, as described above, and can thus protect them. As a result, MPAs have great potential and could enhance adaptation.

2.4.3 Fisheries Management

Similar to MPAs, fisheries management can contribute to resilience building, and the mechanisms at work are comparable. Tools of fisheries management 'include restrictions on access to a fishery, spatial and temporal closures (including MPAs), catch limits, gear restrictions, and limits on the composition (sizes and sex) of allowable catch'.[275] These tools can affect stock size, individual size, and age structure. For instance, larger stock sizes lead to greater genetic and functional diversity, which can result in more resistance, similar to what has been explained above.[276] Diverse genotypes among different populations could vary significantly regarding their ability to withstand ocean change, such as OA. Accordingly, choosing larval cohorts for reproduction and fishing that are more accustomed to warmer or more acidic waters might produce more resistant adults.[277] In addition, fisheries managers could regulate the sizes of each species that are allowed to be caught. Thus, managers promote resilience, where resistance and recovery at the organismal or population level depend on size. If this or similar resilience mechanisms are present in fisheries, a better comprehension of the spatiotemporal (space and time) variability of a population's susceptibility to fishing and/or environmental stressors could be helpful for fishery location and timing.[278] Thus, it becomes clear that, similar to MPAs, fisheries management has the potential to enhance adaptation.

2.4.4 Understanding Adaptation Options and Alternative Ways of Mitigation

It has been shown above that there are various means to achieve adaptation and alternative methods of mitigation concerning OA. Although common examples (blue carbon, fisheries management, MPAs) are mentioned, they are still in their infancy, requiring more research and understanding. Aside from the solutions outlined in the adaptation options above, geoengineering and other ocean interventions could also provide ways to adapt to future changes in the ocean and are currently being explored. However, as emphasised earlier, many techniques investigated thus far can cause harm and have adverse side effects. Additionally, further research is necessary to identify safe techniques in this field. Furthermore, nature-based solutions, in contrast to more technological mitigation options,

[275] University of California, Santa Cruz and others (n 250) 122.

[276] Ibid; cf. Ray Hilborn and others, 'Biocomplexity and Fisheries Sustainability' (2003) 100 *Proceedings of the National Academy of Sciences* 6564.

[277] University of California, Santa Cruz and others (n 250) 122.

[278] Ibid.

offer a range of other ecosystem services, such as coastal protection and nutrient removal. Therefore, nature-based solutions uniquely serve as both mitigation and adaptation measures.

2.5 Finding Approaches to Ocean Acidification Governance with the Scientific Background in Mind

This chapter has sought to familiarise the non-scientific reader with OA, particularly its causes, stressors, and adaptation options. It provides a thorough, though relatively brief, overview to help the reader gain a solid understanding of the scientific background of the problem. A good comprehension of OA as an issue is essential to identify how it is and should be governed. More specifically, scientific knowledge can help identify actors, legal instruments, and ways of governance that can contribute to addressing OA, preventing ocean stress, and facilitating adaptation. OA is a complex and insidious problem that is gradually becoming more evident. Furthermore, much about OA is still not fully understood. Although research in this field is rapidly expanding, many questions remain unanswered. Nevertheless, some facts and characteristics regarding OA are sufficiently understood and must be considered when seeking governance solutions.

OA is a problem that involves different Earth spheres, namely the ocean, atmosphere, and land.[279] Even though the repercussions on the ecosystem can mainly be seen in the oceans, the causes and stressors of the problem can derive from the atmosphere and land. In addition, a time and space dimension must be considered when addressing OA.

Regarding time, it has been shown above that some causes can be addressed more quickly than others. For example, tackling anthropogenic CO_2 emissions has, unfortunately, become a long-term task, while certain land-based activities could be addressed more rapidly as they present a less daunting governance challenge. Specifically, land-based activities could be managed by individual states or regions. These different timeframes indicate that while humankind is confronted with the challenging task of reducing CO2 emissions, it can simultaneously eliminate other causes and stressors. Beginning to address some of these causes and stressors can now 'buy time' in addressing OA more broadly.[280] Creating less stress through either causes or stressors can, for instance, provide ecosystems and species with time to adapt, potentially preventing tipping points from being reached as quickly or at all.

Regarding space, the second dimension, it has been demonstrated above that the problem's causes and various ocean stressors can be traced back to global, regional, and local activities. Similarly, the effects of OA also manifest at all these levels.

[279] Cf. figure 1 for Earth spheres Dahe Qin and others, 'Cryospheric Science: Research Framework and Disciplinary System' (2018) 5 *National Science Review* 255, 257.

[280] Billé and others (n 23) 767; Harrould-Kolieb and Hoegh-Guldberg (n 26) 14.

Therefore, these anthropocentric causes and stressors differ between the varying levels. Additionally, natural variations exist among these levels and even within the same level, depending on the geographic context. The average pH and pH extremes experienced by the open ocean can differ from those in coastal areas. It is also true that the average and extreme pH levels of different parts of a coastline can vary significantly. For example, one coastline might regularly experience upwelling events, while another may encounter infrequent or no upwelling at all. These varying pH averages and extremes complicate the search for a solution to OA. Establishing an OA baseline as a measure would, for instance, be difficult or even impossible. Nonetheless, stakeholders at local and regional levels have the ability to address and begin tackling causes and stressors that can be managed in the short term, such as coastal nutrient input. Beyond the causes and stressors, adaptation options are being investigated but require further research. Effective strategies for utilising these options for OA adaptation must be identified. The degree to which they can be beneficial and their exact mechanisms especially need to be better understood. Nevertheless, there appears to be potential concerning, for example, MPAs, blue carbon, and fisheries management.

What can be learnt from the science behind OA is that there will not be an easy fix for the problem. To mitigate and adapt to the problem of OA, addressing anthropogenic CO_2 emissions from land is essential. However, other causes – such as coastal activities or stressors like fishing – should not be overlooked.

The following chapters will utilise science as a foundation to explore how OA is and should be governed. As described in the introduction, the literature indicates that various actors and instruments from different areas could be involved in addressing the problem. Moreover, when examining the science, it becomes clear that OA is a complex issue, as it pertains not only to the ocean but also to the atmosphere and land. The fact that OA involves different spheres of the Earth suggests that the actors and legal instruments relevant to the governance of OA are, similarly, not restricted to those that govern the ocean but include the atmosphere and land as well. Therefore, OA likely engages a wide range of actors and legal instruments from several areas of international and environmental law.

To approach the question of how OA is governed, this book will first map the existing governance landscape, including the actors and legal instruments that may contribute to addressing OA. Regime complex theory is one approach that can guide the mapping exercise and is effective in describing the current governance landscape. Chapter 3 will turn to this governance landscape and the theory of regime complexity.

CHAPTER 3
Ocean Acidification and Regime Complexity

This book aims to analyse how OA is and should be governed. Therefore, having examined the causes, stressors, and adaptation options for OA in Chapter 2, this chapter seeks to uncover the existing governance landscape. Accordingly, this chapter will map the international and transnational governance landscape for OA.

The main contribution of this chapter to the book will be the creation of the OA governance map. This map identifies multifarious actors and instruments that tackle, or have the potential to tackle, different aspects of OA. As will become apparent throughout the chapter, the governance of OA does not start from a clean slate, meaning that many actors and instruments are already present in this densely occupied landscape.[281] The construction of this map is important in its own right because, for the first time, it provides a snapshot of the currently existing international and transnational governance landscape for OA.

This chapter, based on the map, will argue that the current governance landscape of OA can be described as a regime complex.[282] This characterisation of the governance landscape as a regime complex represents an important step in this book for two reasons. First, describing it as a regime complex provides the foundation upon which a governance framework for OA should be built. As outlined in this chapter, the OA regime complex consists of a large, diverse group of institutions capable of addressing a complex, newly arising issue area. These characteristics will necessitate a governance form that can offer, for example, an adaptable and collaborative approach. As global experimentalist governance advocates these exact characteristics, this chapter will lead to the selection of global experimentalist governance as

[281] Cf. Raustiala and Victor make the point that 'the array of rules already in force channel and constrain the content' in their case of new elemental regimes within regime complexes. Raustiala and Victor (n 55) 280; Simons and Stephens (n 17) 6; Downing (n 19) 267; Baird, Simons and Stephens (n 18) 463.

[282] See also Scott, 'Ocean Acidification' (n 29) 390; Gordon (n 31) 39; Simons and Stephens (n 17) 1; Harrould-Kolieb and Stephens (n 52) 265; Baird, Simons and Stephens (n 18) 459; Kim (n 21) 247.

a suitable match for OA governance, as will be seen in Chapter 4. Chapter 4 will later demonstrate that global experimentalist governance is a realistic continuation of a regime complex. This governance type can build on a regime complex without completely dismantling it and, on the contrary, make a virtue of what is already present in terms of governance. Furthermore, academic literature has shown a close relationship between regime complexes on the one hand and experimentalist forms of governance on the other.[283] The characterisation of OA governance as a regime complex is an important step in the direction of experimentalist governance as a framework for analysis.

Second, the map will inform the selection of case studies in Chapters 5,6, and 7. This book will provide a close examination of the presence of global experimentalist governance within the institutional framework of two institutions capable of addressing OA. The initial mapping included in this chapter is essential for identifying institutions relevant to the domain of OA. Moreover, when the criteria for selecting the institutions to be closely examined are elaborated on later in this book, the results of this mapping exercise will facilitate the selection of pertinent examples.

This chapter proceeds as follows. First, it maps the international and transnational governance of OA (Section 3.1), identifying actors and instruments that, taken together, will be described as institutions. Second, the chapter argues that the current OA governance landscape can be characterised as a regime complex (Section 3.2). Third, to conclude, the chapter will reiterate the importance of describing the governance landscape for OA as a regime complex (Section 3.3).

3.1 Mapping the International and Transnational Landscape for Ocean Acidification

The map presented in this chapter identifies which international and transnational actors have the potential to contribute to tackling the causes, stressors, and adaptation options of OA. As noted in Chapter 2, the concept of 'international' is defined as including bodies comprising more than one state, including multilateral treaty bodies.[284] The concept of 'transnational' includes bodies that facilitate

[283] Chiara Armeni, 'Global Experimentalist Governance, International Law and Climate Change Technologies' (2015) 64 *International and Comparative Law Quarterly* 875, 883; Gráinne De Búrca, Robert O. Keohane and Charles Sabel, 'Global Experimentalist Governance' (2014) 44 *British Journal of Political Science* 477, 479.

[284] Inferred from Thiel and Maslanik, as they say, 'Transnational does not simply signify international; it refers to the organization of power beyond the state (not between states) and is, thus, a relatively open term (…)' Markus Thiel and Jeffrey Maslanik, 'Transnational Actors' in Markus Thiel and Jeffrey Maslanik, *Oxford Research Encyclopedia of International Studies* (Oxford University Press 2010) 2 https://oxfordre.com/internationalstudies/view/10.1093/acrefore/9780190846626.001.0001/acrefore-9780190846626-e-105 accessed 26 July 2023.

cooperation across national borders, but also encompass private entities within their scope.[285] Transnational actors are immensely important in environmental governance, including in relation to OA. For instance, Hale underlines in his paper concerning transnational actors and governance that, in relation to the climate change regime alone, 190 transnational entities had been identified by the United Nations (UN) in 2018.[286] Thus, in addition to international actors, transnational actors are incorporated into the map as they constitute a considerable part of environmental institutions. Each of the actors and instruments included in the map has the potential to tackle aspects of OA and is therefore relevant for OA governance. This reference to 'aspects' of OA includes causes, stressors, and/or consequences. The map has been drawn using the scientific data outlined in Chapter 2.

The following 'map' (Figure 3.1) of the international and transnational landscape in relation to OA includes thirty-one actors and twenty-six instruments (indicated on the left side of the map). The term 'actors' refers to associations of persons, such as international organisations or non-governmental organisations, while the term 'instruments' refers to legal instruments or documents. Together, actors and instruments can be referred to as institutions. Therefore, in some cases, an actor who is the governing body of an instrument is presented separately from that instrument, as in the cases of the OSPAR Convention and the OSPAR Commission, as well as the CAMLR Convention and its Commission. The map is divided into institutions that have (bottom half) or have not (top half) considered OA (TIC) or at least acknowledged the relevance of the issue. Furthermore, the map indicates whether an institution is active on the global, regional, or local level (from left to right). Additionally, the table reveals whether an institution is a private entity (diamond), a state (dot), or a hybrid entity encompassing both (star). The circle represents a group of actors that includes both private and state entities. An actor labelled private consists of at least partially private individuals. Regarding instruments, it pertains to those adopted by civil society and/or the private sector.

The map is not exhaustive. It is limited because it includes instruments and actors identified as relevant to OA governance in the legal and scientific literature, as well as those found through Internet searches. For the Internet research, Google was used as the primary search engine, and the search was conducted in two rounds during April 2020. First, to create an initial overview of any institutions that can tackle OA, the following keywords were used: 'ocean acidification', 'ocean acidification governance', 'ocean acidification organizations/institutions', 'ocean acidification transnational actors', 'ocean acidification actors', 'ocean acidification initiatives', 'CO_2

[285] Kenneth Abbott, 'Strengthening the Transnational Regime Complex for Climate Change' (2013) 3 *Transnational Environmental Law* 57, 60.

[286] Thomas Hale, 'Transnational Actors and Transnational Governance in Global Environmental Politics' (2020) 23 *Annual Review of Political Science* 203, 204.

governance' and 'NO_x and SO_x governance'. Second, after this initial search, each institution found was examined individually to determine if they have the potential to address aspects of OA (causes, stressors, adaptation) and therefore could be included in the map. This second examination included Google searching the institutions, as well as word searching their websites for ocean acidification and the various causes, stressors, and adaptation options outlined in Chapter 2. The two rounds of searches were repeated in February 2023 to update the findings.

Therefore, the map aims to provide the reader with an understanding of the number of actors and instruments that may have potential relevance for OA governance, without claiming to be exhaustive. Abbreviations in Figure 3.1 are explained in Tables 3.1 and 3.2.

Examining the map more closely reveals that efforts to address OA involve a wide array of actors and instruments. Such extensive efforts are expected since the issue of OA spans various Earth spheres, encompasses different dimensions (time, space), and will have repercussions across numerous areas. Moreover, considering that the problem of OA impacts all levels (from local to global) and affects different regions to varying degrees, it is also unsurprising that responses emerge at different levels of governance.

When looking at the 'map' and the list of abbreviations (Tables 3.1 and 3.2), it is evident that many institutions are included. No single instrument or actor holds primary responsibility for addressing OA. As previously noted, instruments and actors were included in the 'map' due to their potential to tackle aspects of OA. More specifically, instruments and actors were included in the 'map' because they have the capacity to address OA and its causes (anthropogenic CO_2 emissions, NO_x, SO_x) directly, such as the climate change regime or MARPOL 73/78, or because they might mitigate stressors like the RFMOs, which could help prevent overfishing. Other instruments or actors may have the potential to address the consequences of OA by implementing adaptation measures, such as the LOTSR, which facilitates the establishment of marine protected areas.

However, while identifying relevant actors or instruments, it could be observed that most of the units shown above have only briefly or superficially mentioned or acknowledged the problem of OA. Nonetheless, given the number and range of actors and instruments identified that have the potential to address at least one aspect of OA, it is expected that the relevance of this topic will be recognised by an increasing number of actors and instruments moving forward. This rising number could include those actors and instruments located in the top half of the map, such as those concerned with transboundary air pollution (CLRTAP) or fisheries (RFMOs). If such actors begin to address the challenge of OA, they would be moved from the top half of the map to the bottom half, where the actors currently considering OA are located. In fact, during the writing of this book, actors and instruments were transitioned from the top to the bottom as they started engaging with OA. RFMOs can be found in both halfs as some of them consider OA while others do not. In the following sections, first the instruments and then the actors included in the map will be examined more closely.

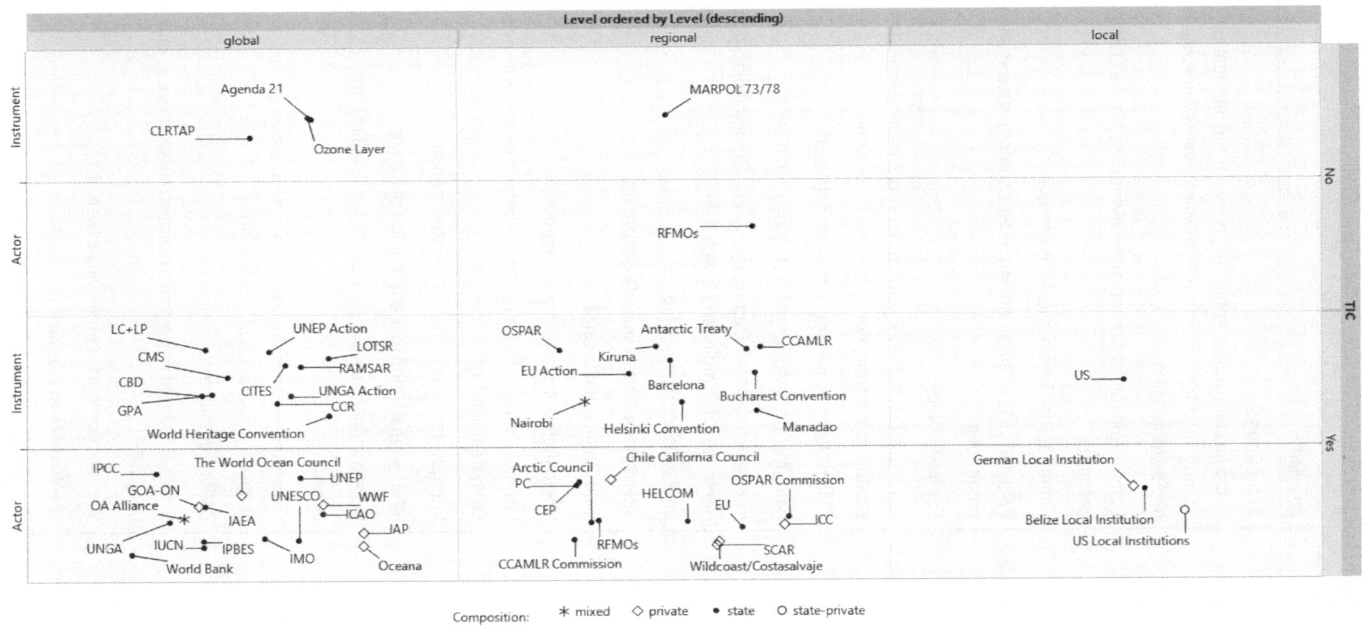

Figure 3.1 Mapping of the actors and instruments in relation to ocean acidification.
Source: Compiled by the author

Table 3.1 Abbreviations of actors.

Abbreviation	Full Name
Arctic Council	Arctic Council
Belize Local Institution	Belize local institution enhancing research and information sharing, monitoring: Coastal Zone Management Authority and Institute (CZMAI)
CCAMLR Commission	Commission for the Conservation of Antarctic Marine Living Resources
CEP	Committee for Environmental Protection
Chile California Council	Regional institution enhancing research, information sharing, monitoring
EU	European Union
German Local Institution	German local institution enhancing research and information sharing, monitoring: German Ocean Foundation
GOA-ON	Global Ocean Acidification Observing Network
HELCOM	Baltic Marine Environment Protection Commission
IAEA	International Atomic Energy Agency and Ocean Acidification International Coordination Center, OA-ICC
IAP	Inter Academy Partnership
ICAO	International Civil Aviation Organization
ICC	Inuit Circumpolar Council
IMO	International Maritime Organization
IPBES	Intergovernmental Science-Policy Platform on Biodiversity and Ecosystem Services
IPCC	Intergovernmental Panel on Climate Change
IUCN	International Union for Conservation of Nature
OA Alliance	International Alliance to Combat Ocean Acidification
Oceana	Oceana
OSPAR Commission	Commission to the Convention for the Protection of the Marine Environment of the North-East Atlantic
PC	Pacific Community
RFMOs	Regional fisheries management organizations (twice as only some have TIC)
SCAR	Scientific Committee on Antarctic Research
The World Ocean Council	The World Ocean Council
UNEP	United Nations Environment Programme

Table 3.1 (cont.)

Abbreviation	Full Name
UNESCO	UNESCO and Intergovernmental Oceanographic Commission
UNGA	United Nations General Assembly
US Local Institutions	US local institutions enhancing research, information sharing, monitoring: including National Oceanic and Atmospheric Administration (NOAA), California Ocean Science Trust, Union of Concerned Scientists, New York State Ocean Acidification Task Force
Wildcoast/Costasalvaje	Regional institution enhancing research, information sharing, monitoring
World Bank	The World Bank
WWF	World Wildlife Fund

Source: Compiled by the author.

Table 3.2 Abbreviations of instruments.

Abbreviation	Full Name
Agenda 21	Agenda 21
Antarctic Treaty	Antarctic Treaty and the 1991 Protocol on Environmental Protection (Madrid Protocol)
CCR	Climate change regime – United Nations Framework Convention on Climate Change, Kyoto Protocol, Paris Agreement
Barcelona	Convention for the Protection of the Marine Environment and the Coastal Region of the Mediterranean and Protocol
OSPAR	Convention for the Protection of the Marine Environment of the North-East Atlantic
CITES	Convention on International Trade in Endangered Species
CBD	Convention on Biological Diversity
CLRTAP	Convention on Long-range Transboundary Air Pollution and Protocols
CMS	Convention on Migratory Species of Wild Animals
CCAMLR	Convention on the Conservation of Antarctic Marine Living Resources
Bucharest Convention/ Black Sea Convention	Convention on the Protection of the Black Sea against Pollution
Helsinki Convention	Convention on the Protection of the Marine Environment of the Baltic Sea Area
World Heritage Convention	Convention on the Protection of the World Cultural and Natural Heritage

Table 3.2 (cont.)

Abbreviation	Full Name
RAMSAR	Convention on Wetlands of International
EU Action	European Union – directives and regulations
GPA	Global Program of Action for the Protection of the Marine Environment from Land-based Activities – including Beijing Declaration, Manila Declaration, Montreal Declaration
MARPOL 73/78	International Convention for the Prevention of Pollution from Ships, 1973 as Modified by the Protocol of 1978
Kiruna	Kiruna Declaration
LOTSR	Law of the Sea Regime – United Nations Convention on the Law of the Sea, Fish Stocks Agreement, UNGA Res 69/292, 72/249
LC+LP	London Convention and Protocols
Manado	Manado Ocean Declaration
Nairobi	Amended Nairobi Convention for the Protection, Management, and Development of the Marine and Coastal Environment of the Western Indian Ocean
Ozone Layer	Ozone Layer Regime – 1985 Vienna Convention for the Protection of the Ozone Layer and its 1987 Montreal Protocol
UNEP Action	United Nations Environment Programme – Regional Climate Change Adaptation Framework for the Mediterranean Marine and Coastal Areas, Regional Seas Programme,
UNGA Action	United Nations General Assembly – Resolutions and Actions under its Auspices – including the Sustainable Development Goals (Goal 14)
US	US Acts – Clean Water Act, Clean Air Act, Federal Ocean Acidification Research and Monitoring Act (FOARAM), Coastal Zone Management Act

Source: Compiled by the author.

Most instruments included in the map have been discussed in the literature surrounding OA to some extent.[287] Authors have referred to these instruments as potentially relevant in addressing the problem. Although many instruments could be used to tackle the issue of OA, two specific instruments at the global level have been referenced by many academic authors writing on this topic: the UNFCCC and the UNCLOS.[288] Even though these two instruments might take centre stage, as

[287] Cf. inter alia Herr and others (n 33); Kim (n 21); Baird, Simons and Stephens (n 18); Simons and Stephens (n 17).

[288] Cf. inter alia Downing (n 19) 250–260; Kim (n 21) 245–248; Lamirande (n 57) 192–198, 202–217.

they are the main instruments that aim to combat CO_2 emissions on one hand and protect the oceans on the other, it is clear from the 'map' that many other instruments are also available.

In general, it can be stated that these other instruments address a range of environmental issues, such as the protection of biodiversity (e.g., CBD, CITES, CMS), safeguarding the marine environment or coastal areas also with respect to specific regions (e.g., LOTSR, Barcelona, Bucharest Convention, CCAMLR), or tackling air and atmospheric challenges (e.g., CCR, CLRTAP). The mapped instruments additionally include those related to geoengineering, addressing the potential risks it poses to the sea. In particular, the London Convention and the 2006 (RES LP.1(1)), 2009 (RES LP.3(4)), and 2013 (RES LP.4(8)) amendments to the London Protocol target these problems. However, other regimes, such as the CBD[289] or, at the regional level, the OSPAR Convention, can also engage with geoengineering.[290] Then, there are various instruments at the regional level that fall under the regional seas programme (e.g., Barcelona, Nairobi, CCAMLR, OSPAR), which aims to protect the shared marine and coastal environments of neighbouring countries.[291]

When examining the actors, it is evident that the majority are interstate actors, particularly UN agencies (e.g., UNGA, IAEA, UNEP). Only a limited number of the actors identified so far are exclusively organised by transnational entities comprising private actors such as GOA-ON, Oceana, and IAP. This may be due to the novelty of the problem. The IPCC and IPBES are internationally organised expert groups. Both the IPCC and the IPBES are intergovernmental bodies that work towards achieving a better scientific understanding of environmental issues such as OA and how to address them.[292] To these two could be added diverse and often temporary programmes and projects that operate at the regional and local levels to organise research to better understand OA (e.g., the Brazil OA Research Network (BROA), the Biological Impacts of OA Program (BIOACID) in Germany, and the United Kingdom's Ocean Acidification Research Programme (UKOA), European Project on Ocean Acidification (EPOCA)). Even though it does not include these temporary projects, the map does feature a number of local actors, for example, from Germany or the United States, which enhance research and information-sharing.

In summary, what can be taken away from mapping the existing governmental landscape is that despite the recent discovery of the problem, there is a wide variety

[289] Biodiversity and Climate Change: C: Ocean Fertilization 2008 (UNEP/CBD/COP/DEC/9/16).

[290] OSPAR Decision 2007/1 to Prohibit the Storage of Carbon Dioxide Streams in the Water Column or on the Sea-bed 2007 (Decision 2007/1); OSPAR Decision 2007/2 on the Storage of Carbon Dioxide Streams in Geological Formations 2007 (Decision 2007/2).

[291] UN Environment, 'Regional Seas Programme – Why Does Working with Regional Seas Matter?' (*UNEP – UN Environment Programme*, 16 August 2017) www.unenvironment.org/explore-topics/oceans-seas/what-we-do/working-regional-seas/why-does-working-regional-seas-matter accessed 10 April 2020.

[292] IPBES, 'About | IPBES Secretariat' (16 March 2017) www.ipbes.net/node/40 accessed 30 July 2023; IPCC, 'About – IPCC' (2023) www.ipcc.ch/about/ accessed 30 July 2023.

of potentially relevant instruments and actors. Additionally, it can be expected that this number will grow, particularly if no specific unit is assigned primary responsibility for addressing this issue. However, despite the problem's clear causes and severe consequences, no international legal framework is, to this day, directly concerned with OA. Therefore, it is evident that there is no integrated regime available to tackle the problem. Instead, given that OA has various scientific causes and stressors relating to different domains such as land, air, and water, and will have consequences for ecosystems and humans alike, various treaties such as the UNFCCC, the UNCLOS, and the CBD, among others, are relevant. Similarly, a range of actors, such as the IMO and the UNEP, could take the lead.

A deeper look at the OA mitigation and adaptation activities on the international plane can be found in Annex B. The information gathered has been included as an annex to avoid interrupting the flow of the main discussion in the book. Many readers will already be familiar with much of the information contained in the annex; even those who are less familiar will find it easier to dip in and out of the material rather than confronting this quantity of information *en masse*. Nevertheless, a quick recap will be provided here.

More specifically, the annex provides information regarding the mandates, missions, and objectives of international actors and relevant instruments. While actors have mandates, objectives, and sometimes missions, instruments often only possess objectives. Typically, mandates are established by foundational treaties, objectives can be found in instruments, and missions or equivalent terms are often utilised by actors who lack a foundational treaty (see also Chapter 5). Additionally, institutions may have extra objectives or missions listed on their websites. The annex outlines three different positions that characterise the relationship between institutions and OA, which are summarised in a table in the annex. These three positions are also discussed below.

An explicit OA mandate/objective/mission indicates that the actor or instrument explicitly addresses OA through, for instance, its founding treaty, its mission, or the objectives it is tasked with pursuing.

Notably, the OAA stands out as the only institution with an explicit mission directly targeting OA, emphasising its specialised focus on this critical environmental issue. The OAA is an international coalition launched at the 2016 Our Ocean Conference to unite governments, organisations, and scientific entities to combat OA.[293] The OA Alliance is a collaborative platform that encourages its members to undertake specific actions and develop strategic plans to address OA. More specifically, members of the OA Alliance commit to creating and implementing OA Action Plans, which include measures such as reducing carbon dioxide emissions, enhancing scientific research, reducing local pollutants, developing adaptation and resilience strategies, and raising public awareness

[293] OA Alliance, 'About' (*OA Alliance*, 2024) www.oaalliance.org/about accessed 7 May 2024; OA Alliance, 'Current Members' (*OA Alliance*, 2022) www.oaalliance.org/current-members accessed 14 September 2022.

and understanding of OA.[294] The fact that there is currently only one actor with an explicit mission to address OA is not surprising, as many of the institutions discussed in the annex have mandates established by their foundational treaties or objectives outlined in the relevant instrument, which are difficult to amend. Therefore, as could be expected, their mandates or objectives have not been adjusted or updated in light of developing environmental threats such as OA.

Even though the OA Alliance is the only entity explicitly established to address OA, other institutions have the potential to mitigate this threat or contribute to adapting to its effects as a result of their mandates/missions/objectives. As highlighted in Chapter 2, policies that lead to a reduction of CO_2 emissions help to curb OA since such emissions are its primary cause. Thus, the second position that characterises the relationship between institutions and OA is an implicit mandate.

An implicit mandate/objective/mission indicates that the actor or instrument implicitly addresses OA through, for instance, its mandate, mission, or the objectives it is charged with pursuing. An implicit OA mandate arises when the actor or instrument lacks an explicit mandate to tackle OA. However, it does have a mandate/objective/mission to address one of the other causes of OA or adaptation options in relation to OA. Therefore, these institutions have either a specific mandate to deal with, for example, CO_2, NO_x/SO_x, land-based pollution, or a broad mandate like 'protect the environment' that is relevant to OA. Thus, the actor or instrument in question is implicitly empowered to tackle OA through its mandate, mission, or objectives. Out of the fourteen institutions reviewed in the annex, all but the OAA, which has an explicit OA mandate, possess implicit mandates to address aspects of OA. For example, the UNFCCC represents a significant global effort to tackle climate change, thereby indirectly addressing OA. The Paris Agreement, adopted under the UNFCCC in 2015 to implement the UNFCCC, advances this framework and aims for a carbon-neutral world by mid-century, setting the stage for significant reductions in greenhouse gases, including CO_2, which is the primary driver of OA.[295] In fact, the climate change regime is the only institution included in the annex with an explicit objective to tackle climate change, including CO_2, the main driver of OA.[296]

Finally, it is relevant to ask which of the institutions with an implicit rather than explicit OA mandate/objective/mission has taken steps to address OA in their work.

Here, ten of the fourteen international institutions with an implicit OA mandate/objective/mission have actively taken steps to address OA, albeit to varying degrees, demonstrating a proactive approach to tackling this issue beyond their established mandates, objectives, or missions. This action underscores the commitment of

[294] OA Alliance, 'Action Plan Toolkit 2024' https://static1.squarespace.com/static/6006d84247a6a51d636dd219/t/661f8d8189290b05c9a25e95/1713343878415/OAlliance_APToolkit2024_A.pdf accessed 7 May 2024; OA Alliance, 'Our Impact' (*OA Alliance*, 2024) www.oaalliance.org/ourimpact accessed 7 May 2024.

[295] Paris Agreement 2015 (UNTS vol 3156) art 2.

[296] United Nations Framework Convention on Climate Change 1992 (1771 UNTS 107) art 2.

these institutions to address OA, even when explicit mandates/objectives/missions are absent. The involvement of diverse sectors (such as shipping via IMO or other sectors via the Climate Change Regime) shows that OA is recognised as a cross-sectoral issue.

Even though only one actor explicitly addresses OA through its mission on the international stage, a broader examination reveals a more engaged landscape. At first glance, a focus on legal mandates might suggest limited international action on OA. However, the combined insights from the map and the annex suggest that many international institutions are empowered to engage with OA, albeit implicitly, and are also actively and expressly engaging with OA in practice. In other words, if one focuses solely on explicit mandates/objectives/missions to tackle OA, few relevant institutions can be found. However, when considering implicit mandates as well, a more crowded, interesting, and promising landscape emerges. This perspective uncovers a richer tapestry of international efforts, where institutions are increasingly recognising and incorporating OA into their agendas, albeit to varying degrees. For instance, while the IMO has minimally addressed OA, mainly mentioning it in a small number of resolutions and guidelines,[297] UNESCO has established the GOA-ON, thereby significantly enhancing global collaboration and data sharing to tackle OA.[298] A recent example of OA being addressed is the Biodiversity Beyond National Jurisdiction Agreement, a new implementing agreement under the UNCLOS. OA is specifically mentioned in this agreement regarding MPAs, even though UNCLOS' broad objective does not mention OA specifically.[299] These

[297] International Maritime Organization (IMO), 'Resolution LP.3(4) – On the Amendment to Article 6 of the London Protocol the Fourth Meeting of Contracting Parties to the 1996 Protocol to the Convention on the Prevention of Marine Pollution by Dumping of Wastes and Other Matter, 1972' wwwcdn.imo.org/localresources/en/KnowledgeCentre/IndexofIMOResolutions/LCLPDocuments/LP.3(4).pdf; International Maritime Organization (IMO), 'Resolution LP.5(14) – On the Provisional Application of the 2009 Amendment to Article 6 of the London Protocol – The Fourteenth Meeting of Contracting Parties to the 1996 Protocol to the Convention on the Prevention of Marine Pollution by Dumping of Waste and Other Matter, 1972' wwwcdn.imo.org/localresources/en/KnowledgeCentre/IndexofIMOResolutions/LCLPDocuments/LP.5(14).pdf; International Maritime Organization (IMO), 'Resolution LP.1(1) On the Amendment to Include CO2 Sequestration in Sub-Seabed Geological Formations in Annex I to the London Protocol'; MEPC, 'MEPC.130(53) – Guidelines for On-Board Exhaust Gas-SOx Cleaning Systems' wwwcdn.imo.org/localresources/en/KnowledgeCentre/IndexofIMOResolutions/MEPCDocuments/MEPC.130(53).pdf accessed 11 February 2024; MEPC, 'MEPC.170(57) – Guidelines for Exhaust Gas Cleaning Systems' wwwcdn.imo.org/localresources/en/KnowledgeCentre/IndexofIMOResolutions/MEPCDocuments/MEPC.170(57).pdf accessed 11 February 2024; MEPC, 'MEPC.184(59) – 2009 Guidelines for Exhaust Gas Cleaning Systems' wwwcdn.imo.org/localresources/en/KnowledgeCentre/IndexofIMOResolutions/MEPCDocuments/MEPC.184(59).pdf accessed 11 February 2024; MEPC, 'MEPC.259(68) – 2015 Guidelines for Exhaust Gas Cleaning Systems' wwwcdn.imo.org/localresources/en/KnowledgeCentre/IndexofIMOResolutions/MEPCDocuments/MEPC.259(68).pdf accessed 11 February 2024; MEPC, 'MEPC.340(77) – 2021 Guidelines for Exhaust Gas Cleaning Systems' wwwcdn.imo.org/localresources/en/OurWork/Environment/Documents/Air%20pollution/MEPC.340%2877%29.pdf accessed 11 February 2024.

[298] UNESCO, 'Ocean Acidification | Intergovernmental Oceanographic Commission' (2024) www.ioc.unesco.org/en/ocean-acidification accessed 4 May 2024.

[299] Agreement under the United Nations Convention on the Law of the Sea on the Conservation and Sustainable Use of Marine Biological Diversity of Areas beyond National Jurisdiction 2023 art 17(c).

examples highlight a trend of growing recognition and integration of OA issues within the work of international institutions, regardless of their explicit mandates/objectives/missions. One of the objectives of this book is to highlight that there is a dense and evolving landscape regarding OA governance and that this landscape will not be revealed in all its rich contours merely by considering the formal mandates of international institutions.

Overall, there has been a positive trend regarding the degree of engagement in OA action on the international plane over the past years (and even since the beginning of writing this book). For example, the annex shows that conversations about OA have started to take off in multiple institutions, particularly at CBD and UNFCCC COPs.[300]

On the flip side, OA is a pressing environmental issue, but the current international landscape addresses different aspects of it unevenly. The annex shows that while some aspects of OA, such as atmospheric CO_2 emissions, receive considerable attention within broader climate change agendas, other critical factors, like land-based pollution, are often neglected or are only beginning to gain more attention.

A significant portion of the response to OA remains concentrated on research and data collection, with less emphasis on facilitating actionable mitigation and adaptation strategies. For instance, although UNESCO is actively engaged in combating OA and has, for example, established the GOA-ON, a global OA observation network, its mandate restricts its activities primarily to scientific research.[301] Similarly, IUCN hosts the Ocean Acidification International Reference User Group (OAiRUG), an expert group that translates the latest scientific findings on OA into policy advice, thereby enhancing global comprehension of the problem of OA. However, IUCN, including OAiRUG, does not take steps to prompt action to tackle OA but is limited to data collection and translation for policy purposes.[302] Even when institutions like the CBD work extensively on OA, the scope of their actions is limited. The CBD can foster the establishment of MPAs and facilitate communication across different international frameworks such as the Climate Change Regime and UNCLOS, but its objectives prevent this institution from transcending these types of activities as it, for example, lacks a mandate to reduce CO_2 emissions.[303]

[300] See, for example, Biosafety Unit, '2030 Targets (with Guidance Notes)' (2024) para 8 www.cbd.int/gbf/targets?fbclid=IwZXh0bgNhZW0CMTAAAR1kVEpA8GTebjE0xr3ptX77yYEK3AlYwieL87FiI0N7YPAsvH4uGtZSUr4_aem_AXPK7NA2pnYXQ1DW2Pe2e0qF3MehsCBa8yuYKLbRWvIbm0s1dbv6MeiYF1cXwWtmQaLJ7XLyU3iVHcW-SYYfeveM accessed 3 May 2024; Woods Hole Oceanographic Institution, 'First Ever Ocean-Focused Pavilion in the Blue Zone' (www.whoi.edu/, 29 April 2024) www.whoi.edu/press-room/news-release/world-leaders-in-ocean-science-and-philanthropy-come-together-to-create-first-ever-ocean-pavilion-at-un-climate-conference/ accessed 29 April 2024; UNESCO, 'The Ocean Pavilion Announces Schedule of Events for COP27 | UNESCO' (29 April 2024) www.unesco.org/en/articles/ocean-pavilion-announces-schedule-events-cop27 accessed 29 April 2024.

[301] Constitution of the United Nations Educational, Scientific and Cultural Organization 1945 (UNTS 4 (p275)) art I(1).

[302] IUCN, 'Ocean Acidification | IUCN' (2024) www.iucn.org/our-work/topic/oceans-and-climate-change/ocean-acidification accessed 6 May 2024.

[303] Kim (n 21) 252; Convention on Biological Diversity 1992 (1760 UNTS 79) arts 1, 2, 6, 8, 10.

Although certain organisations are not limited purely to research roles due to their mandates, this does not necessarily imply they are actively taking measures to address OA. For instance, the IMO is empowered to prevent and control marine pollution from ships.[304] However, despite the significant contribution of the shipping industry to OA through emissions such as CO_2, NO_x/SO_x, and the use of scrubbers, the IMO has not taken specific actions to tackle OA. On the contrary, the IMO has encouraged the use of scrubbers to clean exhaust gas and reduce air pollution, but this technology washes out acid into the ocean water, which contributes to OA (see Chapter 2).

Efforts to manage OA often rely on non-binding instruments or programmatic approaches that lack enforcement and impact. Furthermore, when binding rules are enacted that could tackle the causes of OA, the level of ambition frequently falls short of what is necessary to prevent dangerous acidification levels. While the Climate Change Regime establishes greenhouse gas reduction targets to meet its climate mitigation objective, these targets are not specifically designed to prevent OA, as detailed in Chapter 5 and Annex B. Additionally, the regime generally deals with greenhouse emissions without concrete CO_2 targets, which is the primary driver of OA.[305] This approach allows countries to define their own mitigation plans, known as Nationally Determined Contributions, which do not guarantee the rapid CO_2 reductions needed to mitigate OA effectively.[306] Moreover, the temperature targets set by the climate regime do not directly address OA, as it pertains to ocean chemistry, necessitating specific strategies beyond temperature management.[307] Although OA has been acknowledged within climate change negotiations, beginning formally in 2005 and with increasing recognition in subsequent conferences and IPCC reports, the actual integration of oceanic concerns into climate strategies has only recently gained more traction.[308] This shift is

[304] IMO, 'Convention on the International Maritime Organization' (2019) www.imo.org/en/About/Conventions/Pages/Convention-on-the-International-Maritime-Organization.aspx accessed 14 January 2022; Amendments to the Convention on the International Maritime Organization Relating to the Institutionalization of the Committee on Technical Co-operation in the Convention 1877 (UNTS 1380 (p268)); Convention on the International Maritime Organization 1948 (UNTS 289 (p3)); IMO, 'Strategic Plan for the Organization' (2019) www.imo.org/en/About/Strategy/Pages/Default.aspx accessed 15 January 2022.

[305] See, for example, Harrould-Kolieb and Stephens (n 52) 273; Gordon (n 31) 41.

[306] Paris Agreement art 4.

[307] Gordon (n 31) 43; Harrould-Kolieb and Stephens (n 52) 273.

[308] SUBSIDIARY BODY FOR SCIENTIFIC AND TECHNOLOGICAL ADVICE, 'Paper No. 4 FCCC/SBSTA/2005/MISC.15 – Views on the Report on Progress Made towards Implementing the Initial Ocean Climate Observing System, and on the Final Report on the Analysis of Data Exchange Issues in Global Atmospheric and Hydrological Networks' 8 https://unfccc.int/resource/docs/2005/sbsta/eng/misc15.pdf?fbclid=IwZXh0bgNhZW0CMTAAAR12G4aR6b-oApWNHx5TqD-_UG5i_wzclUaI7wSzWHaP3bzSglDwwo59tf8_aem_Aae5uLN9w4hdzdalgiWRQTjN8H2UN30k3hT5cm6duYHIZbWjGxAPw-mur0htPmM_drpupJOEz2YdS39J1YuUo7yG; Intergovernmental Panel On Climate Change (IPCC), *The Ocean and Cryosphere in a Changing Climate: Special Report of the Intergovernmental Panel on Climate Change* (1st ed., Cambridge University Press 2022) 9, 12, 13, 18, 19, 22, 24, 27 www.cambridge.org/core/product/identifier/9781009157964/type/book accessed 29 April 2024; R. K. Pachauri, Leo Mayer, and Intergovernmental Panel on Climate Change (eds), *Climate Change 2014: Synthesis Report* (Intergovernmental Panel on Climate Change 2015) 69; IPCC, *Global Warming of 1.5°C: IPCC Special Report on Impacts of Global Warming of*

reflected in the incorporation of ocean-based measures in over 70 per cent of the updated Nationally Determined Contributions and the establishment of the Ocean and Climate Change Dialogue at COP 25, highlighting the growing recognition of the oceans' role in global climate dynamics and policy.[309]

There is concern that certain environmental policies aimed at addressing climate change may inadvertently neglect or exacerbate the negative spillovers related to OA. For instance, some geoengineering techniques, while designed to combat climate issues, could pose risks to ocean health and potentially worsen OA. For example, the LC and the LP's 2006 and 2009 (RES LP.1(1)), (RES LP.3(4)) amendments allow for carbon capture and storage.[310] Additionally, although a further amendment from 2013 regulates ocean fertilisation and other marine geoengineering activities, the list of regulated geoengineering activities in annex 4 of the 2013 amendment only includes 'ocean fertilization'.[311] This raises the question of whether other geoengineering activities are permitted or not.[312]

Having presented some of the key findings from the work undertaken to prepare the map above, a summary of which is included in Annex B, this chapter will, as a next step, identify the type of governance landscape that the map represents. As foreshadowed in the introduction, the landscape resembles a regime complex. The understanding that the landscape can be described as a regime complex provides the foundation on which OA governance must be built. Before selecting an appropriate form of governance for OA, it is necessary to define the current landscape and identify the characteristics of the regime complex. Without a clear understanding of the current governance landscape, it is difficult to explore options for future governance. Hence, the rest of this chapter explains what regime complexity is and how and why the map fits this definition.

The chapter will then conclude not only with how regime complexity describes the map above but also by identifying how the regime complex for OA holds characteristics that will require a governance form capable of providing, for example,

1.5°C above Pre-Industrial Levels in Context of Strengthening Response to Climate Change, Sustainable Development, and Efforts to Eradicate Poverty (1st ed., Cambridge University Press 2018) 209, 222 www.cambridge.org/core/product/identifier/9781009157940/type/book accessed 29 April 2024.

309 Kristina Rodriguez, 'A Breakthrough for Oceans: Scaling Nature-Based Solutions for Ocean-Based Climate Policy at COP28' (*Climate Champions*, 9 December 2023) https://climatechampions.unfccc.int/a-breakthrough-for-oceans-scaling-nature-based-solutions-for-ocean-based-climate-policy-at-cop28/ accessed 29 April 2024; United Nations, 'FCCC/CP/2019/13/Add.1 – Report of the Conference of the Parties on Its Twenty-Fifth Session, Held in Madrid from 2 to 15 December 2019' para 31, p. 4 https://unfccc.int/sites/default/files/resource/cp2019_13a01E.pdf?download accessed 8 May 2024.

310 International Maritime Organization (IMO), 'LP.1(1)' (n 297); International Maritime Organization (IMO), 'LP.3(4)' (n 297).

311 IMO, 'Resolution LP.4(8) On the Amendment to the London Protocol to Regulate the Placement of Matter for Ocean Fertilization and Other Marine Geoengineering Activities' wwwcdn.imo.org/localresources/en/KnowledgeCentre/IndexofIMOResolutions/LCLPDocuments/LP.4(8).pdf.

312 Harrould-Kolieb and Stephens (n 52) 278; Karen N. Scott, 'Geoengineering and the Marine Environment' in Rosemary Rayfuse (ed), *Research Handbook on International Marine Environmental Law* (Edward Elgar Publishing 2015) 460 https://china.elgaronline.com/view/edcoll/9781781004760/9781781004760.00033.xml accessed 14 May 2024; Fennel and VanderZwaag (n 47) 352.

an adaptable and collaborative approach. Chapter 4 will demonstrate how global experimentalist governance advocates, among other things, these exact characteristics. Thus, this map and chapter will lead to the selection of global experimentalist governance as a suitable match for OA governance. Additionally, the visualisation of the landscape through the map and Tables 3.1 and 3.2 can offer an overview of potentially relevant institutions. More specifically, this overview is essential, as it will inform the selection of two institutions (Chapter 5) for case studies that can be tested for the presence of global experimentalist governance (Chapters 6 and 7).

3.2 Describing the International and Transnational Landscape for Ocean Acidification

This part will first explain what a regime complex is, based on the various definitions established in regime complex theory (Section 3.2.1), and then examine whether the mapped governance landscape can be described as a regime complex (Section 3.2.2).

3.2.1 Defining the Concept of a Regime Complex

Raustiala and Victor coined the concept of a regime complex and began to develop regime complex theory, drawing on the topic of plant genetic resources.[313] The authors formulated this theory as they identified a need to understand what they called 'regime interaction' due to the continuous proliferation of international institutions.[314] Previously, other authors had discussed either single integrated regimes[315] or hierarchical/nested regimes,[316] which describe a situation in which one institution stands in a hierarchy over others and can therefore resolve disputes with subordinate institutions.[317] Authors had also depicted an alternative form of institutional interaction, termed 'parallel regime'.[318] Regimes are parallel when they are concerned with completely different issue areas.[319] However, according to Raustiala and Victor, theories to describe regime interaction had not yet been

[313] Raustiala and Victor (n 55). [314] Ibid., 277, 278.

[315] Raustiala and Victor mention international environmental cooperation and in particular the Montreal Protocol on Ozone Depletion as a highly discussed single regime. Ibid., 278; as mentioned by Raustiala and Victor, cf. Elizabeth R. DeSombre and Joanne Kaufman, 'The Montreal Protocol Multilateral Fund: Partial Success Story' in Robert O. Keohane and Marc A. Levy (eds), *Institutions for Environmental Aid: Pitfalls and Promise* (MIT Press 1996); Richard Elliot Benedick, *Ozone Diplomacy: New Directions in Safeguarding the Planet* (Enl ed, Harvard University Press 1998); Edward Parson, *Protecting the Ozone Layer: Science and Strategy* (Oxford University Press 2003).

[316] Raustiala and Victor (n 55) 278.

[317] Ibid., 278; Kenneth Abbott, 'Strengthening the Transnational Regime Complex for Climate Change' (2013) 3 *Transnational Environmental Law* 57, 64.

[318] Abbott (n 317) 64, 65; Altieri and Gedan (n 194) 15. [319] Ibid.

developed at that point.[320] Accordingly, the authors chose plant genetic resources as a case to explore regime interaction, a topic that lies at the nexus of different issue areas, including international property, environmental protection, agriculture, and trade.[321] The authors proceed to argue that, instead of being governed by a single regime, plant genetic resources are governed by 'at least five clusters of international agreements – what we call *elemental regimes*'.[322] Thus, according to Raustiala and Victor, a regime is a cluster of international agreements. The authors refer to the collective of these elemental regimes as a 'regime complex'.[323] The authors define a regime complex as:

> [A]n *array* of partially *overlapping and nonhierarchical institutions* governing a particular *issue-area*. Regime Complexes are marked by the existence of *several legal agreements* that are created and maintained in *distinct fora* with participation of *different* sets of *actors*. These *rules* in these elemental regimes functionally *overlap*, yet there is *no* agreed upon *hierarchy* for resolving *conflicts* between rules.[324] [emphasis added]

In other words, the defining elements of this early definition of a regime complex are the presence of multiple, non-hierarchical institutions that have functional overlaps as they govern the same issue area, such as plant genetic resources. Raustiala and Victor further describe that the overlap of the institutions governing the same issue area may exist regarding scope, subject, and/or time.[325] For example, in the case of plant genetic resources, the different elemental regimes (environmental protection, agriculture, international property) can each address plant genetic resources as a subject and thus overlap. At the same time, some elemental regimes, such as environmental protection and agriculture, overlap in scope as they could both address an issue like runoff from agriculture to protect the environment. Lastly, these different elemental regimes need to coexist and operate simultaneously to overlap in time.

Since the paper by Raustiala and Victor, discussions in the literature on regime complexes have gained momentum. Those writing on this theme invariably reference the plant genetic resources paper as the first to define the concept of a regime complex and often reiterate the key elements of the aforementioned definition.[326] However, the concept of a regime complex has also evolved over

[320] Raustiala and Victor (n 55) 278. [321] Ibid. [322] Ibid., 279. [323] Ibid. [324] Ibid., *279.*

[325] Ibid.

[326] Benjamin Faude and Thomas Gehring, 'Chapter 7: Regime Complexes as Governance Systems', *Research Handbook on the Politics of International Law* (Edward Elgar Publishing 2017) 571, 579, 582; Gorana Draguljić, 'The Climate Change Regime Complex: Path Dependence amidst Institutional Change' (2019) 25 *Global Governance*: A Review of Multilateralism and International Organizations 476, 477; Robert O. Keohane and David G. Victor, 'The Regime Complex for Climate Change' (2011) 9 *Perspectives on Politics* 7, 7; Frank Biermann and others, 'The Fragmentation of Global Governance Architectures: A Framework for Analysis' (2009) 9 *Global Environmental Politics* 14, 14; Karen J. Alter and Sophie Meunier, 'The Politics of International Regime Complexity' (2009) 7 *Perspectives on Politics* 13, 13.

the years. This progress can be observed in the writings of the authors discussed below, which add nuance and new perspectives to the original definition of a regime complex (see Table 3.3). Later in this chapter, these new perspectives will be used alongside the original definition to determine whether the governance landscape for OA, as captured in the map, qualifies as a regime complex.

First, authors such as Orsini, Morin and Young have sought to clarify the definition of a regime complex.[327] Yet, these clarifications did not move away significantly from the original understanding developed by Raustiala and Victor. More recently, however, authors have begun to depart more emphatically from the traditional definition. Specifically, the idea that regime complexes must be nonhierarchical has been questioned.[328] Newer understandings of regime complexes, or as Eilstrup-Sangiovanni calls them 'global governance complexes' (GGC), claim that these complexes can vary regarding the nature of the hierarchical relationship between elemental regimes.[329] Hence, a lack of hierarchy does not need to be a defining feature of a regime complex. Instead, these newer framings understand regime complexes, or GGCs, to simply be 'rule sets and agents that assert overlapping authority claims to govern a specific global policy issue'.[330]

Nevertheless, both the old and newer definitions share the concept of a nexus in common. Similar to the nexus of different issue areas described by Raustiala and Victor, the new definitions reiterate and further explain this narrative by stating that while individual institutions address clearly defined issues, collectively these institutions form a complex. Hence, this complex exists at the nexus of various issue areas.[331] For example, international civil aviation occupies the nexus between the international legal regimes for immigration, transport, and travel, to name just a few.[332] Therefore, institutions overlap, as they assert authority to govern specific problems but are also part of adjacent governance systems.[333] In sum, one might question whether a complete absence of hierarchy should be considered a defining characteristic of a regime complex.

Second, the original understanding of a regime complex postulated by Raustiala and Victor, as well as the broader one by Keohane and Victor (see below),[334] largely concentrates on interstate institutions that are empowered to adopt legally binding rules. This shortcoming has been identified by Abbott, who introduced the concept of a 'transnational regime complex'.[335] According to his findings, the

[327] Amandine Orsini, Jean-Frédéric Morin and Oran Young, 'Regime Complexes: A Buzz, a Boom, or a Boost for Global Governance?' (2013) 19 *Global Governance* 27, 29–31.

[328] Cf. Mette Eilstrup-Sangiovanni, 'Ordering Global Governance Complexes: The Evolution of the Governance Complex for International Civil Aviation' (2022) 17 *The Review of International Organizations* 293; Jessica F. Green, 'Hierarchy in Regime Complexes: Understanding Authority in Antarctic Governance' (2022) 66 *International Studies Quarterly* 1.

[329] Eilstrup-Sangiovanni (n 328) 296.

[330] Ibid., 294.

[331] Ibid; Raustiala and Victor (n 55) 278.

[332] Eilstrup-Sangiovanni (n 328) 297; cf. Orsini, Morin and Young (n 327) 30, 31.

[333] Eilstrup-Sangiovanni (n 328) 297.

[334] Keohane and Victor (n 326).

[335] Cf. Kenneth W. Abbott, 'The Transnational Regime Complex for Climate Change' (2012) 30 *Environment and Planning C: Government and Policy* 571; Abbott (n 317).

original understanding of a regime complex presents a limited and incomplete view of governance because it leaves out transnational institutions.[336] This focus on legally binding instruments overlooks the potential of transnational organisations to address the governance gaps left by multilateral and interstate institutions.[337]

Therefore, to gain a comprehensive picture of a regime complex, Abbott argues that the transnational level should also be considered. To identify transnational 'organizations' in his own mapping exercise, Abbott refers to Bulkeley and defines an 'organization' as transnational if three criteria are present. First, they are 'transnational because they operate in more than one country and include private actors and/or subnational units of governance as well as, or rather than, states and interstate organizations'.[338] Second, these institutions participate in governance because they have the authority to engage relevant actors towards common goals. Even though these actors often possess some type of authority, most can only enact non-binding rules.[339] Therefore, the institutions frequently draw on 'regulatory standard setting', which establishes voluntary 'norms of conduct'.[340] Third, provided that they contribute to protecting public goods,[341] they can also be considered 'institutions of governance'.[342] Many new understandings of regime complexes or GGCs align with Abbott and present a less limited understanding of institutions compared to Raustiala and Victor's original conception. The diversity of both actors and instruments is emphasised.[343]

Third, in a widely cited article,[344] Victor and Keohane[345] analyse the regime complex for climate change, an area related to OA, as seen in Chapter 2. Using a definition similar to the one coined by Raustiala and Victor, Keohane and Victor explain that a regime complex is just one form of governance on a continuum of different governance options (see Figure 3.2 for the full governance spectrum). This continuum ranges from single integrated regimes on one end to fragmentation on the other. In the middle, nested regimes – and, importantly, regime complexes – can be found.[346] In addition to placing regime complexes on this spectrum of governance options, the authors also provide a theoretical explanation using so-called forces to clarify why a regime complex emerges in relation to regulatory efforts in some issue areas but not others.[347] These forces are interests, uncertainty, and linkages.[348] By examining these three forces, it becomes possible to understand and explain if and why a certain issue area is likely to yield a regime complex. This analytical framework can be applied in relation to the governance of OA.

336 Abbott (n 335) 574. 337 Abbott (n 317) 59. 338 Abbott (n 335) 572. 339 Ibid.

340 Ibid.

341 Definition of a public good: 'a commodity held in common (usually in plural); (Economics) a commodity or service provided, without profit, to all members of a society (whether by the government or privately)'. Oxford English Dictionary, 'Public Good, n'. www.oed.com/dictionary/public-good_n?tab=meaning_and_use#9927762718 accessed 25 July 2023.

342 Abbott (n 335) 572. 343 Eilstrup-Sangiovanni (n 328) 296; Green (n 328) 2.

344 Abbott (n 335) 583; Abbott (n 317) 65; Orsini, Morin and Young (n 327) 34; Eilstrup-Sangiovanni (n 328) 298, 300, 304.

345 Keohane and Victor (n 326) 8. 346 Ibid., 7. 347 Ibid., 8, 12. 348 Ibid., 8, 9.

The original definition by Raustiala and Victor, along with the three new perspectives presented above, are summarised below in Table 3.3. After exploring the concept of regime complexity, this chapter will analyse whether the governance landscape outlined earlier qualifies as a regime complex.

3.2.2 Ocean Acidification – Governed by a Regime Complex

To evaluate whether the governance landscape mapped for OA qualifies as a regime complex, this chapter utilises the governance options on the continuum described above, as visualised in Figure 3.2. More specifically, the map will be tested against the different governance options to determine which one is present (Section 3.2.2.1). As part of this exercise, in particular, the definition of regime complexity and new perspectives on it will be employed. Then, alongside testing the mapped governmental landscape against the governance options and the definition of regime complexity, the forces identified by Keohane and Victor can further confirm the relevance of regime complex theory for the problem of OA (Section 3.2.2.2). Examining these forces enhances the understanding of the reasons why OA as an issue area yields a regime complex.

3.2.2.1 Ocean Acidification on the Continuum of Governance Options

The first two governance options included in the continuum in Figure 3.2 are integrated and nested regimes. A characteristic of both types of regimes is that one institution is clearly in charge and hierarchically positioned above other institutions. The map indeed shows a wide variety of institutions (both actors and instruments) at different governance levels that consider the topic relevant for their work, *without* any institution taking the lead (at least for now). Based on this, it is evident that the OA governance landscape, as outlined in the map above, does not qualify as an integrated or nested regime.

The third governance option on the continuum in Figure 3.2 is a regime complex, as developed by Raustiala and Victor in their paper on plant genetic resources and described above (see also Table 3.3). According to this understanding, a regime complex has three defining elements. First, institutions should be present. Institutions include a variety of legal agreements that stem from distinct fora and different actors. According to Abbott, this might also include transnational institutions. Second, these institutions are organised in a non-hierarchical fashion.

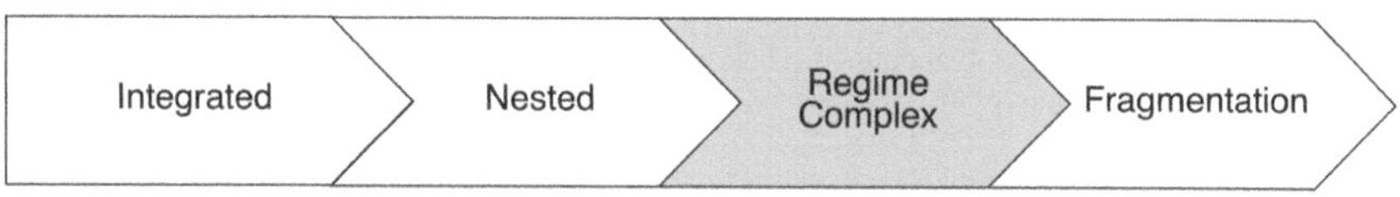

Figure 3.2 Spectrum of governance options.
Source: Compiled by the author

Table 3.3 Regime complex theory and its developments.

<table>
<tr><th></th><th>Original</th><th>Challenge</th><th>Addition</th><th>Addition</th></tr>
<tr><td>Regime complex + new perspectives</td><td>Traditional regime complex (Raustiala and Victor)</td><td>New understandings of regime complex/GGC (Eilstrup-Sangiovanni and Green)</td><td>Transnational regime complex (Abbott)</td><td>Theoretical background to yielding of regime complex (three forces) (Keohane and Victor)</td></tr>
<tr><td>Relationship</td><td>Partially overlapping (scope, subject, time)</td><td>Overlapping authority claims,</td><td>Same as original</td><td rowspan="4">Continuum of governance options (see Figure 3.2)
Explanation of it and why a certain issue area yields a regime complex through three forces: Interests Uncertainty Linkages</td></tr>
<tr><td>Hierarchy</td><td>Nonhierarchical</td><td>Everything from informal hierarchy to no overall architecture</td><td>Same as original</td></tr>
<tr><td>Institution</td><td>Legal agreements with distinct fora and participation of different actors</td><td>Broad definition of institutions (including transnational)</td><td>Institutions: Transnational – operate in more than one country and include privates. Participate in governance – authority and can steer target actors. Institutions of governance – provide public goods</td></tr>
<tr><td>Nexus</td><td>Topic lies at the nexus of different issue areas</td><td>Institutions address delimited issues, GGCs are at the nexus of several issue areas</td><td>Same as original</td></tr>
</table>

Source: Compiled by the author.

However, the importance of this second element, as discussed above, has been questioned by Eilstup-Sangiovanni and Green. Third, the institutions have a functional overlap as they govern the same issue area.

Regarding the first characteristic – institutions – looking at the map reveals a variety of legal instruments and actors that, together, form institutions. Additionally, these institutions focus on the governance of various issue areas, such as climate, air pollution, and fisheries. As described above, the map includes not only state actors but also transnational actors. These transnational actors, according to the framework set out by Bulkeley, consist at least partially of private actors and originate from a minimum of two different countries.

Nonetheless, it becomes clear from the map that the number of actors marked as private or mixed is quite limited. This limitation reflects the paucity of transnational actors that are expressly concerned with and/or have considered OA concerning their work so far. The limited involvement of private actors is particularly pronounced for those that, in addition to being transnational, also have the potential to fulfil one or both of the other two criteria that Bulkeley presents to qualify as an organisation engaged in transnational governance: namely, the second criterion, the potential to participate in governance, and third, the capacity to provide public goods. However, even though the number of transnational actors is currently low, it may, of course, grow in the future. In contrast, other related regime complexes, such as the one for climate change, have attracted significant attention from transnational actors.[349] Since the problem of OA was only presented to the broader public in 2005, more transnational actors will likely become involved in the coming years. Thus, the first characteristic, the presence of institutions, can be confirmed.

Regarding hierarchy, the second characteristic, it has already been identified that there is no single institution in charge of organising the field. Instead, numerous institutions exist, not only at the global level but also at regional and local levels. Furthermore, no clear hierarchy can be observed when examining the map, as most institutions emerge from different issue areas, for example, geoengineering versus land-based pollution. Thus, the various institutions that address or may address OA do not appear to be hierarchically organised and seem to operate in an uncoordinated manner. However, there may be some order or hierarchy among certain institutions within the OA regime complex. For instance, in her paper about Antarctic governance, Green identifies hierarchy within this governance area.[350] Some of the actors/instruments (CCAMLR, SCAR, ATS) included in her analysis are also represented on the map for OA governance. Thus, the informal or formal ordering found by Green concerning Antarctic governance may indeed exist to some extent in the map for OA governance, as the map, for example, includes CCAMLR and SCAR. Therefore, some forms of order or hierarchy cannot be entirely ruled out. Regardless, since the absence of hierarchy as a necessary

[349] Cf. Abbott (n 335). [350] Cf. Green (n 328).

condition for the existence of a regime complex is contested, the potential presence of hierarchical elements does not exclude the existence of a regime complex. In any event, even if it may not conform to the original definition, the governance landscape for OA could satisfy the characteristics of the modified definition of a regime complex by Green/Eilstrup-Sangiovanni if the third characteristic, namely functional overlap, is present.

Connected to this, the third characteristic is functional overlap, more specifically, overlapping authority to govern a specific global policy issue/issue area. The overlap exists regarding scope, subject, and time. For OA, this means an overlap in subject is evident when the different elemental regimes can address OA (or aspects of OA), while there is an overlap in scope if these regimes address the same aspects within OA. Lastly, these different elemental regimes need to coexist and operate simultaneously to also overlap in time.

First, it can be argued that they overlap in subject. The map displays many institutions operating across different fields, such as air and atmosphere, biodiversity protection, and geoengineering. Despite working in these diverse areas, these institutions are all empowered to address certain aspects of OA related to mitigation, stressors, and adaptation. Most institutions listed on the map have only referred to or briefly touched upon OA in their work. As observed on their websites, only a few of these institutions engage further with the topic, going beyond mere acknowledgement of the problem's existence.[351] Although many institutions have not yet declared OA as an issue area on their agenda, they still address certain elements of OA. For instance, although MARPOL 73/78 does not explicitly mention OA, it can address NO_x and SO_x emissions, which are contributors to OA. The fact that institutions have not actively expressed interest in OA merely indicates their lack of awareness regarding the overlapping aspects of OA. Therefore, as long as the institutions address an aspect of OA, they overlap in subject, which is true for most, if not all, institutions included in the map above.

Second, regarding the overlap in scope, several institutions can address the same aspects of OA (see also Chapter 4). The scope of an institution can be described as the reach/boundary of what it can address. If several institutions cover the same specific aspect of OA, this is referred to as an overlap in scope. For example, both the IMO and the CCR tackle CO_2 emissions, albeit from different industrial sectors, while the LOTSR addresses marine protected areas, which are also covered by UNESCO. These examples illustrate that the boundaries of what the different institutions encompass and the aspects of OA they can address overlap. Chapter 5 will further highlight the various overlaps between institutions. Additionally, all

[351] More aware of OA are, for instance, OA Alliance, 'About' (*OA Alliance*, 2021) www.oaalliance.org/about accessed 18 January 2022; IUCN, 'Climate Change and the Ocean' (*IUCN*, 7 October 2015) www.iucn.org/theme/marine-and-polar/our-work/climate-change-and-ocean accessed 20 January 2022; IAEA, OA-ICC, 'Ocean Acidification International Coordination Centre (OA-ICC)' (5 February 2018) www.iaea.org/services/oa-icc accessed 11 January 2022.

institutions on the map coexist and operate simultaneously, thereby overlapping in time. Thus, the third characteristic of a regime complex is evident in the governance landscape for OA.

In summary, the three characteristics of a regime complex are present, albeit with some relatively minor doubts regarding hierarchy and overlap. Furthermore, as described by Raustiala and Victor, as well as Green and Eilstrup-Sangiovanni, the map clearly indicates that OA sits at the nexus of different issue areas, which is typical for a regime complex. The various institutions represented in the map operate within fields such as air and atmosphere, biodiversity protection, or geoengineering. Thus, these institutions engage with governance systems that are adjacent to OA. These existing institutions will influence the governance of OA, as they will 'channel and constrain the content' of OA governance.[352] Thus, it becomes evident that the landscape depicted in the map has not been developed explicitly for OA, but OA governance also does not begin forming on a clean slate as anticipated at the start of this chapter.

When testing the map against the continuum of governance options, and as part of that, against the definition of a regime complex, it is evident that the governance landscape for OA aligns with the three characteristics of a regime complex. However, some doubt has been identified regarding overlap and hierarchy. Therefore, to further confirm this placement within the continuum, the three forces (interest, uncertainty, and linkages) proposed by Keohane and Victor can be assessed in relation to the issue area of OA. Utilising these three forces can also clarify why the issue area of OA has emerged as a regime complex. Understanding the origins of the regime complex can, in turn, be used to identify governance approaches that accommodate the features of a regime complex for OA (see also Chapter 4).

3.2.2.2 Confirmation of a Regime Complex through Interests, Uncertainty, and Linkages

There is a spectrum of governance options, as Figure 3.2 shows and has been described in detail above. The possibilities range from an integrated regime to a nested regime, then a regime complex, and finally fragmentation.[353] Keohane and Victor identify three forces – interests, uncertainty, and linkages – that can help explain where a new problem, such as OA, is likely to be situated on the continuum.[354] Hence, three factors are used to understand why a particular issue area will be addressed through a certain form of governance and why regime complexes are present in some areas but not others.[355] However, it is crucial to recognise that there is not always a clear-cut delineation between the different governance options on the spectrum. On the contrary, an issue area might lean more towards one end

[352] Cf. Raustiala and Victor (n 55) 280, who identify that regulations which are already in force can 'channel and constrain'.

[353] Keohane and Victor (n 326) 7. [354] Ibid., 8, 9. [355] Ibid.

concerning one factor and more towards the other concerning a different factor, while overall still settling in the middle and showing the characteristics of a regime complex. To confirm that OA as a problem is likely to be situated in the middle of the continuum and take the form of a regime complex, the three forces – interests, uncertainty, and linkages – will be explained, and the problem of OA will be tested against them.

3.2.2.2.1 Interests Concerning interests, Keohane and Victor predict the formation of a more integrated regime where the interests of pivotal actors are similar. In contrast, they foresee fragmentation, where those interests largely diverge.[356] In a situation where interests diverge, actors may purposely promote and encourage the emergence of an array of institutions. This behaviour arises because a multitude of regulatory regimes opens the possibility of forum shopping and regime shifting.[357] Certain regulatory regimes may represent a departure from the status quo and eschew path-dependency in favour of a more novel approach.[358] This novel approach may lead to the construction of a normative framework that better protects actors whose interests would not be sufficiently safeguarded by the status quo.[359] Hence, in cases of differing interests, where actors seek to move away from path-dependency, different institutions and the formation of a regime complex are likely to occur.[360]

3.2.2.2.2 Interests and OA The first factor, or 'force' described by Keohane and Victor in their paper is interests. According to their thesis, an integrated and comprehensive regime is more likely to exist when the interests of pivotal actors are aligned rather than conflicting. Where interests diverge, fragmentation of the governance landscape can be expected.[361] The following section will first describe the actors and detail their interests (with examples), and then reach a conclusion regarding how the interests related to OA settle on the spectrum.

When it comes to OA and the actors identified above, it becomes apparent that many different entities are already involved or potentially involved in the regulation of OA. Most of the actors are state actors, but there are also transnational and private ones. The number of actors will likely grow in the future. This is especially true for private and mixed transnational actors, as other transnational regime complexes have developed in this way. Abbott, for example, has identified sixty-eight mixed and private transnational actors in his transnational regime complex for climate change.[362]

Actors may have differing motives when deciding whether to consider OA in their activities. Some motives and underlying interests may conflict or even be incompatible.[363] Therefore, a greater number and variety of actors are likely to generate diverse interests, including economic versus environmental ones. RFMOs are

356 Ibid. 357 Ibid., 9. 358 Ibid; Draguljić (n 326) 477, 479, 480. 359 Cf. ibid.
360 Keohane and Victor (n 326) 9. 361 Cf. ibid., 8, 9, 13. 362 Abbott (n 335).
363 See forum shopping above. In situations where several actors are at play, often some actors will try to forum shop as their interests diverge from the status quo. Alter and Meunier (n 326) 16.

one type of actor obligated to consider various interests. These fisheries organisations are responsible for managing a marine resource on which many countries and people depend for income and food security. Thus, RFMOs have an interest in ensuring the sustainability of fishing.

Nevertheless, to ensure the continuation of fishing as a source of food and income, it must be conducted in a sustainable manner that can take environmental concerns into consideration.[364] However, especially regarding OA, the environmental perspective lags behind. Although RFMOs could protect the natural resistance of the oceans against OA by setting fishing quotas that account for OA (see fisheries management as an adaptation option in Chapter 2), so far, OA has only been considered by some RFMOs to a limited extent.[365] Contrary to that, other actors have prioritised environmental interests over economic ones. These interests can, for example, be observed in relation to GOA-ON. This network has devoted itself to detecting and understanding 'the drivers of ocean acidification' in ocean environments and protecting oceanic ecosystems to avoid exacerbating OA.[366] Sometimes, however, interests cannot be distinctly divided between environmental and economic. Since crucial industries, such as the oyster industry in the United States, are already feeling the repercussions of OA, they have begun to recognise the necessity of protecting the ocean to fulfil their economic aspirations.[367] In such cases, actors tend to consider both economic and environmental interests together.

Regarding OA, it is clear that there are divergent interests at play. Although environmental and economic interests seem incompatible and suggest fragmentation, certain actors – especially businesses – must increasingly consider both economic and environmental interests together to achieve their goal of increasing income. Consequently, some economic actors also pay attention to environmental interests. This attention helps to reduce the degree of divergence between the interests of different actors and create a pocket of convergence, making complete fragmentation in governance less likely. Thus, concerning the first factor, interests, the OA landscape is likely positioned in the middle of the spectrum, though probably with a slight tendency towards greater fragmentation.

3.2.2.2.3 Uncertainty Regarding uncertainty, the second factor highlighted by Keohane and Victor, it can be said that the higher the uncertainty, the more likely a fragmented regime can be expected.[368] Depending on the issue area, various

[364] Cf. Bianca Haas and others, 'Factors Influencing the Performance of Regional Fisheries Management Organizations' (2020) 113 *Marine Policy* 103787, 1, 4, 6.

[365] Scott, 'Ocean Acidification' (n 29) 391; Rosemary Rayfuse, 'Regional Fisheries Bodies and Ocean Acidification' in David L. VanderZwaag, Nilufer Oral and Tim Stephens (eds), *Research Handbook on Ocean Acidification Law and Policy* (Edward Elgar Publishing 2021).

[366] GOA-ON, 'GOA-ON: Approach & Goals' (2023) www.goa-on.org/about/goals.php accessed 25 July 2023.

[367] Jagers and others (n 30) 13.

[368] Keohane and Victor (n 326) 9.

parameters can lead to greater uncertainty. For instance, uncertainty increases in issue areas characterised by complexity.[369] This increase occurs, for example, when the issue at hand requires understanding a complicated scientific background that is not sufficiently researched.[370] Also, the number of actors involved can contribute to increasing uncertainty. When multiple actors are involved, there is greater uncertainty regarding the distribution of costs and benefits stemming from regulation. In cases where extensive cooperation among many actors is needed, governments may increasingly struggle to fulfil their commitments. This weakness is particularly evident in situations involving significant national interest groups. In these cases, uncertainty gives rise to cooperative structures that unite only a select number of states, referred to as clubs.[371]

3.2.2.2.4 Uncertainty and OA As seen above, the second factor described by Keohane and Victor is uncertainty. The hypothesis is that the higher the uncertainty regarding an issue area, the more likely fragmentation will occur. If a problem area is not characterised by a high degree of uncertainty, an integrated regime will probably emerge. Numerous factors contribute to uncertainty, and their nature will vary according to the issue area. However, complexity and the presence of multiple actors are two important examples that increase uncertainty.[372] Below, whether OA, as an issue area, is characterised by a high degree of uncertainty will be considered in order to evaluate the implications of this from a governance perspective.

Certain factors will tend to increase the level of uncertainty regarding the problem of OA. First, the large number of actors involved in this issue will serve to exacerbate uncertainty. As seen in the map, a significant and potentially growing number of actors are engaged in the topic. This generates uncertainty about the distribution of the costs and benefits of cooperation. Second, OA is characterised by a high degree of scientific complexity. Actors tend to be more cautious in their decision-making in situations where problems are challenging to address and difficult to understand. Third, closely related to the trait of scientific complexity, is that of scientific uncertainty. Not only is OA a problem that requires a deep understanding of the scientific background, but this background is also uncertain and unexplored, as noted in Chapter 2. Even though scientists have discovered that OA has occurred before, during the Paleocene–Eocene boundary, the developments observed today are different and happening more rapidly. Thus, the effects and repercussions for the ecosystem and humans cannot be clearly predicted. The leading cause of OA is CO_2; however, other causes and environmental stressors, such as rising temperatures and overfishing, aggravate the situation and further weaken the resilience of the ocean. This multitude of causes and stressors increases uncertainty, as OA cannot be addressed with one simple strategy; rather, solutions must come from a variety of directions. Moreover, OA will affect diverse geographical regions in different

[369] Ibid. [370] Cf. ibid., 13. [371] Ibid., 9, 13. [372] Cf. ibid.

ways and to varying degrees. These characteristics of OA demand intense cooperation and a high level of commitment from a wide variety of actors active in different fields and regions of the world. Solution-finding must continue despite ongoing deficits in scientific understanding of the problem.

Nonetheless, some institutions aim to reduce scientific uncertainty. For instance, the IPCC and the IPBES conduct ongoing research to gather more information about the science behind the causes, stressors, and effects of OA. This new knowledge is then simplified and communicated to make the topic more understandable. Over time, we can expect more scientific certainty. For now, however, a high degree of scientific uncertainty remains.

In short, it can be said that many factors concerning OA lead to an increase in uncertainty. According to Keohane and Victor, this is therefore more likely to result in the formation of smaller cooperative structures, such as so-called clubs, and consequently to increase the fragmentation inherent in the governance landscape. However, uncertainty about OA will diminish (indeed, already has) due to the research being conducted. Growing confidence in the scientific understanding of the different parameters of the problem supports elements of regime complexity instead of complete fragmentation.

3.2.2.2.5 Linkages Concerning the third factor, linkages, Keohane and Victor theorise that an absence of scope for linkages between institutions in an issue area makes a regime complex and even fragmentation more likely.[373] It can be inferred from Keohane and Victor that linkages refer to the ability to connect different issue areas under the same umbrella. In other words, the boundaries around the issue area are partially defined by the linkages that can be made.[374] An example can be found in the 'GAAT/WTO regime, which originally focused on border tariffs and now encompasses a broader array of trade-related measures such as, subsidies, government procurement, and food safety standards'.[375] Therefore, the original regime linked border tariffs with subsidies, government procurement, and food safety, creating deeper cooperation.[376] Hence, the suitability of an issue area for linkages depends on its ability to link diverse regulatory agreements. Linkages can be an option to broaden the scope of deal-making and thus further integration. Those linkages that can multiply benefits from cooperation and induce compliance are especially relevant and encouraged.[377] Thus, the more linkages are available, the more an integrated regime can be expected.

3.2.2.2.6 Linkages and OA The last factor highlighted by Keohane and Victor is linkages. Their theory claims that fragmentation is more likely in cases where there is an absence of scope for linkages in an issue area. Accordingly, an integrated regime is expected when a high number of linkages can be established. A problem area will demonstrate more linkages if it has the ability to connect diverse regulatory

[373] Ibid., 9. [374] Cf. ibid., 9. [375] Ibid. [376] Ibid. [377] Ibid., 9.

agreements.[378] In view of this, it is essential to assess the potential for creating linkages in the area of OA.

To address OA with the aim of mitigating the issue and minimising its repercussions, collaboration will be necessary among a considerable number of actors from various substantive fields and geographical regions. This necessity arises from the inherent nature of the problem. Nevertheless, although OA has been mentioned individually by numerous actors and instruments (see Figure 3.1), collaboration among these different actors can only be observed sporadically thus far.[379] Patchy cooperation creates a strong impression that the issue of OA hinders the formation of linkages. Consequently, the emergence of smaller, specialised regimes, or clubs, can be anticipated. It can be expected that those involved in OA governance will resist an integrated regime, as integration offers fewer advantages compared to fragmentation, making it unworthy for club members to invest time and resources in negotiations or to accept trade-offs.[380] Hence, where participants are reluctant to cooperate, it is probable that linkages will not be formed, leading actors to create clubs instead.

Nevertheless, as the scientific uncertainty surrounding OA decreases and as greater convergence between economic and environmental interests occurs, actors may be expected to unite more in pursuit of a common goal. This convergence may create more opportunities for linkages. Furthermore, states that invest in institutions and their establishment will likely refuse to accept a complete fragmentation of the issue area. These states spend substantial amounts of money because they hope to gain and expect first-mover advantages, for instance.[381]

Thus, it can be said vis-à-vis the third factor (linkages) that even though the OA landscape at first glance does not have a high tendency to create linkages, connections between clubs may nonetheless grow as uncertainty decreases and interests align. Therefore, concerning the third factor, elements of regime complexity may be expected to emerge, shifting the governance landscape to the left on the spectrum in Figure 3.2, thereby avoiding complete fragmentation.

According to the three factors – interests, uncertainty, and linkages – the international and transnational landscape for OA is likely to be neither fully integrated nor completely fragmented but rather situated somewhere in the middle of the spectrum in the domain of a regime complex. However, since the boundaries between the different governance options are fluid, it may be that the OA landscape, while positioned in the middle of the spectrum, will nonetheless show a tendency towards some degree of fragmentation. In other words, the three forces suggest that OA is

[378] Cf. ibid., 9, 13.

[379] One example of linkages between actors included in the table: OSPAR Commission becoming an Affiliate Member of the OA Alliance. OSPAR Commission, 'OSPAR Has Become an Affiliate Member of the International Alliance to Combat Ocean Acidification' (*OSPAR Commission*, 14 December 2022) www.ospar.org/news/oaalliance accessed 28 February 2023.

[380] Similar results for the climate change regime complex were found by Keohane and Victor (n 326) 13.

[381] Similar results for the climate change regime complex were found by ibid.

the kind of problem likely to give rise to a regime complex, albeit one based on a degree of fragmentation.[382] Chapter 4 will analyse how this regime complex might evolve in a manner well suited to the governance of OA.

3.3 Finding a Governance Approach for Ocean Acidification with the Governmental Landscape in Mind

This chapter has mapped the international and transnational landscape for OA. The multifarious institutions included in the map operate in many different issue areas, such as biodiversity protection, transboundary air pollution, and climate change. Within the scope of their work, these institutions address different aspects of the causes, stressors, and/or adaptation to OA. Thus, as predicted at the beginning of this chapter, the challenge of tackling OA does not start from a clean slate. Furthermore, after examining the characteristics of a regime complex and the three forces that make its existence likely, this chapter argues that the governance landscape for OA can be characterised as a regime complex, although it may continue to exhibit a degree of fragmentation. As is typical for a regime complex, the regime complex for OA sits at the nexus of many different issues, including those mentioned above: biodiversity protection, transboundary air pollution, and climate change.

As is typical for all regime complexes, the one concerning OA also involves multifarious institutions, which can be seen on the map. Furthermore, the three forces have demonstrated that OA governance includes, for instance, various interests and uncertainties that complicate reaching an agreement on how to address OA *ex ante*. Global experimentalist governance is one approach that can effectively leverage these characteristics of a regime complex without dismantling it.

After understanding the scientific background of OA (Chapter 2) and armed with the knowledge that the governance landscape for OA can be described as a regime complex, this book will now consider how this governance landscape can evolve to help mitigate the causes and consequences of OA (Chapter 4).

[382] Many others come to the same result. See, for example, Karen Scott comes to the same result in her brief mentioning of OA and regime complexity. Karen N. Scott, 'Ocean Acidification' in Elise Johansen, Signe Busch and Ingvild Ulrikke Jakobsen (eds), *The Law of the Sea and Climate Change* (1st ed., Cambridge University Press 2020) 109, 110 www.cambridge.org/core/product/identifier/9781108907118%23CN-bp-5/type/book_part accessed 10 April 2023.

CHAPTER 4
Global Experimentalist Governance

Chapter 3 shows that the current international and transnational landscape for OA can be characterised as a regime complex. However, the question remains: how will the regime complex for OA evolve? Ideally, governance arrangements should address the causes, stressors, and adaptation options concerning OA. One governance structure that can, according to the literature, develop from a regime complex is global experimentalist governance.[383] As noted in Chapter 3, the regime complex for OA involves, for example, multiple institutions attempting to tackle a newly arising problem. Furthermore, the three forces (interests, uncertainty, linkages) illustrate that OA governance encompasses varying interests and uncertainties, which complicates reaching a consensus on how to address OA *ex ante*.

Global experimentalist governance can build on a regime complex without completely dismantling it, even making a virtue of what is already present in terms of governance. This approach attempts to accommodate the rise of transnational problems and legal and institutional pluralism. In its bid to do so, global experimentalist governance seeks to tackle challenges based on learning and the engagement of various actors across multiple levels, thus allowing for flexible and adaptive governance.[384] Thus, global experimentalist governance is a governance approach well adapted to the characteristics of a regime complex, featuring numerous institutions operating at different levels, and seeking to address a transnational problem that remains partially understood (see also Chapter 3). Hence, global experimentalist governance is expected to evolve from a regime complex, as it can cater to

[383] De Búrca, Keohane and Sabel (n 283) 479; see also: Grainne De Búrca, Robert O. Keohane and Charles Sabel, 'New Modes of Pluralist Global Governance' (2012) 45 *New York University Journal of International Law and Politics* 723, 728.

[384] Gabrielle Goldstein and Christopher Ansell, 'Experimentalist Governance in Global Public Health: The Case of UNAIDS' (2018) 35 *Arizona Journal of International and Comparative Law* 219, 220.

and accommodate its characteristics. These characteristics will be analysed in more detail below.[385]

Global experimentalist governance has been assessed and tested at both national and regional scale[386] and, to a lesser extent, globally.[387] What this theory entails and how far it might provide a promising framework to address OA will be explored in this chapter. Accordingly, this chapter will first outline the definition of global experimentalist governance (Section 4.1) and then discuss the five elements that imbue global experimentalist governance in its ideal form (Section 4.2). Afterwards, in light of these elements, the meaning and functioning of the notion of a penalty default will be explained to finalise the description of the theory (Section 4.3). Having set out the key elements of global experimentalist governance, the next step is to examine the characteristics that define the problem of OA (Section 4.4). This is done to evaluate the extent to which this theory (global experimentalist governance) and problem (OA) are a match (Section 4.5). This 'matching' of theory and problem can help to assess if global experimentalist governance provides a promising framework to address OA. Finally, the chapter will evaluate whether the necessary background conditions for global experimentalist governance to develop and thrive are present in the context of OA (Section 4.6).

4.1 Definition

De Búrca, Keohane, and Sabel describe global experimentalist governance as follows: '[A]n institutionalized transnational process of participatory and multilevel problem-solving, in which particular problems (and the means of addressing them) are framed in an open-ended way, and subjected to periodic revision by various forms of peer review in light of locally generated knowledge'.[388]

Based on this definition, five key elements of global experimental governance have been identified.[389] De Búrca, Keohane, and Sabel use these elements to assess the presence of this form of governance.[390] Further, the literature explains that

[385] Cf. Christine Overdevest and Jonathan Zeitlin, 'Assembling an Experimentalist Regime: Transnational Governance Interactions in the Forest Sector: Assembling an Experimentalist Regime' (2014) 8 *Regulation & Governance* 22, 24–25.

[386] Grainne De Búrca, 'New Governance and Experimentalism: An Introduction' (2010) 2010 *Wisconsin Law Review* 227; Charles F. Sabel and Jonathan Zeitlin, 'Learning from Difference: The New Architecture of Experimentalist Governance in the EU' in Charles F. Sabel and Jonathan Zeitlin (eds), *Experimentalist Governance in the European Union: Towards a New Architecture* (Oxford University Press 2010); Jonathan Zeitlin (ed), *Extending Experimentalist Governance? The European Union and Transnational Regulation* (1st ed., Oxford University Press 2015).

[387] Armeni (n 283); De Búrca, Keohane and Sabel (n 383); Goldstein and Ansell (n 384).

[388] De Búrca, Keohane and Sabel (n 283) 477.

[389] De Búrca et al. refer to experimentalist governance as '(…) an "ideal type" in the sense used by Max Weber'. De Búrca, Keohane and Sabel (n 383) 727.

[390] Armeni (n 283) 880; De Búrca, Keohane and Sabel (n 383) 739; De Búrca, Keohane and Sabel (n 283) 478; Goldstein and Ansell (n 384) 221.

global experimentalist governance and the operation of the five steps are coordinated through an umbrella institution, the so-called central unit. The central unit is responsible for organising the interaction between various actors participating in experimentalism. However, the role of the central unit does not extend beyond this, as it is not to lead but to facilitate global experimentalist governance.[391] Section 4.2 will explain the five elements that constitute the core of global experimentalist governance. Where relevant, the role of the central unit will be discussed.

4.2 The Five Elements of the Ideal Type of Experimentalist Governance

The literature distils five elements present in the ideal type of global experimentalist governance.[392] These five elements can help identify the presence of global experimentalist governance. Since there is no one settled model of this type of governance,[393] an ideal type has been defined instead. Governance models can then be evaluated against this ideal type to determine whether the model in question resembles the ideal type.[394] If all the elements of the ideal type are present in a particular case, one can speak of global experimentalist governance. The elements can be considered necessary features that can be realised through various institutional arrangements.[395] The five elements are as follows:

- The existence of a shared problem;
- Agreement on open-ended goals;
- Delegation to lower levels of governance;
- Mechanisms for gathering feedback and peer review; and
- Flexibility in the adjustment of overarching goals.

Occasionally, authors omit the first step,[396] the shared problem – but as the very definition of a shared problem can be challenging, it will be considered a core element of experimentalist governance in this book. The literature does not provide much detail regarding the explanation of the five elements. Typically, they are mentioned and then directly applied to specific cases. Therefore, the question of how to assess whether an element is fulfilled remains open. The five elements will be explained in detail to guide the reader and facilitate the assessment of their presence. Information about the five elements is inferred from the literature and

[391] Goldstein and Ansell (n 384) 220, 230–232.

[392] Ibid., 221; De Búrca, Keohane and Sabel (n 383) 738, 739; Sabel and Zeitlin, 'Learning from Difference: The New Architecture of Experimentalist Governance in the EU' (n 386) 3; Armeni (n 283) 879, 880.

[393] Armeni (n 283) 879.

[394] Ibid.

[395] Sabel and Zeitlin, 'Learning from Difference: The New Architecture of Experimentalist Governance in the EU' (n 386) 3.

[396] See, for example, Armeni (n 283) 880; Goldstein and Ansell (n 384) 230.

existing case studies.[397] Ideally, this information about each individual element can later help determine whether the element is present in a particular case, specifically concerning the governance of OA. Therefore, the five elements will be discussed in the following order: shared problem (Section 4.2.1), open-ended goals (Section 4.2.2), delegation to lower levels of governance (Section 4.2.3), feedback and peer review (Section 4.2.4), and finally, adjustment of overarching goals (Section 4.2.5).

4.2.1 Shared Problem

The first element of the ideal type of global experimentalist governance is the requirement for a shared problem. More specifically, there should be an awareness among stakeholders that a common issue needs to be addressed.[398]

The literature has discussed global experimentalist governance regarding various concerns.[399] The kinds of problems approached through this form of governance share several common characteristics. These issues are often newly arising, creeping, or persistent.[400] An example of such a problem is climate change, whose effects have been slowly aggravating over many decades. When problems are new, creeping, or persistent, they also tend to exhibit low visibility, as climate change did a few decades ago. This low visibility occurs because there is no abrupt change from one environmental state to another.[401] In many cases, a limited amount of scientific information is available to understand the issue, which can lead to significant uncertainty concerning causes, aggravating factors, and solutions.[402]

Another challenge is the global dimension that such problems usually exhibit.[403] The global dimension refers to the fact that problems can 'only be addressed

[397] Cf. Armeni (n 283); Goldstein and Ansell (n 384); De Búrca, Keohane and Sabel (n 283); De Búrca, Keohane and Sabel (n 383); Sabel and Zeitlin, 'Learning from Difference: The New Architecture of Experimentalist Governance in the EU' (n 386); Vanessa C. Pinsky, Isak Kruglianskas and David G. Victor, 'Experimentalist Governance in Climate Finance: The Case of REDD+ in Brazil' (2019) 19 *Climate Policy* 725; Charles F. Sabel and Jonathan Zeitlin (eds), 'Experimentalist Governance in the European Energy Sector', *Experimentalist Governance in the European Union: Towards a New Architecture* (Oxford University Press 2010).

[398] De Búrca, Keohane and Sabel (n 283) 478.

[399] Goldstein and Ansell (n 384); De Búrca, Keohane and Sabel (n 383); Armeni (n 283); Pinsky, Kruglianskas and Victor (n 397).

[400] Armeni (n 283) 884; Sabel and Zeitlin, 'Experimentalist Governance in the European Energy Sector' (n 397) 72; Charles F. Sabel and Jonathan Zeitlin (eds), 'Emerging Experimentalism in EU Environmental Governance', *Experimentalist Governance in the European Union: Towards a New Architecture* (Oxford University Press 2010) 127.

[401] When there is an abrupt change from one environmental state to another, a so-called tipping point is reached. Tipping points are critical thresholds that, once reached indicate significant and often irreversible changes to the climate system, including the ocean. Egbert H. Van Nes and others, 'What Do You Mean, "Tipping Point"?' (2016) 31 *Trends in Ecology & Evolution* 902, 902–904.

[402] Cf. Pinsky, Kruglianskas and Victor (n 397) 728; Sabel and Zeitlin, 'Experimentalist Governance in the European Energy Sector' (n 397) 65, 72.

[403] Armeni (n 283) 884; Sabel and Zeitlin, 'Emerging Experimentalism in EU Environmental Governance' (n 400) 127.

effectively by internationally coordinated measures'.[404] In the face of political obstacles caused by questions of, for example, sovereignty or common but differentiated responsibilities and respective capabilities, these coordinated measures can be difficult to achieve.[405] Further, the issues governed by global experimentalist governance are considered complex.[406] High complexity means that 'the sources of persistent problems are diffuse and involve a large number of actors, including important indirect contributors. In addition, cause and effect tend to be significantly delayed'.[407] These characteristics make the problems at the centre of global experimentalist governance seemingly impossible to solve, and compelling solutions are difficult to identify – at least *ex ante*.[408]

To qualify as a 'shared' problem, stakeholders should have begun to reflect upon and discuss the problem in question.[409] This requirement implies that experimentalism is most suitable for governance situations where there is no overarching authority in charge that can define common goals.[410] Instead, it is up to the stakeholders to create a common understanding of what the problem entails.[411] Thus, part of the first step of the ideal type of global experimentalist governance is identifying, framing, and defining the issue in a way that experimentalist actors can agree on. Ideally, this process should be informed by the best available data and ongoing monitoring.[412]

In summary, stakeholders recognise a shared problem and understand the outcomes they aspire to, yet they do not know how to achieve them.[413] Once a shared problem has been agreed on, the formulation of open-ended goals – the second element of the ideal type of global experimentalist governance – can be agreed.

4.2.2 Open-Ended Goals

The second element of the ideal type of global experimentalist governance is the presence of open-ended goals. More specifically, stakeholders initially address the shared problem by outlining open-ended and framework-like goals rather than detailed, prescriptive regulations.[414] These open-ended goals are essential due to the often excessive uncertainty and disagreement that prevent the drafting of detailed regulations.

[404] Sabel and Zeitlin, 'Emerging Experimentalism in EU Environmental Governance' (n 400) 127.

[405] Ibid.

[406] Goldstein and Ansell (n 384) 230; Pinsky, Kruglianskas and Victor (n 397) 728; Sabel and Zeitlin, 'Experimentalist Governance in the European Energy Sector' (n 397) 72.

[407] De Búrca, Keohane and Sabel (n 283) 479.

[408] Goldstein and Ansell (n 384) 230.

[409] Cf. De Búrca, Keohane and Sabel (n 283) 478.

[410] Charles F. Sabel and Jonathan Zeitlin, 'Experimentalist Governance', *Experimentalist Governance* (Oxford University Press 2012) 169 http://oxfordhandbooks.com/view/10.1093/oxfordhb/9780199560530.001.0001/oxfordhb-9780199560530-e-12 accessed 31 July 2022.

[411] De Búrca, Keohane and Sabel (n 283) 479.

[412] De Búrca (n 386) 235.

[413] De Búrca, Keohane and Sabel (n 283) 479, 484.

[414] Ibid., 478; Goldstein and Ansell (n 384) 221.

Goals are set through consultation and collaboration among various stakeholders.[415] The actors involved are drawn from different governance levels and include civil society actors.[416] The result of these exchanges is an agreement on broad provisional framework goals and provisional metrics for assessing performance towards their attainment.[417] Metrics are tools designed to evaluate goal achievement and enable stakeholders to quantify their success in reaching these goals. These metrics can consist of specific targets to be achieved over time, adding detail to the metrics and making it easier to track and assess progress.[418] Essentially, alongside the broader framework goals, specific metrics are established. If these metrics are successfully achieved, they not only support the overall framework goals but also indicate a stakeholder's progress towards attaining them. In this way, stakeholders can evaluate their progress more effectively.[419]

While goals should be open-ended and framework-like in nature, both goals and metrics should possess a provisional character.[420] This means that goals are likely to be loosely worded, lacking in detail, and often do not specify particular timescales for their achievement.[421] A way to ensure these features is by creating 'living documents' that remain open to review and updating.[422] Provisionality is necessary as the goals and metrics need to be adaptable to changing circumstances. Over time, they should be shaped by the experiences of actors at lower levels of governance in light of local contexts.[423] In particular, newly discovered technological and scientific knowledge might lead to changes in goals and metrics in the future.[424] Examples of previously used open-ended goals are 'good water quality', 'adequate education', and 'sustainable forests'.[425] As is typical for open-ended goals, those mentioned here do not contain much detail and are loosely worded. To fulfil the ideal type's second element, a central unit should steer and manage the described process.[426] Accordingly, the central unit should facilitate the consultation and collaboration of the multifarious stakeholders. Afterwards, the central unit should establish framework goals while considering the different views expressed during the collaboration process.[427]

In conclusion, loosely defined goals should be identifiable to fulfil the second element of the ideal type. As a next step, solutions to the shared problems should

[415] Goldstein and Ansell (n 384) 230; cf. Joshua Cohen and Charles Sabel, 'Directly-Deliberative Polyarchy' (1997) 3 *European Law Journal* 313.

[416] Goldstein and Ansell (n 384) 230; Sabel and Zeitlin, 'Experimentalist Governance' (n 410) 169.

[417] Goldstein and Ansell (n 384) 230, 235.

[418] Cf. Armeni (n 283) 880; Goldstein and Ansell (n 384) 236.

[419] Cf. Sabel and Zeitlin, 'Experimentalist Governance' (n 410) 170; Armeni (n 283) 880; Goldstein and Ansell (n 384) 238.

[420] Goldstein and Ansell (n 384) 230, 235.

[421] Ibid., 236.

[422] Sabel and Zeitlin, 'Experimentalist Governance' (n 410) 171.

[423] Armeni (n 283) 880.

[424] Ibid.

[425] Sabel and Zeitlin, 'Experimentalist Governance' (n 410) 169; Sabel and Zeitlin, 'Learning from Difference: The New Architecture of Experimentalist Governance in the EU' (n 386) 3.

[426] Goldstein and Ansell (n 384) 235.

[427] Cf. ibid.

be found in accordance with the aforementioned open-ended goals and metrics. This task is delegated to lower levels of governance and constitutes the third element of the ideal type.

4.2.3 Delegation to Lower Levels of Governance

The third element of the ideal type of global experimentalist governance is delegation to actors at lower levels of governance. These lower levels are tasked with developing solutions to achieve open-ended goals through on the ground experience.[428]

More concretely, this means that finding solutions to the shared problem is, at least provisionally, delegated to lower-level units that are more familiar with local or regional conditions.[429] Lower-level actors have the discretion to experiment and adjust their practices and strategies over time.[430] This discretion derives from the framework-like nature of the goals.[431] Discretion reaches far, as actors have the authority to depart from existing rules if they consider it counterproductive to follow them.[432] However, this discretion is not unlimited. Experimentalist actors must work transparently and justify their choices, which are subject to regular review by other actors on the lower level as well as the central unit.[433] If their judgement regarding the inappropriateness of the existing rules persists and is widely shared, this may prompt the reformulation of the old rules.[434]

Solutions and strategies are explored that reflect localised, country, and region-specific needs and circumstances as they are created by actors familiar with the conditions prevailing within them.[435] Hence, experimentation and practical learning occur through a process on the lower level and include trying different options via implementation and planning.[436] This experimentation at the lower levels of governance provides an opportunity to 'learn from differences'.[437] Comparing the diverse pool of strategies and practices experimented with in various geographical areas may offer inspiration and information about what works under certain conditions and what does not.[438] Ultimately, this can 'establish processes that help to generate unimagined alternatives and improve our ability to choose among these alternatives by rigorously exposing each to criticism in light of the others'.[439] Ideally, a broad range of stakeholders should be involved to generate knowledge and a variety of

[428] Pinsky, Kruglianskas and Victor (n 397) 728. [429] De Búrca, Keohane and Sabel (n 283) 478.
[430] Goldstein and Ansell (n 384) 221, 230. [431] Cf. ibid., 237.
[432] Sabel and Zeitlin, 'Experimentalist Governance' (n 410) 174.
[433] De Búrca, Keohane and Sabel (n 283) 478; Goldstein and Ansell (n 384) 230; Sabel and Zeitlin, 'Experimentalist Governance' (n 410) 174.
[434] Sabel and Zeitlin, 'Experimentalist Governance' (n 410) 174.
[435] De Búrca, Keohane and Sabel (n 283) 478.
[436] Goldstein and Ansell (n 384) 235; De Búrca, Keohane and Sabel (n 283) 478.
[437] Goldstein and Ansell (n 384) 229; De Búrca, Keohane and Sabel (n 383) 740.
[438] Sabel and Zeitlin, 'Emerging Experimentalism in EU Environmental Governance' (n 400) 130.
[439] De Búrca, Keohane and Sabel (n 283) 484.

strategies to choose from.[440] It has been 'observed empirically that enrolling diverse sources of knowledge in this process may also produce better solutions'.[441] Thus, global experimentalist governance provides a model through which transnational problems involving multiple stakeholders – which may create significant governance challenges – can be managed.[442]

The long list of potential experimentalist actors includes states, municipalities, civil society representatives, academics, indigenous peoples, community-based organisations, national authorities, local communities, and scientists.[443] The composition of actors working together on the lower level will vary in each geographical area.[444] The inclusion of a variety of actors, such as civil society and local communities, may provide these different groups with a voice, build credibility, promote shared ownership, and encourage a shared future vision.[445] Such an open and transparent governance process involving diverse actors also increases accountability.[446] The reason decision-making in groups promotes accountability is twofold. First, members operate under the scrutiny of their peers, which leads to informal pressure to avoid errors or misuse of power. Second, since providing reasons is essential for group decision-making, and members come from various backgrounds, this ensures that matters taken for granted in homogenous groups are clarified and questioned in more heterogeneous settings.[447] The operation of this element is coordinated and organised by the central unit as it, for example, communicates the shared problem and open-ended goals to the lower levels.[448]

To sum up, global experimentalist governance as a form of governance encompasses participatory and multilevel cooperation, particularly involving lower levels of governance in solution-finding.[449] However, experimentation and the decision-making regarding strategies and practices are subject to feedback and peer review, which represents the fourth element of the ideal type.

4.2.4 Feedback and Peer Review

The fourth element of the ideal type of global experimentalist governance is feedback and peer review.

The literature identifies reporting, peer review, and feedback as core components of this element of the ideal type of global experimentalist governance. Nevertheless,

[440] De Búrca (n 386) 235.

[441] Goldstein and Ansell (n 384) 230; Burris Scott, Clifford Shearing and Michael Kempa, 'Changes in Governance: A Cross-Disciplinary Review of Current Scholarship' (2008) 41 *Akron Law Review* 1, 11.

[442] Goldstein and Ansell (n 384) 229.

[443] De Búrca, Keohane and Sabel (n 283) 477; Pinsky, Kruglianskas and Victor (n 397) 730; De Búrca, Keohane and Sabel (n 383) 741.

[444] Cf. Goldstein and Ansell (n 384) 238. [445] Ibid.

[446] De Búrca, Keohane and Sabel (n 283) 478, 484.

[447] Sabel and Zeitlin, 'Experimentalist Governance' (n 410) 173.

[448] Goldstein and Ansell (n 384) 230; De Búrca, Keohane and Sabel (n 383) 741.

[449] De Búrca, Keohane and Sabel (n 283) 477.

the presentation and order of these components vary from author to author.[450] For the purpose of this book, reporting will be regarded as the first step, peer review as the second step, and feedback as the last step.

First, reporting involves local units sharing information about their performance and, more specifically, their achievement of the framework goals.[451] The information is shared with other local-level actors.[452] However, the specific details to be included in the report depend on the nature of the shared problem, as well as the metrics and goals involved.

Second, following this reporting stage, the information provided by the local units becomes subject to peer review.[453] During peer review, the local units' performances and experiences are compared to one another.[454] In other words, local actors compare their results from experimentation and evaluate each other's progress towards achieving the goals. Consequently, information is pooled, and where possible, best practices may be identified, general lessons noted, and challenges acknowledged.[455] Therefore, the collection, tracking, and dissemination of data, as well as monitoring and evaluation, are fundamental to the process of information gathering and analysis.[456] In addition, collecting case studies for future exemplification and learning can be helpful.[457] Hence, case studies can be used to showcase the types of measures or steps previously taken by others that have been successful. Accordingly, the process allows for pooling information gathered at the lower level, comparing results, identifying best practices, and communicating those to the central unit for consideration.[458]

As a final step, feedback on the results is provided to lower-level units by both their peers and the central unit.[459] As part of this feedback, lower-level units that are not making sufficient progress towards the agreed-upon goals are expected to demonstrate that they are implementing appropriate adjustment measures in place.[460] The feedback and review process can be facilitated in several ways. For instance, initiatives can take the form of annual regional meetings, conferences, or an active secretariat.[461] Accordingly, the otherwise considerable discretion of the lower levels is kept in check by this feedback and peer-review process.[462]

In conclusion, through these three components, experimentalist actors can learn from one another's experiences, although it must be acknowledged that

[450] Goldstein and Ansell (n 384) 229–230; Armeni (n 283) 880; De Búrca, Keohane and Sabel (n 383) 756; De Búrca, Keohane and Sabel (n 283) 478.

[451] Goldstein and Ansell (n 384) 230; Armeni (n 283) 880. [452] Goldstein and Ansell (n 384) 230.

[453] De Búrca, Keohane and Sabel (n 383) 739; De Búrca, Keohane and Sabel (n 283) 478.

[454] Goldstein and Ansell (n 384) 230. [455] Ibid., 239–240; Armeni (n 283) 762, 880.

[456] Goldstein and Ansell (n 384) 239, 240. [457] Ibid., 239. [458] Ibid., 230, 238.

[459] Ibid., 230, 253; Armeni (n 283) 880; De Búrca, Keohane and Sabel (n 283) 478.

[460] Sabel and Zeitlin, 'Experimentalist Governance' (n 410) 170; Zeitlin (n 386) 2.

[461] Goldstein and Ansell (n 384) 239; Armeni (n 283) 762; An active secretariat plays '(...) a "focal point, hub and broker" role, including a key role as a "knowledge administrator for best practice information."' Goldstein and Ansell (n 384) 239.

[462] Sabel and Zeitlin, 'Experimentalist Governance' (n 410) 170; Sabel and Zeitlin, 'Learning from Difference: The New Architecture of Experimentalist Governance in the EU' (n 386) 3.

specific solutions may not always be generalisable.[463] Therefore, global experimentalist governance can be said to transform 'diversity from an obstacle into an asset'.[464] Hence, feedback and peer-review advance systematic learning from diversity while holding actors accountable for their work.[465] Thus, global experimentalist governance is moving away from the typical one-size-fits-all solution.[466] This form of governance is neither top-down nor bottom-up; rather, it is both, as corrections occur in both directions.[467] Following the feedback and peer-review process, the overarching goals can be adjusted, which is the fifth element of the ideal type.

4.2.5 Adjustment of Overarching Goals

The fifth element of the ideal type of global experimentalist governance is the adjustment of overarching goals. As the final step, feedback and peer review continuously inform the substance of the framework goals and/or the metrics used to measure progress towards their attainment. Consequently, goals and sometimes metrics are regularly adjusted.[468]

It is a process of learning by doing.[469] Feedback and peer review will uncover unforeseen details and reveal dead ends as well as new – sometimes generalisable – solutions. This knowledge may raise questions about the previously agreed-upon open-ended goals and metrics.[470] Therefore, an approach based on provisionality applies to goals, metrics, solutions, and even to the problem definition itself.[471] Thus, over time, these goals, metrics, solutions, and the problem definition should evolve in response to what has been learnt from feedback and peer review.[472] The process, in its entirety, can be considered a recursive learning process.[473] Similar to processes in 'mathematics or computer science, whereby the output from one application of a procedure or sequence of operations becomes the input for the next so that iteration of the same process produces changing results'.[474] Recursive learning is considered the most crucial characteristic of experimentalist governance.[475] This feature allows for flexibility and adaptability in order to accommodate changing

463 Sabel and Zeitlin, 'Experimentalist Governance' (n 410) 175.

464 Ibid.

465 De Búrca, Keohane and Sabel (n 283) 479; Pinsky, Kruglianskas and Victor (n 397) 728.

466 Zeitlin (n 386) 10–11.

467 Charles F. Sabel and David G. Victor, *Fixing the Climate: Strategies for an Uncertain World* (Princeton University Press 2022) 10.

468 De Búrca, Keohane and Sabel (n 283) 478.

469 Goldstein and Ansell (n 384) 223.

470 De Búrca, Keohane and Sabel (n 383) 741.

471 Grainne De Búrca and Joanne Scott, 'Introduction: New Governance, Law and Constitutionalism', *Law and New Governance in the EU and the US* (Hart Publishing 2006) 3 www.bloomsburycollections.com/book/law-and-new-governance-in-the-eu-and-the-us accessed 31 July 2022; Sabel and Zeitlin, 'Learning from Difference: The New Architecture of Experimentalist Governance in the EU' (n 386) 3.

472 Goldstein and Ansell (n 384) 227, 235.

473 Ibid., 220.

474 Sabel and Zeitlin, 'Experimentalist Governance' (n 410) 169.

475 Sabel and Zeitlin, 'Experimentalist Governance in the European Energy Sector' (n 397) 65.

circumstances.[476] This is especially needed in issue areas characterised by uncertainty and a complex character.[477]

In conclusion, global experimentalist governance is equipped to tackle problems that are typically complex, global in nature, newly arising, creeping, or persistent, and often have low visibility, at least for some time. These problems may also be poorly understood due to limited scientific information, resulting in high uncertainty. Consequently, the issues at hand often lack obvious solutions. Global experimentalist governance provides a recursive, multilevel learning circle facilitated by reporting, feedback, peer review, and provisionality to address these features. As highlighted throughout, these elements can materialise through various institutional arrangements. While a central unit is envisioned, experimentalist governance encompasses several lower-level units to maintain the ability to learn from one another.[478] The central unit primarily focuses on facilitating information pooling and organising peer evaluations.[479] That said, the central unit can realign reluctant actors through what has been termed a 'penalty default'. The nature and function of the penalty default will be discussed in the following section.

4.3 Penalty Default

Regimes of experimentalist governance sometimes function in 'the shadow of penalty default'.[480] The penalty default is a tool to steer unwilling or reluctant actors.[481] It is a way of penalising non-cooperation.[482] The idea is that control is taken away from actors by threatening to impose alternative rules. More specifically, the central unit threatens to revert to traditional forms of rulemaking that are beyond the actors' control.[483] Usually, the loss of control alarms actors and is, therefore, a less favourable option from an actor's perspective.[484] This threat should encourage actors to reconsider and remind them of the advantages of cooperation.[485] The possibility of bargaining instead of having an imposed, often draconian, one-size-fits-all solution is preferred, as actors can influence the outcome and potentially reach a more favourable resolution. The penalty default, therefore, creates an enticement for actors to cooperate to avoid potentially punitive default regulation.[486]

476 Armeni (n 283) 883.

477 Sabel and Zeitlin, 'Emerging Experimentalism in EU Environmental Governance' (n 400) 128; De Búrca, Keohane and Sabel (n 383) 740.

478 Goldstein and Ansell (n 384) 230, 231.

479 De Búrca, Keohane and Sabel (n 283) 478.

480 Ibid.

481 Zeitlin (n 386) 4; De Búrca, Keohane and Sabel (n 283) 784.

482 Goldstein and Ansell (n 384) 221; De Búrca, Keohane and Sabel (n 283) 478.

483 Sabel and Zeitlin, 'Learning from Difference: The New Architecture of Experimentalist Governance in the EU' (n 386) 5; Sabel and Zeitlin, 'Experimentalist Governance' (n 410) 176; Zeitlin (n 386) 4.

484 Sabel and Zeitlin, 'Learning from Difference: The New Architecture of Experimentalist Governance in the EU' (n 386) 5.

485 De Búrca, Keohane and Sabel (n 383) 739; De Búrca, Keohane and Sabel (n 283) 478.

486 Bradley C Karrkainen, 'Information-Forcing Regulation and Environmental Governance', *Law and New Governance in the EU and the US* (Hart Publishing 2006) 297 www.bloomsburycollections.com/book/

In simpler terms, it can be said that the penalty default leaves the actors with two options.[487] On one hand, actors can choose an outcome that is difficult to predict but may be prejudicial due to an imposed rule. On the other hand, they have the option of cooperation and mutual engagement. The latter alternative gives the actors greater control, allowing them to influence their fate and providing the parties a chance to achieve a workable solution.[488]

An example of a penalty default being used is the European Union Emissions Trading System (EU ETS) for aviation concerning third countries.[489] In its ETS, the EU initially included all airlines operating flights to, from, or within the EU.[490] However, this setup faced opposition from non-EU countries. To address this disapproval, the EU implemented a penalty default mechanism called 'Stop the Clock' for aviation emissions. This mechanism temporarily suspended the inclusion of international flights in the EU ETS for non-European Economic Area (EEA) countries, giving them a chance to cooperate and engage in developing a global solution through the International Civil Aviation Organization (ICAO).[491] By employing this penalty default, the EU incentivised non-EEA countries to negotiate and find a feasible solution, increasing their control and influence over the outcome.[492]

The question remains: Can global experimentalist governance address OA? Before determining whether global experimentalist governance is a suitable approach to tackling the problem of OA, one must examine what type of problem OA is. Accordingly, the following section will identify the characteristics of OA as a problem. Subsequently, the theory of experimentalist governance and the specific problem of OA can then be discussed together.

4.4 The Characteristics of Ocean Acidification

Chapters 1–3 have introduced and described OA as, on the one hand, a scientific problem (Chapter 2) and, on the other, from a governance perspective, as a regime complex (Chapter 3). Section 4.4 will outline how these two generate seven

law-and-new-governance-in-the-eu-and-the-us accessed 30 November 2022; see also Ian Ayres and Robert Gertner, 'Filling Gaps in Incomplete Contracts: An Economic Theory of Default Rules' (1989) 99 *The Yale Law Journal* 87.

487 Sabel and Zeitlin, 'Experimentalist Governance' (n 410) 177.

488 Ibid.

489 Armeni (n 283) 882; see also: J. Scott and L. Rajamani, 'EU Climate Change Unilateralism' (2012) 23 *European Journal of International Law* 469.

490 European Commission, 'Aviation and the EU ETS' (2023) https://climate.ec.europa.eu/eu-action/european-green-deal/delivering-european-green-deal/aviation-and-eu-ets_en accessed 16 July 2023.

491 EU Commission, 'Stopping the Clock of ETS and Aviation Emissions Following Last Week's International Civil Aviation Organisation (ICAO) Council' (*European Commission – European Commission*, 2023) https://ec.europa.eu/commission/presscorner/detail/fr/MEMO_12_854 accessed 16 July 2023.

492 The result of the negotiation was CORSIA, which is a global market-based measure designed to address carbon emissions from international civil aviation. ICAO, 'Carbon Offsetting and Reduction Scheme for International Aviation (CORSIA)' (2023) www.icao.int/environmental-protection/CORSIA/Pages/default.aspx accessed 16 July 2023.

different characteristics, based on the work in Chapters 2 and 3. Hence, this section will be divided into two parts. The first will summarise OA as a scientific problem and identify four characteristics (Section 4.4.1), while the second will recap OA as a regime complex and identify the last three characteristics (Section 4.4.2). Once these characteristics have been identified, a governance form (global experimentalist governance) can be matched to the problem (OA) (Section 4.5). Matching a governance form that can accommodate these characteristics – or even make a virtue of them – is crucial to successfully tackling OA.

4.4.1 Ocean Acidification, a Scientific Problem

The nature of OA as a problem – or more precisely, its causes, stressors, and consequences – can be scientifically explained. The science behind the problem has been thoroughly discussed in Chapter 2 of this book. To evaluate whether OA is a problem that can be addressed through experimentalist governance, some of the key takeaways and defining features detailed in Chapter 2 will be briefly recalled here.

First, OA exhibits the characteristics of a complex problem. A problem can be considered complex when 'the sources of persistent problems are diffuse (...), including important indirect contributors. In addition, cause and effect tend to be significantly delayed'.[493] Despite being a problem whose repercussions are primarily observed in the ocean, the causes and stressors also originate from the atmosphere and land. Therefore, like many environmental issues, there is an interaction between the Earth's spheres, and the problem does not play out in just one of them.[494] Furthermore, OA is not the only stressor the oceans are facing; multiple stressors are likely to intensify one another. The involvement of different environmental spheres and various stressors (indirect contributors) of OA renders it a diffuse problem. Moreover, Chapter 2 has demonstrated that OA is a gradual process, with consequences that only slowly become visible. There is a delay between cause and effect. It is thus evident that OA can be considered a complex problem.

Second, OA's causes and stressors can be traced back to global, regional, and local actions. Additionally, the effects of OA manifest at all these levels. Therefore, searching for solutions through mitigation and adaptation will require the engagement of actors at each level. However, beyond that, natural variation in pH exists between different levels (global/open ocean and local/in the vicinity of the coastline) and even within the same level. In addition to the variety between and within levels, it is clear that some areas are more vulnerable to the effects of OA than others, such as the Arctic/Antarctica or regions that experience upwelling. Hence, two points can be made here. First, to address OA, a multilevel approach is required. Second, a one-size-fits-all solution cannot be expected to work effectively, as generalisations can be problematic even within a specific local area.

[493] De Búrca, Keohane and Sabel (n 283) 479.

[494] See figure 1 for Earth spheres Qin and others (n 279) 257.

Third, techniques to address OA are still insufficiently researched, and behavioural changes that are currently deemed infeasible may be necessary. For instance, regarding mitigation, the step that would lead to the most significant reduction of the problem is an immediate, radical cut in carbon dioxide emissions. However, this is proving to be a daunting task and will not happen immediately. Research on OA mitigation and adaptation is underway, including studies on geoengineering and nature-based solutions to provide more time for the demanding emission-cutting process. Nonetheless, further research is needed before these alternatives can be implemented. It is expected that, due to its multifarious causes, stressors, consequences, and adaptation options, OA will be better understood over time. During this process, it is likely that some drivers can be controlled more quickly than others. For example, it may be less costly and more politically feasible to clean wastewater from agriculture or urbanisation than to achieve substantial cuts in GHG emissions. As explained in Chapter 2, it is up to individual states or regions to manage wastewater, which could otherwise lead to acidification near the coastline. In summary, this indicates that the governance framework must be flexible and easily adjustable to respond swiftly to future advancements in research.

In conclusion, after reminding readers about the different features of OA, four main elements can be identified which characterise OA as a problem:

- OA is a complex problem;
- Addressing OA requires a multilevel approach;
- No one-size-fits-all solution can be expected to work for OA;
- OA governance needs to be adjustable and flexible.

After this summary of OA as a scientific problem, which identified four characteristics, a recap of OA as a regime complex will be provided below to identify the last three characteristics.

4.4.2 Ocean Acidification, a Regime Complex

The governance landscape for OA can be described as a regime complex, as outlined in Chapter 3. Regime complexes have specific characteristics that can be identified. This series of additional features becomes apparent when examining the map created in Chapter 3. Section 4.5 will reiterate these regime complex characteristics to align them with global experimentalist governance.

From the map and list of actors, one can discern that many actors are, and could potentially be, involved in OA governance. These actors have different compositions. They are variously public, private, or mixed. The number of actors is expected to grow in the future, as more institutions are anticipated to engage with OA issues and incorporate this theme into their work. This trend is particularly evident among private and mixed transnational actors, as other transnational regime complexes have developed similarly. Abbott, for example, as presented in Chapter 3, identified sixty-eight mixed and private transnational actors in relation to the transnational regime complex for climate change. Thus, two points can be made here: there is a large number of actors involved, and these actors are diverse rather than homogenous.

There seems to be a growing engagement and agreement among actors that OA is a problem that will endanger oceanic ecosystems and ecosystem services. Institutions increasingly address and voice concerns about the problem. However, due to the varying interests and uncertainties surrounding OA, which are typical for a regime complex and have been identified when discussing the three forces (interests, uncertainty, linkages) in Chapter 3, it is unlikely that actors will engage in integrated governance solutions. Despite recognising OA as a problem, actors will likely struggle to agree on a joint approach because of the different interests and many uncertainties that OA as a problem encompasses. Hence, it is unlikely that there will be any agreed-upon, detailed goals or pathways towards their attainment *ex ante*.

In conclusion, after reviewing different features in relation to the governance landscape of the problem, three main points can be made about OA as a problem:

- A large number of actors are involved;
- Various types of actors are involved;
- No agreement on how to address the problem concerned can be expected *ex ante*.

With these points in mind, one can now return to the question of whether global experimentalist governance may be a useful framework for addressing OA. To determine if the theory of experimentalist governance aligns with the challenge of OA, it is necessary to evaluate whether the identified characteristics of this issue, both as a scientific problem and as a regime complex, can be accommodated by global experimentalist governance. In other words, is there a 'good match' between OA and its existing governance framework and global experimentalist governance? This potential match between OA and global experimentalist governance will be discussed in Section 4.5.

4.5 Matching Ocean Acidification and Global Experimentalist Governance

A total of seven elements have been identified to accurately characterise OA as a problem. These seven points will be examined one by one in the following paragraphs, starting with those related to OA as a scientific problem (Section 4.5.1), followed by those concerning OA as a regime complex (Section 4.5.2). For each point, it will be discussed whether global experimentalist governance is a suitable governance approach, bearing in mind the specific characteristic. To provide visual assistance and clarify the overall argument, the match between the characteristics and global experimentalist governance will be presented in two corresponding Tables 4.1 and 4.2.

4.5.1 Matching the Scientific Problem and Global Experimentalist Governance

Section 4.5.1.1 outlines four distinct characteristics of OA as a scientific problem. These characteristics are presented in Table 4.1. The left side of the table lists the characteristics of OA as a scientific problem, while the right side details various aspects of global experimentalist governance. These aspects, identified earlier in this chapter as the five elements of the ideal type of global experimentalist governance, provide information on the types of problems this governance approach can address and how it intends to do so. This distinction is also illustrated in Table 4.1 using black and white bullet points. Black bullet points indicate the types of problems that global experimentalist governance can tackle, while white bullet points show how this governance type plans to address them. In other words, the table aligns the characteristics with the corresponding aspects of global experimentalist governance to assess if this governance type is suitable for the problem of OA. Following the table, each of the four characteristics of global experimentalist governance will be explored.

Table 4.1 OA science and global experimentalist governance.

OA – scientific problem	Global experimentalist governance
Complex problem	• Newly arising • Creeping or persistent • Low visibility • Complex
Multilevel approach	• Global dimension o Goals set through discourse of stakeholders from various levels o (Multilevel) Experimentation, comparison, feedback, and peer review
No one-size-fits-all solution/Diversity	o Delegation to lower levels of governance o Experimentation, comparison, feedback, and peer review
Adjustable and flexible governance/ uncertainty	• Limited scientific information/uncertainty • No known solution – *ex ante* o Provisionality of goals, metrics, solutions, and problem definition o Experimentation, comparison, feedback, and peer review

Source: Compiled by the author.

• The kind of problems global experimentalist governance addresses.

o How global experimentalist governance can accommodate the features of these problems.

4.5.1.1 Complex Problem

OA is a newly arising and complex problem. Its complexity arises from the fact that it is diffuse, involving different Earth spheres and various stressors. Its causes and effects are delayed, as it is by nature creeping, with repercussions that become slowly visible. Global experimentalist governance has been conceived to address this exact type of issue. As noted above, the problems the theory intends to address are typically newly arising, complex, and creeping, just like OA. Additionally, as is typical for creeping problems, OA has garnered limited public attention as it silently emerges. This low visibility is characteristic of the type of problem that experimentalist governance approaches. Global experimentalist governance may therefore potentially address OA as a complex problem.

4.5.1.2 Multilevel Approach

On one hand, OA is a problem with a global dimension that needs international coordination to be addressed, as a large part of OA is caused by globally emitted CO_2. On the other hand, the causes, stressors, and repercussions of OA can be traced back and observed at the global, regional, and local levels. Additionally, there are natural pH differences at various levels, such as the global level/open ocean and the local level/near the coastline. It is therefore sensible that mitigation and adaptation must be undertaken at all these levels. Thus, OA is a problem best addressed through a multilevel governance approach. As explained in Section 4.2.1, global experimentalist governance addresses problems with a global dimension.

As noted, global experimental governance requires a multilevel approach to address complex and interconnected global problems. First, the theory requires that goals and metrics be set through collaboration among stakeholders of various kinds. These stakeholders also come from different levels of governance. Second, besides goal and metric setting, the recursive learning cycle involving experimentation, comparison, feedback, and peer review is also multilevel. Experimentation occurs locally; results are compared, analysed, and communicated to higher levels for further review. Hence, in essence, global experimentalist governance is conceived as a multilevel process, and a multilevel approach is a necessary part of global experimentalist governance.

4.5.1.3 No One-Size-Fits-All Solution/Diversity

Along with the multilevel approach, it is important to remember that OA, particularly pH, can vary even within a specific geographical locality. For example, two areas near the coastline (local level/regional level) may not share the same average pH and its fluctuations. This diversity is why a one-size-fits-all solution may not be suitable, and generalisation can be problematic. Global experimentalist governance accommodates this diversity and lack of generalisability by delegating the responsibility of finding solutions to issues to actors functioning at a lower level of governance. These localised actors have the discretion and opportunity to test solutions that respond to local circumstances. Similarly, experimentation, comparison, feedback, and peer review ensure that different strategies and solutions can be compared and critically analysed. Ultimately, this may lead to a catalogue of best practices. This catalogue assists stakeholders in selecting practices that are likely to be effective under specific circumstances, such as geographical ones. Therefore, global experimentalist governance can tackle problems that cannot be addressed with a one-size-fits-all solution.

4.5.1.4 Adjustable and Flexible Governance/Uncertainty

OA is a relatively new environmental problem that has not been comprehensively researched. Additionally, mitigation and adaptation responses will often be challenging to implement, as they require extensive and varied behavioural changes. Mechanisms to address some drivers of OA will become available faster than others. For instance, it is less costly and politically more feasible to tackle drivers such as wastewater from agriculture or urbanisation rather than CO_2 emissions. Over time, scientific information will become available to better explain the causes, stressors, consequences, and adaptation options.

At the same time, technology will advance and create new ways to tackle OA. For this reason, OA governance needs to be flexible and easily adjustable. Global experimentalist governance typically addresses problems with limited scientific information and a high level of uncertainty, such as OA. Due to this lack of information, the problems that the theory addresses also lack straightforward solutions *ex ante*. To accommodate this uncertainty, the theory requires provisional goals, metrics, solutions, and problem definitions. Provisionality allows for adjustments once new and additional scientific knowledge or technologies are discovered. Experimentation, comparison, feedback, and peer review facilitate the testing and evaluation of discovered knowledge and technology. This approach allows for real time learning by doing and customisation to new developments. Therefore, global experimentalist governance is designed to tackle problems characterised by inherent uncertainty.

Regarding the key points concerning OA as a scientific problem, it can be said that global experimentalist governance is well adapted to accommodate them. This again makes OA and global experimentalist governance a 'good match'. The points relating to OA as a regime complex will be discussed next. More specifically, Section 4.5.2 will show what has already been indicated in Chapter 3 and reiterated above, namely, that global experimentalists can match the characteristics of OA as a regime complex.

4.5.2 Matching the Regime Complex for Ocean Acidification and Global Experimentalist Governance

Section 4.4.2 outlines three distinct characteristics of OA as a regime complex. All three characteristics are typically found in regime complexes, as described in Chapter 3. These characteristics are presented in Table 4.2. Like Table 4.1, the right side lists various types of aspects of global experimentalist governance, while the left side details the characteristics of the landscape for OA, the regime complex. Again, the black

Table 4.2 OA regime complex and global experimentalist governance.

OA – regime complex	Global experimentalist governance
Large number of actors	o Goals set through discourse of stakeholders from various levels o Finding solutions delegated to lower levels
Various types of actors	o Goals set through discourse of stakeholders from various levels o Finding solutions delegated to lower levels
No agreement *ex ante*	• No known solution – *ex ante*

Source: Compiled by the author.

• The kind of problems that global experimentalist governance addresses.

o How global experimentalist governance can accommodate the features of these problems.

bullet points indicate the types of problems that global experimentalist governance can address, while the white bullet points show how this governance type intends to manage them. Therefore, this section will explore whether global experimentalist governance can accommodate and build upon the characteristics of the regime complex for OA, the current governmental landscape. To achieve this, each of the three characteristics concerning global experimentalist governance will be detailed.

4.5.2.1 Large Number of Actors

The map in Chapter 3 indicates that many actors are already involved in OA governance. As OA sits at the nexus of different issue areas related to the ocean, land, and atmosphere, actors working within these areas show interest in OA. Furthermore, the number of actors is expected to grow as more institutions become interested in OA and incorporate this issue into their work, similar to other regime complexes like the one for climate change. Part of global experimentalist governance involves setting provisional goals and metrics as a result of collaboration among various stakeholders at different levels across issue areas. The actual experimentation of strategies based on these goals and metrics is then delegated to lower levels of governance. The theory facilitates and organises solution-finding, including many actors from various governance levels. Therefore, global experimentalist governance should be able to effectively contend with the large number of actors potentially involved in OA governance and can even make a virtue of this situation.

4.5.2.2 Various Types of Actors

Aside from the presence of many actors, various types of actors are and could be involved in the governance of OA. In particular, these actors are imbued with different compositions. They can be public, private, or mixed. In any case, these actors are not homogeneous. As mentioned earlier, regarding the large number of actors, different stakeholders from various levels are involved in setting goals and metrics. Additionally, the actors at the lower levels responsible for experimentation can be different types of stakeholders. Therefore, global experimentalist governance not only enables but also demands the inclusion of various actors.

4.5.2.3 No Agreements Ex Ante

Regime complexes address issues like OA for which no agreement can be found *ex ante*. This likely disagreement can be traced to differing interests and uncertainties surrounding OA, which are typical of a regime complex. Despite increased engagement with the issue and a growing number of stakeholders expressing their concerns about OA, they will likely struggle to reach a consensus on a unified strategy to tackle OA due to these uncertainties and varied interests. Therefore, it is improbable that there will be goals agreed upon *ex ante*. As noted, global experimentalist governance is a theory that can tackle complex problems characterised by significant uncertainty. These types of issues often lack a readily identifiable solution. Consequently, the theory is well suited to address problems for which a solution cannot be anticipated *ex ante*, as is the case for OA.

After discussing the seven characterising points, it can be determined that global experimentalist governance has the potential to address OA, both because of its characteristics as a scientific problem and considering the current existence of a regime complex. Indeed, OA is typically a problem addressed by global experimentalist governance. Therefore, taking into account the theory of global experimentalist governance and the nature of the OA problem, it can be expected that OA could be effectively tackled in this manner. The following chapters will investigate whether this type of governance is present in the governance landscape of OA. This chapter has shown that global experimentalist governance is guided and organised by a central unit. Accordingly, if global experimentalist governance were present in the OA governance landscape, a coordinating central unit would be established. Hence, two case studies will examine whether two potential central units of global experimentalist governance concerning OA fulfil the elements of the ideal type and thus implement this governance type in practice.

Before moving on to the selection of the two case studies, one final theoretical analysis must be conducted. For global experimentalist governance to emerge and thrive, several conditions should ideally be present. Section 4.6 will therefore identify whether the necessary background conditions for a thriving global experimentalist governance setup are in place for OA.

4.6 Background Conditions

The academic literature on experimentalist governance identifies several conditions that make this governance form more likely to emerge and thrive.[495] Two groups of

[495] Armeni (n 283) 880–882; De Búrca, Keohane and Sabel (n 383) 781–783; De Búrca, Keohane and Sabel (n 283) 483, 484; Goldstein and Ansell (n 384) 230; Sabel and Zeitlin, 'Learning from Difference: The

conditions can be frequently found in the literature. The first comprises two conditions: strategic uncertainty (and technical complexity) and a multipolar or polyarchic power distribution.[496] The second is a set of four conditions: no agreement on rules by governments, governments are not stymied by disagreement, inclusion of non-state actors, and no lack of cooperation between key actors.[497] Both sets of background conditions will be examined in more detail below. First, the set of two will be discussed, including their presence in the case of OA (Section 4.6.1), and afterwards, the same will be done for the set of four (Section 4.6.2). This approach helps to complete the analysis of the extent to which there is a 'match' between experimentalist governance and the problem of OA.

4.6.1 The Set of Two Conditions

The first set of conditions that are believed to increase the likelihood of global experimentalist governance emerging are strategic uncertainty and a multipolar or polyarchic distribution of power. Both of these conditions will be explained below.

First, the literature describes strategic uncertainty in various ways. Goldstein and Ansell define it as a situation 'where there is a need to address a complex problem that is not amendable to resolution through hierarchy or the market'.[498] By contrast, Sabel and Zeitlin note that: '[u]nder strategic uncertainty actors by definition have to learn what their goals should be, and while learning determine how to achieve them. This learning necessarily involves cooperation, since any actor able to fix a strategy independently would do so, and not be in a state of strategic uncertainty'.[499]

Eberlein refers to an example from a specific sector and claims that 'Evidence from the electricity sector suggests that experimentalist techniques were most important at the very beginning of the process of market creation, in a technically complex and new policy domain, when strategic uncertainty (...) were at the highest level'.[500]

Despite these quotes being slightly different, they seem to share a commonality: strategic uncertainty arises when a problem lacks a known or clearly defined solution. This scenario often applies to problems that are complex or technical in nature. Consequently, uncertainty exists regarding which strategy to apply in order to address the problem. Thus, strategic uncertainty indicates that actors confront

New Architecture of Experimentalist Governance in the EU' (n 386) 9; Sabel and Zeitlin, 'Experimentalist Governance in the European Energy Sector' (n 397) 61, 72.

[496] Sabel and Zeitlin, 'Learning from Difference: The New Architecture of Experimentalist Governance in the EU' (n 386) 9; Sabel and Zeitlin, 'Experimentalist Governance in the European Energy Sector' (n 397) 61, 72.

[497] Armeni (n 283) 880–882; De Búrca, Keohane and Sabel (n 383) 781–783.

[498] Goldstein and Ansell (n 384) 230.

[499] Sabel and Zeitlin, 'Learning from Difference: The New Architecture of Experimentalist Governance in the EU' (n 386) 9.

[500] Sabel and Zeitlin, 'Experimentalist Governance in the European Energy Sector' (n 397) 72.

a complex issue. In grappling with such a problem, actors must determine which goals they should pursue and comprehend how to achieve them. Therefore, uncertainty surrounds both the goals themselves and the means to accomplish them.[501] It can be concluded that while 'normal' uncertainty can be managed by adhering to established protocols, strategic uncertainty frequently necessitates innovative approaches due to the complexity of the problem and interactions with other issues. Hence, the distinction between 'normal' and strategic uncertainty lies in the complexity of the problem, which necessitates cooperation, as no individual actor can tackle the issue independently.[502]

The question of the presence of strategic uncertainty is straightforward in the case of OA. This chapter has already noted that OA is a complex problem due to its diffuse character, the involvement of many actors in causing, exacerbating, or responding to the issue, and the delay between cause and effect. Due to the problem's novelty (at least for audiences outside the natural sciences community) and its complexity, finding strategies to tackle OA *ex ante* is difficult. Consequently, as the problem advances, actors must learn and test which tools are effective in achieving a decline in acidification or in responding to its effects. What is helpful is often far from obvious. Therefore, actors must collaborate and try different strategies to address the issue. As new scientific knowledge and technologies are discovered and strategies are tested, actors will hopefully be better equipped to confront OA. Additionally, despite variations across and within different governmental levels, OA is a global problem with causes and stressors that stem from many sources (similar to climate change). As assumed within strategic uncertainty, the problem cannot be tackled by only one actor. The many actors involved (presently or potentially) were depicted in the map in Chapter 3. In conclusion, OA is a problem characterised by strategic uncertainty.

Second, the definitions of multipolar or polyarchic power distribution are more similar to each other than those describing strategic uncertainty. For example, Sabel and Zeitlin explain, 'multipolar or polyarchic distribution of power implies that no single actor has the capacity to impose her own preferred solution without taking into account the views of the others'.[503] Eberlein, as well as Goldstein and Ansell, have similar definitions. All of them underline that the term refers to a situation where no single actor is empowered to make decisions.[504] In the same vein, Goldstein and Ansell further explain that 'our world has grown less State-centered and more polyarchic, with multiple agencies, entities, and sites of governance in any

[501] Sabel and Zeitlin, 'Learning from Difference: The New Architecture of Experimentalist Governance in the EU' (n 386) 9.

[502] Ibid; Sabel and Zeitlin, 'Experimentalist Governance in the European Energy Sector' (n 397) 61, 72; Goldstein and Ansell (n 384) 230.

[503] Sabel and Zeitlin, 'Learning from Difference: The New Architecture of Experimentalist Governance in the EU' (n 386) 9.

[504] Goldstein and Ansell (n 384) 230, 252; Sabel and Zeitlin, 'Experimentalist Governance in the European Energy Sector' (n 397) 65.

given policy space'.[505] 'This polyarchy has in turn required a shift from traditional regulatory tools (… and) instead employ flexible and revisable standards'.[506] Thus, polyarchy can lead to a demand for new governmental approaches.

The presence of multipolar or polyarchic power distribution is evident in the case of OA. The governance landscape for OA exhibits the characteristics of a regime complex, involving a multitude of different actors. Since OA is a global issue, albeit with variations across various levels – from the global/open ocean to local/coastal areas – it is unlikely that one actor alone can solve it; cooperation, as discussed earlier in this chapter, is essential. Hence, the second background condition of the set of two conditions is also present.

Regarding the two conditions mentioned in the literature, it can be concluded that both are present in the case of OA. According to the literature, these two conditions increase the likelihood of global experimentalist governance emerging and thriving. This likelihood reinforces the view that the current regime complex for OA could potentially evolve towards global experimentalist governance.

4.6.2 The Set of Four Conditions

In addition, the literature mentions four conditions that make global experimentalist governance more likely to appear and thrive. These will be discussed below.

According to Armeni, as well as De Búrca, Keohane and Sabel,[507] the first of these conditions is that governments cannot agree on or formulate a comprehensive set of rules. Additionally, even if rules were formulated, governments would be unable to monitor compliance with them effectively. This scenario, involving a lack of rules and effective monitoring, often occurs in situations where actors cannot predict how rules affect the local level and especially where those rules are subject to changes that, for example, follow technological or scientific advancements.[508]

Regarding the first precondition, OA is a problem that is insufficiently researched and characterised by geographical diversity in its manifestations. For this reason, it is challenging for governments to formulate rules, let alone monitor compliance with them. In fact, as of 2025, no rules specifically regulating OA can be found in international law. The map depicting the governmental landscape for OA shows that an increasing number of actors are becoming aware of the problem. However, the task of identifying solutions to this issue is still in its infancy. Likewise, the responsibility for adopting measures among the different actors involved is only just beginning to emerge. Given the problem's high level of scientific uncertainty, even if rules were to emerge, they would necessarily need to be flexible to accommodate changes. Hence, this first precondition relating to the absence of a comprehensive set of rules is present.

[505] Goldstein and Ansell (n 384) 228.
[506] Ibid.
[507] Armeni (n 283) 880; De Búrca, Keohane and Sabel (n 383) 781.
[508] Armeni (n 283) 880.

The second condition acts as the counterpart to the first. Despite their inability to agree on rules, governments must not be stymied by dissent over basic principles. Consequently, there should be a 'thin consensus'.[509]

Determining the presence of the second condition is more challenging. Due to the novelty of the problem, actors' positions have only recently begun to develop on the international plane. However, as is typical for a regime complex, and as discussed in Chapter 3, the various actors included in the map have diverging interests. Nonetheless, it is evident that actors are becoming more aware of OA and are gradually engaging in identifying solutions to this problem. As a basic principle, these solutions primarily address CO_2 as a driver of OA. It is clear that a significant and growing number of actors are currently involved. Indeed, all the actors in the bottom half of the map presented in Chapter 3 are already, albeit to varying degrees, addressing or mentioning OA. Thus, there is at least a thin consensus on the need to address OA and in particular CO_2 as the primary driver of OA.[510] A similar consensus has developed over time regarding climate change, a related and equally life-altering issue. In any case, the reactions and actions of institutions will be examined in more detail in the following chapters, especially during the institutional case studies (Chapters 5–7). Therefore, the second condition can be considered fulfilled.

The third background condition partially resembles what has been discussed under the third element of the ideal type of global experimentalist governance. However, as mentioned, in particular, by Armeni and De Búrca, et al.[511] it may also be usefully highlighted here. This background condition underlines how experimentalist regimes need to include non-state actors in agenda-setting and problem-solving. Otherwise, both problem-solving and agenda-setting are more likely to be unsuccessful. The inclusion of those actors is especially needed in problem areas characterised by extended uncertainty or diversity. Local actors will be able to identify and approach issues that are likely ignored or left unaddressed by central state actors. Furthermore, the involvement of different actors provides legitimacy.[512] De Búrca underlines the importance of this condition (along with monitoring) as she calls them 'crucial features of an experimentalist-governance system'.[513]

Concerning the third condition, the map has shown that various types of actors, including public, private, and mixed entities, are involved in the governance of OA. The subsequent chapters will demonstrate that these multifarious actors are also engaged in agenda-setting and problem-solving. The current governance landscape suggests that this condition can be considered fulfilled. However, as further explained in subsequent chapters, a broader range of actors will be necessary, particularly local ones who understand the specific contextual circumstances and local conditions.

[509] Armeni calls this a 'thin consenus' (ibid., 881).

[510] Cf. for example, these actors have underlined the importance of OA as a problem: IUCN, 'Climate Change and the Ocean' (n 351); OA Alliance, 'About' (n 351); IAEA, OA-ICC (n 351).

[511] Armeni (n 283) 882; De Búrca, Keohane and Sabel (n 383) 782.

[512] Armeni (n 283) 882.

[513] As part of her normative proposal, De Búrca argues that participation and monitoring are crucial to experimentalist governance. De Búrca (n 386) 235.

Fourth and last, experimentalist governance will struggle when there is a lack of cooperation among key actors due to their reluctance or unwillingness to collaborate. Thus, this background condition emphasises the importance of cooperation between actors. For example, a lack of cooperation can arise when veto powers impede consensus, allowing hidden agendas or strategies to thrive. The aforementioned penalty default can serve as a tool to encourage cooperation in this context. The hope is that actors will engage in experimentalist governance and information-sharing to avoid unfavourable rules.[514] In their paper 'New Modes of Pluralist Global Governance', De Búrca et al. add as an alternative fourth condition that the problem should not be one of 'high politics'. By 'high politics', the authors mean 'situations where government are in direct control of relevant decisions'.[515] An example would be control over nuclear weapons.[516]

OA governance is just beginning to evolve, making it difficult to predict how future dynamics will play out. That being said, similar to climate change, OA as an environmental problem might complicate cooperation between diverse actors with various interests and significant uncertainty. This challenge arises especially due to the difficulty in distributing responsibility for mitigation measures among actors, for instance, because of the varying contributions of actors to the problem of OA. However, these diverse interests at stake, such as political and economic ones, can render the penalty default a powerful device to keep reluctant actors in line.[517] Therefore, even in cases where actors behave out of line, cooperation is unlikely to be entirely hindered. In fact, some cooperation, for example, between actors at different levels (global and regional), can already be observed.[518] In addition, as pointed out by De Búrca et al., OA is also not a matter of high politics comparable to, for instance, nuclear weapons. Thus, considering the already observed cooperation and the fact that OA does not involve high politics, the fourth condition is also present.

Section 4.6.1 shows that the two different sets of background conditions can be considered present. According to the literature, it is likely that global experimentalist governance will develop for OA. Whether this is the case will be explored in the institutional case studies.

4.7 Global Experimentalist Governance and Ocean Acidification – a Good Match

Based on the scientific background (Chapter 2) of the problem and the identified regime complex for OA (Chapter 3), this chapter identifies a governance approach

[514] Armeni (n 283) 880–882; De Búrca, Keohane and Sabel (n 383) 781–783; De Búrca, Keohane and Sabel (n 283) 483, 484.

[515] De Búrca, Keohane and Sabel (n 383) 783.
[516] Ibid.

[517] Similar results were found by Armeni with regard to global climate governance. Armeni (n 283) 882.

[518] See, for example, OSPAR Commission (n 379).

that aligns well with OA, as both features can be accommodated by global experimentalist governance. Seven elements have been defined to describe OA as a problem. These points outline the characteristics of OA both as a scientific issue and as a regime complex. Global experimentalist governance emerges as a suitable mode of governance for OA. More specifically, experimentalist governance addresses the nature of OA as a complex and poorly understood problem. Additionally, global experimentalist governance can tackle this type of issue through its structure, including delegation, peer review, and the like. For example, global experimentalist governance can respond to the necessity of a multilevel approach by engaging actors or stakeholders from various governmental tiers. Thus, the chapter proposes that global experimentalist governance could leverage the regime complex for OA and its characteristics without dismantling it. In fact, global experimentalist governance could capitalise on the existing landscape for OA.

The theoretical background provided in this chapter regarding experimentalist governance demonstrates that the existence of this governance form can be tested against the five steps of the ideal type. Nevertheless, to evaluate these five elements, one or more actors must be selected. Thus, as indicated, after identifying a possible governance solution, namely global experimentalist governance, this serves as a step towards determining which of the many actors are particularly relevant for the governance of OA. If global experimentalist governance is present within one of the actors, the actor pooling information and organising revisions can be considered the centre. Therefore, the question is: Which of all the actors identified during the mapping exercise should be tested? The answer to this question will be developed in Chapter 5.

CHAPTER 5

Actors and Instruments Tackling Ocean Acidification

Chapter 4 has demonstrated that global experimentalist governance aligns well with OA. In fact, global experimentalist governance can build on the existing regime complex for OA without dismantling it and can even make a virtue of OA's currently fragmented governance landscape. However, even if global experimentalist governance is a good match for OA, the question remains regarding the extent to which this governance form already exists in addressing the problem of OA. To begin answering this question, this chapter will select two case studies, namely, the OA Alliance and the IMO, to evaluate against the five elements of the ideal type of global experimentalist governance outlined in Chapters 6 and 7. As discussed in Chapter 4, these five elements serve as reference points for assessing whether and to what extent global experimentalist governance is present within an institution. The shortcomings, from an experimentalist perspective, will also be identified. It is hoped that the two case studies conducted in this book will provide insights not only for the institutions under examination, the OA Alliance and IMO, but also for other institutions regarding the usefulness and challenges of applying global experimentalist governance to OA.

All institutions included on the map presented in Chapter 3 could serve as case studies, as they address aspects of OA (see Chapter 3, Annex B). The institutions in the bottom half of the map already consider OA to some extent. Therefore, to explain why this book focuses on the OA Alliance and the IMO as case studies, this chapter will first distinguish between institutions that, in accordance with the science behind OA, are merely suitable to address OA and those with significant potential to tackle the problem (Section 5.1). Second, a table based on the map will be presented (Chapter 3) of institutions that could be suitable as case studies (Section 5.2). Third, to arrive at the case selection, different institutions from the table that have significant potential to tackle the problem regarding causes, stressors, and adaptation will be discussed (Section 5.3). Finally, a justification for why the OA Alliance and the IMO have been selected from all the institutions present in the map will be offered (Section 5.4).

5.1 Suitable Institutions and Institutions with Significant Potential

As shown in the map in Chapter 3, a wide range of institutions operate in various issue areas, such as biodiversity protection, transboundary air pollution, and climate change. Therefore, these institutions address different aspects of the causes, stressors, and/or adaptation to OA within the scope of their work. In particular, the institutions in the lower half of the map have started to consider OA as an issue relevant to their work. Hence, many institutions presented on the map could serve as case studies concerning the presence of global experimentalist governance in tackling OA.

The first step in choosing a case study is to distinguish between institutions that are merely suitable for addressing this problem and those that possess significant potential to do so. The science presented in Chapter 2 shows that OA has diverse causes, stressors, and adaptation options. Various human activities contribute to this problem, while others can induce mitigation or adaptation to OA. For instance, both coastal activities and emissions lead to an increase in CO_2 and, thus, OA. Therefore, to tackle OA effectively, an institution should ideally be equipped to address the causes, stressors, and adaptation options. These causes, stressors, and adaptation options will also be referred to as 'concerns' in this chapter.

Based on the science (Chapter 2), three concerns have been identified that manifest if an institution can tackle OA through its mandate and objectives; the mandate/objective then helps in understanding whether an institution is suitable or has significant potential to deal with OA. In this regard, potential means that the institution can, according to its mandate or objectives, address OA (and its causes, stressors, and adaptation options), but there is so far no evidence that it is doing so. Accordingly, the two key premises for distinguishing institutions as merely being suitable to address OA as opposed to having significant potential to do so are as follows:

- An institution can be considered **suitable** for tackling OA when it can, according to its objective(s) or mandate, address only one single activity relevant to one OA concern.
- An institution can be considered to have **significant potential** to tackle OA if it can address:
  - One concern in depth (for example, different activities within one concern) and/or
  - Several concerns simultaneously, thus achieving breadth (for example, stressors and adaptation).

These key premises are visualised in Tables 5.1 and 5.2. Table 5.1 demonstrates how an institution is suitable to tackle OA when it can address any single activity relevant to the causes or stressors of OA or pursue adaptation to its effects. Furthermore, Table 5.1 indicates that an institution has significant potential to address the problem when it can address the concerns (causes, stressors, or adaptation options) in depth and/or in breadth. Table 5.2 illustrates both depth (represented as the light grey box) and width (represented as the dark greybox).

An institution addresses concerns broadly when it tackles more than one (at least two) of them. For instance, if an institution simultaneously tackles an activity leading to one of the causes (such as land-based pollution contributing to CO_2 input from coastal activities) and an activity generating additional stress (such as overfishing), it addresses OA broadly. Therefore, if an institution is empowered by its mandate or objective(s) to address at least two of the concerns (causes, stressors, or adaptation options), it can be classified as dealing with the concerns broadly and thus can be considered to have significant potential to tackle OA.

An institution addresses concerns in depth when it tackles multiple activities, but only within a single concern. For instance, if an institution addresses several activities contributing to issues such as land-based pollution and CCS, which both potentially lead to CO_2 entering ocean water, it engages with a concern deeply. Therefore, if an institution is empowered by its mandate or objectives to address various activities within one concern (causes, stressors, or adaptation options), it can be classified as engaging with those concerns comprehensively and thus also as having significant potential to tackle OA. Consequently, by examining an institution's mandate and/or objectives, it can be determined whether it is merely suitable or possesses significant potential to address OA.

Institutions with significant potential may be intriguing candidates for further study, as they are better prepared to address OA. Therefore, if an actor's has substantial potential to tackle OA, already existing or possibly developing experimentalist governance may be expected to be particularly potent in addressing the issue.

With this distinction in mind, the next step is to present suitable institutions from the map in Chapter 3 in a table that explains whether they are empowered to address causes, stressors, and/or adaptation options. Once this overview is

Table 5.1 Institution's ability to deal with OA.

	Suitable	Significant potential
Mandate/Objective	One single activity	Breadth
		Depth

Source: Compiled by the author.

Table 5.2 Significant potential – visualisation of width and depth.

Concerns		Activities	
Causes	CO_2	Anthropogenic CO_2 emissions	Electricity Transportation Industry
		Geoengineering and CCS	Direct injections Nutrient fertilisation CCS
		Coastal activities	Suboptimal coastal planning Land-based pollution Land-use change Land-use Deforestation
	NO_x and SO_x	Anthropogenic emissions	Energy transformation Energy consumption Industry processes Shipping
		Scrubber	Scrubbing
Stressors		Anthropogenic emissions	Electricity Geoengineering, coastal activities, shipping Industry
		Geoengineering, coastal activities, shipping	Fishing Pollution
		Fishing	Dangerous and disruptive fishing Overfishing
Adaptation		Blue carbon	
		Management of fishing activities	
		Marine protected areas	

Source: Compiled by the author.

clear, Section 5.3 will detail different institutions with significant potential regarding causes, stressors, and adaptation will be detailed in order to select two of them as case studies.

5.2 Suitable Actors and Instruments in One Table

The objective of Section 5.2 of this chapter is to identify actors and instruments that are suitable for addressing OA. The tool chosen to provide an overview of these units is a table, which will be presented and explained in the following sections. This overview facilitates the discussion of some of the institutions and actors with significant potential in Section 5.3, allowing for the justification of the selection of the OA Alliance and the IMO as case studies for in-depth consideration in subsequent Chapters 6 and 7.

Table 5.3 presented here is based on the map and list of actors and instruments created during the mapping exercise conducted in Chapter 3. It shows whether an actor and instrument can address causes, stressors, and adaptation options related to OA. As explained above, this depends on the unit's mandate and/or objectives. While actors have mandates and objectives, instruments possess only objectives. However, both mandates and objectives will be further explained below. The layout of the table illustrates which actors and instruments are suitable. Since all of the institutions can address at least one activity within causes, stressors, or adaptation options related to OA, they can all be considered suitable for tackling OA.

Table 5.3 will be explained in detail in the sections below. After that, first the three concerns causes, stressors, and adaptation (Section 5.2.1) will be examined. Second, the selection and arrangement of the actors and instruments will be clarified (Section 5.2.2) before explaining how the two terms 'objective(s)' and 'mandate' and the meaning of markings (X, R) used in the table can be understood (Section 5.2.3.)

5.2.1 The Concerns

The top horizontal row of the table is divided into two columns: institutions and concerns. Then below, I further divide the row relating to institutions into actors and instruments, while the category of concerns is divided into causes, stressors, and adaptation. These three concerns have been selected based on the information provided in Chapter 2, which explains the scientific background of OA. An institution receives a mark in one of the columns (causes, stressors, adaptation) if the mandate or objective of the individual institution addresses at least one activity within that concern. It should be noted that while Table 5.2 indicates the specific activities under each concern, Table 5.3 simply shows the concern to ensure legibility. In the following paragraphs, it will be clarified which activities a mandate or objective must include to receive a mark.

5.2.1.1 Causes

In accordance with the scientific background provided in Chapter 2, the causes considered in the table are CO_2 and NO_x/SO_x. An actor or instrument receives a mark in the causes column if it has the potential to prevent or reduce activities that

Table 5.3 Actors and instruments suitable for tackling OA (as of December 2023).

Institutions			Concerns			
			Causes			
Actors		Instruments	NO_x/SO_x	CO_2	Stressors	Adaptation
			Global			
GOA-ON				R		R
IAEA				R	R	R
ICAO			X	X	X	
IMO			X	X	X	
		LC+LP	(X)	X	X	
		MARPOL 73/78	X	X	X	
		LOTSR	X	X	X	X
IUCN				X	X	X
		RAMSAR				X
OA Alliance				X	X	X
Oceana (International)				X	X	X
RFMOs					X	(X)
UNEP			X	X	X	X
		GPA		X	X	
		CMS			X	(X)
		CBD				X
	IPBES		R	R	R	R
	IPCC			R	R	R
		CCR		X	X	(X)
		Manado		X	X	X
UNESCO				X	X	X
		World Heritage Convention	X	X	X	X
UNGA			X	X	X	X
		CLRTAP	X	(X)	(X)	
WWF				X	X	X
			Regional			
SCAR				R	R	R
CEP			X	X	X	X
		Antarctic Treaty	X	X	X	X
CCAMLR				X	X	X
		CAMLR			X	X
Arctic Council			X	X	X	X
ICC			X	X	X	X
OSPAR Commission			X	X	X	X
		OSPAR	X	X	X	X

Source: Compiled by the author.

Note: X – unit's mandate/objective addresses the concern; R – unit's mandate/objective is limited to research regarding concern.

either produce such compounds or carry any of these materials into the ocean (see Figures 2.1 and 2.2 and Table 2.1). The activities considered relevant in this context differ for the various chemical materials.

Concerning CO_2, the activities that need to be prevented or reduced – and would therefore qualify for a mark in the table under CO_2 if addressed by an actor and/or instrument – are those generating CO_2 emissions, geoengineering, and relevant coastal activities. Among these three activities, CO_2 emissions play the most crucial role for OA. These emissions are produced and have effects on a global level. Relevant coastal activities significantly affect local and regional levels (i.e., near the coastline). However, geoengineering plays a minor role at this stage when assessed in terms of its contribution to the total amount of CO_2 entering the water.

Activities that should be prevented or at least reduced concerning NO_x/SO_x include those that generate emissions and utilise exhaust gas cleaning systems (also known as scrubbers) on ships. Shipping is a significant source of NO_x and SO_x emissions, which contribute to OA. Therefore, ships are encouraged to adopt scrubbing practices to lower NO_x and SO_x emissions during operation. If an actor or instrument addresses any of the activities mentioned, it receives a mark in the causes or, more specifically, in the NO_x/SO_x column of the table.

5.2.1.2 Stressors

In addition to the causes, the table also includes a column for stressors. Institutions receive a mark in the stressors column if they have the potential to prevent or reduce one or several of the activities that lead to ocean stress. Increased stress can exacerbate the effects of OA on the oceanic ecosystem. The first activity causing stress is the release of anthropogenic GHG emissions, as these contribute to climate change, which, in turn, leads to sea-level rise and ocean warming, among other impacts. These consequences of climate change generate additional ocean stress. The second group of activities that can worsen stress involves the release of nutrients into the water, including geoengineering, certain coastal activities, and shipping. The latter two activities can also result in other forms of pollution entering the water, while shipping additionally threatens the oceans through harmful materials found in scrubber effluents, oil spills, dumping, ballast water, and similar issues. The final activities that qualify for a mark in the stressor's column are fishing and harmful or disruptive fishing practices.

5.2.1.3 Adaptation

The final category of concern included in the table is adaptation. Adaptation refers to activities that help the ocean adjust to acidification. Three activities have proven beneficial in this regard: the protection, restoration, or planting of blue carbon-storing plants; the creation of marine protected areas; and the readjustment of fishing practices. If an actor's or institution's mandate involves one or more of these activities, it receives a mark in the adaptation column of the table.

The meaning of the three concerns – namely, causes, stressors, and adaptation – as shown in the top horizontal rows on the right side of the table has been defined. The following paragraphs outline institutions (specifically actors and instruments) as found in the top horizontal rows on the left side of Table 5.3.

5.2.2 The Selection and Arrangement of Actors and Instruments

The units collected in the two columns headed actors and instruments are based on the list created during the mapping exercise in Chapter 3. Due to the large number of actors and instruments, not all featured in the original list (Tables 3.1 and 3.2) have been included in Table 5.3 to provide a clear and understandable overview. Hence, the list has been narrowed down to twenty actors and fourteen of the previously highlighted instruments. The following section will explain which units have been chosen over others and why. It will also explain how some actors and instruments are linked and therefore presented side by side in the table.

Underneath the first light grey horizontal rows, the next dark grey row is divided into global and regional categories. Global and regional refer to the actors and instruments operating at a global versus regional level, based on the map created in Chapter 3.

Many global actors and instruments from the original list are included in this table. The ones not chosen have either failed to engage with OA in their work or are not well suited to addressing this problem because, based on their mandates or objectives, they would not receive a mark related to any of the three concerns columns. Examples that fall into either group are the Ozone Layer Regime and CITES. For instance, even though the Ozone Layer Regime, including the Montreal Protocol, controls substances depleting the ozone layer as part of the atmosphere, none of these controlled substances are CO_2, NO_x, or SO_x.[519] Therefore, despite addressing an atmospheric pollution problem, the Ozone Layer Regime does not receive a mark in any of the concern columns of the table. In addition, OA has not been mentioned in the work of the Ozone Layer Regime. Aside from these institutions, the IAP is not included in the table since dealing with acidification does not form part of its permanent mandate but rather constitutes a temporary research interest for this institution. Furthermore, the World Bank is omitted since it has, as a bank, a different strategy for approaching OA. The World Bank undertakes investments, and its influence on climate and ocean issues appears through the conditions the bank prescribes for a country to receive funds.[520]

In contrast, the other actors included in the table, among other things, advance research or propose new regulations independent of monetary incentives for

[519] Montreal Protocol on Substances that Deplete the Ozone Layer (with annex) 1987 (UNTS vol 1522) Annex A.

[520] The World Bank, 'What We Do' (*World Bank*, 2022) www.worldbank.org/en/what-we-do accessed 10 January 2022; The World Bank, 'Environmental and Social Policies' (*World Bank*, 2022) www.worldbank.org/en/projects-operations/environmental-and-social-policies accessed 10 January 2022.

countries, as discussed below. Due to the World Bank's different functioning, it will not be included in the table. Similarly, the World Ocean Council is also excluded from the table. The World Ocean Council is a 'global, cross-sectoral ocean industry leadership alliance committed to "Corporate Ocean Responsibility."'[521] Due to this solely industrial focus, it does not lend itself well compared to the other actors with a much broader focus on problem-solving in the land-ocean-atmosphere nexus.

Moreover, the majority of regional or local actors and instruments have been excluded from the table. To limit the total number of units, only a few regional examples have been selected. As outlined in Chapter 2, not all regions of the world are currently equally affected by acidification, nor will the effects be distributed evenly across regions in the future. The Arctic and Antarctica have been found to be more vulnerable and are particularly sensitive to environmental changes, such as OA. Thus, the effects of acidification have been, and will likely continue to be, observed in these two areas first. The Arctic and Antarctica can be considered significant regions for OA; therefore, the actors and instruments that focus on these territories have been included in the table.

As can be seen, the columns for actors and instruments are side by side and organised in relation to each other. Instruments are placed next to the actor they are linked to. When an organisation is positioned next to an instrument, this means that the organisation developed the instrument, administers it, relies on or refers to it, or provides facilities for the instrument. For instance, the IMO administers the LC+LP, developed MARPOL 73/78, and is referred to by UNCLOS. On some occasions, organisations are also related to each other. UNEP used to provide the secretariat for IPBES, and it still employs all staff at the IPBES secretariat, for example.[522]

As a next step, it is essential to explain how the mandates and objectives of the chosen institutions have been ascertained. Based on the respective mandates and objectives, the type of mark that an actor receives in the columns labelled causes, stressors, and adaptation is determined.

5.2.3 Understanding Mandates/Objectives and Markings in the Table

As previously mentioned, while actors have mandates and objectives, instruments only have objectives. Accordingly, actors and instruments are chosen and receive markings in one of the three concern columns of the table if they are suited, according to their mandate/objectives, to deal with causes, stressors, or adaptation to OA. More precisely, they are suited if they can at least address a single activity

[521] World Ocean Council, 'About Us' (*World Ocean Council*, 2023) www.oceancouncil.org/about-us/ accessed 16 March 2023.

[522] IPBES, 'History of the Establishment of IPBES' (*IPBES Secretariat*, 17 January 2020) https://ipbes.net/history-establishment accessed 14 January 2022.

within causes, stressors, or adaptation options to OA, as outlined above. The paragraphs below illustrate how the mandates and objectives of the different actors and instruments were identified, including the difficulties encountered during this process. The text below will also explain the markings in the columns derived from these mandates and objectives. Actors will be focused on first before turning to instruments.

Regarding actors, mandates (including objectives) are found in the founding documents of actors.[523] Though often included there, objectives are also elaborated, for example, on an actor's website.[524] However, not all actors have accessible founding documents. This is particularly true for private or mixed public–private actors, as they do not necessarily maintain an accessible statute, founding treaty, or founding resolution. This issue can sometimes render the task of identifying and defining the mandate and objectives of actors challenging. Thus, if a founding document, statute, or resolution is unavailable, the goals stated on the institution's website become the sole source for understanding the actor's mission. Additionally, even when a foundational document is accessible, the actor's previously established targets may not align with some of its current activities. This is the case for the IAEA, for example. The IAEA was created to oversee and ensure that atomic energy is used solely for peaceful and non-military purposes.[525] However, the agency currently engages in work, specifically research-related tasks on OA, which is not explicitly stated in the statute.[526] Hence, for the purpose of this table and to define the mandates and objectives of the actors, information has been gathered from sections of each institution's website (often labelled as 'What we do' or 'About us', and so on) and their founding treaty, statute, or resolution if available. Based on the information on the web pages and documents, the problems that an individual organisation aims to address were identified.

Identifying the objectives of the instruments in the table is more straightforward than determining those of the actors. The instruments themselves are used to reveal their primary objectives, which are often found in the preamble or one of the first articles.

Concerning the mandates and objectives, it must be emphasised that they are subject to change in the future. In particular, the mandates of actors can quickly evolve, especially in cases where a mandate is not defined by a founding treaty or has moved away from the goals originally set, as in the case of the IAEA. Adding to 'What we do' or 'Our Goals' can be accomplished rapidly. For instance, during this research, initially, many actors did not focus on adaptation options at all. However, in recent years, mitigation and adaptation using blue carbon ecosystems

523 See, for example, Convention on the International Maritime Organization Art 1(a).

524 See, for example, IMO, 'Strategic Plan for the Organization' (n 304).

525 IAEA, 'History' (8 June 2016) www.iaea.org/about/overview/history accessed 11 January 2022; Statute of the International Atomic Energy Agency 1956 (UNTS 276 (p3)) article II.

526 IAEA, OA-ICC (n 351).

(see Chapter 2) have gained momentum and been incorporated into the focus of many of the actors listed in the table. In contrast to the rapidly evolving mandates and objectives of actors, the objectives of instruments tend to change at a slower pace. To update the objective(s) of, for example, a legal instrument, amendments (such as the introduction of a new annex) would likely be necessary, which presents a larger hurdle. The table was last amended in winter 2023/2024. For further updates on the latest OA-related actions on the international stage, see Annex B (May 2024).

As mentioned above, the actors and instruments receive marks in the table if they address an activity within one of the concerns of OA, namely causes, stressors, and adaptation, within their mandates and objectives. A mark can either be just an X or the letter R. The X indicates that the unit is addressing the area of concern in various ways, including through proposals for new regulations, while the R signifies that the unit's overall mandate is limited to research, coordination of research, information gathering, mainstreaming of information, and similar activities. In cases where either letter is in brackets, it shows that, although it fits the unit's mandate well, the unit is not actually dealing with this area of concern. For example, as of today, RFMOs have not addressed adaptation to OA yet, such as through climate-friendly fisheries management.[527] However, since this type of adaptation would fall precisely within the ambit of their work, the RFMOs received an X in brackets in the table under adaptation.

As can be seen, all actors and instruments included in the table have at least one mark, indicating that they can each address at least one activity related to OA and may therefore be considered suitable for addressing the problem of OA. In fact, most actors and instruments have multiple marks across or within different concerns, giving them significant potential to tackle OA. Consequently, Section 5.3 will discuss several institutions with multiple marks and significant potential to address OA in relation to causes, stressors, and adaptation. This discussion will highlight previously explained elements, such as the reasons institutions received a mark, how actors and instruments are interconnected, and, most importantly, their significant potential. For a compact overview of the activities related to OA on the international stage, see also annex B.

5.3 Actors and Instruments with Significant Potential to Deal with Ocean Acidification

Most of the actors and instruments included in the table have multiple marks across concerns or within a single concern and, therefore, significant potential to tackle OA as they can address the concerns in breadth and/or depth. Although the table displays thirty-four different institutions, and not all of them can be examined in

[527] Cf. Scott, 'Ocean Acidification' (n 29) 404; however, some of them have considered OA as part of their scientific research. See Rayfuse (n 365).

detail, this section will discuss various ways institutions with several marks and significant potential can address OA's causes, stressors, and adaptation options. This discussion of what institutions could do (through their mandate/objectives) to address the concerns can, for example, illustrate why institutions received marks and how they can thus tackle the concerns in depth and/or breadth, thereby giving them significant potential to address OA.

Accordingly, the three concerns (causes, stressors, and adaptation options) will guide the discussion. First, institutions that can address the causes of OA will be discussed (Section 5.3.1). Second, institutions that can tackle the problem's stressors will be examined (Section 5.3.2) before finally looking at the institutions that potentially address adaptation to the problem (Section 5.3.3).

Thus, several institutions included in the table will be examined throughout this section. Due to space constraints, only five different types of institutions (IMO, IUCN, OA Alliance, UNEP, UNESCO) and their related instruments will be addressed. Excluding institutions that operate at the regional level, as well as those with only one X or that solely focus on research, nine organisations remain (ICAO, IMO, IUCN, OA Alliance, Oceana, UNEP, UNESCO, UNGA, WWF).

Among these nine, three UN-affiliated institutions and two non-profit organisations will be examined in more detail. Choosing UN-affiliated and non-profit institutions enables an analysis of differently composed and structured actors. Exploring global experimentalist governance within various types of institutions may reveal issues stemming from these differing attributes.

In addition, instead of analysing the broadly focused UNGA, the IMO, as one of the institutions operating in the transport sector, will be discussed (instead of ICAO), as well as UNEP and UNESCO. The UNGA's mandate and objectives are extensive, and OA would likely represent a comparably small part of its wide-ranging activities. Among the two institutions in the transport sector, the IMO was selected because it can address both NO_x and SO_x emissions from air pollution and scrubbing, unlike ICAO (see Chapter 2).

Moreover, the OA Alliance and the IUCN were selected over Oceana and WWF. The OA Alliance is the only institution explicitly focused on OA and will thus be discussed. The IUCN was selected due to its extensive network of various members, including governmental members, NGOs, and indigenous peoples. In contrast to this diverse network, Oceana and WWF primarily depend on individual memberships.[528] A network comprising multiple types of actors is more likely to exhibit global experimentalist governance features (see Chapter 4). Nevertheless, it is important to remember that the table presents more institutions

[528] IUCN, 'Indigenous Peoples | IUCN' (2024) www.iucn.org/our-work/topic/indigenous-peoples accessed 20 February 2024; IUCN, 'Government Partners | IUCN' (2024) www.iucn.org/about-iucn/partners-and-donors/government-partners accessed 20 February 2024; WWF, 'Funding and Financial Overview | WWF' (*World Wildlife Fund*, 2024) www.worldwildlife.org/about/financials accessed 20 February 2024; Oceana, 'Financials' (*Oceana*, 2024) https://oceana.org/financials/ accessed 20 February 2024.

with significant potential than those being discussed. For a more comprehensive overview of institutions not mentioned here, see annex B. The significance of the units not selected for further discussion should not be underestimated. To evaluate and conclude on significant potential, Section 5.3.1 will, for simplicity, discuss actors alongside their associated instruments.

5.3.1 Actors and Instruments Dealing with the Causes of Ocean Acidification

The two groups of compounds considered causes of OA in the table are CO_2 and NO_x/SO_x. To be regarded as having significant potential to address the causes of OA, institutions must be empowered to prevent or reduce at least two activities that produce or transport these materials into the ocean. If institutions can address two activities related to the causes, they are viewed as tackling the causes in depth and possessing significant potential. Conversely, if an institution only addresses one activity within the causes, it lacks significant potential unless it also tackles another concern (discussed below), thus addressing the issues broadly (focusing on breadth rather than depth). Therefore, to demonstrate that an actor and its associated instruments address the causes in depth, it must engage with a minimum of two different activities that produce and transport those materials. Some actors and instruments that achieve depth this way, and will therefore be introduced below, include the IMO, the OA Alliance, and UNEP along with their associated instruments. First, the actors and instruments that can address NO_x/SO_x will be presented (Section 5.3.1.1) before examining CO_2 (Section 5.3.1.2). Finally, the discussion of causes will be concluded (Section 5.3.1.3).

5.3.1.1 Organisations and Instruments Addressing NO_x/SO_x

Activities that lead to the introduction of NO_x/SO_x into ocean water must be prevented or reduced by actors through recourse to their associated instruments. First, emissions – particularly those from shipping, which are a significant source of NO_x/SO_x contributing to OA – require action. Second, beyond emissions, stakeholders and instruments should also address scrubbing, which directly releases NO_x/SO_x into ocean water. While UNEP and the IMO, along with their associated instruments, include both CO_2 and NO_x/SO_x in their mandates and objectives, the OA Alliance focuses solely on CO_2 and will only be discussed later in the CO_2 section. This lack of engagement with NO_x/SO_x by the OA Alliance is also reflected in the table. Therefore, the following paragraphs will elaborate on which activities leading to the introduction of NO_x/SO_x and CO_2 into ocean water these institutions address.

5.3.1.1.1 Actors and Instruments Dealing with Emissions of NO_x/SO_x When looking at the table, it is evident that a comparatively limited number of actors and instruments address NO_x/SO_x. However, as noted, the IMO, as an actor, is targeting shipping emissions. The IMO is a specialised agency of the United Nations (UN).

This agency is responsible for the safety and security of shipping and for the prevention of pollution by ships. The IMO has 175 member states.[529]

One of the purposes of the IMO, as defined by article 1(a) of the Convention on the International Maritime Organization, is 'to encourage and facilitate the general adoption of the highest practicable standards in matters concerning (…) *prevention and control of marine pollution from ships* [emphasis added]'.[530]

Even though the prevention and control of pollution from ships, as mentioned in this article, was not included in the original text, it has grown in importance for the organisation. Accordingly, this goal was added with the 1977 amendment to the IMO Convention as environmental concerns, particularly pollution, became an obvious issue after the Torrey Canyon disaster.[531] In addition to the text of the convention, the environment and pollution are included in the IMO's mission statement as published on its website, which explains that: 'the mission (…) is to promote safe, secure, *environmentally sound*, efficient and sustainable shipping through cooperation. This will be accomplished by adopting the highest practicable standards of (…) *prevention and control of pollution from ships* [emphasis added]'.[532]

To achieve the purposes of the convention, including the prevention and control of pollution, the IMO should, pursuant to Part II, article 2(b) of the IMO Convention: 'provide for the drafting of conventions, agreements, or other suitable instruments, and to recommend these to Governments and to intergovernmental organisations, and to convene such conferences as may be necessary'.[533]

From both the IMO Convention and the mission statement, it can be inferred that the environment (in general) and marine pollution from ships (in particular) have emerged as important issue areas for the organisation. Furthermore, the IMO's mandate provides the organisation with the tools to strive for improvements regarding these issues by offering the capacity to recommend legal instruments such as conventions or agreements. For these reasons, the IMO received an X in the NO_x/SO_x column of the table.

Correspondingly, one of the organisation's most important achievements – not just regarding pollution from ships in general, but more specifically with respect to air pollution from ships – is MARPOL 73/78.[534] According to the IMO's own

[529] IMO, 'International Maritime Organization' (2019) www.imo.org/ accessed 17 March 2023.

[530] IMO, 'Convention on the International Maritime Organization' (n 304); Amendments to the Convention on the International Maritime Organization Relating to the Institutionalization of the Committee on Technical Co-operation in the Convention; Convention on the International Maritime Organization.

[531] IMO, 'Convention on the International Maritime Organization' (n 304); IMO, 'Brief History of IMO' (2019) www.imo.org/en/About/HistoryOfIMO/Pages/Default.aspx accessed 14 January 2022; Amendments to the Convention on the International Maritime Organization relating to the institutionalization of the Committee on Technical Co-operation in the Convention.

[532] IMO, 'Strategic Plan for the Organization' (n 304).

[533] IMO, 'Convention on the International Maritime Organization' (n 304); Amendments to the Convention on the International Maritime Organization Relating to the Institutionalization of the Committee on Technical Co-operation in the Convention; Convention on the International Maritime Organization.

[534] International Convention for the Prevention of Pollution from Ships, 1973, as modified by the Protocol of 1978 (MARPOL 73/78); IMO, 'Brief History of IMO' (n 531).

website, this is one of the organisation's key legal instruments.[535] MARPOL 73/78 targets ocean pollution from ships, including accidental and routine pollution. The convention, which combines the 1973 Convention and the Protocol of 1978, entered into force on 2 November 1983. Another protocol amending the instrument was adopted in 1997, and annex VI was added, entering into force on 19 May 2005. Over the years, the convention has been updated further with amendments.[536]

This instrument aims to 'prevent pollution of the marine environment by the discharge of harmful substances', as established as the general obligation in article 1. In this regard, harmful substance refers, pursuant to the definitions in article 2(2) MARPOL 73/78, to a substance that 'if introduced into the sea, is liable to create hazards to human health, to harm living recourses and marine life', and discharge includes 'any release howsoever caused from a ship', according to article 2(3)(a). As discussed in Chapter 1, air pollution through NO_x/SO_x emissions harms living resources and marine life and is released from ships into the air. Therefore, these emissions must be prevented according to MARPOL 73/78. In fact, the instrument dedicates an entire annex (annex VI) to the prevention of air pollution from ships. Annex VI, first adopted in 1997, limits NO_x/SO_x, which are among other air pollutants, the principal contaminants in ships' exhaust gas.[537] Hence, MARPOL 73/78 is suitable for addressing one of the causes of OA and thus received an X in the table under the NO_x/SO_x column.

The other instrument more loosely connected to the IMO that received an X in the NO_x/SO_x column is the Law of the Seas Regime (LOTSR). Regarding the reduction of NO_x/SO_x emissions, UNCLOS is the most suitable instrument of the LOTSR to address this cause of OA. UNCLOS was adopted in 1982 and contains regulations concerning the law and governance of the oceans. Its regulations cover all uses of the seas, including the exploitation of natural resources. Furthermore, UNCLOS is phrased in an open way that permits further development in this area of law.[538] As mentioned and seen in the table, UNCLOS is connected to the IMO.

Nevertheless, this connection is loose, as the IMO, rather than having developed the instrument, is only referred to by it.[539] The IMO is explicitly mentioned in article 2 of annex VIII of UNCLOS but referred to as 'the competent international organization' in several articles.[540] In particular, the IMO is mentioned concerning the adoption of shipping rules addressing, among other things, the prevention and

[535] IMO, 'Brief History of IMO' (n 531).

[536] International Convention for the Prevention of Pollution from Ships, 1973, as modified by the Protocol of 1978 (MARPOL 73/78).

[537] IMO, 'Prevention of Air Pollution from Ships' (2019) www.imo.org/en/OurWork/Environment/Pages/Air-Pollution.aspx accessed 15 January 2022.

[538] IMO, 'United Nations Convention on the Law of the Sea' (2019) www.imo.org/en/ourwork/legal/pages/unitednationsconventiononthelawofthesea.aspx accessed 17 March 2023.

[539] IMO, 'The United Nations Convention on the Law of the Sea (UNCLOS) and the International Maritime Organization' (2019) www.imo.org/en/MediaCentre/SecretaryGeneral/Pages/itlos.aspx accessed 17 January 2022.

[540] Ibid; *United Nations Convention on the Law of the Sea (UNCLOS) 1982 arts. 211(1), 216(1), 217(4) etc.*

control of pollution from vessels.[541] In addition, the IMO references UNCLOS on their website on several occasions.[542] For example, UNCLOS is mentioned under 'our work' in the 'legal affairs' section.[543] Hence, even though UNCLOS is not an IMO instrument, it is the competent organisation for preventing and controlling pollution from vessels.[544] As described above, vessel pollution is relevant for OA as it cannot just introduce compounds that lead to OA into the water but also create ocean stress. Therefore, for the sake of simplicity and the purpose of this chapter, the actor IMO and the instrument UNCLOS (LOTSR) will be considered together.

Rules regarding the prevention and control of pollution of the marine environment can be found in Part XIII of UNCLOS. Article 192 UNCLOS establishes that '[s]tates have the obligation to protect and preserve the marine environment'. Articles 194 and 212 set rules for pollution through the atmosphere, while article 211 includes rules for pollution from vessels. Essentially, pursuant to all mentioned articles, states shall create measures, regulations, laws, rules, or standards necessary to 'prevent, reduce and control pollution of the marine environment from any source',[545] including from or through the atmosphere.[546] As seen in these articles, UNCLOS provides that states are obliged to control and prevent pollution and shall create rules accordingly. Thus, the convention received an X in the NO_x/SO_x column of the table. However, from the articles, it also becomes evident that states need to create further instruments to achieve the goals set by UNCLOS. Nevertheless, the convention calls for states to address emissions causing OA and provides the basis for them to do so.

In conclusion, the IMO, utilising its associated instruments, has the capability to create tools addressing pollution from vessels, including the emission of NO_x/SO_x, unlike most other actors or instruments. In fact, as discussed above, this area of work is one of the organisation's primary concerns. The instruments related to it either prevent air pollution from vessels directly, as in the case of MARPOL 73/78, or mandate further actions to address pollution from vessels, as is the case with UNCLOS. Thus, the IMO and its associated instruments can tackle an activity that causes OA (i.e., NO_x/SO_x emissions), particularly the emissions of these chemical materials from shipping.

UNEP highlights emissions of NO_x/SO_x on its website under '[w]hat we do' in relation to two focuses of its work: air and transport. First, when looking through the 'Air' section of the website, it can be seen that UNEP is, for example, working

[541] IMO, 'Convention on the International Maritime Organization' (n 304) preprint 211(1); IMO, 'The United Nations Convention on the Law of the Sea (UNCLOS) and the International Maritime Organization' (n 539).

[542] IMO, 'The United Nations Convention on the Law of the Sea (UNCLOS) and the International Maritime Organization' (n 539); IMO, 'United Nations Convention on the Law of the Sea' (n 538).

[543] Ibid.

[544] For further discussion on the relationship between UNCLOS and IMO, see also Harrould-Kolieb and Stephens (n 52) 276.

[545] United Nations Convention on the Law of the Sea (UNCLOS) preprint 194(1).

[546] Ibid arts. 194(3)(a), 212.

on air pollution. Accordingly, as suggested by the UN Environment Assembly, UNEP regularly undertakes assessments of member states' progress regarding improving air quality. Hence, UNEP produced and updated the 2016 Actions on Air Quality report, creating a picture of national efforts towards better air quality. The update will also be accompanied by, for instance, country-specific case studies.[547] The Actions on Air Quality report considers NO_X and SO_X to be part of the air pollution problem.[548] In addition, under 'transport' and more specifically, under 'global clean ports', UNEP addresses pollution from ports as a source of air pollution, especially for coastal areas. On the website, emissions from NO_X and SO_X are specifically mentioned.[549] These examples show that UNEP is working on the reduction of the emissions of NO_X and SO_X. For this reason, UNEP received an X in the column for these compounds.

5.3.1.1.2 Actors and Instruments Dealing with Scrubbing Scrubbing is a technique that can remove certain harmful materials, such as SO_X, from the exhaust gases of ships. Following this procedure, the materials are disposed of as acid wash in the ocean. The functioning of this technique has been thoroughly explained in Chapter 2.[550] Despite the technique's adverse effects on the ocean, none of the actors discussed under causes – namely, the IMO and its instruments, the OA Alliance, UNEP, and related instruments – include scrubbing as a problem area in setting out their objectives. As scrubbing is not recognised as a problem by these actors in their objectives, this technology, including open-loop scrubbers, the type of scrubber most relevant for OA, can still be used. The only limitation (as will be seen below) is guidelines, albeit weak ones, promulgated by the IMO.[551]

In fact, scrubbing, as a technique, was developed to secure compliance with stricter standards for noxious materials in exhaust gases from ships. Notably, under the auspices of the IMO, a new limit on the sulphur content of fuel oil came into force in 2020, which is considered a milestone for improving air quality.[552] However, despite scrubbing potentially being a harmful technique in the context

[547] UNEP, 'Actions on Air Quality Report Update' (*UNEP – UN Environment Programme*, 25 March 2020) www.unep.org/explore-topics/air/what-we-do/taking-stock-global-efforts/actions-air-quality-report-update accessed 18 March 2023.

[548] Environment, 'Actions on Air Quality' (*UNEP – UN Environment Programme*, 2 July 2017) www.unep.org/resources/assessment/actions-air-quality accessed 18 March 2023.

[549] Environment, 'Why Does Global Clean Ports Matter?' (*UNEP – UN Environment Programme*, 26 July 2017) www.unep.org/explore-topics/transport/what-we-do/global-clean-ports/why-does-global-clean-ports-matter accessed 18 March 2023.

[550] Cf. Turner and others (n 121); Endres and others (n 168); Dulière, Baetens and Lacroix (n 170) For a full discussion on scrubbers compare above: B.I.3.b.bb.

[551] MEPC, 'MEPC.170(57) – Guidelines for Exhaust Gas Cleaning Systems' (n 297); MEPC, 'MEPC.184(59) – 2009 Guidelines for Exhaust Gas Cleaning Systems' (n 297); MEPC, 'MEPC.130(53) – Guidelines for On-Board Exhaust Gas-SOx Cleaning Systems' (n 297); MEPC, 'MEPC.259(68) – 2015 Guidelines for Exhaust Gas Cleaning Systems' (n 297); MEPC, 'MEPC.340(77) – 2021 Guidelines for Exhaust Gas Cleaning Systems' (n 297).

[552] IMO, 'IMO 2020 – Cutting Sulphur Oxide Emissions' (2019) www.imo.org/en/MediaCentre/HotTopics/Pages/Sulphur-2020.aspx accessed 17 January 2022.

of OA, this issue has not been addressed, and scrubbing is encouraged by the IMO and its instruments. The reason for this is that scrubbing is viewed as a tool to manage high levels of sulphur in exhaust gases and meet the required limits.[553] Thus, despite the IMO and its related instruments addressing marine pollution, and the LC/LP, in particular, focusing on geoengineering, CCS, and dumping in general, as will be seen below, there are no specific global rules targeting scrubbing. Accordingly, the LC/LP received an X in brackets in the table, as it is an instrument addressing other forms of dumping, meaning that while it does not cover scrubbing as an issue, it could.

The only limitation on scrubbers can be found in guidelines formulated by the IMO that address certain parameters such as pH in scrubber discharge water.[554] However, the voluntary nature of these guidelines, coupled with the initial absence of numerical criteria in 2005 and the modest enhancements made by 2008, suggests a lack of stringent oversight.[555] The 2008 amendments propose 6.5 as a minimum outlet pH level and limit the pH variance between inlet and outlet to 2 pH units while the ship is at berth, in a port, harbour, or estuary.[556] The logarithmic nature of the pH scale means that even seemingly minor deviations can result in substantial increases in acidity (see Chapter 2); for instance, a discharge pH of 6.5 is significantly more acidic than the average seawater pH of 8.1, exacerbating the risk to marine ecosystems from acidification. Even though numerical criteria have been introduced, these criteria are so weak that they cannot actually prevent acidification and therefore make no difference from an OA perspective. In addition, these numerical criteria were not updated during revisions in the years after.[557] The exponential increase in ships equipped with scrubbers, from three in 2008 to over 4,300 by 2020, underscores the pressing need for more robust regulations.[558]

Nevertheless, some states have exercised their rights under UNCLOS to implement measures within their ports and coastlines to limit the release of wash water

[553] Ibid; IMO, 'Equivalents (S_{Ox} Scrubber, Etc.) – Regulation 4' (2019) www.imo.org/en/OurWork/Environment/Pages/Equivalents-(Sox-scrubber,-etc.)---Regulation-4.aspx accessed 17 January 2022.

[554] MEPC, 'MEPC.170(57) – Guidelines for Exhaust Gas Cleaning Systems' (n 297); MEPC, 'MEPC.130(53) – Guidelines for On-Board Exhaust Gas-SOx Cleaning Systems' (n 297); MEPC, 'MEPC.184(59) – 2009 Guidelines for Exhaust Gas Cleaning Systems' (n 297); MEPC, 'MEPC.259(68) – 2015 Guidelines for Exhaust Gas Cleaning Systems' (n 297); MEPC, 'MEPC.340(77) – 2021 Guidelines for Exhaust Gas Cleaning Systems' (n 297).

[555] MEPC, 'MEPC.170(57) – Guidelines for Exhaust Gas Cleaning Systems' (n 297); MEPC, 'MEPC.130(53) – Guidelines for On-Board Exhaust Gas-SOx Cleaning Systems' (n 297); Bryan Comer, Elise Georgeff and Liudmila Osipova, 'Air Emissions and Water Pollution Discharges from Ships with Scrubbers' (International Council on Clean Transportation (ICCT) 2020) 7, 8, 9 https://theicct.org/wp-content/uploads/2021/06/Air-water-pollution-scrubbers-dec2020.pdf.

[556] MEPC, 'MEPC.170(57) – Guidelines for Exhaust Gas Cleaning Systems' (n 297) 10.1.2.1(i); Comer, Georgeff and Osipova (n 555) 9.

[557] MEPC, 'MEPC.184(59) – 2009 Guidelines for Exhaust Gas Cleaning Systems' (n 297); MEPC, 'MEPC.259(68) – 2015 Guidelines for Exhaust Gas Cleaning Systems' (n 297); MEPC, 'MEPC.340(77) – 2021 Guidelines for Exhaust Gas Cleaning Systems' (n 297); Comer, Georgeff and Osipova (n 555) 11.

[558] Comer, Georgeff and Osipova (n 555) 11.

from vessels.[559] Although the IMO and its instruments could address this cause of OA as part of their mandate and objectives, they have not yet established limitations to prevent acidification. Rather than addressing scrubbing, it is promoted as a method to reduce air pollution.

It should be noted that scrubbing has drawn attention as an issue at the regional level, particularly by the Arctic Council, which is positioned at the lower end of the table. One of the projects – more specifically, a survey of current practices conducted by PAME, a working group of the Arctic Council – is titled 'wastewater discharges from vessels in the arctic'.[560] However, even this project, as defined by its objective, is limited to investigating current practices to gain a better understanding scrubbing better.[561] Hence, at this stage, the Arctic Council is not regulating scrubbing, but rather trying to understand it.

So far, the IMO and its associated instruments, along with UNEP, include NO_x/SO_x emissions in their mandates and objectives. Addressing these emissions alone does not provide significant potential. Nevertheless, these instruments can also tackle other activities relating to the three concerns of OA, as shown in the table and further demonstrated below. Generally, NO_x/SO_x as a contributor to OA is often excluded from the mandates and objectives of many actors and instruments. As one of the few entities that can address this issue, even the IMO only partially addresses this lesser-known cause of OA through its mandates and objectives, particularly as its focus is limited to the shipping industry. However, it will be shown that the IMO, along with the other organisations and related instruments introduced at the beginning of the causes section, can address various activities contributing to the second cause of OA (namely, CO_2).

5.3.1.2 Organisations and Instruments Addressing CO_2

Regarding CO_2, three different activities need to be reduced or halted: CO_2 emissions, certain coastal activities, and geoengineering. While geoengineering plays a minor role in the total share of CO_2 leading to OA currently, CO_2 emissions and coastal activities are larger contributors to the total amount of CO_2 being released or absorbed into the water, albeit on different levels (global vs. regional/local). In the following paragraphs, the three organisations that include emissions in their mandates/objectives will be examined before discussing which ones address relevant coastal activities. Lastly, the organisations that approach geoengineering will be considered. If UNEP or the IMO (and associated instruments) address at least one other activity related to CO_2, the two institutions can be regarded as having significant potential, as they can address two activities within the causes. Addressing

[559] IMO, 'IMO 2020 – Cutting Sulphur Oxide Emissions' (n 552).

[560] Arctic Council, 'Wastewater Discharges from Vessels in the Arctic' (*Arctic Council*, 2022) https://arctic-council.org/projects/wastewater-discharges-from-vessels-in-the-arctic-a-survey-of-current-practices/ accessed 17 January 2022.

[561] Ibid.

two activities within the causes implies that the institutions are tackling this concern in depth. Concerning the OA Alliance, since this institution does not handle NO_x/SO_x, it would need to include at least two activities related to CO_2 in its mandate/objectives to address the causes in depth (and have significant potential).

5.3.1.2.1 Actors and Instruments Dealing with CO_2 Emissions Today, many institutions recognise the threat that climate change and associated GHG emissions, including CO_2, pose to the Earth's environment. Since OA is an effect of climate change, every institution or mechanism that addresses CO_2 can, to some extent, mitigate it, as discussed in Chapters 1 and 2. This relationship is also reflected in the table, where nearly every actor or mechanism received an X in the CO_2 column, and many of the included units aim to tackle climate change in one way or another.

The institution – or, more accurately, the instrument – most prominently involved in reducing GHG emissions (including CO_2) is the UNFCCC, along with the entire CCR, including the Paris Agreement. The regime is clearly suitable for addressing CO_2 emissions, as this is part of the very reason for its creation. While its contribution to the prevention of OA has been discussed elsewhere in detail[562] (see also Chapter 1), this discussion will not be elaborated upon here. Instead, attention will be drawn to another lesser-known institution addressing CO_2 emissions: the OA Alliance, which also has an X in the CO_2 column. As its name indicates, among all the institutions considering CO_2 in the table, only the OA Alliance is purely dedicated to tackling OA (see also Section 5.4).[563]

The OA Alliance is a growing coalition of governments and organisations dedicated to reducing OA as a threat to coastal communities and livelihoods.[564] According to the institution's website, one of its main strategies for addressing OA and climate impacts on the ocean is cutting CO_2 emissions. To achieve this goal, the OA Alliance calls on its members to create so-called Action Plans.[565] For instance, one of the institution's objectives for these Action Plans is to '[r]educe atmospheric carbon dioxide emissions, the number one cause of ocean acidification'.[566] The institution's members are tasked with setting up their Action Plans in accordance with the targets, similar to the Paris Agreement's nationally determined contributions (NDCs), and the OA Alliance facilitates this procedure.[567] Therefore, the OA Alliance received an X in the column of the table for CO_2. In addition to emissions, the OA Alliance is also addressing relevant coastal activities, as will be seen below.

Along with the UNFCCC and the OA Alliance, the IMO can also tackle CO_2 emissions. In line with its pollution reduction purpose, the IMO's Marine

[562] Baird, Simons and Stephens (n 18); Harrould-Kolieb, 'Ocean Acidification and the UNFCCC: Finding Legal Clarity in the Twilight Zone' (n 57); Harrould-Kolieb and Herr (n 57); Kim (n 21); Oral (n 47).

[563] Cf. OA Alliance, 'About' (n 351).

[564] Ibid; cf. OA Alliance, 'Current Members' (n 293) The Alliance has forty-two governmental members operating on different levels of governance.

[565] OA Alliance, 'About' (n 351). [566] Ibid.

[567] OA Alliance, 'Action Plans' (*OA Alliance*, 2021) www.oaalliance.org/action-plans accessed 19 January 2022.

Environment Protection Committee adopted a new Chapter 4 to annex VI of MARPOL 73/78 in 2011, named 'Regulations on energy efficiency for ships'. According to the IMO's website, this chapter constitutes the 'first ever mandatory global GHG reduction regime for an entire industry sector'.[568] In addition to MARPOL 73/78, the IMO as an organisation has made the reduction of greenhouse gases produced by the shipping industry an important target. Through its Marine Environmental Protection Committee, the organisation adopted a resolution (MEPC.304(72)) in April 2018, establishing an initial IMO strategy on the reduction of GHG emissions from ships, which was then followed in October of the same year by the Programme of follow-up actions of the Initial Strategy up to 2023.[569] Then, in July 2023, the IMO adopted the Revised GHG Strategy (MEPC.377(80)).[570] This move affirms the organisation's urgent goal to reduce GHG emissions, including CO_2 produced by the shipping industry.[571] The new and revised strategy has enhanced targets for reducing GHG emissions.[572] More specifically, it includes a higher common ambition to 'reach net-zero GHG emissions from international shipping by or around (…) 2050'.[573] To achieve this goal, the organisation has set indicative checkpoints for 2030 and 2040.[574] At the MEPC's 83rd meeting in 2025, a pivotal agreement was reached regarding a 'net zero framework' (even though adoption is still pending in October 2025). This framework outlines the legal text designed to meet the objectives established by the revised strategy.[575] Following what has been said above, both MARPOL 73/78 and the IMO got an X in the CO_2 column of the table.

5.3.1.2.2 Actors and Instruments Dealing with Coastal Activities As explained in Chapter 2, certain coastal activities, such as coastal pollution and suboptimal

[568] IMO, 'Greenhouse Gas Emissions' (2019) www.imo.org/en/OurWork/Environment/Pages/GHG-Emissions.aspx accessed 19 January 2022.

[569] Ibid; IMO, 'IMO's Work to Cut GHG Emissions from Ships' (2019) www.imo.org/en/MediaCentre/HotTopics/Pages/Cutting-GHG-emissions.aspx accessed 24 August 2023; International Maritime Organization (IMO), Marine Environmental Protection Committee (MEPC), 'Initial IMO Strategy on Reduction of GHG Emissions from Ships' https://unfccc.int/sites/default/files/resource/250_IMO%20submission_Talanoa%20Dialogue_April%202018.pdf accessed 24 August 2023.

[570] International Maritime Organization (IMO), Marine Environmental Protection Committee (MEPC), '2023 IMO Strategy on Reduction of GHG Emissions from Ships' wwwcdn.imo.org/localresources/en/MediaCentre/PressBriefings/Documents/Clean%20version%20of%20Annex%201.pdf; IMO, 'Revised GHG Reduction Strategy for Global Shipping Adopted' (2019) www.imo.org/en/MediaCentre/PressBriefings/pages/Revised-GHG-reduction-strategy-for-global-shipping-adopted-.aspx accessed 24 August 2023.

[571] IMO, 'Greenhouse Gas Emissions' (n 568).

[572] IMO, 'Revised GHG Reduction Strategy for Global Shipping Adopted' (n 570); International Maritime Organization (IMO), Marine Environmental Protection Committee (MEPC) (n 570).

[573] IMO, 'Revised GHG Reduction Strategy for Global Shipping Adopted' (n 570); see also: International Maritime Organization (IMO), Marine Environmental Protection Committee (MEPC) (n 570) para 3.3.4.

[574] International Maritime Organization (IMO), Marine Environmental Protection Committee (MEPC) (n 570) para 3.4; IMO, 'Revised GHG Reduction Strategy for Global Shipping Adopted' (n 570).

[575] IMO, 'Circular Letter No.5005 – Draft Revised Marpol Annex Vi (Secretariat)' wwwcdn.imo.org/localresources/en/MediaCentre/HotTopics/Documents/Circular%20Letter%20No.5005%20-%20Draft%20Revised%20Marpol%20Annex%20Vi%20%28Secretariat%29.pdf accessed 7 May 2025.

coastal planning, can lead to enhanced OA. While CO_2 emissions are a known cause of OA, the contribution of coastal activities to OA has received less attention in instruments and from various actors. Nevertheless, all three actors discussed concerning the causes of OA aim to contribute to reducing these activities.

Apart from being linked to the CCR, the UNEP is also related to the GPA, which is particularly important for reducing relevant coastal activities. On UNEP's website (under 'Oceans and Seas'), the actor explains that it hosts the GPA to address land-based pollution.[576] Land-based pollution, as a form of coastal activity, is one of the actions that carry nutrients into the water, which then results in OA. After initially tackling nine different 'source categories' of pollution, the GPA, since the 2012 Manila Declaration, has focused only on three source categories: marine litter, nutrient management, and wastewater.[577] Thus, this example shows that UNEP (and the GPA specifically) are addressing damaging coastal activities as one of their goals, and both of these units received an X in the CO_2 column of the table. Additionally, this demonstrates that UNEP and its related instruments can address various activities causing OA, such as the reduction of CO_2 emissions and coastal activities.

Second, the OA Alliance calls for its members to create Action Plans, as has already been observed regarding CO_2 emissions. Another objective that OAA members are meant to achieve with these Action Plans, aside from reducing emissions, is to 'reduce local pollutions that exacerbate ocean acidification'.[578] For example, as noted on the OA Alliance website, local and land-based pollution introduces nutrients into the water, which ultimately convert into CO_2, further acidifying the oceans.[579] The OA Alliance is targeting coastal activities and urging its members to address them, which is another reason the institution received an X in the CO_2 column.

As an actor responsible for overseeing shipping, the IMO cannot address activities related to land, such as coastal activities, within its mandate/objectives. However, the IMO, following its mandate to prevent pollution of the marine environment, specifically through instruments, is addressing activities that have similar effects to coastal activities and lead to OA. MARPOL 73/78 and the LC/LP address pollution and dumping at sea, which, if not prevented, could have similar repercussions to coastal activities and, more specifically, land-based pollution. Pollution and dumping at sea can, for instance, release nutrients into the

576 UNEP, 'Addressing Land-Based Pollution' (*UNEP – UN Environment Programme*, 15 August 2017) www.unep.org/explore-topics/oceans-seas/what-we-do/addressing-land-based-pollution accessed 19 January 2022.

577 Ibid; UNEP, 'Governing the Global Programme of Action' (*UNEP – UN Environment Programme*, 16 August 2017) www.unep.org/explore-topics/oceans-seas/what-we-do/addressing-land-based-pollution/governing-global-programme accessed 19 January 2022.

578 OA Alliance, 'About' (n 351); OA Alliance, 'Action Plans' (n 567).

579 OA Alliance, 'ACTION #3: Reduce Local Pollution That Exacerbates OA Action 3' (*OA Alliance*, 2023) www.oaalliance.org/action-3 accessed 24 August 2023.

water similarly to coastal activities. These nutrients can lead to acidification (see Chapter 2 for a complete explanation).

Because UNCLOS can be linked to the IMO (and is discussed alongside it in this chapter), it is important to note that UNCLOS explicitly mentions pollution from land-based sources. Pollution from land-based sources is addressed by the convention in a general article for the prevention, reduction, and control of pollution (194(3)(a) UNCLOS), which was examined earlier, as well as in article 207 UNCLOS, which is entirely dedicated to this issue. Pursuant to article 207, '[s]tates shall adopt laws and regulations to prevent, reduce, and control pollution of the marine environment from land-based sources'.[580] As noted above, UNCLOS typically calls for states to create laws and regulations instead of setting concrete targets itself. Nevertheless, UNCLOS provides a foundation for these laws and regulations and encourages states to address this type of coastal activity. In fact, the table includes an instrument that constitutes a law or regulation as described by the article, namely OSPAR, which is part of the regional section of the table. OSPAR's article 3 states that the contracting parties shall take 'all possible steps to prevent and eliminate pollution from land-based sources'.[581] Thus, it can be inferred that the IMO and its related instruments can address yet another activity leading to OA. In addition to the IMO and the other instruments, UNCLOS also received an X in the CO_2 column of the table.

5.3.1.2.3 Actors and Instruments Dealing with Geoengineering The last activity discussed here that leads to OA due to CO_2 is geoengineering. Considered in relation to the causes, only one of the actors addresses geoengineering, namely the IMO through the LC/LP.[582] The IMO has administered the LC since 1977, and these instruments are jointly dedicated to controlling and preventing marine pollution through dumping.[583] While the LC and the LP's 2006 and 2009 amendments jointly specify CCS as a technique to mitigate the repercussions of CO_2, the units, particularly the 2013 amendment to the LP, strictly regulate ocean fertilisation and other marine geoengineering activities.[584] The 2013 amendment to the LP introduces,

[580] United Nations Convention on the Law of the Sea (UNCLOS) preprint 207(1).

[581] Convention for the Protection of the Marine Environment of the North-East Atlantic 1992 (2354 UNTS 67) preprint 3.

[582] Convention on the Prevention of Marine Pollution by Dumping of Wastes and Other Matter 1972 (1046 UNTS120); London Protocol to the Convention on the Prevention of Marine Pollution by Dumping and Other Matter 1996 (36 ILM 1 (1977)).

[583] IMO, 'Convention on the Prevention of Marine Pollution by Dumping of Wastes and Other Matter' (2019) www.imo.org/en/About/Conventions/Pages/Convention-on-the-Prevention-of-Marine-Pollution-by-Dumping-of-Wastes-and-Other-Matter.aspx accessed 19 January 2022.

[584] IMO, 'LP.4(8)' (n 311); IMO, 'Resolution LP.1(1) – ON THE AMENDMENT TO INCLUDE CO2 SEQUESTRATION IN SUB-SEABED GEOLOGICAL FORMATIONS IN ANNEX 1 TO THE LONDON PROTOCOL.Pdf' wwwcdn.imo.org/localresources/en/KnowledgeCentre/IndexofIMOResolutions/LCLPDocuments/LP.1(1).pdf accessed 14 May 2024; IMO, 'Resolution LP.3(4) – 2009 AMENDMENT TO ARTICLE 6 OF THE 1996 PROTOCOL TO THE CONVENTION ON THE PREVENTION OF MARINE POLLUTION BY DUMPING OF WASTES AND OTHER MATTER 1972' https://cil.nus.edu.sg/wp-content/uploads/2019/02/2009-Amd-to-London-Prot.pdf accessed 14 May 2024.

for the first time, a definition of geoengineering as it adds paragraph 5*bis* to article 1 of the LP. In addition, the same amendment also created article 6*bis* to the LP, which, in para 1, among other things, stipulates that '[c]ontracting Parties shall not allow the placement of matter into the sea (...) for marine geoengineering activities listed in annex 4'. The list in annex 4 includes 'ocean fertilization' and defines it in para 1.1. as a geoengineering activity, which accordingly forbids the placement of matter into the sea as part of this activity. The preceding discussion indicates that strictly regulating geoengineering, such as ocean fertilisation, is one of the LC/LP's intentions, which is why the units received an X in the table in the CO_2 column.

5.3.1.3 Causes – Conclusion

This concludes the causes section of this chapter, which has generated several findings. It has been shown that actors and instruments focus more on CO_2 than NO_x/SO_x. The prevention of scrubbing, for instance, as part of NO_x/SO_x, is not included in institutions' mandates or objectives and is, on the contrary, currently encouraged. On the other hand, CO_2 emissions are a well-explored threat and are accordingly addressed by a variety of units. Regarding coastal activities, some of the actors and instruments considered here specifically address land-based pollution, while other coastal activities (like land use change) described in Chapter 2 received less attention. Lastly, geoengineering has only gained attention through the IMO's LC/LP. As things stand, this activity is only a minor contributor to OA, and addressing it is therefore less urgent than other activities.

Examining the actors and their associated instruments, it is evident that all of them demonstrate significant potential to address OA, as they can all deal with one of the concerns (namely, the causes of OA) in depth. They all engage in several activities related to one of the causes, and some address both causes (NO_x/SO_x and CO_2). The IMO and its instruments encompass both NO_x/SO_x and CO_2 emissions, as well as geoengineering and coastal activities, albeit through UNCLOS in their mandate/objectives. Consequently, the IMO and associated instruments jointly consider various activities concerning CO_2 and both causes. The OA Alliance does not address NO_x/$SO_{x;}$ however, it includes a range of activities related to CO_2 in its mandate/objectives, specifically emissions and coastal activities. Lastly, UNEP and its instruments focus solely on various activities contributing to OA via CO_2 – namely, emissions and coastal activities. This alone indicates that the discussed actors (UNEP, IMO, OA Alliance) can address one of the concerns (i.e., causes) in depth and therefore exhibit significant potential to tackle OA.

In addition, some of these actors and instruments will be revisited in the stressors and adaptation section of this chapter. All actors with their associated instruments mentioned in the causes section cannot only tackle the causes in depth but also address other concerns, as illustrated in the table. Being able to deal with several of the concerns simultaneously indicates an ability to address the concerns in terms of width, meaning these actors can approach them not only in depth but also broadly. In any case, they show significant potential to handle OA.

5.3.2 Actors and Instruments Dealing with the Stressors

The stressors can be divided into three groups of activities: climate change (Section 5.3.2.1), activities releasing nutrients and other pollutants (Section 5.3.2.2), and activities related to fishing (Section 5.3.2.3). Afterwards, the stressors will be concluded (Section 5.3.2.4). Just as described for the causes above, institutions must, to be regarded as having significant potential to address the stressors of OA, be empowered to prevent or diminish at least two activities discussed under this concern. If institutions can engage with two activities within the stressors, they address the stressors in depth and have significant potential to tackle OA. If an institution only addresses one activity within the stressors, it does not have significant potential unless it additionally tackles another concern (either the causes discussed above or the adaptation discussed below) to deal with the concerns in breadth. Thus, to demonstrate that an actor and its related instruments address the stressors in depth, that actor should engage with a minimum of two of the different activities that induce ocean stress. The IMO, UNEP, and the IUCN (and their associated instruments) are able to achieve depth, a point that will be examined further below. If the IMO and UNEP address only one activity within this concern (stressors), they also address the concerns in breadth (and have significant potential), as they also address the causes, as seen above.

5.3.2.1 Climate Change as an Ocean Stressor

Climate change – or, more specifically, the emission of GHGs (including CO_2) – has repercussions that further stress the ocean. Examples of such repercussions include ocean warming and sea-level rise. All three organisations considered regarding the stressors can address climate change according to their mandates. It has already been shown that the IMO and its instruments, as well as UNEP with its instruments, can tackle emissions of CO_2 and climate change in general. Therefore, this argumentation will not be repeated here. Nonetheless, the IUCN also engages in activities related to climate change, and since it has not yet been surveyed, the following paragraphs will detail this institution.

The IUCN is an actor composed of government and civil society organisations.[585] The union's objectives can be found in Part II of the IUCN Statute, and its article 2 stipulates that '[t]he objectives of IUCN shall be to influence, encourage and assist societies (…) to conserve the integrity and diversity of nature'.[586] While the conservation of nature appears to be a broad and general objective, the actor provides clarifications regarding its work on their website. It states that since the 2000s, the IUCN has also been addressing global challenges such as climate

[585] IUCN, 'About' (*IUCN*, 10 September 2018) www.iucn.org/about accessed 20 January 2022.

[586] IUCN, *Statutes of 5 October 1948… (Including Rules of Procedure…) and Regulations…Last Amended on 13 December 2023* (IUCN, International Union for Conservation of Nature 2023) pt II article 2 https://portals.iucn.org/library/node/51397 accessed 6 May 2024.

change, presenting climate change as one of the 'themes' of the IUCN.[587] Thus, it becomes evident that climate change is an issue that this actor addresses under the conservation objective mentioned in the statute. The IUCN's website is complex and constantly changing, but it demonstrates that the union is active and has created projects in many different areas related to nature conservation.

Another theme that the IUCN addresses is 'Ocean and Coasts'.[588] Regarding this theme, the union organises its work into six categories, one of which is 'Ocean and climate change'.[589] Unlike most other actors in this category, the IUCN approaches (apart from OA), ocean warming, ocean deoxygenation and marine heat waves. These latter three are repercussions of climate change and stressors of the ocean.[590] Therefore, it can be seen that the IUCN includes both climate change and its repercussions for the ocean in its conservation mandate. The tools the union has to pursue its goals are manifold and framed in article 3 of the statute mentioned above. Pursuant to article 3, 'to attain these objectives, IUCN' must contribute 'to the preparation of international agreements relevant to the conservation of nature and natural resources and encourages states to adhere to these agreements'. Hence, the union works on and even has the option to contribute to the preparation of conservation instruments in the area of climate change and its repercussions, which is the reason it can deal with ocean stress and received an X in the table.

5.3.2.2 Nutrient- and Pollutant-Releasing Activities as Ocean Stressors

The second group of activities generating ocean stress involves the release of nutrients and, in some cases, other pollutants into the ocean water. The activities included here are geoengineering, relevant coastal actions, and shipping. The three institutions discussed in the stressors section of this chapter can all address one or more of these activities based on their mandates and objectives.

As previously discussed, the IMO and its instruments address geoengineering (LC/LP) and relevant coastal activities, particularly pollution from land-based sources, albeit through UNCLOS, as well as pollution and dumping from shipping (MARPOL 73/78, LC/LP). Thus, the IMO and its related instruments will not be further discussed concerning this group of ocean stressors. The same applies to UNEP and its instruments since, as previously noted, UNEP addresses coastal activities with the help of the GPA. The actors and their related instruments received an X in the OA stressors column of the table.

However, one instrument related to UNEP that has not been discussed here so far is the Manado Ocean Declaration. This declaration was published in 2009

[587] IUCN, 'Themes' (*IUCN*, 13 August 2015) www.iucn.org/theme accessed 20 January 2022; IUCN, 'IUCN – A Brief History' (*IUCN*, 6 October 2017) www.iucn.org/about/iucn-a-brief-history accessed 20 January 2022.

[588] IUCN, 'Our Work | IUCN' (2025) https://iucn.org/our-work accessed 13 May 2025.

[589] IUCN, 'Ocean and Climate Change | IUCN' (2025) https://iucn.org/our-work/topic/ocean-and-climate-change accessed 13 May 2025.

[590] Ibid.

during the World Ocean Conference by ministers and heads of delegations.[591] Manado and the GPA also target pollution reductions through the declarations made within this document. For example, point 4 of the declaration states, '[w]e will strive to reduce pollution of ocean, coastal and land areas'. In addition, point 9 includes a declaration that the parties 'will strive to implement sustainable development (…) through (…) a precautionary approach (…) in addressing the adverse effects of climate change on oceans, and in this regard, we will take adequate measures to reduce sources of marine pollution'. Lastly, pollution is also included in point 16, which declares: 'We will promote the Large marine Ecosystem approach (…) due to its wide vision considering pollution'. Thus, an X was added to Manado in the stressors column.

In addition to climate change and its repercussions, the IUCN also discusses the theme of capturing and storing carbon dioxide from the atmosphere under the headings 'Climate Change' and, more specifically, 'Ecosystem-based mitigation'.[592] Furthermore, another of category related to the 'Ocean and Coasts' theme is 'Plastic and other Pollution'.[593] As a form of pollution, marine plastics have diverse sources, including certain coastal activities and shipping. In addition to plastics, the website also mentions nutrient loading as another form of pollution, for example.[594] Hence, as part of their conservation mandate, the IUCN also works to contribute to the preparation of conservation instruments to work on geoengineering (carbon capture) and coastal activities. This presents another reason why the actor can tackle stressors and has an X in the respective column.

5.3.2.3 Activities Relating to Fishing as Ocean Stressors

The last of the activities leading to ocean stress are unregulated fishing and dangerous or disruptive fishing practices. All three institutions discussed in this section address this stressor – namely, the IMO with the related LOTSR and UNEP through the CMS (Convention on Migratory Species) and Manado. IUCN features a section on 'Fisheries and Aquaculture' under its 'ocean coasts' theme on its website. As fishing is a complex area of law in its own right, it should be noted that this section can only touch upon the most relevant aspects for OA regarding this topic.

The LOTSR – or more specifically, UNCLOS, the UN Fish Stocks Agreement, and the new Biodiversity Beyond National Jurisdiction (BBNJ) Agreement – address fishing. UNCLOS follows a zonal division of the world's oceans; notably, two of the zones are covered by specific articles regulating fishing, namely the exclusive economic zone (EEZ) and the high seas.[595] While in the EEZ, the coastal state has

591 Manadao Ocean Declaration 2009.

592 IUCN, 'Ecosystem-Based Mitigation | IUCN' (10 March 2025) https://iucn.org/our-work/topic/ecosystem-based-mitigation accessed 13 May 2025.

593 IUCN, 'Plastic and Other Pollution | IUCN' (15 June 2022) https://iucn.org/our-work/topic/plastic-and-other-pollution accessed 13 May 2025.

594 Ibid.

595 United Nations Convention on the Law of the Sea (UNCLOS) Parts V, VII.

a sovereign right to explore, exploit, conserve, and manage the natural resources, including fish. On the high seas, the freedom of fishing prevails as states can exercise their sovereignty.[596]

Accordingly, the coastal state is responsible for conservation in the EEZ, which includes preventing overexploitation and regulating the utilisation of living resources, including fish.[597] Furthermore, states shall coordinate and cooperate to achieve conservation concerning stocks occurring within several EEZs or an EEZ and the high seas or in cases of highly migratory species.[598] In addition, the articles governing the EEZ include special rules concerning anadromous and catadromous stocks.[599]

On the high seas, states must take measures, such as agreeing on an allowable catch limit to conserve living resources pursuant to article 119 UNCLOS. According to the article, to do so, states shall 'take measures (…) designed, on the best scientific evidence available to the States concerned, to maintain or restore populations of harvested species at levels which can produce the maximum sustainable yield'.[600] It can be seen that UNCLOS provides guidelines to coordinate fishing, which could reduce the contribution of fishing to ocean stress.

However, as has been seen, UNCLOS often only calls for further creation of regulations and measures.[601] Consistent with this, the UN Fish Stocks Agreement was subsequently created. As its name says, it is an 'Agreement for the Implementation of the Provisions of the United Nations Convention on the Law of the Sea of 10 December 1982 Relating to the Conservation and Management of Straddling Fish Stocks and Highly Migratory Fish Stocks'. Its objective is, according to its article 2, 'to ensure the long-term conservation and sustainable use of straddling fish stocks and highly migratory fish stocks' and to this end, further defines what states ought to do to achieve this goal.[602] In June 2023, another implementing agreement under UNCLOS was adopted that focuses on areas beyond national jurisdiction and, in particular, the conservation as well as sustainable use of marine biological diversity within these areas. The full name of the draft agreement is 'Agreement under the United Nations Convention on the Law of the Sea on the conservation and sustainable use of marine biological diversity of areas beyond national jurisdiction' ('High Seas Treaty'). Among other things, it focuses on marine protected areas.[603]

[596] Ibid arts. 56(1)(a), 87(1)(e). [597] Ibid arts. 61, 62. [598] Ibid arts. 63, 64.

[599] Ibid arts. 66, 67. [600] Ibid., 119(1)(a).

[601] For example, with regard to the conversation of straddling and highly migratory stocks, UNCLOS demands States to cooperate directly or through an International Organization. Ibid., 63(2), 64.

[602] Agreement for the Implementation of the Provisions of the United Nations Convention on the Law of the Sea of 10 December 1982 Relating to the Conservation and Management of Straddling Fish Stocks and Highly Migratory Fish Stocks (UN Fish Stocks Agreement) 1995 (UNTS vol 2167, p 3).

[603] UN, 'Intergovernmental Conference on Marine Biodiversity of Areas beyond National Jurisdiction' www.un.org/bbnj/ accessed 21 January 2022; Agreement under the United Nations Convention on the Law of the Sea on the Conservation and Sustainable Use of Marine Biological Diversity of Areas beyond National Jurisdiction.

This will be returned to again further along. Hence, the LOTSR can deal with acidification of the oceans and received an X in the stressors column.

The CMS[604], a convention related to UNEP, as its secretariat is provided and administered by it, could be fit to address fishing as a stressor.[605] Article II contains the convention's fundamental principles, and in paragraph 1, '[t]he Parties acknowledge the importance of migratory species being conserved and of Range States agreeing to take action to this end'. The fundamental principle is followed by the parties' acknowledgement that there is a 'need to take action to avoid any migratory species becoming endangered' in paragraph 2 of the same article. In addition, paragraph 3(b)(c) also calls on the parties to 'provide immediate protection' and commits them to 'endeavor to conclude Agreements' regarding migratory species.[606] Since there is agreement that migratory species need protection, this convention can also lead to action to protect migratory fish species. Such action could then potentially reduce fishing as an activity, creating stress for the ocean. Thus, the instrument received an X in the table under stressors.

In addition to the CMS, another instrument linked to UNEP, the Manado Declaration, also includes fishing in its remit. Point 4, mentioned above, declares the parties 'will strive to reduce pollution of ocean, coastal and land areas and to promote sustainable management of fisheries'. Point 16 also mentions fishing in promoting an 'approach that enhances [fishing] due to its wide vision considering pollution'. These aspects all commit the parties to sustainable fishing, potentially reducing this industry as an ocean stressor. Thus, UNEP and its related instruments can address another damaging activity leading to ocean stress.

The IUCN, under its 'Ocean and Coasts' theme, has a section on 'Fisheries and Aquaculture'.[607] According to its website, the IUCN aims to shape global policies for sustainable fisheries and aquaculture management, tackling issues such as illegal, unreported, and unregulated (IUU) fishing and the impacts of climate change, including OA, on aquaculture. Additionally, it offers guidance on sustainable aquaculture practices and fosters connections with marine protected areas.[608] Thus, IUCN can also address fishing as a stressor.

5.3.2.4 Stressors – Conclusion

From the stressors section, it can be inferred that, as mentioned before, climate change is addressed by many actors with their associated instruments, while geoengineering and shipping, as nutrient or pollution-releasing stressors, are handled to a lesser extent. Relevant coastal activities and fishing are addressed by all units.

[604] Convention on the Conservation of Migratory Species of Wild Animals 1979 (UNTS 1651).

[605] 'The Secretariat of the Convention | CMS' (2020) www.cms.int/en/about/secretariat accessed 20 January 2022.

[606] Convention on the Conservation of Migratory Species of Wild Animals.

[607] IUCN, 'Fisheries and Aquaculture | IUCN' (15 June 2022) https://iucn.org/our-work/topic/fisheries-and-aquaculture accessed 13 May 2025.

[608] Ibid.

Regarding actors and instruments, it is evident that all actors, along with their associated instruments, can engage in various activities that contribute to ocean stress. The IMO and its instruments collectively address all three activities: climate change, nutrient and other pollutant-releasing stressors, and fishing (albeit through UNCLOS). Similarly, UNEP and its instruments, as well as IUCN, also tackle these three groups of activities. In conclusion, all units discussed here address several activities leading to ocean stress and can therefore examine this concern (stressors) in depth, demonstrating significant potential. As mentioned, the IMO and UNEP cover various activities within this concern (stressors) and the causes. Consequently, they also tackle the concerns in breadth (and have significant potential). Although the IUCN has not been discussed under causes, the table indicates that this institution also includes other concerns in its mandate/objectives. Thus, the IUCN also confronts the concerns in breadth (and holds significant potential).

5.3.3 Actors and Instruments Dealing with Adaptation

Three activities are particularly relevant to tackling OA's negative consequences: the reorganisation and adjustment of fishing activities (covered in Section 5.3.3.1), the conservation, restoration, and protection of sources storing blue carbon (Section 5.3.3.2), and the creation of marine protected areas (Section 5.3.3.3). These three areas will be discussed before a final section on adaptation (Section 5.3.3.4). As mentioned previously, a lot is changing regarding adaptation, and these changes are occurring rapidly. To possess significant potential, institutions must be empowered to work on at least two activities discussed under adaptation. If institutions can consider two activities within adaptation, they address the topic in depth and have significant potential. However, if an institution only considers one activity within adaptation, it does not have significant potential unless it additionally addresses another concern (either causes or stressors discussed above) and thus deals with the concerns in breadth. Therefore, to demonstrate that an actor and its related instruments consider adaptation in depth, it should work on a minimum of two adaptation activities. The actors and instruments chosen for this concern are the IMO, the IUCN, and UNESCO. Regarding significant potential through breadth, it has already been argued above that the IMO and the IUCN address both causes and stressors. However, UNESCO is discussed for the first time.

5.3.3.1 Reorganisation and Adjustment of Fishing Activities

The discussion regarding OA stressors has already demonstrated that the LOTSR (explored together with the IMO) can address fishing through UNCLOS and the UN Fish Stocks Agreement. It has also been indicated that IUCN is working on this adaptation option. However, LOTSR and IUCN are the only institutions introduced as part of the adaptation section that can tackle fishing. UNESCO will be covered under blue carbon and marine protected areas.

5.3.3.2 Protection, Restoration, and Conservation of Blue Carbon Ecosystems

Two actors address blue carbon in their mandates and work. First, for instance, under its 'Ocean and Coasts' theme and more specifically under the 'Ocean and Climate' category of this theme, the IUCN mentions blue carbon as a good illustration of a nature-based solution.[609] Hence, the IUCN actively engages with blue carbon as part of its conservation mandate, as explained above. To promote this activity, the IUCN partners with, among others, IOC–UNESCO – which will be discussed in more detail later on in this section – the Blue Carbon Initiative, and the International Blue Carbon Partnership.[610] Together, they focus on 'guidance for international and national policy making, as well as on how to finance blue carbon projects and programmes'.[611] In addition, the IUCN approaches blue carbon through one of the instruments linked to it (namely, RAMSAR[612]). This linkage is based on the fact that the instrument's secretariat is located at the IUCN.[613]

The convention's mission can be found on its website and in the articles of the convention's text. The website states that Ramsar's mission is 'the conservation and wise use of all wetlands through local and national actions and international cooperation'.[614] When referring to wetlands, the convention adopts a broad definition, encompassing everything from coral reefs to marshes and mangroves.[615] This mission is confirmed by articles 3.1, 4.1, and 5 of the Ramsar Convention.[616] Thus, although the convention does not specifically mention blue carbon protection, it protects plants known for their ability to store carbon, such as mangroves. In any case, Ramsar can help protect the ocean from further acidification by preserving these wetlands. The IUCN and the convention received an X in the outcome section of the table since they can address the repercussions of OA.

Second, UNESCO also addresses blue carbon as an activity. Pursuant to article I(1) of its constitution, the original purpose of UNESCO is 'to contribute to peace and security by promoting collaboration among the nations through education, science and culture'.[617] To achieve this goal, the organisation has a whole catalogue of tools. For example, the constitution states, 'the Organization will: (a) Collaborate in the work (…) through all means of mass communication and

[609] IUCN, 'Ocean and Climate Change | IUCN' (n 589).

[610] IUCN, 'Blue Carbon' (*IUCN*, 4 May 2017) www.iucn.org/theme/marine-and-polar/our-work/climate-change-and-ocean/blue-carbon accessed 23 January 2022; International Partnership for Blue Carbon, 'Our Partners | Blue Carbon Partnership' (8 April 2022) https://bluecarbonpartnership.org/the-partnership/blue-carbon-partner-organisations/ accessed 13 May 2025.

[611] IUCN, 'Blue Carbon' (n 610).

[612] Convention on wetlands of international importance, especially as waterfowl habitat 1971 (UNTS 996 (p245)).

[613] RAMSAR, 'The Secretariat | Ramsar' (2014) www.ramsar.org/about/the-secretariat accessed 24 January 2022.

[614] RAMSAR, 'The Convention on Wetlands and Its Mission | Ramsar' (2014) www.ramsar.org/about/the-convention-on-wetlands-and-its-mission accessed 24 January 2022.

[615] Ibid. [616] Convention on wetlands of international importance especially as waterfowl habitat.

[617] Constitution of the United Nations Educational, Scientific and Cultural Organization.

to that end recommend such international agreements as may be necessary'.[618] UNESCO has a very broad remit, but it becomes clear that its work's foundation is education, science, and culture. To reach its goals, the organisation can, under certain circumstances, recommend international agreements. As part of UNESCO's rather broad mandate, and based on the education and science branch of its foundation, the organisation created a commission, the IOC–UNESCO, to enhance cooperation to 'generate knowledge about the nature and resources of the ocean and coastal areas and to apply that knowledge to management, sustainable development, marine environment protection, and decision-making processes within its Member States'.[619]

Part of the work of IOC–UNESCO involves partnering with the International Partnership for Blue Carbon and co-hosting the Blue Carbon Initiative mentioned above.[620] Overall, IOC–UNESCO aims to 'protect, manage or restore' blue carbon ecosystems while working towards this objective on scientific and policy levels.[621] Due to its efforts related to blue carbon, it received an X in the outcome column. (See also annex B for more information on UNESCO).

In addition, UNESCO is connected to the World Heritage Convention as UNESCO's General Conference adopted the convention on 16 November 1972.[622] The World Heritage Convention establishes what type of cultural or natural sites qualify for inclusion on the World Heritage List.[623] 'Natural heritage' is defined in article 2 of the World Heritage Convention. The third option included in the article defines natural heritage as 'natural sites or precisely delineated natural areas of outstanding universal value from the point of view of science, conservation or natural beauty'. This definition is broad and 'natural sites or precisely delineated natural areas' could potentially include blue carbon ecosystems such as mangrove forests. As outlined by the website set up by UNESCO for the convention, the instrument follows five strategic objectives regarding these sites. One of these strategic objectives is 'conservation', more specifically, the conservation of world heritage.[624] This objective can be confirmed when looking at the World Heritage Convention itself. In fact, article 4 of the World Heritage Convention states, 'Each State Party (…) recognizes that the duty of ensuring (…) protection, conservation, (…) of the cultural and natural heritage (…) belongs primarily to that State. It will do all it can to this end'. Thus, with the help of this instrument,

[618] Ibid., I(2)(a).

[619] UNESCO, 'One Planet, One Ocean' (*UNESCO*, 6 May 2013) https://en.unesco.org/themes/one-planet-one-ocean accessed 24 January 2022.

[620] UNESCO, 'Blue Carbon | IOC UNESCO' https://ioc.unesco.org/topics/blue-carbon accessed 24 January 2022; International Partnership for Blue Carbon (n 610).

[621] UNESCO, 'Blue Carbon | IOC UNESCO' (n 620).

[622] UNESCO, 'The World Heritage Convention' (*UNESCO World Heritage Centre*, 2023) https://whc.unesco.org/en/convention/ accessed 20 March 2023; Convention Concerning the Protection of the World Cultural and Natural Heritage 1972 (UNTS 1037 (p151)).

[623] Convention Concerning the Protection of the World Cultural and Natural Heritage art cf. article 11(1).

[624] UNESCO, 'The World Heritage Convention' (n 622).

blue carbon ecosystems could be protected and conserved. Hence, the convention received an X in the adaptation column.

5.3.3.3 Creation of Marine Protected Areas

All three actors and related instruments introduced in this section promote the creation of MPAs. First, in addition to fishing, the LOTSR (discussed together with IMO) can encourage the establishment of MPAs. One of the main themes of the newly drafted High Seas Treaty under UNCLOS is MPAs.[625] The treaty's objective is: 'conservation and sustainable use of marine biological diversity of areas beyond national jurisdiction'.[626] Article 1 of the draft defines the terms used in the treaty. MPAs, one of the tools to achieve this objective, have their own definition: '"Marine protected area" means a geographically defined marine area that is designated and managed to achieve specific long-term biodiversity conservation objectives and may allow, where appropriate, sustainable use provided it is consistent with the conservation objectives'.[627]

In addition, article 1(1) also clarifies that MPAs fall under the collective term 'Area-based management tool'. Part III of the High Seas Treaty is entirely dedicated to these 'Area-based management tools, including marine protected areas'. Article 17, the first article of Part III, outlines the objectives regarding this part of the treaty. One of the objectives (article 17(a)) is to '[c]onserve and sustainably use areas (…) including through the establishment of a comprehensive system of area-based management tools, with (…) networks of marine protected areas'. It becomes obvious that marine protected areas, including their establishment, are central to the new High Seas Convention. This is another reason the LOTS regime receives an X under adaptation. However, it is vital to note that the aforementioned Part III, which addresses MPAs, even mentions ocean acidification. Article 17(c) reads: '[p]rotect, preserve, restore and maintain biodiversity and ecosystems, including with a view to enhancing their productivity and health, and strengthen resilience to stressors, including those related to climate change [and] ocean acidification'.[628]

This reference builds on the discussions in Chapter 2, specifically that MPAs can contribute to resilience building, including against stresses such as OA.

[625] See IUCN, 'BBNJ Knowledge Series' (*IUCN*, 27 November 2020) www.iucn.org/theme/marine-and-polar/our-work/international-ocean-governance/unclos/bbnj-knowledge-series accessed 23 January 2022; IUCN, 'Marine Biodiversity of Areas beyond National Jurisdiction (BBNJ)' (*IUCN*, 7 August 2018) www.iucn.org/theme/environmental-law/our-work/oceans-and-coasts/marine-biodiversity-areas-beyond-national-jurisdiction-bbnj accessed 23 January 2022; cf. Draft Agreement under the United Nations Convention on the Law of the Sea on the Conservation and Sustainable Use of Marine Biological Diversity of Areas beyond National Jurisdiction 2023.

[626] Agreement under the United Nations Convention on the Law of the Sea on the Conservation and Sustainable Use of Marine Biological Diversity of Areas beyond National Jurisdiction art 2.

[627] Ibid., 1(9).

[628] Draft Agreement under the United Nations Convention on the Law of the Sea on the Conservation and Sustainable Use of Marine Biological Diversity of Areas beyond National Jurisdiction art 17(c).

Therefore, the High Seas Treaty provides for the establishment of MPAs to achieve, among other objectives, resilience, which is precisely what is necessary to adapt to OA.

Second, IUCN deserves another X in the outcome column, as the union under the 'Protected areas and land use' theme has a category called 'Marine Ecosystems' where MPAs are clearly mentioned.[629] Thus, the union deals with marine protected areas as part of its conservation mandate. More specifically, the IUCN, among other things, works on the development and expansion of these areas of the ocean through advocacy and interaction with local stakeholders.[630]

Last, UNESCO mentions MPAs on its website. Hence, UNESCO seems to also promote MPAs as part of its broad mandate. More specifically, MPAs are mentioned in 'Ocean' under the 'Our Expertise' tab.[631] There, the 'World Heritage Marine Programme' is referenced. Part of this programme entails establishing new MPAs and conserving existing ones within the fifty marine sites on UNESCO's World Heritage List.[632] Hence, as many heritage sites have been created with the help of the convention, UNESCO aims to take the next step by making these sites MPAs or protecting those that already qualify as such. Therefore, it can again be seen that UNESCO is promoting an adaptation option and receives an X in the adaptation column of the table.

5.3.3.4 Adaptation – Conclusion

Regarding adaptation, it is noted that the management of fishing activities is debated under the LOTS regime and IUCN. As initially predicted, blue carbon is becoming increasingly popular and well-known among institutions, and a growing number of initiatives have started to emerge. Both the IUCN and UNESCO promote blue carbon initiatives. However, MPAs have also recently gained considerable attention due to the newly released High Seas Treaty.

Regarding the institutions, the IMO (albeit through the LOTSR) is active in fishing and MPAs, while the IUCN addresses fishing, blue carbon, and MPAs, and finally, UNESCO focuses on blue carbon and MPAs. The institutions introduced in the adaptation section all demonstrate significant potential. All actors and associated instruments are actively engaged in various activities and can therefore address the concern (adaptation) in depth. As mentioned earlier, the IMO and the IUCN also engage in multiple activities across different concerns, thus addressing these issues in breadth and showing significant potential.

[629] IUCN, 'Marine Ecosystems | IUCN' (15 June 2022) https://iucn.org/our-work/topic/marine-ecosystems accessed 13 May 2025.

[630] IUCN, 'Marine Protected Areas' (*IUCN*, 7 October 2015) www.iucn.org/theme/marine-and-polar/our-work/marine-protected-areas accessed 24 January 2022.

[631] UNESCO, 'The Ocean We Need for the Future We Want | UNESCO' (2023) www.unesco.org/en/ocean accessed 20 March 2023.

[632] UNESCO, 'World Heritage Marine Programme' (*UNESCO World Heritage Centre*, 2023) https://whc.unesco.org/en/marine-programme/ accessed 20 March 2023.

Although UNESCO has not been discussed in the context of causes or stressors, it is evident from the table that this institution encompasses other concerns within its mandate/objectives. Consequently, UNESCO also addresses these issues in breadth and possesses significant potential.

5.4 Choosing Actors for Case Studies to Test the Presence of the Ideal Type of Global Experimentalist Governance

This chapter aimed to select actors for further case studies. More precisely, this study will identify whether and to what extent the elements of the ideal type of global experimentalist governance are present within the governance of the chosen actors. Accordingly, after explaining which institution would theoretically be ideal for addressing OA – one that can tackle causes, stressors, and adaptation – this chapter distinguishes between institutions that are merely suitable and those that have significant potential to address OA. Institutions with significant potential are prioritised for further study, as they possess the greatest capacity to tackle all three concerns. Therefore, based on the map developed in Chapter 3, Table 5.3 was created, listing institutions that could potentially be used for case study selection.

However, the majority of the actors and instruments included in the table received multiple marks across various concerns or within a single concern, indicating their significant potential to tackle OA, as they can address the concerns in depth and/or breadth. Thus, based on the earlier assumption, a majority of the thirty-four different institutions could serve as interesting case studies. However, not all of them can be examined in detail. Therefore, in this book, only two actors will be discussed due to time and space constraints. Hence, to determine the case selection, different institutions on the map with significant potential were analysed regarding causes, stressors, and adaptation.

To this end, the IUCN, UNEP, IMO, UNESCO, and OAA have been examined in more detail, while ICAO, WWF, Oceana, and UNGA have been excluded for the reasons mentioned above. This discussion of how institutions tackle concerns through their mandate/objectives demonstrates why these institutions received marks and how they could address the concerns in depth and/or breadth, thereby granting them significant potential to deal with OA. All of the actors, partly through their interconnected instruments, have the potential to address OA as a problem both in depth and breadth, as seen during the discussion and when reviewing the table. The IUCN has been analysed and can tackle stressors (climate change, nutrients and pollution, fishing) and adaptation (fishing, blue carbon, MPA), while UNEP was discussed and can manage both NO_X/SO_X (emissions) and CO_2 (emissions, coastal), as well as the stressors (climate change, nutrients and pollution, fishing). UNESCO has been mentioned and can address adaptation (blue carbon, MPA), and the OAA was noted regarding the causes (emissions, coastal). Lastly, the IMO can deal with the causes (NO_x/SO_x (emissions), CO_2 (emissions, coastal, albeit through LOTSR), geoengineering), stressors (climate change, nutrients and pollution, fishing (through LOTSR)), and adaptation (fishing, MPAs (all through LOTSR)).

While discussing how the remaining five institutions under consideration address various concerns, it became evident that all of them – IMO, OAA, UNEP, UNESCO, and IUCN – represent interesting case studies due to their significant potential and distinct approaches to OA. Hence, it is important to acknowledge that there is no definitive reasoning that distinctly elevates IMO and OAA above the others. Nevertheless, the reasons why the OA Alliance and IMO are compelling and relevant cases regarding the governance of OA will be explained below and are based on insights from the discussion of the five actors above. However, this does not imply that the other institutions would not also serve as equally interesting case studies.

As indicated above, due to the constraints of this book, only two institutions will be chosen for a case study: the OA Alliance and the IMO. Figure 5.2 shows how these two institutions possess significant potential. The selection criteria discussed in this chapter are outlined in the top half of Figure 5.1, while the bottom half presents three additional reasons for selecting the OA and IMO, which will be discussed below.

First, based on the assumption that an institution should have significant potential and tackle as many activities as possible through its mandate/objective, various actors, particularly the five discussed further, would lend themselves as interesting case studies. Therefore, significant potential alone cannot be relied upon when selecting a case. The IMO and the OAA possess significant potential to address OA, as they can cover the topic in depth and breadth (see Figure 5.2 for visualisation). However, according to the science, not all concerns are equally important, and it is especially noteworthy that CO_2 is the primary reason for OA. Hence, institutions that can specifically address CO_2 should be prioritised.

However, as discussed above, nearly all the institutions can address CO_2. Additionally, it has been shown in Chapter 1 and the discussion above that CO_2, specifically the CCR, has gained more attention than any of the other aspects of OA. Therefore, this book will focus on the OA Alliance as a case study instead of further engaging with the already crowded discussion surrounding the CCR. The OA Alliance is a relatively new and growing institution that is solely focused on OA and addresses many activities, including CO_2 emissions and coastal activities.[633]

Apart from that, the CCR and specifically the Paris Agreement do not establish reduction targets for GHG emissions. In particular, there are no specific targets for CO_2 emissions, the primary driver of OA. Instead, states decide at the national level about their commitments, which then take the form of 'nationally

[633] OA Alliance, 'About' (n 351).

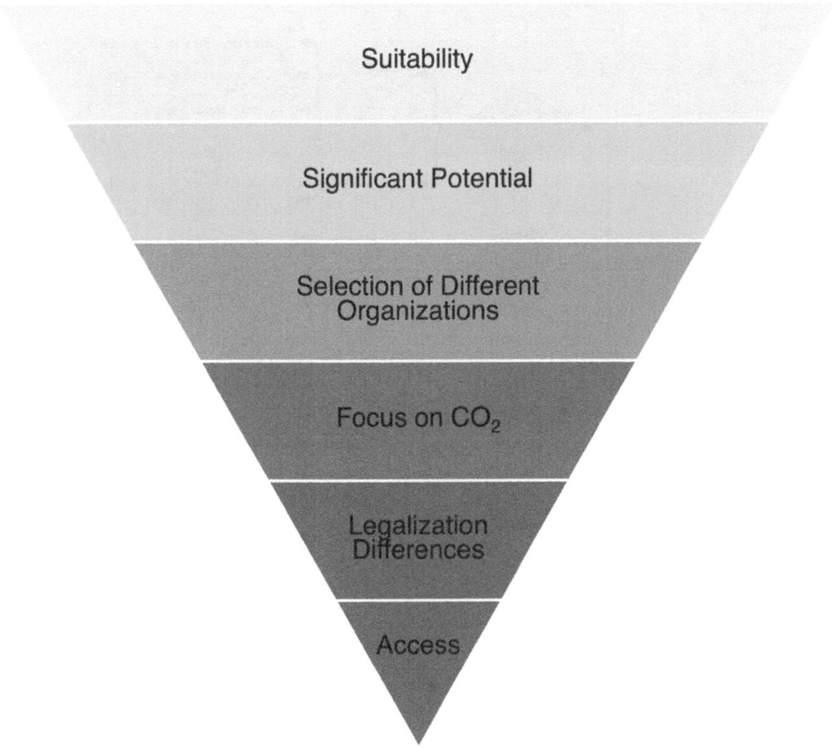

Figure 5.1 Case study selection criteria.
Source: Compiled by the author

determined contributions' to achieve the global temperature limit.[634] Thus, states are free to determine which gases they prioritise and to what extent.[635] Thus, emissions reduction to reach the Paris Agreement's long-term temperature goal, even on a 1.5 degrees pathway (article 2 (a)), could be achieved in many different ways. However, the impacts on the ocean would differ depending on which route is chosen to achieve the temperature goal. More specifically, the impact on the ocean will depend on which GHGs are reduced, to what extent, and how fast.[636] In fact, if states have the option to select certain types of emissions, as is currently the case for NDCs, they might focus on, for instance, methane instead of CO_2, as methane is a GHG that has seventy-two times the global warming potential of an equivalent amount of CO_2 would have.[637]

[634] Cf. Scott, 'Ocean Acidification' (n 29) 395; Paris Agreement art 2.
[635] See, for example, Gordon (n 31) 41.
[636] Cf. Harrould-Kolieb, 'Implications of the Paris Agreement for Action on Ocean Acidification within the UNFCCC' (n 57) 30.
[637] Gordon (n 31) 41.

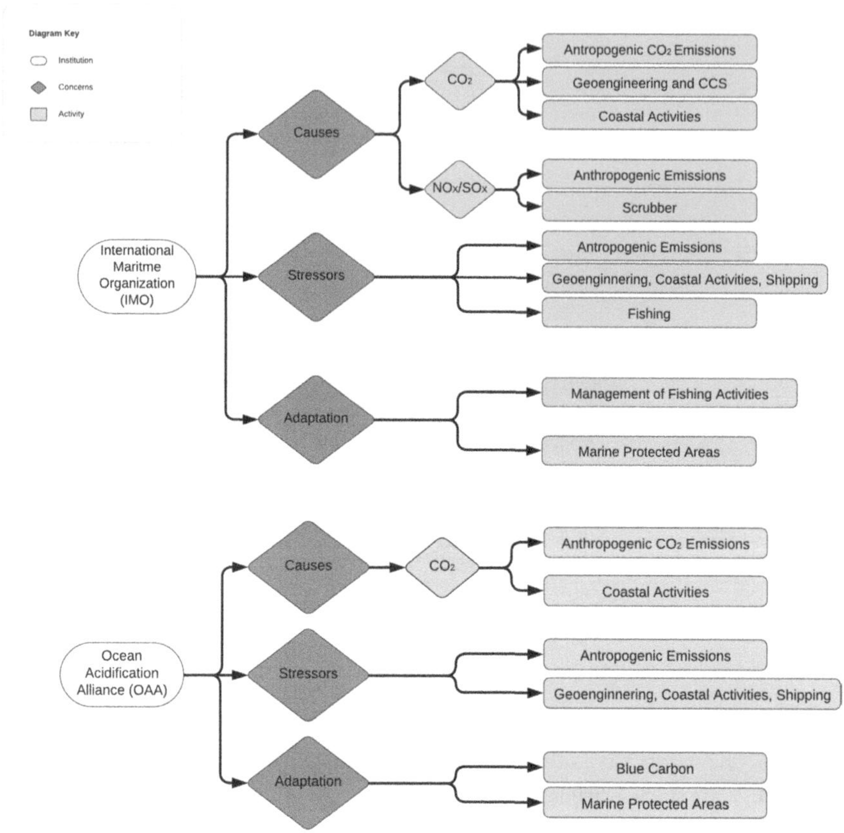

Figure 5.2 Visualisation of breadth and depth for IMO and OAA.
Source: Compiled by the author

As a result, even though OA can be reduced through the CCR, the setup of the regime is not guaranteed to lead to the necessary reduction of CO_2 to address OA.[638] On the contrary, the OA Alliance specialises in OA and aims at its reduction (see also Annex B). In fact, the OA Alliance is the only entity among those studied in Annex B that has an explicit mandate to address OA, making it an interesting case study. Additionally, the IMO will be selected as a case because transportation, specifically the shipping sector, is a continually growing contributor to both CO_2 and NO_x/SO_x emissions.[639] In fact, regarding CO_2 emissions globally, transport is

[638] See, for example, ibid.

[639] Jasper Faber and others, 'Fourth IMO GHG Study 2020 – Full Report and Annexes' (International Maritime Organization (IMO) 2021) wwwcdn.imo.org/localresources/en/OurWork/Environment/Documents/Fourth%20IMO%20GHG%20Study%202020%20-%20Full%20report%20and%20annexes.pdf accessed 27 August 2023; cf. Beatriz Garcia, Anita Foerster and Jolene Lin, 'Net Zero for the International

the second largest contributor, only surpassed by heating/electricity.[640] In addition, shipping is one of the sectors excluded from the much-discussed CCR.[641] The OA Alliance and the IMO not only possess significant potential but also represent two novel and relevant case studies regarding OA.

Second, ideally, the two actors chosen for further study should differ from one another. Disparities indicate distinct styles of governance, and it will be interesting to see if global experimentalist governance will manifest in one actor rather than the other, in both, or in neither. If an actor, such as the IMO or OA Alliance, has significant potential to address OA, then existing or potentially developing experimentalist governance would be particularly effective in tackling the issue. Global experimentalist governance could already be in place or may develop in the future within either or both actors. Moreover, by selecting different cases, a broader range of challenges that institutions might face when applying this governance form to address OA will emerge. Thus, the two case studies can offer insights not only for the OA Alliance and IMO but also for other institutions regarding the usefulness and challenges of applying global experimentalist governance to OA. The IMO and the OA Alliance represent different institutions. It has been noted that the IMO is a specialised UN agency with a large membership.[642] The OA Alliance, in contrast, is a comparatively new and growing actor in both membership and scope.[643] Furthermore, while the IMO has the capacity to adopt instruments that obligate states, the OA Alliance lacks the ability to oblige members through binding instruments.[644] As such, they exhibit different degrees of legalisation.

Third, after deciding that the two institutions are suitable case studies due to their focus on CO_2 and varying degrees of legalisation, individuals working in or with these two organisations were accessible to the author upon request. These contacts facilitated interviews and the collection of additional information, enabling a deeper analysis of the actors. Therefore, Chapters 6 and 7 will discuss the OAA and the IMO, respectively.

Shipping Sector? An Analysis of the Implementation and Regulatory Challenges of the IMO Strategy on Reduction of GHG Emissions' (2021) 33 *Journal of Environmental Law* 85, 86.

[640] Our World in Data, 'CO_2 Emissions by Sector' (*Our World in Data*, 2022) https://ourworldindata.org/grapher/co-emissions-by-sector accessed 1 October 2023.

[641] Michael Traut and others, 'CO_2 Abatement Goals for International Shipping' (2018) 18 *Climate Policy* 1066, 1066.

[642] Cf. IMO, 'International Maritime Organization' (n 529).

[643] Cf. OA Alliance, 'About Us' (*OA Alliance*, 2022) www.oaalliance.org/about accessed 14 September 2022.

[644] IMO, 'Convention on the International Maritime Organization' (n 304) art Part II, article 2(b); Amendments to the Convention on the International Maritime Organization Relating to the Institutionalisation of the Committee on Technical Co-operation in the Convention; Convention on the International Maritime Organization; What do Members Commit to when they Join as Members? OA Alliance, 'FAQs' (*OA Alliance*, 2022) www.oaalliance.org/faqs accessed 14 September 2022.

CHAPTER 6

Case Study I

The Ocean Acidification Alliance

As anticipated in Chapters 4 and 5, this chapter will conduct a case study on the International Alliance to Combat Ocean Acidification (the OA Alliance or OAA). It aims to ascertain whether global experimentalist governance is present for OA within the OAA as an institution. Thus, the chapter will test the OAA against the five elements of the ideal type of global experimentalist governance. This chapter was informed by data obtained from the OA Alliance website, supplemented by four interviews with a representative of the OA Alliance, and further added to by short follow-up conversations (see Annex A). The chapter will briefly introduce the OAA as an institution (Section 6.1), analyse if the five elements of the ideal type of global experimentalist governance are fulfilled in the case of the OAA (Section 6.2), and finally identify if the penalty default functions as a tool within the Alliance (Section 6.3).

6.1 What Is the OA Alliance

The OAA was launched in 2016 at the Our Ocean Conference.[645] The OA Alliance was founded by four subnational governments working together as the Pacific Coast Collaborative (PCC). The PCC is a collaborative effort comprised of leaders from the US states of California, Oregon, and Washington, along with British Columbia in Canada, focusing on energy, climate, and ocean health.[646] This initiative was a direct response to the growing evidence regarding the adverse impacts of climate and ocean change along the North American West Coast. One of those effects was the onset of OA and the associated repercussions on oyster

[645] OA Alliance, 'About Us' (n 643).
[646] OA Alliance, 'FAQs' (n 644) Whose idea was this, to create the alliance?

hatcheries along the coastline in the mid 2000s.[647] In April 2023, the OA Alliance became an initiative of the United Nations Foundation.[648]

Thus far, the OAA has over 145 members from 25 countries, including both governmental and affiliate members. Governmental members consist of sovereign tribal, indigenous, First Nation, municipal, state, and national governments. These national government members comprise large, developed countries from the Global North, including the United States, the UK, and France, as well as small island developing states such as Seychelles, Fiji, and the Cook Islands. The affiliate membership of the OAA includes a diverse range of organisations, from NGOs to seafood industry leaders and local university academics (see also Section 6.2.3).[649] Today, around 300 million people and 366,000 kilometres of coastline are represented by the various members of the Alliance.[650] Since its inception, the OAA has established leadership bodies, including an Advisory Body and an Executive Committee. Overall, the Alliance is dedicated to 'taking urgent action to protect coastal communities and livelihoods from the threat of ocean acidification and other climate–ocean impacts'.[651] In line with this commitment, its mission is to '[t]ransform planning and response to climate-ocean change', and its vision is '[t]o increase ambition for climate action and ensure resilience of marine ecosystems and coastal communities'.[652] To this end, it calls upon members to create an OA Action Plan and provides support and information by sharing resources such as the OA Action Plan Toolkit, technical information exchange, and in-person meetings.[653] More detail about the ways in which the Alliance operates will be provided as this chapter sets out to ascertain the extent to which it practices global experimentalist governance for OA in Section 6.2.

6.2 Testing If the OA Alliance Fulfils the Five Elements of the Ideal Type of Global Experimentalist Governance

In Chapter 4, it was argued that global experimentalist governance is a suitable approach to tackle the problem of OA. This chapter also engaged with how to determine whether global experimentalist governance is present. The five elements of the ideal type of global experimentalist governance can be used to test if this

[647] Ibid; OA Alliance, 'About Us' (n 643).

[648] 'UN Foundation Welcomes OA Alliance!' (*OA Alliance*, 2024) www.oaalliance.org/news/ker0yxuif79nfwz7671tab5iryhacg accessed 18 April 2025.

[649] OA Alliance, 'About Us' (n 643); OA Alliance, 'Current Members' (n 293); OA Alliance, 'OA Alliance Initiative, Executive Committee, Articles of Governance 2023 (Internal Document Provided by OAA Personnel)' 1.

[650] OA Alliance, 'Become a Member and Welcome Packet' (*OA Alliance*, 2022) 2 www.oaalliance.org/general-3 accessed 14 September 2022.

[651] OA Alliance, 'About Us' (n 643).

[652] OA Alliance, 'About Us' (*OA Alliance*, 2024) www.oaalliance.org/about accessed 17 April 2025.

[653] OA Alliance, 'FAQs' (n 644) under: How will the OA Alliance engage and support its members?

type of governance exists within an institution. Thus, the institution, in this case, the OAA, must be 'graded' against the five core elements of global experimentalist governance. Therefore, the following sections will analyse element by element whether the OAA fulfils the criteria identified in Chapter 4. The elements will be discussed in the following order: shared problem (Section 6.2.1) open-ended goals (Section 6.2.2) delegation to lower levels of governance (Section 6.2.3) feedback and peer review (Section 6.2.4) adjustment of overarching goals and metrics (Section 6.2.5). For each element, a short recap of the theory will be given before analysing the presence of the element in the OAA.

6.2.1 Shared Problem

The first element of the ideal type of global experimentalist governance is stakeholder recognition and the definition of a shared problem.[654] The OAA identifies and defines OA as a shared problem, as detailed in Chapter 4, and is explained in the following paragraphs.

The OAA consists of various types of stakeholders. Under the auspices of the OAA, stakeholders come together to address the problem of OA. Two requirements must be present to satisfy the first element of the ideal type of global experimentalist governance. First, the nature of OA as a problem must be such that it is suitable for being tackled through global experimentalist governance. Second, the problem must be 'shared' in the sense that stakeholders have created a common perception of what the problem entails. Each of these requirements will be discussed further below.

The first requirement – OA as a problem that lends itself to being tackled through global experimentalist governance – has been discussed earlier in Chapter 4. Section 4.5 addresses whether experimentalist governance, as a theory, is a suitable match for OA. It was clarified here that global experimentalist governance is appropriate for addressing OA as a problem. The characteristics that make a problem suitable for global experimentalist governance, such as a global dimension, complexity, and uncertainty, are also present concerning OA. The discussion concluded that OA is the kind of issue that may be addressed by global experimentalist governance. For instance, the theory advocates for an adaptable and collaborative approach that can leverage OA's characteristics as a scientific problem and a regime complex. Hence, OA is a problem that can be addressed through global experimentalist governance, satisfying the first requirement.

The second requirement is that the problem must be shared. For a problem to qualify as 'shared', stakeholders must begin to reflect on and discuss it, as outlined in Chapter 4. More precisely, this discussion and reflection should lead to a definition of the issue that experimentalist actors collectively agree upon. OA has gained increasing attention in recent years. Institutions have expressed their concern since

[654] De Búrca, Keohane and Sabel (n 283) 478, 479.

OA poses a threat to the oceanic ecosystem and ecosystem services. The mapping exercise in Chapter 3 has indicated that several institutions already reference OA in relation to their work. This number is expected to rise as more institutions become aware of the issue. Regarding the OAA, the very establishment of the OAA – an institution created specifically to address OA – demonstrates that various stakeholders recognise it as a problem that requires attention.

In addition to discussion and reflection, as mentioned above, stakeholders should also create a common perception of the problem. Such a common perception can manifest in the identification and phrasing of a shared definition of the issue at hand by stakeholders. The OAA identifies OA as a problem and provides explanations and definitions in several places on its website and the documents available on it.[655] The Toolkit, for instance, describes several sources of OA but identifies the number one cause of OA as emissions from CO_2.[656] More specifically, it says: 'The addition of CO_2 to the ocean from burning fossil fuels is making seawater more acidified; we call this process 'ocean acidification' or OA. The chemical reactions that occur lower the pH of seawater and decrease the availability of carbonate, which many species like shellfish, finfish, and coral need to grow, reproduce, and thrive'.[657]

Similar to this definition, other definitions in the Welcome Packet and the Submission to the UNFCCC Ocean and Climate Change Dialogue from June 2022 explain OA, focusing on the CO_2 absorbed from the atmosphere into seawater. These documents further clarify that the chemical material (CO_2) combines with water upon absorption, producing carbonic acid, which acidifies the oceans.[658] The definitions often mention other climate change-driven alterations to the ocean as well as local pollutants that exacerbate OA. These local pollutants, along with other ocean stressors and OA, are causing unprecedented damage to the oceans.[659] According to the definitions, the OAA concentrates on atmospheric CO_2 but acknowledges other ocean stressors and local pollutants as problematic.

In conversations with OAA personnel, it was revealed that the OAA has recently started to develop a 'Glossary of Key Terms' concerning OA. Along with the definition of OA, these terms also include notions such as land-based pollution, which are

[655] OA Alliance, 'Advancing Ocean & Coastal Adaptation – Submission to the UNFCCC Ocean and Climate Change Dialogue, June 2022' https://static1.squarespace.com/static/6006d84247a6a51d636dd219/t/6287d1b38414cb73a19d50c3/1653068212622/OAlliance_UNFCCCOceanDialogue2022_Submission.pdf accessed 4 October 2022; OA Alliance, 'Become a Member' (*OA Alliance*, 2024) www.oaalliance.org/becomeamember accessed 18 April 2025; OA Alliance, 'OA Alliance Action Plan Toolkit' https://static1.squarespace.com/static/6006d84247a6a51d636dd219/t/661f8d8189290b05c9a25e95/1713343878415/OAlliance_APToolkit2024_A.pdf accessed 18 April 2025; State of California, Province of British Columbia, State of Oregon, State of Washington, 'LetterGovernors – Welcome Letter' (2016) https://static1.squarespace.com/static/6006d84247a6a51d636dd219/t/604211fed050703aae69c45d/1614942721743/LetterGovernors.pdf accessed 18 April 2025.

[656] OA Alliance, 'OA Alliance Action Plan Toolkit' (n 655) 6.

[657] Ibid.

[658] OA Alliance, 'Become a Member and Welcome Packet' (n 650) 5; OA Alliance, 'Advancing Ocean & Coastal Adaptation – Submission to the UNFCCC Ocean and Climate Change Dialogue, June 2022' (n 655) 2.

[659] OA Alliance, 'Become a Member and Welcome Packet' (n 650) 5; OA Alliance, 'OA Alliance Action Plan Toolkit' (n 655) 9.

relevant for explaining OA and embedding it within the larger framework of ocean water quality issues (such as warming or rising sea levels). The purpose of the glossary is to enable members to understand and share a common way of communicating about OA as a pressing issue.[660] Therefore, the OAA has identified a problem (namely, OA) and has arrived at an agreed definition for it, as highlighted above. In addition to this definition, the glossary of terms can help create a shared vocabulary regarding OA, making it easier to understand and communicate the problem. As a result, the stakeholders participating in the OAA have developed a common perception of the issue they wish to address.

Even though it is not a necessary condition for qualifying the problem as 'shared', accurate data and ongoing monitoring should inform the processes leading to a common perception. The OAA realises this by organising regular workshops, webinars, technical information exchanges, and similar.[661] These serve to inform stakeholders about many topics, including the latest scientific developments, thus allowing them to stay up to date. Data provided by the institution continuously informs stakeholder agreement on a shared understanding of OA. When new stakeholders join, they receive guidance from the Alliance through the exchange of information concerning recent and relevant science and best practices.[662] Hence, there is a continuous flow of information about scientific data and technological advancements for both existing and new members.

Concerning the first element of the ideal type of global experimentalist governance, both requirements relating to the existence of a recognised problem and 'shared' acknowledgement of its nature and importance are present. As is typical for problems tackled by this form of governance, stakeholders, such as those of the Alliance, recognise the existence and nature of the problem but are unsure how to address it.

6.2.2 Open-Ended Goals

The second element of the ideal type of global experimentalist governance is that stakeholders target the shared problem through open-ended, framework-like goals.[663] Indeed, following the theory of global experimentalist governance, the OAA has identified goals that can be considered open-ended and framework-like (Section 6.2.2.1). These goals are informed and created through the participation of stakeholders from various levels of governance (Section 6.2.2.2). The Alliance's goals and their mode of creation will be described in the following paragraphs.

[660] Interview with OAA Personnel #1, 'OAA Expert Information Exchange #1' (July 2023).

[661] OA Alliance, 'Workshops and Webinars' (*OA Alliance*, 2023) www.oaalliance.org/webinars accessed 13 January 2023; OA Alliance, 'FAQs' (n 644) under: How will the OA Alliance engage and support its members?

[662] OA Alliance, 'FAQs' (n 644) under: How will the OA Alliance engage and support its members?

[663] De Búrca, Keohane and Sabel (n 283) 478; Goldstein and Ansell (n 384) 221.

6.2.2.1 Open-ended and Framework-like Goals

The broad framework goals and metrics to assess progress towards their attainment should be provisional to align with the theory described earlier. While metrics are produced to facilitate the evaluation of the achievement of the goals and take the form of more specific targets, the goals themselves are often loosely worded, lacking detail, and do not include specific timescales. Another way to ensure these features, especially provisionality, is by creating 'living documents', which are open to review and updating. First, the OAA's goals can be found on the website of the Alliance and in various documents prepared by it and sent to members. More precisely, these goals are outlined in the Welcome Packet and the various documents included in this, including the Global Call to Action. Second, metrics are added to the goals, which can provide targets to assess progress towards achieving the goals in the OA Action Plan Toolkit and the Getting Started Document. Third, both the metrics and the goals are provisional.

6.2.2.1.1 Goals First, upon joining the Alliance, new members receive a Welcome Packet containing basic information. The Welcome Packet entails four documents: a general letter (Overview of OA Action Plans), an Invitation Letter from the governors of California, Washington, and Oregon, along with the premier of British Columbia, the Global Call to Action, and a Letter of Commitment affirming the new members' decision to join.[664] Goals are mentioned throughout the Welcome Packet.

The general letter states that the OAA's task is to '[t]ogether, we are increasing ambition for climate action and transforming response to climate-ocean change'.[665] Members are expected to prepare a so-called Action Plan to create ambition for emissions mitigation and address local OA. These plans guide members and help them proactively respond to OA and its impacts.[666] More concretely, the Welcome Packet clarifies that Action Plans can help to achieve the following:

- Reduce atmospheric carbon dioxide emissions, the number one cause of ocean acidification.
- Advance scientific understanding of climate–ocean impacts.
- Reduce local pollutions that exacerbate ocean acidification.
- Protect the environment and coastal communities from climate–ocean impacts.
- Expand public awareness.
- Sustain international and multi-governmental support for addressing this global problem.[667]

[664] OA Alliance, 'Become a Member and Welcome Packet' (n 650) 2; OA Alliance, 'OA Welcome Packet Government Members' 2 https://static1.squarespace.com/static/6006d84247a6a51d636dd219/t/65c39872ea60216b8dffd847/1707317370464/OA_WelcomePacket_GOVERNMENT_2024.pdf accessed 18 April 2025.

[665] OA Alliance, 'OA Welcome Packet Government Members' (n 664) 2.

[666] OA Alliance, 'Ocean Acidification Alliance Action Plan' (*OA Alliance*, 2024) www.oaalliance.org/oaactionplan accessed 18 April 2025; OA Alliance, 'OA Welcome Packet Government Members' (n 664) 2, 3.

[667] OA Alliance, 'OA Welcome Packet Government Members' (n 664) 3.

These six objectives are mentioned at several points in the Welcome Packet, including in the Letter of Commitment.[668] Furthermore, the Global Call to Action, which is essentially the founding document of the OA Alliance, along with the goals that the state's Action Plans should achieve individually, also outlines five goals that the Alliance and its members aim to achieve both individually and collectively. Although these five goals are phrased slightly differently, their content largely overlaps with the other six listed above.[669] All of the goals mentioned by the OAA, including the six goals cited above, can be described as framework-like and open-ended. The language used to define the goals is broad, incorporating terms that lack specificity, such as 'advance', 'reduce', or 'protect'.

Although they seek to induce action, none of the words or goals describe how or to what extent something should be advanced, reduced, or protected. They do not provide concrete measures to be taken or timeframes to abide by. For example, 'reduce atmospheric carbon dioxide emissions' does not indicate by when they should be reduced or by how much. In other words, the goals do not provide much detail. This absence of precision and clarity allows room for members to engage in interpretation, elaboration, and experimentation. Besides the goals, the Welcome Packet itself does not seem to offer any metrics for assessing progress towards the overarching goals. Feedback and peer review can become more challenging as members lack the tools to measure their own or others' success.

In addition to their own goals discussed above, the OAA also endorses and follows open-ended goals set within other frameworks.[670] Apart from that, as pointed out by OAA personnel in conversations, the OAA also contributes to these open-ended goals by raising awareness and making contributions related to science, policy, and financing needs.[671] Examples of these other frameworks include the UN Agenda for Sustainable Development (in particular goals 13 and 14), the UNFCCC, the Convention on Biological Diversity Aichi Targets, and the UN Decade of Ocean Science.[672]

6.2.2.1.2 Metrics Second, while the Welcome Packet does not contain metrics, to make the creation of Action Plans more viable, the Alliance shares resources

[668] Ibid., 4.

[669] OA Alliance, 'International Alliance to Combat Ocean Acidification: A Global Call to Action' https://static1.squarespace.com/static/6006d84247a6a51d636dd219/t/64d2bc821c15727478d960d9/1691532419019/OA_CALL+TO+ACTION_2016.pdf accessed 18 April 2025; OA Alliance, 'OA Welcome Packet Government Members' (n 664) 2; OA Alliance, 'FAQs' (n 644).

[670] As an example of endorsement and support, the OAA has suggested themes for the UNFCCC Ocean and Climate Dialogue which address mitigation and adaptation measures, see OA Alliance, 'Our Impact' (*OA Alliance*, 2022) www.oaalliance.org/ourimpact accessed 4 October 2022; and OA Alliance, 'Advancing Ocean & Coastal Adaptation – Submission to the UNFCCC Ocean and Climate Change Dialogue, June 2022' (n 655).

[671] Interview with OAA Personnel #1 (n 660).

[672] OA Alliance, 'Posters – OA Action Supports International Frameworks' (*OA Alliance*, 2022) www.oaalliance.org/posters accessed 4 October 2022; OA Alliance, 'Our Impact' (n 670).

similar to metrics, including the OA Action Plan Toolkit and a Getting Started Document.[673] These two documents provide more detail regarding the six goals mentioned above. In addition to the Toolkit and the Document, the OAA facilitates learning from other members' general expertise and experiences. The Alliance also provides illustrations of OA mitigation and adaptation strategies at different scales and initiates technical information exchange through webinars, workshops, and in-person meetings.[674] Together with the Toolkit and the Getting Started Document, this additional information can illustrate the order in which steps should be taken. While the information provided by the two documents and the webinars hardly qualifies as specific targets, it can serve as a basis for comparison among different members. This key data can be used to compare where members are in the process of achieving the goals, thereby facilitating a review of members' relative performance. In short, the information provided by the Toolkit, the Getting Started Document, and the webinars, among others, is the closest the OAA has to metrics.

For example, the OA Action Plan Getting Started Document outlines the simple order of steps that members should follow once they join the OAA to establish their Action Plan. These steps include milestones such as '[i]dentify local resources and concerns' or '[b]egin outlining the existing or future actions you might include'.[675] For some steps, examples are also provided; for instance, regarding the outlining of future actions, it suggests 'mitigate causes' or 'assess vulnerabilities'.[676] However, neither the steps nor the examples offer further detail. The reason for this lack of detail is stated at the top of the document, which clarifies that not all Action Plans will share the same framework or structure, as no single solution fits all.[677] This approach is typically seen in global experimentalist governance.

The OA Action Plan Toolkit is a reference aid containing additional information to develop the Action Plans and pursue the abovementioned goals. The Toolkit serves as both a guide and inspiration, suggesting various actions that members can take. Moreover, not all plans resulting from the Toolkit are expected to look identical due to the diverse circumstances related to the issue of OA.[678] As noted above, this acknowledgement of diversity in the Alliance's Toolkit is

[673] OA Alliance, 'OA Alliance Action Plan Toolkit' (n 655); OA Alliance, 'OA Getting Started' (2022) https://static1.squarespace.com/static/6006d84247a6a51d636dd219/t/60196febec250f31a6dc64cd/1612279790011/OAGettingStarted_8.5x14.pdf accessed 4 October 2022; OA Alliance, 'Ocean Acidification Alliance Action Plan' (n 666).

[674] OA Alliance, 'Become a Member' (n 655); OA Alliance, 'OA Alliance Action Plan Toolkit' (n 655); OA Alliance, 'OA Getting Started' (n 673); See also webinars specifically to facilitate the creation of action plans: OA Alliance, 'Unveiling OA Action Plans' (*OA Alliance*, 2023) www.oaalliance.org/webinars/qsks3gbjjcc9xwjsqwhk18laxldwxv accessed 28 July 2023; OA Alliance, 'U.S. State-Led OA Action Planning in the Mid-Atlantic' (*OA Alliance*, 2023) www.oaalliance.org/webinars/nmdyihmf9ge6hgq9742dhr7jd3xmis accessed 28 July 2023.

[675] OA Alliance, 'OA Getting Started' (n 673). [676] Ibid. [677] Ibid.

[678] OA Alliance, 'OA Alliance Action Plan Toolkit' (n 655); OA Alliance, 'Ocean Acidification Alliance Action Plan' (n 666).

characteristic of global experimentalist governance. The OA Action Plan Toolkit is structured around the six different goals, addressing each one individually. For each goal, there is a non-exhaustive list of examples of actions taken by members to achieve that goal.[679]

The metrics described above clearly define further steps that ideally contribute to achieving the six goals. Nevertheless, the information provided in the two documents, the webinars, and so on, does not introduce detailed requirements or targets regarding actions to be taken. To remedy this lack of specificity, in December 2021, the OAA set out to establish metrics to measure performance at the OA Alliance Strategic Planning Meeting.[680] More specifically, in their internal summary and outcome document, provided by personnel of the OAA, it is mentioned that the OAA should '[a]sk members to report out annually on key metrics we identify (such as [net-zero goals; nutrient reductions; stormwater infrastructure; shoreline habitat restoration; and effective marine management])'.[681] According to OAA personnel, the document 'helps outline the metrics we would like to further solidify moving forward – particularly to help illuminate the valuable content and specific items relevant to OA Action Plan development'.[682] Thus, even though the OAA has started making the metrics more concrete, the metrics remain unspecific as of the time of writing.

Overall, it is evident that the OAA has introduced or endorsed broad, open-ended framework goals. However, despite providing members with additional information on how to achieve these goals, these metrics currently lack specificity.

6.2.2.1.3 Provisionality Third, the set goals and metrics are provisional. A way to guarantee this feature is by creating 'living documents', which are open to review and updating. The Executive Committee, part of the OAA leadership, is tasked with providing input 'on OA Alliance programming to advance the work plan'[683] and the Alliance's long-standing goals and obligations.[684] This wording suggests that the work plan, which comprises webinars, training, meetings, tools, and products, is designed to be flexible and adjustable, allowing for advancements as needed.[685] Nevertheless, it is unclear under which conditions or when the work plan can be advanced. Apart from that, the wording does not clarify whether goals or metrics can be adjusted.

That being said, the Alliance values and emphasises the importance of incorporating the latest scientific information into its activities. It also supports so-called international science and monitoring activities, including those by the Global Ocean Acidification Observing Network (GOA-ON), the Ocean Acidification

[679] OA Alliance, 'Ocean Acidification Alliance Action Plan' (n 666); OA Alliance, 'OA Alliance Action Plan Toolkit' (n 655) 5–16.

[680] OA Alliance, 'OA Alliance Strategic Planning Meeting December 2021 Summary and Outcomes (Internal Document Provided by OAA Personnel)' 5.

[681] Ibid. [682] Interview with OAA Personnel #1 (n 660).

[683] OA Alliance, 'About Us' (n 643) Leadership. [684] Ibid. Leadership.

[685] OA Alliance, 'FAQs' (n 644) Leadership.

International Reference User Group (OAiRUG), and the UN Decade of Ocean Science endorsed OA Research for Sustainability (OARS) programme.[686] Activities in this regard include 'scientific information exchange and best practices in the areas of research, monitoring and modeling'.[687] For example, in the context of the OARS programme, the OA Alliance is responsible for leading outcome number 2 to 'identify data and evidence needs for OA mitigation and adaptation strategies, from local to global'.[688] The OA Alliance has produced a white paper setting out a framework for leading this activity.[689] It can be assumed that this knowledge gathering is intended to inform the Alliance's goals and next steps.

Nevertheless, this remains an assumption, and the website does not clarify these processes. Therefore, even though it is likely that goals and metrics are provisional, it is not completely clear from the information on the website. However, in conversations with OAA personnel, it was confirmed that both the goals and the metrics found in the Toolkit are considered living documents open to review and adjustment.[690] Regarding the goals more generally, the personnel confirmed that 'goals and programmatic focus of OA Alliance activities may evolve as science, technology, or members' experiences evolve'.[691] An example of how goals evolved over time was also given during the interview: the case of marine carbon dioxide removal (mCDR) strategies.[692] While mCDR was originally (2016) not included in the relevant research for advancing the goals of the OAA, because of the increase in science and technology in that area and members' experiences, mCDR has gained focus within the OAA.[693] MCDR may '(…) – one day – be updated as an express goal, 'support and advance science and research of mCDR' for example'.[694] In addition to the goals, the Toolkit was also updated in 2020 to integrate what has been learned from conversations with members. For instance, more attention was given to land-based pollution, adaptation, and enhancing resilience.[695]

The above indicates that the OAA establishes metrics that currently lack specificity, along with open-ended and framework-like goals. Both the metrics and the goals are provisional, as required by the theory of global experimentalist governance.

[686] Ibid. How does the OA Alliance connect with other existing international efforts related to ocean acidification?; GOA-ON, 'GOA-ON: OA Research for Sustainability (OARS)' (2023) www.goa-on.org/oars/overview.php accessed 29 July 2023.

[687] OA Alliance, 'FAQs' (n 644) How does the OA Alliance connect with other existing international efforts related to ocean acidification?

[688] GOA-ON, 'GOA-ON : OARS – White Papers' www.goa-on.org/oars/white_papers.php accessed 29 July 2023; Jessie Turner and Richard Bellerby, 'Outcome #2: Identify Data and Evidence Needs for OA Mitigation and Adaptation Strategies, From Local to Global' www.goa-on.org/oars/docs/oars-outcome_2-white_paper-2023.pdf accessed 29 July 2023.

[689] GOA-ON, 'GOA-ON : OARS – White Papers' (n 688); Turner and Bellerby (n 688).

[690] Interview with OAA Personnel #1 (n 660). [691] Ibid.

[692] OA Alliance, 'Perspective on Marine Carbon Dioxide Removal and Related Research' https://static1.squarespace.com/static/6006d84247a6a51d636dd219/t/64d2b154b25a557b3828ac3e/1691529556581/OAA_Perspectives+on+mCDR_FINAL.pdf accessed 15 August 2023; Interview with OAA Personnel #1 (n 660).

[693] Interview with OAA Personnel #1 (n 660). [694] Ibid. [695] Ibid.

6.2.2.2 Goals Created through the Participation of Stakeholders from Various Levels of Governance

In alignment with the theory of global experimentalist governance, the aforementioned goals should have been set through a process that involved the participation of diverse stakeholders from various governance levels. Over time, these goals should be shaped by stakeholders' experiences, including newly discovered technological and scientific knowledge. A wide variety of stakeholders came together to create, and now comprise, the OAA.

The OAA was created in response to growing evidence that climate and ocean change negatively impact the ecosystem and economy. The leaders of the PCC, including the US states of California, Oregon, and Washington, as well as the Canadian province of British Columbia, invited other national and subnational entities to collaboratively establish the OAA together.[696] Hence, the Alliance was founded by various stakeholders from different levels of governance, ranging from the national to the subnational level. That being said, on the website, it is not directly stated who formulated the goals described above. Nevertheless, according to the website, the documents included in the Welcome Packet that mention the goals of the Alliance (for example, the Invitation Letter and the Global Call to Action) have been created by the members of the OAA to welcome and engage new members.[697]

Furthermore, interviews with OAA personnel confirm that the original goals outlined in the Call to Action in the Welcome Packet were drafted, revised, and agreed upon by the founding members.[698] Today, the OAA has gained various types of government and affiliate members, including states, tribes, ports, and cities (see also Sections 6.1 and 6.2.3). All members must, at a minimum, agree to these goals, as all new members subscribe to the objectives set by the Alliance upon joining. Thus, the goals are established through stakeholder participation from various governance levels, and new members commit to these goals.

As seen above, goals are provisional and can be continuously shaped by lived experiences, including those of a diverse membership and science. Additionally, the Alliance underlines the importance of science, as mentioned above, and assists new members by providing information regarding 'the most recent and relevant science and best practices'.[699] Personnel also confirmed that goals have been shaped over time by, for instance, stakeholders' experiences; accordingly, various updates were drafted, revised, and agreed upon in 2019/2022 by the Executive Committee.[700] Thus, over time, goals have been set and shaped by stakeholders' experiences, including technological and scientific knowledge.

[696] OA Alliance, 'FAQs' (n 644) under: Whose idea was this, to create the Alliance?

[697] OA Alliance, 'OA Welcome Packet Government Members' (n 664); OA Alliance, 'International Alliance to Combat Ocean Acidification: A Global Call to Action' (n 669); State of California, Province of British Columbia, State of Oregon, State of Washington (n 655).

[698] Interview with OAA Personnel #1 (n 660).

[699] OA Alliance, 'FAQs' (n 644) under: How will the OA Alliance engage and support its members?

[700] Interview with OAA Personnel #1 (n 660).

Concerning the second element of the ideal type of global experimentalist governance, it can be said that the OAA sets open-ended framework-like goals and metrics. However, the metrics lack specificity. Both the goals and the metrics are provisional. The goals have also been created in a manner that involves the participation of various types of stakeholders and are updated according to members' experiences, as well as developments in science and technology.

6.2.3 Delegation to Lower Levels of Governance

The third element of the ideal type of global experimentalist governance is the so-called delegation to lower levels of governance.[701] Following the theory, the OAA fulfils the requirements of the third element by delegating the identification of solutions to the shared problem to lower-level stakeholders. These stakeholders have the discretion to experiment and adjust practices, provided they operate transparently (Section 6.2.3.1). Furthermore, the lower-level stakeholders of the Alliance are diverse, as demanded by the theory (Section 6.2.3.2).

6.2.3.1 Delegation to Lower-Level Stakeholders with Discretion

As part of the third element of global experimentalist governance, solutions to the shared problem should initially be delegated to lower levels of governance, such as by involving stakeholders who are more familiar with local or regional conditions. Second, these lower-level stakeholders have the discretion to experiment with various strategies and practices to address and tackle the problem. Over time, they can adapt these strategies and practices as they learn more about the issue and potential responses to it. Third, in exchange for this discretion, stakeholders must operate transparently. The theory necessitates that to fulfil the transparency requirement, stakeholders should, among other things, justify their choices while experimenting with different options. The OAA leaves this experimentation, aimed at achieving the aforementioned goals, entirely to its various members, including lower levels of governance. However, the website does not clarify the specific role of these lower levels, as will be explained below.

6.2.3.1.1 Delegation First, regarding delegation, the OAA highlights the important role played by actors operating at lower levels of governance. As introduced earlier, the Welcome Packet and Toolkit outline the goals the OAA is pursuing, which should be realised through Action Plans. Members are encouraged to create these Action Plans with the help of the OAA.[702] The members of the OAA come from various types and levels of governance, including lower levels. These levels of government include national entities such as the French Republic and extend down to local tribes like the Makah Tribe.[703] Therefore, lower levels are

[701] Pinsky, Kruglianskas and Victor (n 397) 728.

[702] OA Alliance, 'Become a Member' (n 655).

[703] OA Alliance, 'Current Members' (n 293).

included in developing methods to achieve the goals, as they are invited to create Action Plans.[704] However, the website does not clarify what role lower levels of governance are expected to play. More concretely, the question arises as to what extent solution-finding in pursuit of the agreed goals is delegated to those members. This question will be discussed further below. It appears that members from all levels of governance should act and create Action Plans. Nevertheless, the Welcome Packet and Toolkit emphasise the role of local levels of governance. This focus on the local level can be seen in several parts of these documents.

For instance, the Alliance's goal number 2, mentioned in both the Welcome Packet and specifically in the Toolkit, is: 'Advance Scientific Understanding of Climate Ocean Impacts, Locally and Globally'.[705] As one of the goals refers specifically to lower levels of governance, it becomes clear that this governance level is an important focus for the OAA. This focus can also be seen in other parts of the Alliance's work. For instance, the Alliance also hosts virtual workshops, which are part of the resources the OAA provides members to create Action Plans and achieve the OAA's goals. Among other things, the workshops focus on 'What Role Can Local And Regional Government Play?'[706] Similarly, the OAA features presentations and actions from 'Tribal and Indigenous Communities of the Front Lines'.[707] Apart from that, they underline the importance of local governments and especially coastal communities for combating OA with posters and infographics.[708] The spreading of this information by the OAA emphasises the role of local and regional actors in combating and adapting to OA. Moreover, the website includes a list of possible local actions that members should aim to undertake. These local actions encompass activities on different levels of governance, many of which are focused mainly on lower levels. An example of an action focused on a lower level would be: 'Creating a local or regional ocean acidification task force or commission to study local impacts, develop strategies to mitigate and adapt'.[709]

The OAA delegates tasks to its members, including those operating at a lower level of governance. Although it is not stated explicitly that lower levels are responsible for experimenting with solutions to the goals, the OAA appears to focus on these levels. The Alliance recognises the importance of lower levels, and work at these levels is encouraged. Given the support the OAA provides its

704 OA Alliance, 'Ocean Acidification Alliance Action Plan' (n 666).

705 OA Alliance, 'OA Alliance Action Plan Toolkit' (n 655) 7.

706 OA Alliance, 'What Role Can Local and Regional Government Play?' (*OA Alliance*, 2022) www.oaalliance.org/webinars/blog-post-title-four-6spzs accessed 5 October 2022.

707 OA Alliance, 'OA Alliance Webinar – Tribes and Indigenous Communities on the Front Lines' (*OA Alliance*, 2023) www.oaalliance.org/webinars/tribes-and-indigenous-communities-on-the-front-lines accessed 29 July 2023.

708 OA Alliance, 'What Can Local Governments Do to Address Ocean and Coastal Acidification?' (2022) https://static1.squarespace.com/static/6006d84247a6a51d636dd219/t/6246cc9c062150292b3ac6de/1648807071761/OA_LocalGovernments_11x17.pdf accessed 5 October 2022.

709 OA Alliance, 'FAQs' (n 644) What do members commit to when they join as members?

members, this demonstrates an expectation that all levels of governance should be involved, underscoring the significance of lower-level actors contributing to the identification of solutions.

6.2.3.1.2 Discretion Second, the theory requires that lower-level stakeholders have the discretion to experiment with different strategies and practices. Members of the OAA are tasked with creating Action Plans aimed at achieving the goals set by the Alliance.[710] The OAA provides assistance in developing these Action Plans through webinars and the like.[711] In particular, the Toolkit suggests steps and actions that can be taken for each goal.[712]

However, apart from this guidance, members, including those at lower levels of governance, are free to explore and implement their preferred approaches to address OA. The OA Alliance website even has a dedicated examples page that shows how different members have completed OA Action plans.[713] The page illustrates that members are trying to reach the goals of the Action Plans in many different ways. It includes all types of members, including those working at lower levels, such as the City of Vancouver, the Port of Seattle, or the Gullah Geechee Nation.[714] Regarding Action 1 of the Toolkit – reduce atmospheric emissions of CO_2 – several stakeholders, including the states of New York and Maine, along with the City of Vancouver and the Port of Seattle, are all working towards reducing emissions in various, sometimes overlapping ways. For example, the City of Vancouver focuses on energy supply and transportation, while the Port of Seattle is undertaking a blue carbon pilot project.[715] Thus, there seems to be discretion for the stakeholders involved to experiment.

6.2.3.1.3 Transparency Third, in exchange for this discretion, stakeholders must work transparently. After their creation, members' Action Plans are included on the website and presented to new members as examples.[716] In addition, Action Plans and information provided by members are shared in webinars, technical information exchanges, workshops, among others.[717] The Alliance therefore 'strengthens the outcomes of member-to-member information sharing'.[718] Through their Action Plans, members show how they are 'proactively responding

[710] See, for example, OA Alliance, 'Become a Member' (n 655). [711] Ibid.

[712] OA Alliance, 'OA Alliance Action Plan Toolkit' (n 655) 5–16.

[713] OA Alliance, 'Member Examples' (*OA Alliance*, 2024) www.oaalliance.org/member-examples accessed 18 April 2025.

[714] Ibid.

[715] Port of Seattle, 'Port of Seattle Ocean Acidification Action Plan' https://static1.squarespace.com/static/6006d84247a6a51d636dd219/t/6122fa91597e8b6a0dfa797b/1629682324883/Port_OA_Action_Plan.pdf accessed 18 April 2025; OA Alliance, 'Case Study: City of Vancouver, British Columbia, Canada' https://static1.squarespace.com/static/6006d84247a6a51d636dd219/t/6481f79f94380172778dbfc8/1686239140858/OA_CaseStudy_VANCOUVER.pdf accessed 18 April 2025; OA Alliance, 'Member Examples' (n 713).

[716] OA Alliance, 'FAQs' (n 644) under: How will the OA Alliance engage and support its members?; OA Alliance, 'Member Examples' (n 713); OA Alliance, 'Become a Member' (n 655).

[717] OA Alliance, 'Become a Member' (n 655). [718] Ibid.

to the impacts of OA and promoting solutions that advance knowledge into local action'.[719] In more detail, '[a]n OA Action Plan encompasses the actions that OA Alliance members will take (or are taking) to better understand the impacts of OA to their region and accelerate OA mitigation, adaptation, and resilience nearshore'.[720] Hence, through the various channels mentioned above, members' Action Plans with their diverse responses and actions are shared and openly accessible. This fulfils the element of transparency. Members from all levels, including the lowest levels, are free to experiment with what suits them best, but they must make that information publicly available.

6.2.3.2 The Large Variety of Stakeholders

In line with the theory of global experimentalist governance and specifically element number three, a broad range of stakeholders should ideally be involved in experimentation and the identification of solutions. These stakeholders can include, for instance, civil society and local communities. As discussed above, including these groups is particularly valuable, as it may provide them with a voice, build credibility, promote shared ownership over solutions, encourage a shared future vision, and increase accountability. The OA Alliance has many different types of members, as indicated by the list on the Alliance's website, which has already been mentioned above.[721]

As indicated above (see Section 6.1), governmental members of the Alliance come from all levels and types of government. These members include tribes, First Nations, ports, cities, regions, provinces, and countries, all of which share a concern about the repercussions that OA might have. All these governmental actors aim to advance the science behind OA and identify effective response strategies.[722] In addition to these governmental members, the OAA has affiliate members striving to advance knowledge and draw attention to the issue. These affiliate members include local universities, NGOs, industry, businesses, to name a few.[723] Overall, the Alliance welcomes and includes members at 'all stages of learning about and responding to ocean acidification'.[724] Hence, the Alliance encompasses a wide variety of stakeholders, consistent with the theory of global experimentalist governance.

Concerning the third element of the ideal type of global experimentalist governance, it can be concluded that the OAA delegates tasks to its members, including those operating at lower levels of governance. However, while global experimentalist governance as a theory calls for the lower levels to be in charge of finding solutions, the OAA appears to allocate this responsibility to every level. Consequently, it is questionable whether only the lower levels are chiefly responsible for

[719] OA Alliance, 'Ocean Acidification Alliance Action Plan' (n 666). [720] Ibid.

[721] OA Alliance, 'Current Members' (n 293). [722] Ibid. Government Members.

[723] Ibid. Affiliate Members.

[724] OA Alliance, 'FAQs' (n 644) What is the international alliance to combat ocean acidification and what will it do?

finding solutions to the goals. In any case, the OAA seems to focus on those levels. Furthermore, regarding the lower levels' discretion to experiment, the OAA grants all members, including the lowest levels, with the discretion to experiment with strategies and solutions. In alignment with global experimentalist governance, these strategies and solutions must be shared with other members to ensure transparency. Ultimately, as is typical for global experimentalist governance, the OAA engages in participatory and multilevel cooperation.

6.2.4 Feedback and Peer Review

The fourth element of the ideal type of global experimentalist governance is feedback and peer review.[725] To fulfil this element of the theory, Chapter 4 notes that reporting will be regarded as the first step (Section 6.2.4.1), peer review as the second step (Section 6.2.4.2), and feedback as the last step (Section 6.2.4.3).

6.2.4.1 Reporting

According to the theory, reporting involves local units sharing information about their performance concerning their achievement of the metrics and goals. This information is meant to be shared with other local-level actors.

The, within the metrics section, already mentioned internal Strategic Planning Meeting in December 2021, and more precisely, its Summary and Outcomes document mentions reporting under 'Bigger questions and Metrics'.[726] It has been seen that the OAA has goals and metrics. Although metrics currently lack specificity, the OAA has started making metrics more concrete. More specifically, the Summary and Outcomes document foresees annual reporting on key metrics, including specific targets regarding 'net-zero goals; nutrient reductions; stormwater infrastructure; shoreline habitat restoration; and effective marine management'.[727] However, since the metrics have yet to undergo the process of becoming more specific, reporting on achievements concerning them is inevitably limited as things stand.

One may even go further, as OAA personnel confirmed during interviews that reporting is not yet being systemically conducted. Regarding reporting, they say that '[i]t hasn't happened as of yet, though we are beginning to develop and socialize member surveys and intake forms to help capture this information and report on metrics'.[728] Even though member surveys have recently started,[729] without

[725] De Búrca, Keohane and Sabel (n 283) 478; Goldstein and Ansell (n 384) 221.

[726] OA Alliance, 'OA Alliance Strategic Planning Meeting December 2021 Summary and Outcomes (Internal Document Provided by OAA Personnel)' (n 680) 5.

[727] Ibid. [728] Interview with OAA Personnel #1 (n 660).

[729] OA Alliance, 'OA Alliance Member Communications Survey 2020 (Internal Document Provided by OAA Personnel)'; OA Alliance, 'Supporting Member Messaging Comms Survey 2021 (Internal Document Provided by OAA Personnel)'.

specific metrics in place, reporting, as required by this element of the ideal type of global experimentalist governance, is minimal and only in the process of being set up. In particular, even with member surveys in place that carry information back to the central unit, reporting between local-level actors is lacking.

6.2.4.2 Peer Review

After reporting, the information provided by the local units becomes subject to peer review. Local actors compare their results from their experimentation and evaluate each other's progress towards achieving the goals. In this process, information is pooled, allowing for the identification of best practices, the recording of general lessons, and the acknowledgement of challenges. The gathered information is then communicated to the central unit for consideration.[730]

With reporting on metrics still in its infancy and currently limited to the central unit, peer review becomes challenging. Nevertheless, even in the absence of comprehensive reporting, the Alliance has processes that resemble the comparison and evaluation of results, particularly through the pooling of information, including best practices, as required by the theory. Within the Alliance, webinars, in-person meetings, and workshops facilitate the comparison, evaluation, and pooling of information. More specifically, during these events, the OAA showcases and exchanges expertise, experiences, and technical information.[731] In particular, the Alliance promotes information exchanges regarding recent scientific developments and best practices (see paragraph below) and provides access to already designed Action Plans and case studies.[732] These case studies can offer examples and foster learning. Thus, case studies serve to compare and review different cases and consolidate measures or steps previously employed by others that have proven successful.

As a result, information collected by members, along with scientific and technological data, is presented and exchanged. This showcasing and exchange of expertise and information during meetings facilitates communication and review, as well as the pooling of information as suggested by the theory. Concerning the pooling of information and best practices, the Alliance has already catalogued actions and steps in the Toolkit. The Toolkit indicates that actions and steps could be undertaken to achieve the overarching goals set by the OAA. Although not explicitly stated in the Toolkit, Alliance personnel describe it as a living document.[733] As such, the Toolkit can be revised and expanded as experimentation, science, and technology advance. Therefore, the OAA and its members pool information, review the data, and create best practices. Despite the efforts outlined here, best practices cannot truly be synthesised from reporting, comparison,

[730] Goldstein and Ansell (n 384) 230, 238.
[731] OA Alliance, 'FAQs' (n 644) How will the OA Alliance engage and support its members?; OA Alliance, 'Become a Member' (n 655).
[732] Ibid; OA Alliance, 'Member Examples' (n 713).
[733] Interview with OAA Personnel #1 (n 660).

and review, as the metrics are not concrete enough. According to OAA personnel, best practices are instead created from 'annual one-on-one calls with members, member-driven webinars and workshops'.[734] When the OA Alliance mentions '"best practices" [they] can also be described as developing and sharing systems for identifying local information needs for purpose'.[735]

In addition, the OAA states on its website that '[a]s the science, research and observed impacts (...) continue to grow, there is need for increased knowledge exchange and expertise on the substance and process for developing local, regional and national responses'.[736] Thus, the Alliance recognises the need to exchange knowledge and expertise on both substance and processes at multiple levels as the science and understanding of OA increases.

The OAA clearly has processes in place that resemble peer review, including comparison, evaluation, and pooling of information. Nevertheless, without specific metrics and reporting on these metrics, comparison, evaluation, and pooling cannot live up to the ideal type of global experimentalist governance. For instance, without reporting, the comparison and evaluation of measures between members do not allow the members to identify best practices as envisioned by the theory; rather, it is the Alliance (central unit) that collects these best practices. However, the theory intends for local actors to evaluate the results of experimentation by appraising each other's progress and identifying best practices. Only after this process is the gathered information supposed to be communicated to the central unit for consideration.

6.2.4.3 Feedback

As the final step of the feedback and peer-review element of the ideal type of global experimentalist governance, feedback on the results needs to be provided to the lower-level units by both their peers and the central unit. Similar to the previous step, although feedback can only be provided to a certain extent, as reporting, comparison, evaluation, and pooling of best practices are present but limited, the OAA has processes that resemble feedback as required by the theory. The feedback and review process can be facilitated in several ways.

It has been observed that the OAA is sufficiently aware of members' actions to sometimes identify best practices.[737] Through the aforementioned webinars, in-person meetings, and workshops, as well as Action Plans created by members, the OAA learns about members' activities. For instance, Action Plans are published on the website and presented during meetings. This process enables the Alliance to gain insight into both the process and the completed Action Plans. Consequently, the OAA is well acquainted with the strategies of the individual members. However, it raises questions about how thoroughly members' strategies

[734] Ibid. [735] Ibid. [736] OA Alliance, 'FAQs' (n 644) Why is the OA Alliance needed?
[737] Cf. Interview with OAA Personnel #1 (n 660).

in general, and their Action Plans specifically, can be evaluated by the OAA (or other members), particularly after the plans are finalised. Thus, even though there is communication across different levels (as seen under peer review), including the lower levels, it remains uncertain to what extent the OAA can assess their approaches and provide feedback on potential improvements.

Additionally, the exchange of different types of information, including access to Action Plans, previously conducted case studies, and more, is intended to assist members in creating, reviewing, and adjusting their own plans based on what has worked for others. However, it is not stated anywhere that members are expected to consider other members' experiences. The website does not specify the extent to which members must take into account the recommendations or best practices of the Alliance and other members. In fact, the only commitment that Alliance members make upon joining is to create a unique Action Plan, which should align with one or more of the goals (see element two, open-ended goals) of the Alliance.[738]

OAA personnel clarified in interviews that, at least regarding Action Plans, feedback from both members and the OAA (central unit) is provided to other members. For example, the Executive Director of the Alliance offers feedback during the drafting process and even sits on the Steering Committee for OA Action Plans.[739] Regarding members' feedback to other members, OAA personnel said, 'We have also cross-pollinated members – sharing OA Action Plan drafts or providing direct introductions across governments to those leading the OA Action Plan drafting process'.[740]

Therefore, after considering both the website and interviews, it can be said that members' actions are known to the Alliance and other members. Some feedback is provided, however, only in relation to Action Plans. According to Alliance personnel, members take recommendations and feedback regarding Action Plans seriously, even though a formal requirement to consider feedback is lacking.[741] Nevertheless, since feedback is expected to be provided after reporting, comparison, evaluation, and pooling of best practices, and those processes are not being conducted as envisioned by the theory, feedback can also only be limited. For example, feedback cannot focus on the selected members' best practices, as those were chosen by the OAA instead, as noted above.

To conclude the fourth element of the ideal type of global experimentalist governance, it can be said that the Alliance does have forms of reporting, comparison, evaluation, pooling of best practices, and feedback, but not in the ways the theory requires. However, it seems that this could change in the future as the Alliance plans to make metrics concrete and require more systematic reporting of them. Once those metrics are specified and reporting is required, the subsequent steps in the process could also be accomplished as envisioned by this element of the ideal type of global experimentalist governance.

[738] See OA Alliance, 'FAQs' (n 644) under: What do members commit to when they join the Alliance?
[739] Interview with OAA Personnel #1 (n 660). [740] Ibid. [741] Ibid.

6.2.5 Adjustment of Overarching Goals

The fifth and final element to be discussed is that feedback and peer review should continuously inform the framework's goals, metrics, and even the problem definition itself, which are regularly adjusted.[742] This is because knowledge collected during the process may raise questions about the previously agreed open-ended goals and metrics. In other words, goals, metrics, and the problem definition should evolve over time in response to what has been learned from feedback and peer review. This chapter has shown that the OAA has six framework goals, metrics (albeit unspecific ones), and the problem definition mentioned above.

The Alliance's long-standing goals and obligations are provided through the Executive Committee of the OAA.[743] The Executive Committee can also provide input 'to advance the work plan' as discussed above under element 2 ('open-ended goals') and, more specifically, 'provisionality'.[744] As previously mentioned, this work plan includes webinars, training sessions, meetings, tools, and products.[745] This task assigned to the Executive Committee suggests that the work plan – including tools and products, such as the Toolkit, which includes the (unspecific) metrics – is not rigid but can be adjusted. This possibility of reviewing and adjusting the Toolkit and its metrics was confirmed in conversations with OAA personnel.

It was also confirmed during interviews that the goals of the OAA are adjustable.[746] Personnel specifically mentioned that the goals of the OA Alliance can evolve in accordance with developing science, technology, and members' experiences.[747] An example of how goals evolved over time was even given – namely, mCDR (marine carbon dioxide removal) strategies.[748] Originally, mCDR was not included in the relevant research for advancing the goals of the OAA, but the issue gained attention because members' experiences, as well as advancements in science and technology in the area, are increasing.[749] Additionally, the Toolkit was updated in 2020 to integrate what has been learned from members in conversations, and more attention was given to land-based pollution, adaptation, and resilience.[750]

In summary, the Alliance's goals, metrics, and so forth, are open to review and adjustment, specifically in accordance with evolving science and technology and members' experiences. However, since the feedback and peer-review cycle do not currently meet the standards of the ideal type of global experimentalist governance, these processes cannot adequately inform adjustments. Before concluding this discussion of the five elements and thus the presence of global experimentalist governance in the OAA, the potential existence of a penalty default will be briefly considered.

[742] De Búrca, Keohane and Sabel (n 283) 478. [743] OA Alliance, 'About Us' (n 643) Leadership.
[744] Ibid. Leadership. [745] OA Alliance, 'FAQs' (n 644) Leadership.
[746] Interview with OAA Personnel #1 (n 660). [747] Ibid.
[748] OA Alliance, 'Perspective on Marine Carbon Dioxide Removal and Related Research' (n 692); Interview with OAA Personnel #1 (n 660).
[749] Interview with OAA Personnel #1 (n 660). [750] Ibid.

6.3 Penalty Default

As noted earlier, the penalty default is a tool to guide unwilling or reluctant actors and penalise non-cooperation.[751] More specifically, the central unit threatens to revert to traditional forms of rule-making that are beyond the actors' control if they refuse to cooperate.[752] The option of bargaining instead of having an imposed official solution is preferred, as actors can influence the outcome and potentially reach a more favourable solution.[753] Given the nature of the OAA, it is doubtful that the actor can impose a penalty default on its members.

The OAA is an actor where different types of stakeholders from various levels of governance come together to tackle OA on a voluntary basis. According to the Alliance's website, all that members commit to upon joining and supporting the Call to Action is to create an OA Action Plan. Action Plans should address at least one of the goals outlined in the Call to Action.[754] In addition, the website underlines that joining the OAA does not have any legal effects or impose any legally binding obligations.[755] Considering the voluntary basis of the OAA and the fact that their joining will have no legal effects, it is unlikely that the OAA would or even could threaten to revert to traditional forms of rule-making in case of non-cooperation. Instead, members are simply 'encouraged' to work together with others to approach OA.[756] From what has been described in this chapter, it can be said that the work of the Alliance is primarily focused on influencing policy at the national and international levels by exchanging information and identifying and disseminating best practices and standards on a voluntary basis. Hence, the OA Alliance is not operating under the so-called shadow of the penalty default.[757]

6.4 Global Experimentalist Governance within the OA Alliance

To conclude, the OAA has been assessed against the five elements of global experimentalist governance to determine if its architecture and functioning align with this ideal type. This chapter has analysed each element to see if the OAA resembles the architecture of global experimentalist governance.

There is an agreement among Alliance members regarding a shared problem, and goals and metrics have been established to address this issue. Nevertheless, the

[751] Zeitlin (n 386) 4; De Búrca, Keohane and Sabel (n 283) 478, 784; Goldstein and Ansell (n 384) 221.

[752] Sabel and Zeitlin, 'Learning from Difference: The New Architecture of Experimentalist Governance in the EU' (n 386) 5; Sabel and Zeitlin, 'Experimentalist Governance' (n 410) 176; Zeitlin (n 386) 4.

[753] Karrkainen (n 486) 297; see also Ayres and Gertner (n 486).

[754] OA Alliance, 'FAQs' (n 644) What do Members Commit to When They Join as Members?

[755] Ibid. Will It Cost to Join the Alliance, am I Making a Binding Commitment of Time or Future Resources?

[756] Ibid. What Do Members Commit to When They Join as Members?

[757] See De Búrca, Keohane and Sabel (n 283) 478.

metrics currently lack specificity and do not set precise targets that can be used to evaluate members' performance. Although the Alliance intends to develop more concrete targets in the future, this is not the case at present. The lack of specificity in the metrics also complicates reporting on them and diminishes the value of peer review and feedback for members. Therefore, insufficiently precise metrics can undermine the reporting process, peer review, and feedback, thus rendering the recursive learning process of global experimentalist governance less effective. As this process is an essential feature, it reduces the realisation of global experimentalist governance within the OA.

However, the Alliance has established processes that facilitate learning, as seen throughout this chapter. In addition, as evidenced by internal documents and insights gained during conversations with OAA personnel, the OAA aims to make metrics concrete and implement more formal reporting requirements in the future. This change could enhance the presence of experimentalist governance in the OAA and should therefore be encouraged. Thus, in the future, the architecture of the Alliance could more closely resemble the ideal type of global experimentalist governance. Nonetheless, it remains uncertain whether the OAA has the capacity to devise a penalty default given the voluntary nature of cooperation within it and the absence of legal powers.

CHAPTER 7

Case Study II

The International Maritime Organization

Chapters 2 and 5 have already touched upon the ways in which shipping contributes to the causes of OA and other ocean stressors. In particular, exhaust gases produced by the shipping industry include CO_2, NO_x, and SO_x. Once these compounds enter the ocean, as outlined in Chapter 2, they cause OA. Worldwide, transportation is the second largest contributor of CO_2, surpassed only by heating/electricity.[758] Shipping, as part of transportation, is a continually growing source of CO_2 emissions.[759] In addition, shipping is one of the sectors excluded from the much-discussed CCR and therefore requires separate consideration.[760]

Also, NO_x and SO_x are emitted by the shipping industry.[761] In fact, shipping is likely the most significant source of NO_x and SO_x emissions concerning their contribution to OA. Highly trafficked shipping lanes, harbours, and coastal areas are particularly affected by OA due to their proximity to the sources of these gases. Research indicates pH decreases because of NO_x and SO_x in these heavily trafficked areas, which have dimensions comparable to CO_2-driven acidification.[762] Apart from that, SO_x, and to some extent, NO_x, are directed through so-called scrubbers directly into ocean waters. Following the introduction of regulations to reduce NO_x and SO_x emissions,[763] exhaust gas cleaning systems, such as scrubber technology – including harmful but cheaper open-loop scrubbers – have been implemented to ensure compliance with these regulations.[764] This technology particularly removes SO_x from the exhaust gas to be released into the atmosphere and disposes of it as

758 Our World in Data (n 640).

759 Faber and others (n 639).

760 Traut and others (n 641) 1066.

761 Turner and others (n 121); Hassellöv and others (n 107); Hunter and others (n 107).

762 Hassellöv and others (n 107) 2731; Turner and others (n 121) 369.

763 International Convention for the Prevention of Pollution from Ships, 1973, as modified by the Protocol of 1978 (MARPOL 73/78) annex VI, Reg. 13, Reg. 14.

764 Cf. Turner and others (n 121) 369, 370; Endres and others (n 168) 1, 2.

acid wash into the ocean.[765] Therefore, the water released back into the ocean after the process has a very low pH.[766] In addition, shipping can also contribute to ocean stress. For instance, as noted in Chapter 2, shipping can release nutrients (through scrubbing)[767] and other pollutants into the ocean and endanger the marine environment through oil spills or dumping.[768]

This brief summary demonstrates that shipping is a sector contributing to OA and other ocean stressors. The actor in charge of regulating shipping, which has the capacity to act on reducing the causes and stressors of OA emitted by this sector, is the IMO. Thus, in the following section, the IMO will be introduced along with the relevant instruments within its purview that can address the causes of OA and other ocean stressors (Section 7.1). Subsequently, the IMO's response to climate change will be discussed in detail to evaluate the extent to which global experimentalist governance is reflected in its responses to the issue of OA (Section 7.2). Then, the presence of penalty defaults within the IMO will be considered (Section 7.3) before concluding (Section 7.4). This chapter draws on information obtained from the IMO website and eight interviews with IMO delegates and experts (see Annex A).

7.1 The IMO

The International Maritime Organization, or IMO, is a specialised agency of the United Nations responsible for regulating international shipping.[769] The IMO was established on 6 March 1948 after a convention that founded the IMO was adopted during an international conference in Geneva.[770] Before receiving its current name in 1982, the IMO was known as the Inter-Governmental Maritime Consultative Organization. The IMO held its first meeting in 1959.[771]

Regarding the structure of the IMO, the Secretary-General leads the IMO, supported by a secretariat based in London at the headquarters of the organisation.[772] In addition, the assembly comprises all of the IMO's member states.[773] The Assembly is responsible for approving the work programme, voting on the budget, and financial agreements.[774] Apart from that, the IMO Council, which oversees

[765] Endres and others (n 168) 5, 6; Turner and others (n 121) 370.
[766] Endres and others (n 168) 6; Turner and others (n 121) 370; Dulière, Baetens and Lacroix (n 170) 9.
[767] Endres and others (n 168) 3, figure 1; Turner and others (n 121) 376.
[768] Vikas and Dwarakish (n 192) 384.
[769] Under: 'What Is the International Maritime Organization (IMO)?' IMO, 'Frequently Asked Questions' (2019) www.imo.org/en/About/Pages/FAQs.aspx accessed 1 September 2023.
[770] Under: 'What Is the International Maritime Organization (IMO)?' ibid.
[771] Under: 'What Is the International Maritime Organization (IMO)?' ibid.
[772] IMO, 'Convention on the International Maritime Organization' (n 304) arts 12, 33, 44(a).
[773] Ibid., 13.
[774] Under: 'How Is IMO Structured?' IMO, 'Frequently Asked Questions' (n 769).

the organisation's work, is its executive organ.[775] The IMO has five main committees, one of which is the Marine Environment Protection Committee (MEPC).[776] In addition, the Intersessional Working Group on Reduction of GHG Emissions from Ships (ISWG-GHG) addresses the reduction of GHG emissions from shipping (including CO_2), and the results of the working group are then considered during meetings of the Marine Environmental Protection Committee.[777] Calling the Intersessional Working Group facilitates quicker agreement on this highly debated issue.[778] As of 2024, the IMO has 175 member states (including three Associate Members: the Faroe Islands, Hong Kong, and Macau), 66 intergovernmental organisations with observer status, and 88 international non-governmental organisations with consultative status.[779]

The IMO was established to regulate and create an international framework aimed at improving shipping safety.[780] Nowadays, the focus of the IMO extends beyond shipping safety, as highlighted in Chapter 5, encompassing environmental concerns, among other topics.[781] These environmental issues, including pollution, were incorporated with the 1977 amendment to the IMO Convention, as these considerations emerged as significant problems following the Torrey Canyon disaster.[782] More specifically, one of the current objectives of the IMO is to prevent and control marine pollution from ships, as defined by article 1(a) of the IMO Convention and the IMO's mission statement.[783] The convention and the mission statement indicate that the overall environment and marine pollution from ships, in particular, have become critical areas of concern for the organisation. To achieve this objective, the IMO has developed various legal instruments. The following paragraphs will provide a brief summary of the primary instruments through which the IMO addresses the causes of OA, specifically NO_x/SO_x and CO_2 (for a longer explanation, see Chapter 5). Additionally, it will be demonstrated that

775 Under: 'How Is IMO Structured?' ibid.

776 Under: 'How Is IMO Structured?' ibid; IMO, 'Marine Environment' (2019) www.imo.org/en/OurWork/Environment/Pages/Default.aspx accessed 1 September 2023.

777 See, for example, IMO, 'Intersessional Working Group on Reduction of GHG Emissions from Ships (ISWG-GHG 15), 26–30 June' (2019) www.imo.org/en/MediaCentre/MeetingSummaries/Pages/Intersessional-Working-Group-on-Reduction-of-GHG-Emissions-from-Ships-(ISWG-GHG-15),-.aspx accessed 1 September 2023; IMO, 'Marine Environment Protection Committee (MEPC)' (2019) www.imo.org/en/MediaCentre/MeetingSummaries/Pages/MEPC-default.aspx accessed 1 September 2023.

778 Garcia, Foerster and Lin (n 639) 91, 92.

779 IMO, 'Member States, IGOs and NGOs' (2019) www.imo.org/en/About/Membership/Pages/Default.aspx accessed 1 September 2023; IMO, 'Member States' (2019) www.imo.org/en/OurWork/ERO/Pages/MemberStates.aspx accessed 1 September 2023.

780 IMO, 'Brief History of IMO' (n 531).

781 Ibid.

782 IMO, 'Convention on the International Maritime Organization' (n 304); IMO, 'Brief History of IMO' (n 531); Amendments to the Convention on the International Maritime Organization Relating to the Institutionalization of the Committee on Technical Co-operation in the Convention.

783 IMO, 'Convention on the International Maritime Organization' (n 304); Amendments to the Convention on the International Maritime Organization Relating to the Institutionalization of the Committee on Technical Co-operation in the Convention; Convention on the International Maritime Organization; IMO, 'Strategic Plan for the Organization' (n 304).

the IMO is also engaged in geoengineering, which, as discussed in Chapter 2, can also contribute to OA. Finally, the potential for the IMO to address other causes of ocean stress will be briefly described.

To tackle air pollution from ships (including NO_x/SO_x), MARPOL 73/78 was drafted.[784] MARPOL 73/78 is the IMO instrument that targets ocean pollution from ships, including accidental pollution and pollution from operational routines. According to the general obligation in article 1, this instrument prevents pollution from 'harmful substances' through 'discharge'. In line with the definitions in article 2(2) MARPOL 73/78, these 'harmful substances' include substances that can, for example, damage living resources and marine life. In addition, any release of a 'harmful substance' from a ship is considered a 'discharge' according to article 2(3)(a) and therefore needs to be prevented. Air pollution via NO_x/SO_x falls under these definitions and accordingly needs to be prevented, as noted in Chapter 5. In fact, the instrument dedicates annex VI to preventing air pollution from ships and limits NO_x/SO_x, which are among the primary air pollutants in ships' exhaust gas.[785]

In contrast to these clear regulations aimed at tackling air pollution through NO_x/SO_x, marine pollution via NO_x/SO_x from scrubbing has not been recognised as an issue that the IMO should address, despite its negative consequences for the ocean. Although voluntary guidelines exist, there are no limitations relevant to OA concerning the use of scrubber technology, particularly open-loop scrubbers, which are most pertinent for OA. Conversely, scrubbing began to be mainstreamed to ensure compliance with stricter air quality standards in 2020 when, under the auspices of the IMO, a new limit on the sulphur content of fuel oil came into force.[786] Therefore, scrubbing is viewed as a legitimate method for reducing high sulphur levels and meeting established air pollution limits.[787] Thus, despite the IMO's objective to prevent pollution, there are no specific regulations addressing scrubbing.

The IMO has raised its focus on reducing greenhouse gases from ships ever since the additional Chapter 4 on energy efficiency for ships to annex VI of MARPOL was adopted by the MEPC in 2011[788]. Accordingly, in April 2018, the same committee adopted Resolution MEPC.304(72) to set up the initial IMO strategy on reducing GHG emissions from ships, followed in October 2018 by the Programme of follow-up actions to this Initial Strategy up to 2023.[789] In July 2023, the IMO

784 International Convention for the Prevention of Pollution from Ships, 1973, as modified by the Protocol of 1978 (MARPOL 73/78); IMO, 'Brief History of IMO' (n 531).

785 IMO, 'Prevention of Air Pollution from Ships' (n 537).

786 IMO, 'IMO 2020 – Cutting Sulphur Oxide Emissions' (n 552).

787 Ibid; IMO, 'Equivalents (SOx Scrubber, Etc.) – Regulation 4' (n 553).

788 IMO, 'Greenhouse Gas Emissions' (n 568).

789 Ibid; IMO, 'IMO's Work to Cut GHG Emissions from Ships' (n 569); International Maritime Organization (IMO), Marine Environmental Protection Committee (MEPC) (n 569).

adopted the Revised GHG Strategy (MEPC.377(80)).[790] This revised strategy has stricter targets for the reduction of GHG emissions.[791] It comprises a higher common ambition 'to reach net-zero GHG emissions from international shipping by or around, i.e. close to, 2050'.[792] To reach this target, the IMO has set indicative checkpoints for 2030 and 2040.[793] Building on the strategies, the MEPC's 83rd meeting in 2025 resulted in a landmark agreement on a 'net zero framework'. This framework establishes the legal text that is intended to achieve the goals set by the revised strategy.[794] The agreement was reached after Saudi Arabia called for a vote, with sixty-three member states voting in favour and sixteen against, the decision threshold being a simple majority.[795] Since the net zero framework is set to become a new chapter V of MARPOL annex VI, it must be formally adopted in October 2025.[796] The net zero framework, as intended by the revised strategy, aims to regulate emissions, including a global levy on a portion of shipping's GHG emissions, a shift away from liquefied natural gas as a marine fuel, and targeted revenue use for zero-emission fuels and equitable transition projects.[797] While expected to generate $11–12 billion annually and push the sector towards net zero by 2050, the agreement's limited emission reductions, complex design, and potential funding gaps may hinder its effectiveness without further support, especially in developing countries. Key implementation details will emerge through guidelines before their expected enforcement in 2027.[798]

Geoengineering is another set of activities that, once operational, will contribute to OA and other ocean stress. As seen in Chapter 2, these activities, although still largely in their infancy, are gaining attention and potential. The IMO has already begun to address geoengineering through the LC/LP.[799] These two instruments otherwise tackle pollution control and prevention regarding dumping.[800] While CCS is allowed under the LC and the LP's 2006 and 2009 amendments, these

790 International Maritime Organization (IMO), Marine Environmental Protection Committee (MEPC) (n 570); IMO, 'Revised GHG Reduction Strategy for Global Shipping Adopted' (n 570).

791 IMO, 'Revised GHG Reduction Strategy for Global Shipping Adopted' (n 570); International Maritime Organization (IMO), Marine Environmental Protection Committee (MEPC) (n 570).

792 Ibid., para 3.3.4.

793 International Maritime Organization (IMO), Marine Environmental Protection Committee (MEPC) (n 570) para 3.4; IMO, 'Revised GHG Reduction Strategy for Global Shipping Adopted' (n 570).

794 IMO, 'Circular Letter No.5005 – Draft Revised Marpol Annex Vi (Secretariat)' (n 575).

795 Tristan Smith and others, 'An Overview of the Discussions from IMO's 83rd Marine Environment Protection Committee' 3 www.shippingandoceans.com/post/phase-out-of-fossil-fuels-in-shipping-begins-in-earnest.

796 IMO, 'IMO Approves Net-Zero Regulations for Global Shipping' (2025) www.imo.org/en/MediaCentre/PressBriefings/pages/IMO-approves-netzero-regulations.aspx accessed 7 May 2025.

797 IMO, 'Circular Letter No.5005 – Draft Revised Marpol Annex Vi (Secretariat)' (n 575) 53–65; See also: Smith and others (n 795).

798 Smith and others (n 795) 3, 4.

799 Convention on the Prevention of Marine Pollution by Dumping of Wastes and Other Matter; London Protocol to the Convention on the Prevention of Marine Pollution by Dumping and Other Matter.

800 IMO, 'Convention on the Prevention of Marine Pollution by Dumping of Wastes and Other Matter' (n 583).

instruments (specifically the 2013 amendment to the LP) strictly regulate ocean fertilisation and other marine geoengineering activities.[801] More concretely, the 2013 amendment to the Protocol includes a definition of geoengineering, adding paragraph 5*bis* to article 1 of the LP. In addition, the 2013 amendment added article 6*bis* to the LP. Pursuant to paragraph 1 of this article, parties shall not permit the release of 'matter' into ocean waters for marine geoengineering activities included in the list in annex 4. The list in annex 4 mentioned in this paragraph includes 'ocean fertilization', which is defined in para 1.1. as a geoengineering activity that forbids the placement of matter (without defining what matter is) into the sea as part of this activity.

Through the presented instruments, the IMO can also mitigate other ocean stress, including the negative repercussions of climate change, such as ocean warming (including MARPOL 73/78, MEPC.377(80)), pollution such as oil pollution (MARPOL 73/78), dumping (LC./LP.), or scrubber effluents (MARPOL 73/78 or LC/LP).

Despite the shipping sector's significant contribution to OA and the various legal frameworks the IMO has established to address the issue, the organisation has only tangentially acknowledged OA as a significant problem. OA is rarely mentioned on the IMO's website, making information about it difficult to find. On the IMO website, OA is only mentioned on a few occasions. Even when it is referenced, the discussions generally sidestep a direct focus on OA, often considering it alongside other issues or listing it among examples.[802] Nevertheless, the IMO clearly recognises the relationship between climate change and OA, and on one occasion acknowledges the link between air pollution from SO_x and OA on its website.[803] In addition to these rare mentions across various pages of the website, a few references to OA can be found in publicly available documents on the site. Regarding SO_x and OA, these documents indicate that the IMO also acknowledges the connection between sulphur scrubbers and OA. For instance, one recent document outlines guidelines for member states on how to assess the environmental and health risks associated with the discharge from scrubbers.[804] OA is cited once, indicating that pH levels of discharge water should be assessed with OA in

[801] International Maritime Organization (IMO), 'LP.1(1)' (n 297); International Maritime Organization (IMO), 'LP.3(4)' (n 297).

[802] IMO, 'IMO and Its Role in Protecting the World's Oceans' (2019) www.imo.org/en/MediaCentre/HotTopics/Pages/oceans-default.aspx accessed 30 August 2023; IMO, 'IMO 2020 – Cleaner Shipping for Cleaner Air' (2019) www.imo.org/en/MediaCentre/PressBriefings/pages/34-IMO-2020-sulphur-limit-.aspx accessed 15 December 2023; 'Ocean Change Requires Solutions – UN Oceans Envoy' (2019) www.imo.org/en/MediaCentre/PressBriefings/Pages/26-oceansenvoy.aspx accessed 15 December 2023.

[803] IMO, 'IMO 2020 – Cleaner Shipping for Cleaner Air' (n 802); IMO, 'IMO and Its Role in Protecting the World's Oceans' (n 802); 'Ocean Change Requires Solutions – UN Oceans Envoy' (n 802).

[804] MEPC, 'MEPC.1-Circ.899 – 2022 Guidelines for Risk and Impact Assessments of the Discharge Water from Exhaust Gas Cleaning Systems' para 6.6.2 wwwcdn.imo.org/localresources/en/OurWork/Environment/Documents/Air%20pollution/MEPC.1-Circ.899.pdf accessed 12 February 2024.

mind.[805] Apart from that, some resolutions related to geoengineering and the LC./LP include references to OA.[806] All these resolutions mention OA in the preambulatory clauses and express general concerns regarding climate change and OA generally.[807] Additionally, two of the resolutions refer to CCS as a potential measure to mitigate climate change and OA.[808] Nevertheless, these are the only references to OA, and the resolutions do not address the potential dangers that CCS poses to the ocean, including increased acidification (see Chapter 2).

During an interview with an internal IMO expert,[809] this apparent lack of concern for OA was confirmed; according to the expert, OA has not been an integral part of the conversations surrounding geoengineering within the Joint Group of Experts on the Scientific Aspects of Marine Environmental Protection (GESAMP).[810] The group advises the IMO regarding marine environmental protection and, as part of its work, strives to comprehend the impacts of geoengineering on the marine environment. In particular, GESAMP advises the parties to the London Protocol and identifies those techniques that should be added to the list in annex 4.[811] Overall, the IMO acknowledges the problem and its relation to climate change, air pollution, and scrubbers through at least SO_x, to the extent that it is occasionally mentioned on the organisation's website or in a few documents. However, the IMO does not have a strong focus on OA and takes no direct action to tackle it. The IMO neither recognises the significant contribution of the shipping sector to OA nor takes responsibility for addressing this contribution. On the contrary, the IMO currently suggests using scrubbers as a technique with no OA relevant limitations, despite their negative influence on the ocean and their ongoing contribution to OA.

Although the organisation takes no specific action to tackle OA, the IMO does regulate OA-relevant aspects of shipping through its efforts to address climate change, air pollution, and geoengineering. Actions taken in these areas reduce some of the causes of OA, albeit indirectly. For this case study, the question remains whether and to what extent global experimentalist governance can be identified within the IMO's areas of work (climate change, air pollution, and geoengineering).

In her paper published in the International and Comparative Law Quarterly, Armeni already tested the 2013 marine geoengineering amendments to the LP against global experimentalist governance.[812] Her analysis of these amendments

805 Ibid.

806 International Maritime Organization (IMO), 'LP.3(4)' (n 297); International Maritime Organization (IMO), 'LP.5(14)' (n 297); International Maritime Organization (IMO), 'LP.1(1)' (n 297).

807 International Maritime Organization (IMO), 'LP.3(4)' (n 297); International Maritime Organization (IMO), 'LP.5(14)' (n 297); International Maritime Organization (IMO), 'LP.1(1)' (n 297).

808 International Maritime Organization (IMO), 'LP.3(4)' (n 297); International Maritime Organization (IMO), 'LP.5(14)' (n 297).

809 Interview with Internal IMO Expert #1 (n 142).

810 Ibid.

811 IMO, 'GESAMP' (2019) www.imo.org/en/ourwork/environment/pages/gesamp.aspx accessed 16 December 2023.

812 Armeni (n 283).

reveals that while there is potential to apply experimentalist governance approaches, there is limited room for cooperation between decision-makers and civil society.[813] Due to this limitation, the ideal type of global experimentalist governance cannot be considered present. Nevertheless, despite this lack of fulfilment of the pure model of this governance form, the regulatory framework for ocean fertilisation under the London Protocol could represent a 'slow shift towards global experimentalist governance'.[814] As Armeni has conducted a thorough analysis of this work by the IMO, this book will not engage in another analysis. However, knowing that Armeni can identify a shift to global experimentalist governance indicates that this governance approach is not foreign to the work of the IMO and might also be found in other areas of work.

With this finding, this chapter focuses on the IMO's responses to climate change and air pollution as possible avenues to determine whether global experimentalist governance is present. Due to space and time constraints, the focus here will be on climate change rather than air pollution. The IMO's response to climate change is selected for three reasons. First, OA is an impact of climate change, and CO_2 is the primary driver of OA, making the IMO's response to climate change a suitable starting point for the analysis. Second, even though the IMO rarely mentions OA, the organisation acknowledges a clear relationship between OA and climate change. On the other hand, only SO_x is identified as a cause of OA, while NO_x remains undiscussed. Additionally, instead of being viewed critically due to their negative repercussions for the ocean environment and therefore regulated by the IMO, scrubber technologies are regarded as a legitimate means to comply with the stricter air pollution regulations. Lastly, as discussed below, with its Initial GHG Strategy, the IMO has begun encouraging states to create and submit so-called National Action Plans (NAPs) to the IMO website. A NAP is, according to Garcia, Foerster, and Lin, 'a national policy or program by which IMO Member States define specific measures to be implemented domestically in order to meet the Strategy's emission reduction targets'.[815] These NAPs resemble the NDCs of the Paris Agreement, which have already been identified as forming part of a global experimentalist governance approach.[816]

Hence, as both the Paris Agreement and the IMO national plans delegate the identification of solutions to specified problems at the national level, it is likely that both NDCs and NAPs form part of the same governance approach. However, even though the IMO's response to climate change is chosen as the focus for discussion, this choice does not imply that features of global experimentalist governance cannot be found elsewhere at the IMO, including in its responses to air pollution through NO_x and SO_x. What is clear, however, is that the IMO has not yet begun to confront the tensions between addressing air pollution through the

[813] Ibid., 899, 904. [814] Ibid., 896, 904. [815] Garcia, Foerster and Lin (n 639) 93.

[816] Ibid., 95; cf. Geng Qin and Hanzhi Yu, 'Rescuing the Paris Agreement: Improving the Global Experimentalist Governance by Reclassifying Countries' (2023) 15 *Sustainability* 3207.

use of scrubbers and responding to OA. These are precisely the kinds of complexities that global experimentalist governance might help to address.

Accordingly, the remainder of the chapter will concentrate on the IMO's response to climate change to identify the extent to which global experimentalist governance is present within its responses to the problem of OA.

7.2 The IMO's Response to Climate Change (Actions against CO_2 Emissions)

Climate change is, in terms of its nature, very similar to OA. It is a global, highly complex scientific problem that has generated a regime complex.[817] Due to these characteristics, OA, as discussed in Chapter 6 and Section 5 of Chapter 4, is susceptible to being addressed through global experimentalist governance. The broader topic of climate change has been examined from the perspective of global experimentalist governance. For example, in their discussion of global experimentalist governance in global public health, Goldstein and Ansell describe the problem of climate change as an example of a 'fundamental transition problem'. They argue that such problems are characterised by complexity and political pluralism, and as a result, more traditional approaches to governance cannot effectively address them.[818] Hence, 'new transnational governance', such as global experimentalist governance, is necessary to tackle such problems.

Similarly, Quin and Yu conclude that climate change necessitates a novel form of governance and discuss possible improvements to the existing framework for global experimentalist governance within the Paris Agreement.[819] At the beginning of the paper, these authors briefly describe the global experimentalist governance design found within the Paris Agreement.[820] Although they recognise that challenges remain in realising global experimentalist governance within the Paris Agreement, they firmly believe that this governance approach can indeed address the problem.[821] Hence, climate change is not merely an issue that can, in the abstract, be tackled through global experimentalist governance due to its characteristics (similar to OA), but this is already occurring in other fora, such as the CCR or, more specifically, the Paris Agreement.

The question arises whether the IMO, like the institutions established by the Paris Agreement, engages in global experimentalist governance in its efforts to tackle CO_2. To answer this question, this chapter will analyse the IMO's initiatives to mitigate GHG (and especially CO_2) emissions from shipping. First, it will provide an overview of how climate change is understood and addressed within the IMO (Section 7.2.1). Second, the Initial and Revised GHG strategies will be

[817] Keohane and Victor (n 326). [818] Goldstein and Ansell (n 384) 220.
[819] Qin and Yu (n 816). [820] Ibid., 2–4. [821] Cf. ibid., 14, 15; Goldstein and Ansell (n 384) 220.

examined as significant instruments that address climate change (Section 7.2.2). Third, the diverse stakeholders involved at various levels of governance within the IMO will be discussed (Section 7.2.3). Lastly, this chapter will consider whether the IMO, through reporting, peer review, and feedback, manages to balance and include these multifarious stakeholders in the fight against climate change (Section 7.2.4). The presence of global experimentalist governance will be explored in relation to these different IMO work procedures.

7.2.1 Understanding and Addressing Climate Change in the IMO

Before arriving at the IMO, discussions regarding climate change as an issue partially caused by CO_2 emissions began in other forums. In response to increasing evidence that CO_2 emissions lead to negative climatic impacts, the UNFCCC was agreed upon in 1992 during the United Nations Conference on Environment and Development in Rio de Janeiro.[822] A few years later, in 1997, the Kyoto Protocol, which aimed to reduce GHG emissions, including CO_2, was adopted and entered into force in 2005 under the UNFCCC umbrella.[823] However, due to their global nature, the Kyoto Protocol addressed emissions from international shipping (and aviation) differently than other GHG emission sources. Instead, action regarding international shipping was to be pursued directly by the IMO.[824] In addition, no further reference is made to the IMO in the 2015 Paris Agreement or the decisions that implement the Paris Agreement. Hence, the question arises: when and how did the IMO commence its battle against climate change? As will be explored in the next paragraph, it has been a lengthy process that is still ongoing.

Considerations of CO_2-induced climate change started in the IMO when, in 1997, Conference Resolution 8 on CO_2 emissions from ships was adopted by the International Conference of Parties to the MARPOL Convention.[825] Among other things, the resolution invites 'the Marine Environment Protection Committee to consider what CO_2 reduction strategies might be feasible in light of the relationship between CO_2 and other atmospheric and marine pollutants'.[826] In addition, in December 2003, Resolution A.963(23) adopted by the IMO Assembly on 'IMO Policies and practices related to the reduction of greenhouse gas emissions from ships' urged 'the Marine Environment Protection Committee to identify and develop the mechanism or mechanisms needed to achieve the limitation or

[822] UNFCCC; IMO, 'Historic Background' (2019) www.imo.org/en/OurWork/Environment/Pages/Historic-Background.aspx accessed 6 October 2023.

[823] Kyoto Protocol to the United Nations Framework Convention on Climate Change 1997 (2303 UNTS 3).

[824] Ibid article 2(2); IMO, 'Historic Background' (n 822).

[825] International Conference of Parties to the MARPOL Convention, 'MP/CONF.3/35 Resolution 8 1997' wwwcdn.imo.org/localresources/en/MediaCentre/PressBriefings/Documents/MP%20CONF.3%2035%20Resolution%208%201997%20CO2.pdf accessed 6 October 2023; IMO, 'Historic Background' (n 822).

[826] International Conference of Parties to the MARPOL Convention (n 825) para 3.

reduction of GHG emissions from international shipping'.[827] After these calls, in 2011, IMO's MEPC adopted a new Chapter 4 to annex VI of MARPOL 73/78 named 'Regulations on energy efficiency for ships'. This chapter aims to reduce the amount of CO_2 emissions from international shipping. According to the IMO's website, it constitutes the 'first ever mandatory global GHG reduction regime for an entire industry sector'.[828]

Then, in April 2018, the IMO, through its Marine Environmental Protection Committee, adopted a resolution (MEPC.304(72)) that established an initial IMO strategy for reducing GHG emissions from ships (Initial Strategy).[829] The Initial Strategy serves as the foundation for international shipping decarbonisation, facilitated by the MEPC.[830] According to IMO's website, '[t]he Initial Strategy envisages for the first time a reduction in total GHG emissions from international shipping (...)'.[831] In October of the same year, the Initial Strategy was followed by the Programme of follow-up actions of the Initial Strategy up to 2023.[832] As planned, in July 2023, the IMO adopted the Revised GHG Strategy (MEPC.377(80)) (Revised Strategy or 2023 Strategy).[833] Building on this, the MEPC's 83rd meeting in 2025 resulted in a landmark 'net zero framework' agreement, introducing a global emissions levy on part of the emissions, discouraging LNG use, and allocating revenues to clean fuels and equitable transition efforts. However, challenges persist regarding its limited impact, complex design, and funding adequacy. Implementation guidelines are expected by 2027.[834] In addition, as the net zero framework is set to become a new Chapter V of MARPOL annex VI, it must first be adopted formally in October 2025.[835]

This string of events shows that climate change has been increasingly and incrementally recognised as a concern to be discussed and reflected under the auspices of the IMO. Ever since the Kyoto Protocol called upon the IMO to tackle the decarbonisation of international shipping, stakeholders through the Assembly and Environmental Protection Committee have begun to address this issue, and

[827] IMO Assembly, 'Resolution A.963(23) – IMO Policies and Practices Related to the Reduction of Greenhouse Gas Emissions from Ships' para 1 wwwcdn.imo.org/localresources/en/KnowledgeCentre/IndexofIMOResolutions/AssemblyDocuments/A.963(23).pdf accessed 6 October 2023.

[828] IMO, 'Greenhouse Gas Emissions' (n 568); MEPC, 'Resolution MEPC.203(62) – Amendments to the Annex of the Protocol of 1997 to Amend the International Convention for the Prevention of Pollution from Ships, 1973, as Modified by the Protocol of 1978 Relating Thereto (Annex 19)' wwwcdn.imo.org/localresources/en/OurWork/Environment/Documents/Technical%20and%20Operational%20Measures/Resolution%20MEPC.203%2862%29.pdf accessed 6 October 2023.

[829] IMO, 'Greenhouse Gas Emissions' (n 568); IMO, 'IMO's Work to Cut GHG Emissions from Ships' (n 569); International Maritime Organization (IMO), Marine Environmental Protection Committee (MEPC) (n 569).

[830] IMO, 'Historic Background' (n 822). [831] Ibid.

[832] IMO, 'Greenhouse Gas Emissions' (n 568); IMO, 'IMO's Work to Cut GHG Emissions from Ships' (n 569); International Maritime Organization (IMO), Marine Environmental Protection Committee (MEPC) (n 569).

[833] International Maritime Organization (IMO), Marine Environmental Protection Committee (MEPC) (n 570); IMO, 'Revised GHG Reduction Strategy for Global Shipping Adopted' (n 570).

[834] Smith and others (n 795); IMO, 'Circular Letter No.5005 – Draft Revised Marpol Annex Vi (Secretariat)' (n 575).

[835] IMO, 'IMO Approves Net-Zero Regulations for Global Shipping' (n 796).

discussions are ongoing. Nevertheless, despite these discussions, no definition of climate change has been agreed upon at the IMO. Instead, for example, both the Initial and the Revised Strategy, when mentioning climate change, refer to elements of the climate change regime such as UNFCCC or the Paris Agreement.[836] For instance, both strategies explain the context in which they are situated and mention that this includes 'their existing instruments related to (…) climate change, including the UNFCCC and its related legal instruments, including the Paris Agreement'.[837] Thus, IMO stakeholders are guided by these agreements and the definitions provided therein. In fact, the climate change regime, and more specifically, the UNFCCC, already define climate change: 'Climate change' means a change of climate which is attributed directly or indirectly to human activity that alters the composition of the global atmosphere and which is in addition to natural climate variability observed over comparable time periods.[838]

Thus, although IMO stakeholders did not create a separate definition of climate change within the IMO, they have agreed to follow the existing definition in international law. Therefore, there is a common agreement among different IMO stakeholders regarding what climate change is and how it is caused. This agreement is an essential part of global experimentalist governance, as it demonstrates that stakeholders share a common problem definition. While relying on the broad definition of climate change coined by the UNFCCC, research commissioned by the IMO continues to be conducted to better understand the shipping sector's contribution to the issue.

More concretely, accurate data and ongoing monitoring inform governance processes within the IMO. In keeping with Resolution MEPC.67(37), which underscores the necessity of evidence-based decision-making and the principle of a precautionary approach, the IMO has commissioned studies since the year 2000 to assess GHG emissions from international shipping and explore ways to reduce them.[839] The four published studies have been prepared by prominent research organisations worldwide, including academic institutions and consultancy firms.[840] These studies have been conducted under the oversight of the IMO Secretariat and a panel of member governments and were approved by

[836] International Maritime Organization (IMO), Marine Environmental Protection Committee (MEPC) (n 570) para 1.6, annex; International Maritime Organization (IMO), Marine Environmental Protection Committee (MEPC) (n 569) 1.5, annex.

[837] International Maritime Organization (IMO), Marine Environmental Protection Committee (MEPC) (n 569) para 1.5.1, annex; International Maritime Organization (IMO), Marine Environmental Protection Committee (MEPC) (n 570) para 1.6.1, annex.

[838] UNFCCC art 1.2.

[839] MEPC, 'MEPC.67(37) – Guidelines on Incorporation of the Precautionary Approach in the Context of Specific IMO Activities (Annex 10)' wwwcdn.imo.org/localresources/en/KnowledgeCentre/IndexofIMOResolutions/MEPCDocuments/MEPC.67(37).pdf accessed 7 October 2023; IMO, 'Historic Background' (n 822); IMO, 'IMO GHG Studies' (2019) www.imo.org/en/OurWork/Environment/Pages/IMO-GHG-studies.aspx accessed 7 October 2023.

[840] For example, UMAS, Dallan Maritime University, icct, see Faber and others (n 639).

the Marine Environmental Protection Committee.[841] IMO GHG studies guide stakeholders and inform the processes within the IMO, including the meetings and discussions of the Marine Environmental Protection Committee. Both the Initial and the Revised Strategy refer to the IMO GHG emissions studies.[842] Furthermore, the Revised Strategy emphasises the importance of researching and monitoring GHG emissions from international shipping to achieve the strategy's objectives (including the reduction of GHG emissions).[843] Thus, it becomes evident that accurate data and monitoring are crucial for IMO processes, particularly those accompanying the strategies to reduce GHG emissions (including CO_2) from shipping. Accordingly, Section 7.2.2 will further analyse the Initial and Revised GHG strategies as instruments to address climate change induced by shipping.

7.2.2 The Initial and Revised IMO GHG Strategy

As explained above, the IMO addresses climate change through its GHG strategies (and possibly through the net zero framework in the future if adopted), establishing goals to tackle the issue. The question at hand is whether the IMO's approach is imbued with features of global experimentalist governance regarding climate change and specifically CO_2 emissions. For global experimentalist governance to be deemed present, certain characteristics should be evident within the strategies. The goals must be open-ended and framework-like (see Chapter 4). Such goals can be found in both the Initial and Revised versions of the strategy. The Initial Strategy was the first emissions reduction target for the entire shipping sector.[844] While the Initial Strategy 'was the first milestone set out in the Road map for developing a comprehensive IMO strategy on reduction of GHG emissions from ships',[845] the 'adoption of the 2023 IMO GHG Strategy is the latest milestone set out in the Road Map'[846] (at least until the adoption of the net zero framework following the goals set in the revised strategy). In accordance with this statement, 'the 2023 IMO GHG Strategy revokes the 2018 Initial IMO GHG Strategy'.[847] Therefore, only the goals and metrics of the 2023 Strategy will be discussed.

[841] IMO, 'IMO GHG Studies' (n 839); IMO, 'Marine Environment Protection Committee (MEPC) 75, 16–20 November (Virtual Session)' (2019) www.imo.org/en/MediaCentre/MeetingSummaries/Pages/MEPC-75th-session.aspx accessed 13 January 2024.

[842] International Maritime Organization (IMO), Marine Environmental Protection Committee (MEPC) (n 569) para 1.6, 4.7.13, annex; International Maritime Organization (IMO), Marine Environmental Protection Committee (MEPC) (n 570) para 1.8, annex.

[843] International Maritime Organization (IMO), Marine Environmental Protection Committee (MEPC) (n 570) para 1.10.3, annex.

[844] Garcia, Foerster and Lin (n 639) 85.

[845] International Maritime Organization (IMO), Marine Environmental Protection Committee (MEPC) (n 570) para 1.4, annex.

[846] Ibid., 1.5, annex.

[847] Ibid., 6, annex 15.

The Revised Strategy establishes 'Objectives of the 2023 IMO GHG Strategy' under para 1.10 of the annex. These objectives clarify what the Revised Strategy aims to achieve.[848] More specifically, the strategy pursues three objectives:

1. enhancing IMO's contribution to global efforts by addressing GHG emissions from international shipping,
2. identifying actions to be implemented by the international shipping sector, as appropriate,
3. identifying actions and measures, as appropriate, to help achieve the above objectives, including incentives for research and development and monitoring of GHG emissions from international shipping.[849]

In addition, and in line with these three objectives, the 'Vision' of the 2023 Strategy states: 'IMO remains committed to reducing GHG emissions from international shipping and, as a matter of urgency, aims to phase them out as soon as possible'.[850] This vision elaborates on a goal for the 2023 Strategy. Members should strive to reduce GHG emissions as soon as possible. Furthermore, the three objectives set goals that should be achieved through the measures outlined by the strategy. It is, therefore, clear that the strategy sets out goals, but the question remains whether these goals can be considered open-ended and framework-like.

To answer this question, it must first be recalled what it means for a goal to be open-ended and framework-like. While this question is challenging, generally, if the words used to describe the goals are broad and non-specific (and perhaps do not include a specific timeframe) (Chapter 4), goals can be considered open-ended and framework-like. For example, terms like 'enhancing', 'identifying', or 'reducing', without further clarification as to the extent to which this should be achieved, are often employed. Therefore, examining the goals set out above, they can all be regarded as open-ended and framework-like. The goals neither provide concrete measures to be taken nor timeframes to adhere to. For instance, 'reducing GHG emissions (...) as soon as possible' does not indicate how or by exactly when this should occur. This lack of precision allows for a fundamental aspect of global experimentalist governance, namely the option for actors at lower levels to experiment with how best to achieve the goal.

One potential downfall of open-ended and framework-like goals is that achieving them can become difficult to measure, and comparing levels of attainment among different lower-level actors can be challenging (see Chapter 4). To address this shortcoming and facilitate the evaluation of goal achievement, the IMO should establish more specific metrics according to global experimentalist governance theory. Within the IMO GHG strategies, these metrics are detailed in the Revised Strategy para 3 (levels of ambition, indicative checkpoints, and guiding

[848] Ibid., 1.10. [849] Ibid., 1.10.1–3, annex. [850] Ibid., 2, annex.

principles) as well as under para 6 (the follow-up actions).[851] All of these components of the 2023 Strategy provide greater detail regarding the goals outlined in the vision and related to the objectives discussed above. In addition, if the net zero framework is adopted in October 2025, it will provide even more details on how to achieve the strategic goals.[852]

The 2023 Strategy pursues defined levels of ambition. For example, 'carbon intensity of international shipping [is] to decline to reduce CO_2 emissions per transport work, as an average across international shipping, by at least 40% by 2030, compared to 2008'.[853] This establishes more concrete targets and can facilitate measuring progress towards achieving the goals. While the goals themselves only state 'contribution to global efforts by addressing GHG emissions' or 'reducing GHG emissions', the levels of ambition specified in the strategy provide clearer targets and time frames, such as a carbon intensity decline of at least 40 per cent by 2030 (compared to 2008).

In the same vein, the indicative checkpoints included in the strategy provide more specific targets. According to the 2023 Strategy, the indicative checkpoints have been set to ensure net zero GHG emissions from shipping[854] 'by or around, i.e. close to, 2050'.[855] There are two specific targets within the indicative checkpoints: one for 2030 and one for 2040. By 2030, total annual GHG emissions should be reduced by at least 20 per cent, striving for 30 per cent (compared to 2008). By 2040, the reduction should be at least 70 per cent and striving for 80 per cent.[856] In contrast to terms such as 'enhancing' and 'reducing', which are used in the established goals, these indicative checkpoints include very concrete numbers that can, like those in the levels of ambition, facilitate the measurement of progress towards achieving the goals.

Lastly, in addition to the levels of ambition and the indicative checkpoints, the follow-up actions included in the 2023 Strategy provide a table outlining key stages towards adopting a new strategy by 2028.[857] The table presents milestones that should be achieved between 2023 and 2028 and includes specific meetings to discuss these milestones. More specifically, one of the next steps for the IMO is to agree on further measures to achieve GHG emissions reduction, with the table indicating when these measures should be adopted (2025) and enter into force (2027).[858] Hence, the follow-up actions also establish specific targets that should be reached in the pursuit of the overall goal, namely to reduce and phase out GHG emissions as soon as possible.

Hence, the Revised GHG Strategy provides not only general, open-ended, and framework-like goals but also more specific metrics to facilitate evaluating the

[851] Ibid., 3, 6, annex.
[852] IMO, 'Circular Letter No.5005 – Draft Revised Marpol Annex Vi (Secretariat)' (n 575) 53–65.
[853] International Maritime Organization (IMO), Marine Environmental Protection Committee (MEPC) (n 570) para 3.3.2, annex.
[854] Ibid., 3.4, annex. [855] Ibid., 3.3.4, annex. [856] Ibid., 3.4.1–2, annex.
[857] Ibid., 6.2, annex. [858] Ibid.

achievement of these goals, as is typical in global experimentalist governance. This evaluation serves as the basis for updating the goals and metrics. Thus, the goals and metrics can be viewed as provisional, which is again an integral part of global experimentalist governance.

The Revised Strategy emphasises at several points that it is indeed subject to review. Right from the very beginning, the strategy states that the Marine Environmental Protection Committee '[a]grees to keep the 2023 IMO GHG Strategy under review'.[859] Additionally, para 7 of the strategy is dedicated to the 'Periodic Review of the Strategy'.[860] More concretely, paragraph 7.1 explains that '[t]he IMO GHG Strategy should be subject to a five-yearly review with the first review due in 2028'.[861] For instance, 7.3 clarifies, specifically regarding levels of ambition, that the reviews of these levels should consider updated emissions estimates, future IMO GHG studies, and inventories to evaluate the already reached progress towards net zero GHG emissions.[862] Therefore, the Revised Strategy, including its goals and metrics, can be reviewed and is thus characterised by provisionality.

The processes of global experimentalist governance also require stakeholder involvement from various levels of governance. Section 7.2.3 will discuss the extent to which stakeholders are involved in the IMO processes and how this involvement occurs.

7.2.3 Involvement of Multifarious Stakeholders from Different Levels of Governance

Different stakeholders are involved in the IMO's work against climate change at various stages. Therefore, this section will first discuss the extent to which diverse stakeholders are involved in setting the goals (Section 7.2.3.1). Second, the section will analyse how the search for solutions and means to attain open-ended goals is delegated to a variety of stakeholders operating at different levels of governance, particularly the national level, through so-called NAPs (Section 7.2.3.2).

7.2.3.1 Goal Setting through the Marine Environmental Protection Committee and Its Intersessional Working Group

The goals outlined in the Revised Strategy have been established through discussions in the Environmental Protection Committee and its Intersessional Working Group on the Reduction of GHG Emissions from Ships.[863] IMO discussions are led

[859] Ibid., 5, annex 15. [860] Ibid., 7, annex. [861] Ibid., 7.1, annex. [862] Ibid., 7.3, annex.

[863] IMO, 'Intersessional Working Group on Reduction of GHG Emissions from Ships (ISWG-GHG 15), 26–30 June' (n 777); IMO, '2023 IMO Strategy on Reduction of GHG Emissions from Ships' (2019) www.imo.org/en/OurWork/Environment/Pages/2023-IMO-Strategy-on-Reduction-of-GHG-Emissions-from-Ships.aspx#:~:text=The%202023%20IMO%20GHG%20Strategy%20envisages%2C%20in%20particular%2C%20a%20reduction,at%20least%2040%25%20by%202030 accessed 3 October 2023.

by the committee chair and involve representatives from the 175 member states.[864] Nevertheless, committee sessions are also attended and closely monitored by the sixty-six intergovernmental organisations with observer status and eighty-eight international non-governmental organisations with consultative status. These organisations offer IMO Member States expertise in their respective areas of work,[865] hold the MEPC accountable by increasing transparency, and represent various stakeholders across different levels of governance.

Utilising expertise from a diverse group of stakeholders is one of the cornerstones of global experimentalist governance. For example, the Asian African Legal Consultative Organization (AALCO), the Caribbean Community (CARICOM), and the Council of Europe represent different regions of the world and are among the intergovernmental organisations with observer status.[866] Greenpeace International, the International Association of Independent Tanker Owners (INTERTANKO), and the Inuit Circumpolar Council are some international non-governmental organisations that enjoy consultative status.[867] These examples of non-governmental organisations illustrate the close involvement of various stakeholders, such as environmentalists, industry, and indigenous peoples. At the same time, these six organisations also come from different levels of governance. While Greenpeace[868] operates at a global level, CARICOM,[869] AALCO[870], and the Council of Europe[871] are active at the regional level. Additionally, INTERTANKO[872] focuses on sectoral industry governance, and the Inuit Circumpolar Council[873] represents indigenous Inuit communities.

Thus, it is evident that multifarious stakeholders, both intergovernmental and non-governmental, are engaged in discussions at the IMO, including those related to GHG emissions reduction in the Marine Environmental

[864] IMO, 'Member States, IGOs and NGOs' (n 779); IMO, 'Member States' (n 779); cf. IMO, 'Marine Environment Protection Committee (MEPC 70), 24–28 October (Closing Remarks)' (2019) www.imo.org/en/MediaCentre/SecretaryGeneral/Pages/MEPC-70-closing.aspx accessed 13 January 2024.

[865] IMO, 'Relations with Observer Organizations' (2019) www.imo.org/en/OurWork/ERO/Pages/Relations-with-Observer-Organizations.aspx accessed 4 October 2023.

[866] IMO, 'Intergovernmental Organizations Which Have Concluded Agreements of Cooperation with IMO' (2019) www.imo.org/en/OurWork/ERO/Pages/IGOsWithObserverStatus.aspx accessed 11 October 2023.

[867] IMO, 'Non-Governmental International Organizations Which Have Been Granted Consultative Status with IMO' (2019) www.imo.org/en/OurWork/ERO/Pages/NGOsInConsultativeStatus.aspx accessed 11 October 2023.

[868] Greenpeace International, 'Who We Are' (*Greenpeace International*, 2024) www.greenpeace.org/international/about/ accessed 13 January 2024.

[869] CARICOM, 'Home – Heads of Government Conference (HGC)' (2023) <https://hgc.caricom.org/> accessed 13 January 2024.

[870] AALCO, 'Member States | Asian African Legal Consultative Organization' (2024) www.aalco.int/Members accessed 13 January 2024.

[871] The Council of Europe, 'The Council of Europe at a Glance – Portal – Www.Coe.Int' (*Portal*, 2024) www.coe.int/en/web/portal/the-council-of-europe-at-a-glance accessed 13 January 2024.

[872] INTERTANKO, 'Membership – INTERTANKO' (2024) www.intertanko.com/about-us/membership accessed 13 January 2024.

[873] ICC, 'ICC's Political Universe… | Inuit Circumpolar Council Canada' (2024) www.inuitcircumpolar.com/about-icc/icc-political-universe/ accessed 13 January 2024.

Protection Committee. As mentioned earlier, the entire 2023 Strategy will undergo review, and these assessments will continue under the auspices of the Marine Environmental Protection Committee and its Intersessional Working Group.[874] Therefore, stakeholders are expected to keep influencing these processes in alignment with the aspirations of global experimentalist governance. Concurrently, scientific data plays a crucial role in these processes, as demonstrated by the preparation and reliance on different IMO GHG studies. Consequently, goals are established through the involvement of stakeholders from various levels of governance.

7.2.3.2 Delegation of Solution Finding to Lower Levels through NAPs

One of the most promising aspects of the Initial Strategy from a global experimentalist governance perspective is the call for NAPs, as these assign lower levels of governance the task of experimenting in search of solutions to reduce GHG emissions from shipping. As part of the (short-term)[875] measures that are intended to 'directly reduce GHG emissions' or 'which support action to reduce GHG emissions' under paragraph 4.7, the Initial Strategy encourages the creation of so-called NAPs.[876] More specifically, 'national action plans to develop policies and strategies to address GHG emissions from international shipping',[877] and these NAPs should be created in accordance with guidelines.[878]

These guidelines were created and can be found in MEPC.327(75) and were revised and revoked by MEPC.367(79).[879] Also, the Revised Strategy reiterates the role of NAPs, including MEPC.327(75) and MEPC.367(79) in appendix 1, which outlines short-term measures and provides an overview of previous IMO work to address GHG emissions.[880] Thus, while further measures (mid- and long-term) are being developed, responsibility for identifying and enacting measures is delegated to the national level.[881] Member states, as a lower level of governance, are tasked by the IMO with creating the NAPs to target the reduction

[874] See, for example, International Maritime Organization (IMO), Marine Environmental Protection Committee (MEPC) (n 570) paras 5, annex 15.

[875] Definition of short-term measures found in the Initial Strategy: 'possible short-term measures could be measures finalized and agreed by the Committee between 2018 and 2023. Dates of entry into force and when the measure can effectively start to reduce GHG emissions would be defined for each measure individually' International Maritime Organization (IMO), Marine Environmental Protection Committee (MEPC) (n 569) para 4.1.1, annex.

[876] Ibid., 4.7, 4.7.6, annex. [877] Ibid., 4.7.6, annex. [878] Ibid.

[879] MEPC, 'Resolution MEPC.327(75) – Encouragement of Member States to Develop and Submit Voluntary National Action Plans to Address GHG Emissions from Ships (Annex 4)' wwwcdn.imo.org/localresources/en/OurWork/Environment/Documents/Air%20pollution/Resolution%20MEPC.327(75).pdf accessed 12 October 2023; MEPC, 'Resolution MEPC.367(79) – Encouragement of Member States to Develop and Submit Voluntary National Action Plans to Address GHG Emissions from Ships (Annex 12)' wwwcdn.imo.org/localresources/en/KnowledgeCentre/IndexofIMOResolutions/MEPCDocuments/MEPC.367(79).pdf.

[880] International Maritime Organization (IMO), Marine Environmental Protection Committee (MEPC) (n 570) paras 8, appendix 1, annex, 4.1.1, annex.

[881] Cf. MEPC, 'MEPC.367(79)' (n 879) paras 5, annex.

of GHG emissions.[882] According to the strategy, many different types of stakeholders, as mentioned by Resolution MEPC.367(79), should be involved in the process of creating NAPs. Resolution MEPC.367(79) requests, 'Member States to bring this resolution to the attention of all stakeholders on a national scale, including Administrations, ports, ship designers, engine manufacturers, fuel suppliers, seafarers and other interested groups'.[883] Thus, the Marine Environmental Protection Committee suggests that the creation of NAPs should involve different kinds of stakeholders. The Committee in the Resolution also recognises that these stakeholders are 'working together to strengthen cooperation through the whole value chain to create favorable conditions along specific shipping routes to reduce GHG emissions from ships'.[884]

Additionally, stakeholder involvement in practice was clarified during interviews with delegates.[885]

The cooperation of multifarious stakeholders envisioned by the resolution could be confirmed through interviews and video resources on the GreenVoyage website.[886] For instance, during interviews, delegates and internal IMO experts emphasised the significance of stakeholders in the NAP creation progress.[887] The experts stated that as many stakeholders as possible should be included in the process and that they can differ depending on the country.[888] The country delegates identified various stakeholders essential for their NAP creation process, including industry, landowners, ports, scientists, cities and mayors, tech professionals, indigenous peoples, and civil society, to name a few.[889] Thus, consistent with the aspirations of global experimentalist governance, the NAPs enable the delegation of solution-finding to lower-level stakeholders within each member state, granting them the autonomy to experiment with different approaches to climate change on their own terms. In other words, the development of NAPs, which outline a country's

[882] 'National Action Plans' (2019) www.imo.org/en/ourwork/environment/pages/relevant-national-action-plans-and-strategies.aspx accessed 12 October 2023.

[883] MEPC, 'MEPC.367(79)' (n 879) paras 8, annex 12.

[884] Ibid., Prambulatory clause No. 9, annex 12.

[885] Interview with IMO Delegate #2, 'IMO Delegate Interview #2' (December 2022); Interview with IMO Delegate #3, 'IMO Delegate Interview #3' (December 2022); Interview with IMO Delegate #1, 'IMO Delegate Interview #1' (December 2022); Interview with IMO Delegate #4, 'IMO Delegate Interview #4' (December 2022); Interview with IMO Delegate #5, 'IMO Delegate Interview #5' (December 2022).

[886] GreenVoyage2050, 'National Action Plan to Address GHG Emissions from Ships: GreenVoyage2050' (2023) tit Video Resources: under Process <https://greenvoyage2050.imo.org/national-action-plan/> accessed 12 October 2023; Interview with Internal IMO Expert #2, 'Internal IMO Expert Interview #2' (December 2022); Interview with IMO Delegate #1 (n 885); Interview with IMO Delegate #2 (n 885); Interview with IMO Delegate #3 (n 885); Interview with IMO Delegate #4 (n 885); Interview with IMO Delegate #5 (n 885).

[887] Interview with IMO Delegate #1 (n 885); Interview with IMO Delegate #2 (n 885); Interview with IMO Delegate #3 (n 885); Interview with IMO Delegate #4 (n 885); Interview with IMO Delegate #5 (n 885); Interview with Internal IMO Expert #2 (n 886).

[888] Interview with Internal IMO Expert #2 (n 886).

[889] Interview with IMO Delegate #1 (n 885); Interview with IMO Delegate #2 (n 885); Interview with IMO Delegate #3 (n 885); Interview with IMO Delegate #4 (n 885); Interview with IMO Delegate #5 (n 885).

practices and targets for addressing GHG emissions, is inclusive and draws upon the expertise of stakeholders within a member state. However, while some member states continue to involve stakeholders after the initial NAP of the member state has been created to revise it and draft an updated version, it remains uncertain whether this is true for all member states.[890] However, continuous engagement with stakeholders is crucial to align the process with global experimentalist governance. Furthermore, delegation necessitates that lower-level stakeholders be granted the discretion to experiment. In return, these stakeholders must commit to being transparent about their work (see Chapter 4).

When testing different strategies, these lower levels of governance engage in experimentation while retaining their discretion, in line with global experimentalist governance theory. Resolution MEPC.367(79) concerning NAPs suggests in paragraph 2 what NAPs could entail.[891] For example, these could include 'activities to further enhance the energy efficiency of ships'.[892] Nevertheless, the resolution makes it very clear that NAPs are not limited to the examples provided in the paragraph.[893] Thus, discretion is not taken away from the actors involved in establishing the NAP. In addition, the Marine Environmental Protection Committee, through this Resolution, asks the secretariat to 'continue to provide guidance and any further action which may be taken (…) to assist Member States (…) in developing National Action Plans'.[894] This guidance is targeted, albeit not exclusively, towards developing countries.[895] Just as with the list of examples in paragraph 2 of the Resolution MEPC.367(79) mentioned above, providing assistance is not obligatory where it is offered. Member States are not required to take it into account. In fact, some specific guidance initiatives are referred to in this Resolution and reiterated by the 2023 Strategy.[896]

One initiative supporting the reduction of GHG emissions, including CO_2, is GreenVoyage 2050.[897] GreenVoyage, more concretely the IMO – Norway GreenVoyage 2050 Project, has prepared a guide to facilitate the development of NAPs. For instance, the guide includes step-by-step instructions with information for all phases, from planning to creating a NAP to implementing the NAP.[898] Nevertheless, as mentioned above, member states have discretion in deciding whether to follow the guidance and to what extent. Of the nine countries that have already uploaded their NAP to the IMO website, it was revealed during an interview with a delegate[899] that at least one country neither used nor was aware of the GreenVoyage Guide while creating their NAP.[900] Apart from that, during interviews,[901] it was confirmed that delegates view NAPs as an opportunity

[890] Interview with IMO Delegate #1 (n 885).
[891] MEPC, 'MEPC.367(79)' (n 879) paras 2, annex 12.
[892] Ibid., 2(b), annex 12.
[893] Ibid., 2, annex 12.
[894] Ibid., 6, annex 12.
[895] Ibid.
[896] Ibid., 4, 6, annex 12; International Maritime Organization (IMO), Marine Environmental Protection Committee (MEPC) (n 570) paras 4, appendix 2, annex.
[897] MEPC, 'MEPC.367(79)' (n 879) paras 4, 6, annex 12.
[898] 'National Action Plans' (n 882); GreenVoyage2050 (n 886).
[899] Interview with IMO Delegate #1 (n 885); 'National Action Plans' (n 882).
[900] Ibid.
[901] Interview with IMO Delegate #2 (n 885); Interview with IMO Delegate #5 (n 885).

to experiment with new strategies. For instance, if these strategies succeed at a lower level of governance, this might convince industry or IMO delegates of the feasibility of these practices.[902]

However, in exchange for this discretion, stakeholders must also work transparently. Hence, while experimenting with different options, stakeholders should, for instance, justify their choices. The Marine Environmental Protection Committee, in Resolution MEPC.367(79), invites member states to share their experiences concerning the planning and creation of NAPs with the IMO as soon as possible and to provide updates thereafter.[903] The Marine Environmental Protection Committee recognises, among other things, the value of 'promoting experience and information-sharing and cooperation for all national stakeholders'.[904] Therefore, the committee also asks the secretariat to create a web page dedicated to NAPs that can support information-sharing.[905] As mentioned above, thus far (May 2025), nine member states have added their NAPs to the website.[906] In addition, some countries that have already created NAPs share their experiences on the GreenVoyage website.[907] Hence, members should and do share their NAPs and experiences surrounding the creation of NAPs publicly. Therefore, while members have the liberty to experiment in search of solutions, there is nonetheless a clear expectation that they make that information available.

Overall, the NAPs provide an almost ideal setup for global experiment governance. NAPs allow for delegation to member states and the multifarious stakeholders at the subnational level, along with the discretion needed for these stakeholders to continue experimenting and utilising their experiences. Furthermore, there is an expectation that member states and their stakeholders operate with transparency. This process of delegation, experimentation, and transparency aligns well with the theory of global experimentalist governance (as seen in Chapter 4). However, since only nine countries (out of 175 member states) have shared their NAPs, this governance approach is either not widely practised or the member states do not share information about their NAPs with the IMO Secretariat.

As will be seen in Section 7.2.4, the lack of engagement, or at least the sharing, of NAPs on the website, is not the only reason why global experimentalist governance is not fully realised within the IMO's response to climate change. The involvement of various stakeholders at different governance levels is an integral part of the experimentation process; thus, flexibility and adaptability in the governance process according to the gathered knowledge and experience are necessary. Stakeholders need to adapt and revise various strategies and lessons learned to accommodate their differing circumstances. To ensure that experimentation is not in vain but instead influences the setting of provisional goals and metrics,

[902] Ibid. [903] MEPC, 'MEPC.367(79)' (n 879) paras 1, 3, Preambulatory clause No. 10, annex 12.
[904] Ibid Preambulatory clause No. 12, annex 12.
[905] Ibid., 7, annex 12; 'National Action Plans' (n 882). [906] 'National Action Plans' (n 882).
[907] GreenVoyage2050 (n 886) tit Video Resources.

a recursive learning process is considered integral to global experimentalist governance. Consequently, a mechanism to ensure the effective functioning of this learning cycle, including reporting, reviewing, and feedback (see below), becomes essential. However, as Section 7.2.4 will show, arrangements within the IMO, and specifically NAP processes, are deficient in this respect.

7.2.4 Balancing Many Stakeholders through Reporting, Peer Review, and Feedback

As many stakeholders at different governance levels ideally participate in global experimentalist governance, the theory establishes a process to balance and navigate their roles within this framework. Whether the IMO provides for and facilitates processes that conform to the ideal of global experimentalist governance to promote learning among different actors, such as reporting (Section 7.2.4.1), peer review (Section 7.2.4.2), and feedback (Section 7.2.4.3) (for details, see Chapter 4), will be analysed in the later sections.

7.2.4.1 Reporting

It has already been highlighted that through Resolution MEPC.367(79), the IMO Secretariat has, upon request, created a website for member states to provide information regarding the creation of their NAPs.[908] Accordingly, member states are invited to submit their NAPs to the IMO and provide updates.[909] The IMO, and more specifically, the Marine Environmental Protection Committee, in the preambulatory clauses of Resolution MEPC.367(79) annex 12, places a high value on the diverse experiences within member states and on information-sharing. Given this, it recommends that member states share their experiences and information.[910] In keeping with this, member states are expected to provide their NAPs to the IMO Secretariat so they can be shared among member states, thus creating the potential for them to learn from one another. As previously noted, nine NAPs have been submitted to the IMO and are now published on the website.[911] Many more are currently being prepared.[912] In addition, at least one member state is working on updating their plan that has already been published on the website.[913] Apart from the NAPs published on the website, some governments have also provided videos for GreenVoyage with more information regarding their NAPs.[914]

908 MEPC, 'MEPC.367(79)' (n 879) paras 7, Annex 12; 'National Action Plans' (n 882).
909 MEPC, 'MEPC.367(79)' (n 879) paras 1, 3, Annex 12; 'National Action Plans' (n 882).
910 MEPC, 'MEPC.367(79)' (n 879) para Preambulatory clauses No. 10, 12, annex 12.
911 'National Action Plans' (n 882).
912 Interview with IMO Delegate #4 (n 885); Interview with IMO Delegate #6, 'IMO Delegate Interview #6' (December 2022); GreenVoyage2050, 'Partnering Countries: GreenVoyage2050' (2023) https://greenvoyage2050.imo.org/partnering-countries/ accessed 14 October 2023; Interview with Internal IMO Expert #2 (n 886).
913 Interview with IMO Delegate #1 (n 885).
914 GreenVoyage2050 (n 886) tit Video Resources.

It is evident that reporting information back to the IMO and GreenVoyage to be shared on the websites, and thus with other member states, is highly encouraged. A small but hopefully increasing number of member states are indeed sharing their information in this manner. It is promising to see that more states are preparing NAPs, as this may indicate a shift towards global experimentalist governance not just on paper but also in practice.

7.2.4.2 Peer Review

To align with global experimentalist governance, the information reported by member states should undergo peer review. During this process, actors should compare and evaluate each other's progress towards achieving shared but open-ended goals. This approach facilitates the identification of best practices. As noted in the reporting section, information about countries' NAPs is publicly available on various websites (IMO and GreenVoyage) for comparison and evaluation. The Revised Strategy under paragraph 4, which addresses the measures and, more specifically, 'other candidate mid-term GHG reduction measures',[915] mentions as part of 'informed policymaking' that a 'feedback mechanism to enable lessons learned on implementation of measures to be collated and shared through a possible information exchange on best practice' should be developed.[916] However, a feedback mechanism of this nature is not referenced concerning NAPs or short-term measures in the Revised Strategy or Resolution MEPC.367(79). Hence, upon reviewing the 2023 Strategy and the resolution, it can be concluded that no system is currently in place to compare and evaluate information and collect best practices based on what has been assembled on the IMO NAP website.

Despite the lack of guidance and encouragement from the Revised Strategy and Resolution MEPC.367(79) to compare, evaluate, and create best practices, the GreenVoyage guide and website appear to build on precisely that. Internal IMO experts who created the guide explain that it was part of a longer process.[917] To write the guide, experts referred to the GEF-UNDP-IMO GloMEEP Project and IMarEST Ship Emissions Toolkit, 2018 Guides No. 1 and 3.[918] In addition, the experts in charge were inspired by policy guides to reduce GHG emissions already in place elsewhere. They also organised a workshop to discuss and test their vision for the guide with a group of countries. During the workshop, they

[915] The revised strategy explains that '[i]n addition to the basket of candidate mid-term GHG reduction measures, the Organization should continue to develop other mid-term GHG reduction measures to reduce GHG emissions from ships'. International Maritime Organization (IMO), Marine Environmental Protection Committee (MEPC) (n 570) para 4.9, annex.

[916] Ibid., 4.9.2, annex.

[917] Interview with Internal IMO Expert #2 (n 886).

[918] Ibid; GreenVoyage2050 (n 886); GEF-UNDP-IMO GloMEEP and IMarEST, 'Ship Emissions Toolkit Guide No. 01 – Rapid Assessment of Ship Emissions in the National Context (GEF-UNDP-IMO GloMEEP and IMarEST)' https://gmn.imo.org/wp-content/uploads/2018/10/ship_emissions_toolkit-g1-online.pdf accessed 15 October 2023; GEF-UNDP-IMO GloMEEP and IMarEST, 'Ship Emissions Toolkit Guide No.3: Development of a National Ship Emissions Reduction Strategy'. https://gmn.imo.org/wp-content/uploads/2018/10/ship_emissions_toolkit-g3-online.pdf accessed 15 October 2023.

presented draft tools and collected information and feedback from the participating countries. The gathered information was then used to revise the guide. Overall, they describe the process as trial and error.[919] Even though the guide is now in place, GreenVoyage continues to organise training events and workshops. These events target the New Pilot Countries[920] undergoing the NAP development process. Lessons learned and feedback from other countries that have already gone through the NAP creation process will be used during training.[921] Therefore, the GreenVoyage guide reflects best practices regarding the creation of a NAP, structured to best tackle GHG emissions. These best practices have been collected and continue to be shared during events as a tool to help countries develop their NAPs and reduce GHG emissions, including CO_2. Information and experiences from various countries contributed to the creation of the guide. However, best practices were identified through the collection of information and experiences by a few IMO experts. Hence, it was not local actors who compared and evaluated each other's progress in achieving the goals, which led to this collection of best practices as suggested by the ideal type of global experimentalist governance.

Accordingly, in interviews,[922] delegates provided varying answers when asked about the NAPs of other member states and how extensively they had consulted or exchanged information with them. For example, two delegates[923] stated that they cooperate or will cooperate within their region in the process of compiling a NAP and beyond.[924] One of those delegates emphasised that they believe NAPs play an important role in facilitating the sharing of best practices. They think that the IMO serves as a good platform for sharing information and strategies, and once this country begins developing its NAP, it will consult the NAPs that have already been published on the website.[925] The other delegate (from a country that already has an NAP) believes that sharing information about NAPs can be beneficial, as developing countries can use this knowledge to create their NAPs. The delegate mentioned the GreenVoyage guide as a resource that can assist developing countries.[926] However, another delegate states that their country is not consulting with other nations. This country is said to believe that there is no value in such consultations, as every country is different.[927] A final delegate was not entirely sure but

919 Interview with Internal IMO Expert #2 (n 886).

920 According to the GreenVoyage website, new pilot countries are: 'those which will, as a first step, undertake the development of a national maritime emissions assessment, establishing a baseline and build the information base, laying the foundation for targeted actions to reduce emissions from shipping. These will provide the basis for the development of a robust and informed national emission reduction strategy and National Action Plan (NAP) to address GHG emissions from ships'. GreenVoyage2050 (n 912).

921 IMO, 'New Guidance for National Emissions Reduction' (2019) www.imo.org/en/MediaCentre/Pages/WhatsNew-1697.aspx accessed 15 October 2023.

922 Interview with IMO Delegate #1 (n 885); Interview with IMO Delegate #2 (n 885); Interview with IMO Delegate #3 (n 885); Interview with IMO Delegate #5 (n 885).

923 Interview with IMO Delegate #5 (n 885); Interview with IMO Delegate #2 (n 885).

924 Ibid.

925 Interview with IMO Delegate #2 (n 885).

926 Interview with IMO Delegate #5 (n 885).

927 Interview with IMO Delegate #3 (n 885).

did not think the country in question formally consulted with others. They also are not planning to reach out or compare their work to that of other countries to revise their NAP. This lack of interest stems from their belief that looking to the experiences of other countries holds little value, as NAPs address national policies and each country has its own. However, the delegate added that, on occasion, other states have contacted them regarding their country's NAP.[928]

Therefore, while some states value the accessibility of information on the IMO NAP website and see the benefit in consulting it when creating their NAPs, others do not recognise the importance of reporting and comparing NAPs. Internal IMO experts have confirmed the existence of these varying attitudes among member states. They agree that different countries face different situations. However, they also emphasise that even though one cannot copy-paste what works in one country to the next, it is still valuable to understand what other countries are doing. Comparisons between similarly situated countries (for example, developing nations) could be especially useful.[929] Thus, the lack of consistency in the responses received to questions posed by the author indicates that the participants involved do not always grasp the value of the peer-review process. Without an appreciation of its significance, participants are unlikely to engage, creating a deficit in the process from the perspective of global experimentalist governance.

Although processes resembling peer review are in place, best practices are not systematically collected by comparing and evaluating information about the nature and results of experimentation at the lower level. Best practices are not routinely communicated to the central unit from lower levels of governance. Instead, experts linked to the central unit compile the best practices themselves, similar to the approach used in the OAA (the previous case study). Thus, overall, even though the GreenVoyage guide and website compile best practices and some delegates seem to consider the NAPs published on the IMO NAP website as best practices, it cannot be concluded that peer review is occurring systematically and universally.

7.2.4.3 Feedback

According to global experimentalist governance theory, feedback on the results of peer review should be provided to lower-level actors by both their peers and the central unit. Even if the feedback process were in place at the IMO, feedback could only be given to a certain extent, as comparison, evaluation, and pooling of best practices are not entrenched or sufficiently widespread to meet the expectations created by global experimentalist governance. Although NAPs are already published on the IMO website, and thus the IMO is aware of the NAPs, the only processes that resemble feedback regarding NAPs can be found within the IMO GreenVoyage project.

[928] Interview with IMO Delegate #1 (n 885).

[929] Interview with Internal IMO Expert #2 (n 886).

An essential part of the GreenVoyage Project is to provide guidance and accompany partnering countries through the entire process of creating and implementing an NAP. The project works with twelve countries in phase 1 and nine additional countries in phase 2. Representatives from all countries receive training, participate in workshops, and undertake other activities.[930] Through this close guidance, feedback is provided to participating countries. However, this guidance for the small number of partner countries in the GreenVoyage project cannot fulfil the requirement of feedback on the results from the central unit, as required by the ideal type of global experimentalist governance. In addition, feedback from other local units is not provided at all.

This lack of a proper peer review and the insufficiency of the feedback mechanism also complicate one of the essential aspects of global experimentalist governance – namely, the adjustment of overarching goals. Because there is no proper peer review and an inadequate feedback mechanism in place, the overarching goals cannot be adjusted accordingly. Nevertheless, one delegate underlined during interviews[931] that widespread national action through NAPs by many member states may eventually put pressure on other member states, which can facilitate the creation of mandatory rules on the international level. However, the delegate also states that this needs time, and for now, NAPs are voluntary and complementary actions.[932] This voluntary and complementary nature of NAPs also means that the idea of penalty default, a tool to steer unwilling or reluctant actors and penalise non-cooperation, as explained in Chapter 4,[933] is not relevant for this aspect of the IMO's work, as will be discussed in Section 7.3.

7.3 Penalty Default

The penalty default is a tool to steer unwilling or reluctant actors and penalise non-cooperation, as explained in Chapter 4.[934] As mentioned above, NAPs are created under the auspices of the Marine Environmental Protection Committee. The Marine Environmental Protection Committee is responsible for tackling GHG emissions, including CO_2 from shipping. The Initial Strategy is considered the 'first milestone' on the long road to achieving a reduction of GHG emissions from ships, while the Revised Strategy is regarded as the latest milestone (until potential adoption of the net zero framework).[935] Alongside this IMO-level process, member states are encouraged to establish NAPs on a voluntary basis, as explained above. Thus, the rule-making process continues at the IMO level

930 GreenVoyage 2050 (n 912). 931 Interview with IMO Delegate #4 (n 885). 932 Ibid.
933 Zeitlin (n 386) 4; De Búrca, Keohane and Sabel (n 283) 478, 784; Goldstein and Ansell (n 384) 221.
934 Ibid.
935 International Maritime Organization (IMO), Marine Environmental Protection Committee (MEPC) (n 570) para 1.4, 1.5, annex.

without considering whether member states are developing NAPs. Hence, even if actors cooperate and NAPs are created, the IMO will persist with traditional forms of rule-making within the IMO and the Marine Environmental Protection Committee. In conclusion, because traditional rule-making is always present and, therefore, cannot be used as a threat, no matter how well member states cooperate, the penalty default becomes ineffective regarding NAPs.

Nevertheless, given the recent developments in the EU ETS, which, as of 2024, also includes shipping, the penalty defaults may still become relevant.[936] Lower-level actors may pressure the IMO to take the task of reducing the climate change impacts of shipping more seriously to avoid a fragmentation of rule-making due to actions at a regional or national level. In other words, individual states or regions may adopt unilateral measures, creating a penalty default. Unilateral action has already been observed concerning the aviation sector (EU ETS on aviation for third countries) and described in Chapter 4. In the context of the EU ETS, a penalty default called 'Stop the Clock' was implemented. Initially, all operating flights to, from, or within the EU were included in its ETS. However, facing opposition from non-EU countries, the EU temporarily 'stopped the clock' and suspended the inclusion of international flights in the EU ETS for non-EEA countries. This move aimed to encourage collaboration for a global solution through ICAO. In a parallel development, the EU recently expanded the scope of the EU ETS to include shipping emissions from 2024.[937] This new development means that from 'January 2024, the EU's Emissions Trading System (EU ETS) will be extended to cover CO_2 emissions from all large ships (of 5,000 gross tonnage and above) entering EU ports'.[938] However, there will be a gradual phase-in that is staggered over three years.[939] Nevertheless, this move could potentially result in another 'stop the clock' scenario. However, it is important to note that the latest efforts towards rule-making at the IMO and the potential adoption of the net zero framework seem to reduce the likelihood of these unilateral actions (at least those aimed at putting pressure to achieve a global solution).

7.4 Global Experimentalist Governance within the IMO

This chapter has shown that the shipping sector significantly contributes to OA. Even though the IMO has a variety of legal frameworks under which OA could be addressed, the organisation neither properly acknowledges the shipping sector's contribution to the problem nor tackles OA directly. On the contrary, the IMO recommends using scrubbers to comply with stricter air pollution

[936] Cf. European Commission, 'Reducing Emissions from the Shipping Sector – European Commission' (2024) https://climate.ec.europa.eu/eu-action/transport/reducing-emissions-shipping-sector_en accessed 14 January 2024.
[937] Ibid. [938] Ibid. [939] Ibid.

regulations, despite their negative effects on the ocean. Although no targeted action is taken, the IMO recognises the connection between climate change and OA, as well as between air pollution through SO_X. Additionally, on a few occasions, the IMO mentions OA in relation to geoengineering and the LC/LP, albeit without acknowledging the potentially dangerous consequences of these techniques for the ocean environment. This acknowledgement has, however, not led to any concrete action directly against OA. While the IMO has not initiated specific measures to tackle OA, the organisation is regulating OA-relevant aspects of shipping through its efforts to address climate change and air pollution, as well as geoengineering (which indirectly addresses OA). Therefore, this case study focused on one of these areas of action – climate change – to examine whether and to what extent global experimentalist governance can be identified.

After discussing the IMO's response to climate change caused by GHG emissions, including CO_2, and evaluating it from the perspective of global experimentalist governance, it can be concluded that the architecture and functioning of this response resemble this model only to a certain extent. IMO member states and observers within the MEPC agree that climate change is a shared problem they need to tackle. Accordingly, goals and metrics have been set to reduce and phase out GHG emissions, including CO_2. These goals and metrics are provisional, as required by the theory of global experimentalism. The theory also calls for provisionality to allow for the updating of goals and metrics based on, for instance, the latest science and technology, and such provisionality is evident in the IMO. However, this is perceived as carrying a certain risk within the organisation. Some member states fear that the possibility of revision may lead to so-called 'backsliding'.[940] In other words, states and observers worry that ambitious goals or metrics might be relaxed during further revision. This fear of backsliding demonstrates that, as the theory suggests, provisionality can create an uncertain future for goals and metrics, presenting a risk of setbacks. This problem will be discussed further in the conclusion of this book.

Nevertheless, the provisionality of the goals and metrics persists, and by utilising NAPs, the process of finding solutions to the shared problem has been delegated to lower levels for experimentation. However, these NAPs are, similar to the OA Action Plans within the OA Alliance, not only voluntary but also complementary to initiatives undertaken within the IMO. The NAPs are intended to include only interim actions that will occur pending the adoption of additional measures at the IMO level. Considering this complementarity, it can be questioned whether the task of finding solutions is genuinely delegated to lower levels.

Regardless, the NAP architecture fails to meet the ideal type of global experimentalism during the feedback and peer-review stages. Although there is some reporting of NAPs (albeit limited), there is no comparison of the reported

[940] 'Marine Environment Protection Committee (MEPC) – 79th Session'.

information nor any identification or dissemination of best practices. Instead, best practices have been compiled outside the IMO by experts developing the GreenVoyage guide and creating content for the GreenVoyage website. However, this collection of best practices does not align with the ideal type of global experimentalist governance. The previous case study demonstrated that a deficient approach to feedback and peer review renders the recursive learning process ineffective. This process is a crucial aspect of the theory, and defects undermine the realisation of global experimentalist governance within the IMO.

This chapter set out to analyse IMO's actions to address OA and, in particular, to assess whether global experimentalist governance is being employed to tackle the issue. It concludes that only some aspects of global experimentalist governance are utilised within the IMO to confront the complex challenge and closely related issue of climate change. Since the IMO's response to climate change only resembles global experimentalism to a certain extent, there is limited evidence to suggest that it would adopt such an approach when it comes to addressing the pressing issue of OA explicitly and directly.

CHAPTER 8
Conclusion

This book has examined the problem of OA and its governance. It demonstrates that OA is a complex issue that touches upon various spheres on Earth – namely, the ocean, atmosphere, and land. It also exhibits different dimensions in time and space; for instance, some causes of OA can be addressed faster than others and traced back to global, regional, and local activities. Similarly, OA is a problem that potentially involves a vast array of actors. The multifaceted nature of OA should be reflected in its governance.

This book has shown that addressing OA and understanding its governance is a complicated and challenging exercise that involves knowledge not only of the legal and policy aspects of the problem but also of its scientific background. The question of how OA is and should be governed, in light of the nature of the problem, has guided this book. To answer this question, the book begins by providing an overview of the scientific underpinnings of OA. Next, the current governance landscape vis-à-vis OA, conceived as a regime complex, is presented. After considering both the science and the current governance landscape, it becomes apparent that global experimentalist governance is an effective approach that can build on the existing landscape and accommodate the scientific background of OA. For this reason, the presence of global experimentalist governance is examined through two case studies, the OAA and the IMO. To reflect on what has been analysed and argued in this book, this conclusion will first summarise the findings (Section 8.1). Then, it will discuss remaining questions (Section 8.2) and present some reflections on the research question (Section 8.3) before finally setting out limitations and some suggestions for further research (Section 8.4).

8.1 Summary of the Main Findings

OA is a problem that can be scientifically explained. Without a sound understanding of the nature of the problem and its causes, it is difficult to identify governance solutions capable of addressing the issue at its roots. Thus, scientific findings can serve as a foundation to explore how OA should be governed. For this reason, Chapter 2 provided an overview of the problem and presented its scientific background before delving into the question of OA governance. It is essential to understand where the problem originates, including knowledge about the causes, stressors, and adaptation options related to OA. Chapter 2 discussed these aspects and demonstrated that OA is a complex and creeping issue. OA also comes with a considerable amount of uncertainty, as much remains poorly understood. Although scientific research on OA is expanding quickly, many questions still await answers. Despite this ongoing uncertainty, the chapter presented the facts and characteristics concerning OA that are understood and must be considered when seeking governance solutions. As mentioned above, the chapter emphasised that OA involves more than just various Earth spheres and dimensions. Hence, the science indicates that many actors and instruments may be relevant to the governance of OA. These actors and instruments govern not only the ocean but also the atmosphere and land.

In the course of the analysis in the book, it became clear that OA governance does not start with a clean slate. There are already institutions (actors/instruments) in place that contribute, and can contribute, to tackling different aspects of OA. In keeping with this, Chapter 3 mapped the international and transnational landscape for OA. The map includes multifarious institutions operating in various cognate issue areas, such as biodiversity protection, transboundary air pollution, and climate change, all of which are connected to OA. The institutions mapped address different aspects of the causes, stressors, and/or adaptation to OA. Regime complex theory guided this mapping to describe the governance landscape for OA. As indicated above, and as is typical for a regime complex, OA involves multiple institutions and sits at the nexus of many different issues. The chapter confirmed that OA yields a regime complex and has shown that OA governance involves diverse and sometimes conflicting interests and uncertainties, which makes reaching an agreement on how to address OA *ex ante* challenging. With the understanding that the governance landscape for OA can be described as a regime complex and armed with information about the scientific background presented in Chapter 7, the book then considered how this governance landscape should evolve to contribute to mitigating the causes and consequences of OA next.

Reading about global and transnational governance made it evident that global experimentalist governance has the potential to address the problem of OA. Therefore, Chapter 4 explored and explained the concept and identified five elements that constitute the ideal type of global experimentalist governance. Additionally, given the nature of OA and the current governance landscape of the issue (characterised as a regime complex), seven key elements that describe OA as a concern were outlined. Subsequently, these seven elements were aligned with the theory of global experimentalist governance. Global experimentalist governance appears to be a suitable match for OA because it can accommodate these seven characteristics of OA as both a scientific problem and a regime complex. For example, OA as an issue involves numerous actors from different levels of governance, as illustrated by the map in Chapter 3. Global experimentalist governance can tackle this challenge, as it facilitates a multilevel governance approach that engages actors or stakeholders from various governance levels. Overall, the chapter concluded that global experimentalist governance has the potential to build on the existing regime complex for OA and even has the ability to make a virtue of the currently fragmented governance landscape.

Next, the book turned to evaluating global experimentalist governance vis-à-vis OA. Chapter 5 aimed to identify actors that would allow for the evaluation of the presence of global experimentalist governance concerning the five elements that constitute the ideal type of global experimentalist governance. This chapter addressed which of the numerous actors identified during the mapping exercise should be selected to 'test' the presence of global experimentalist governance. The chapter began by explaining that an institution can be considered suitable to tackle OA if it is capable of addressing causes, stressors, and adaptation (concerns). Following this insight, the chapter established a taxonomy to determine which institutions are merely suitable and which have significant potential to tackle OA. A table of institutions that could be selected as case studies was created based on the map developed in Chapter 3. However, most of the institutions included in the table received multiple marks concerning different concerns (or within one concern), providing them significant potential to tackle OA broadly and/or in depth. Therefore, to select case studies, various institutions (IUCN, UNEP, IMO, UNESCO, OAA) with considerable potential to address OA were analysed regarding causes, stressors, and adaptation. Due to time and space constraints, only two actors could be selected for further study. The OA Alliance and the IMO were chosen after considering not only suitability and significant potential but also their diverse institutional setup, their focus on CO_2, their differences in legalisation, and lastly, the willingness of these organisations to grant access to the author. Thus, Chapters 6 and 7 included case studies on the OAA and the IMO, respectively.

Chapter 6 evaluated the architecture and functioning of the OAA against the five elements of the ideal type of global experimentalist governance. Although there is consensus among Alliance members regarding the existence of a shared problem when it comes to OA, and goals and metrics have been established to address this issue, the current metrics lack specificity to establish precise targets. Without such targets, it becomes challenging to evaluate members' performance in addressing the problem. This limitation also hinders the subsequent steps inherent in global experimentalist governance, including the feedback and peer-review process. Given that feedback and peer review are essential for the recursive learning process, this diminishes the realisation of global experimentalist governance within the OAA. Nevertheless, the Alliance is working towards making its metrics more concrete and implementing more formal reporting requirements. Such changes could enhance the presence of experimentalist governance in the OAA, suggesting that in the future, the architecture of the Alliance might more closely resemble the ideal type of global experimentalist governance.

Chapter 7 examined the extent to which the IMO applies global experimentalist governance to tackle the problem of OA. However, as the IMO does not directly address OA, it first considered which areas of the IMO's work are relevant to OA and, consequently, where OA could be integrated within their efforts. Subsequently, the working procedures within the IMO's response to climate change – through which the IMO indirectly addresses OA – were analysed to identify features of global experimentalist governance. Similar to the OAA, the structure and functioning of the IMO's response to climate change do not fully resemble the ideal type of global experimentalist governance. The IMO's member states and the organisation's observers agree that climate change is a shared problem that requires collective action. Therefore, goals and metrics have been established and are provisional, as stipulated by the theory of global experimentalist governance. The quest for solutions to this common problem has been delegated to lower-level actors for experimentation. This delegation is facilitated through NAPs. These NAPs are voluntary and intended to complement the activities of the IMO. Moreover, the NAP architecture fails to meet the ideal type of global experimentalist governance at the feedback and peer-review stage. Specifically, a comparison of the reported information and the collection of best practices does not take place. Again, since these elements are vital for global experimentalist governance, deficiencies in this process hinder the realisation of this governance approach within the IMO. It thus becomes apparent that the IMO's response to climate change reflects the architecture and functioning of global experimentalist governance only to a certain extent.

8.2 Discussion of Remaining Questions

The case studies have shown that while features within the OAA and IMO resemble global experimentalist governance, neither of the examined actors fully realises the theory's ideal type. This raises the question of what hinders these actors from completely realising the elements of the ideal type. Accordingly, this conclusion will consider the types of factors that may impede the realisation of global experimentalist governance in the OAA/IMO's approach to OA as a problem. Considering the obstacles that may block the fulfilment of the ideal type of global experimentalist governance may provide insights not only for the institutions under examination – the OA Alliance and the IMO – but also for other institutions that can address OA.

8.2.1 Global Experimentalist Governance within the OA Alliance

The OA Alliance did not fulfil all elements of global experimentalist governance, particularly the second element: agreement on open-ended goals and specific metrics. Global experimentalist governance theory recommends establishing open-ended goals alongside specific metrics that can evaluate actors' progress towards achieving them. The Alliance sets both goals and metrics. While the goals are open-ended and align with global experimentalist governance theory, the metrics lack sufficient specificity to establish precise targets. This absence of specific targets complicates the evaluation of members' performance, undermining not just the second step of the ideal type but also the entire feedback and peer-review cycle. That said, setting metrics as specific targets aimed at reducing OA is a challenging task.

The very nature of OA as a problem and the insufficiency of data concerning the phenomenon of OA make setting precise OA thresholds difficult. It can even be debated whether setting pH thresholds would be the right path, as other forms of measurement might be more targeted.[941] Throughout this book, it has been shown that OA is a complex problem. For instance, average and peak pH values differ between the open ocean and coastlines, as well as between different water layers. At the same time, pH values also vary between coastlines; for instance, some experience upwelling with extreme pH events while others do not.

Furthermore, different ecosystems, species, and life stages exhibit varying tolerance to changing pH levels. Additionally, OA is not the only ocean stressor; sea-level rise and ocean warming, among others, are also increasingly threatening the oceans. Chapter 2 illustrated that the interactions among these different stressors are not sufficiently understood. Overall, more research, particularly monitoring through time series and in situ (field) experiments and observations, is needed before concrete OA thresholds can be agreed on.[942] These examples merely illustrate why setting concrete metrics regarding OA is problematic. Accordingly, although the OA Alliance is attempting to solidify its metrics, as described in the first case study, it will take time before targets that fulfil the requirements of the ideal type of global experimentalist governance can be established. However, challenges in setting metrics with concrete targets should not come as a surprise, especially when dealing with a newly emerging and relatively recent environmental issue. Establishing concrete reduction targets or thresholds for any environmental problem necessitates a certain amount of research, and OA is no exception.

Nevertheless, as indicated above, governing complex problems is precisely what global experimentalist governance is designed to address, as illustrated in Chapter 4. Experimenting and learning through the comparison of various strategies at the local level can inform the necessary adjustments of prematurely

[941] For example, the planetary boundary level for OA is defined in 'terms of the marine saturation level, Ω, of aragonite, a form of calcium carbonate.' See Christoph Butz and others, 'Towards Defining an Environmental Investment Universe within Planetary Boundaries' (2018) 13 *Sustainability Science* 1031, 1035; Johan Rockström and others, 'A Safe Operating Space for Humanity' (2009) 461 *Nature* 472.

[942] Cf. for example, Abed El Rahman Hassoun and others, 'Ocean Acidification Research in the Mediterranean Sea: Status, Trends and Next Steps' (2022) 9 *Frontiers in Marine Science* 892670; Phillip Williamson and Carol Turley, 'Ocean Acidification in a Geoengineering Context' (2012) 370 *Philosophical Transactions of the Royal Society A: Mathematical, Physical and Engineering Sciences* 4317.

established, yet provisional, metrics and goals. As all lower-level stakeholders experiment with different strategies, specific metrics are essential to evaluate whether they are on the right track to achieving the overarching goals. Both metrics and goals can then be adjusted as needed, in line with what can be learned from experimentation, developing science, and technology. Thus, in cases where the problem is complex and the science is insufficiently understood, as is the case for OA, global experimentalist governance, along with its recursive learning cycle, is the only reasonable approach to address these issues. However, other institutions attempting to tackle OA will likely face the same challenges as the OA Alliance. Global experimentalist governance may, therefore, hold promise as a strategy to manage these scientific uncertainties and complexities.

8.2.2 Global Experimentalist Governance within the IMO

Like many institutions, the IMO has not directly considered or addressed OA in its work. Instead, the IMO approaches OA indirectly through its focus on geoengineering, air pollution, and climate change, as detailed in Chapter 7. Thus, the presence of global experimentalist governance can only be evaluated in relation to these indirect methods of addressing OA. Two questions then arise: If the IMO chooses to tackle OA directly, which factors should be taken into careful consideration? Why has the IMO not fully recognised the ideal type of global experimentalist governance?

Regarding the first question, if the IMO were to include OA in its work, the question of how best to do so would require a thorough analysis. That being said, two points can be briefly presented in this conclusion: the first relating to emissions and the second relating to scrubber effluents.

First, similar to what other authors have pointed out regarding the climate change regime,[943] the IMO should set strict reduction targets for CO_2 emissions, specifically since CO_2 is the main contributor to OA. Achieving emissions reduction to meet the Paris Agreement's long-term temperature goal, even on a 1.5°C pathway, could be accomplished in many different ways. However, the impacts on the ocean would differ depending on the route chosen to achieve the temperature goal. More specifically, the impact on the ocean will depend on how much and how quickly CO_2 is being reduced.[944] Global concentrations of atmospheric CO_2 can, at a maximum, reach 450 ppm (parts per million[945]). Even at that level,

[943] Gordon (n 31) 41; Simons and Stephens (n 17) 8.

[944] Cf. Harrould-Kolieb, 'Implications of the Paris Agreement for Action on Ocean Acidification within the UNFCCC' (n 57) 30.

[945] PPM – parts per million means that for every 1 million atmospheric molecules 450 parts are CO_2 molecules. Cf. NOAA, Global Monitoring Laboratory, 'Carbon Cycle Greenhouse Gases – Trends in CO_2' (2024) https://gml.noaa.gov/ccgg/trends/weekly.html#:~:text=Data%20are%20reported%20as%20a,parts%20per%20million%20(ppm) accessed 15 January 2024.

dangerous negative impacts on the marine ecosystem might not be prevented.[946] If emissions reduction targets were to stabilise atmospheric CO_2 at 450 ppm, this would translate to a stabilisation of an ocean surface pH of approximately 8.01.[947] Unfortunately, in 2021, atmospheric CO_2 already exceeded 414 ppm (meaning 92 per cent of the capacity has been reached).[948]

Nevertheless, it should be noted that while these numbers are good indicators, finding a threshold that signifies safe or dangerous conditions is difficult to define for OA.[949] Defining a threshold for pH in a manner similar to 2°C for warming (atmospheric levels of approximately 450 ppm CO_2 equivalent) is challenging. For the reasons explained throughout this book, OA is not uniform; pH changes and impacts are contextual, both spatially and temporally. Therefore, it is unlikely that there will be a global tipping point for OA.[950] Even if CO_2 is stabilised at 450 ppm, it is expected that there is still a danger of significant and large-scale OA impacts.[951]

Hence, OA-specific action needs to be taken swiftly, and Harrould-Kolieb and Hoegh-Guldberg underline that '[s]ubstantial losses are expected for coastal livelihoods and industries if 1.5°C of average global warming is exceeded, even if this overshoot is only temporary'.[952] Also, an IPCC Special Report on the impacts of global warming of 1.5°C warns that 'multiple lines of evidence that ocean warming and acidification corresponding to 1.5°C of global warming would impact a wide range of marine organisms and ecosystems, (...) (*high confidence*)'.[953] Therefore, regarding emissions, the IMO ought to set specific targets for CO_2 emissions, the leading cause of OA. While setting these specific targets, thresholds relevant for acidification – rather than just temperature change – should be considered, as these are likely to differ significantly. These thresholds should be seen as indicative and provisional, susceptible to adjustment over time in accordance with new and developing scientific findings. Here, global experimentalist governance would be a suitable approach to inject the necessary adaptability and flexibility.

Second, the IMO should discourage or set strict limitations on the use of exhaust gas cleaning systems, known as scrubbers, particularly open-loop scrubbers, to remove SO_x and, less frequently, NO_x from exhaust gas emitted into the atmosphere.[954] A significant pH reduction in seawater is expected due to this technology, especially in heavily trafficked areas of the sea, as explained in detail in Chapter 2.[955] Open-loop scrubbers discharge the removed SO_x as acid wash

946 Williamson and Turley (n 942) 4327. 947 Ibid., 4325. 948 Findlay and others (n 5) 1.
949 Williamson and Turley (n 942) 4327. 950 Ibid. 951 Ibid.
952 Harrould-Kolieb and Hoegh-Guldberg (n 26) 13.
953 Ove Hoegh-Guldberg and others, 'Impacts of 1.5°C of Global Warming on Natural and Human Systems' in V. Masson-Delmotte and others (eds), *Global Warming of 1.5°C: IPCC Special Report on Impacts of Global Warming of 1.5°C above Pre-industrial Levels in Context of Strengthening Response to Climate Change, Sustainable Development, and Efforts to Eradicate Poverty* (Cambridge University Press 2018) 178.
954 Endres and others (n 168) 5, 6; Turner and others (n 121) 370.
955 Dulière, Baetens and Lacroix (n 170) 8.

into the ocean.[956] While open-loop scrubbers are the cheapest and most commonly used option, they are also the most harmful. These scrubbers use seawater to clean SO_x from exhaust gas, but the water released back into the ocean after the process has a very low pH.[957] Scrubbers, particularly open-loop scrubbers, should be avoided even with the aim of complying with regulations designed to address the emissions problem.[958] Even though there are voluntary guidelines proposing a minimum outlet pH level of 6.5 and limiting the pH variance between inlet and outlet to 2 pH units while the ship is in port, these guidelines are weak.[959] The logarithmic nature of the pH scale implies that even seemingly minor deviations can lead to substantial increases in acidity. Consequently, a discharge pH of 6.5 is significantly more acidic than the average seawater pH of 8.1. Thus, the introduced numerical criteria cannot realistically prevent acidification and therefore make no difference from an OA perspective.

Thus, if the IMO intends to address OA specifically, it should, at a minimum, establish appropriate CO_2 reduction targets for OA. Additionally, the IMO should discourage the use of scrubbers, particularly open-loop scrubbers. Neither of these two measures is currently operational within the IMO as of 2025.

Regarding the second question, namely, why the IMO has not fully realised the ideal type of global experimentalist governance, it is necessary to focus on two issues, namely, the apprehension of both delegation and provisionality, as well as on the report/feedback/peer-review cycle. More concretely, within the IMO, especially where the IMO applies experimentalist structures, IMO member states do not all seem committed to the nascent experimentalist architecture. Instead, a reluctance to experiment can be observed.

While the IMO delegates the search for solutions to the national level through NAPs, these NAPs are voluntary and seen as complementary to actions at the IMO level. Consequently, NAPs are primarily intended to generate short-term actions, while further measures are outlined at the IMO level. In this context, there is some hesitation to delegate the search for solutions to lower levels of governance, specifically national governments. Indeed, only a few member states have developed NAPs and communicated them to the IMO Secretariat for sharing on the IMO website.

Apprehension regarding experimentalist structure can also be seen in the member states' reluctance towards provisionality. Following global experimentalist governance theory, the established goals and metrics are provisional, allowing for adjustments based on the latest scientific findings and technological developments. However, as the case study explains, member states seem to attribute

[956] Endres and others (n 168) 5, 6; Turner and others (n 121) 370.

[957] Ibid; Dulière, Baetens and Lacroix (n 170) 9.

[958] Cf. *International Convention for the Prevention of Pollution from Ships*, 1973, as modified by the Protocol of 1978 (MARPOL 73/78) annex VI, Reg. 13, Reg. 14.

[959] MEPC, 'MEPC.170(57) – Guidelines for Exhaust Gas Cleaning Systems' (n 297) 10.1.2.1(i); Comer, Georgeff and Osipova (n 555) 9.

a certain risk to this provisionality. Some member states fear that the possibility of revision may lead to so-called backsliding.[960] Backsliding would entail that ambitious goals or metrics might be diluted during further revision.

Lastly, the NAP architecture is not structured in a manner that promotes feedback and peer review. The reporting of NAPs is carried out only to a limited extent. While best practices are being gathered, this is occurring through IMO experts in the GreenVoyage guide and on the GreenVoyage website, rather than by lower-level participants who analyse reported information and compile best practices. Nevertheless, this method of collecting best practices is not envisioned by the ideal type of global experimentalist governance. Since feedback and peer review are crucial components of the recursive learning process, shortcomings in these processes hinder the realisation of global experimentalist governance within the IMO.

After discussing the shortcomings of both the OA Alliance and the IMO in relation to global experimentalist governance, it can be stated that these institutions only partially realise the different aspects of the theory. While neither the OA Alliance nor the IMO has fully implemented global experimentalist governance, their engagement with its principles offers valuable insights for future governance strategies. Indeed, analysing the activities of these two institutions confirms that global experimentalist governance serves as an appropriate response for OA. Based on these findings, the following section revisits the original research question: how OA, as a complex and uncertain problem, is and should be governed.

8.3 How Is and Should OA Be Governed?

In line with the research question posed in Chapter 1, this book explores how OA is and should be governed, given the nature of the problem it presents. Without repeating the entire argumentation of this book, it can be said that after examining the science behind OA (including causes, stressors, and adaptation options) as well as the current governance landscape, global experimentalist governance emerges as an appropriate response to OA. In short, OA is a complex issue that requires a multilevel approach alongside adjustable and flexible governance. Thus, many actors operating at different levels of governance are positioned to join the quest for a better understanding of the problem and how it can be addressed. Furthermore, the current governance landscape for OA is characterised by regime complexity and, consequently, by the presence of diverse actors of various types operating at different levels. Therefore, it is fortunate that global experimentalist governance can build upon elements of the existing OA regime complex and that fragmentation in governance responses to OA can be viewed as an advantage in this context.

[960] 'Marine Environment Protection Committee (MEPC) – 79th Session' (n 940).

In the case studies, it has been observed that at least two of the actors included in the regime complex map created in Chapter 3 are already applying certain features of global experimentalist governance, although not always with great ambition and certainly not in full. More specifically, the institutions tested lack specific metrics, as well as reporting, peer review, and feedback mechanisms. The reasons for this incomplete application of the theory seem to stem from apprehension towards experimentation and the complexity of OA as a problem. On one hand, the apprehension towards the experimentalist structure represents a challenge inherent to the institution and its members and cannot be addressed through the theory itself. On the other hand, the complexity of OA relates to the core problem and can be addressed through features of global experimentalist governance, such as provisional metrics and goals. After discussing the actors' issues with various aspects of the theory in detail, it can be confirmed that global experimentalist governance is an appropriate governance approach for OA, as it provides the flexibility and adaptability that such a complex problem requires.

8.4 Limitations and Recommendations for Future Research

This section will discuss two limitations of the book, which could be addressed by further research. First, due to time and space constraints, this book had to limit the number of case studies to two: the OA Alliance and the IMO. As Chapter 5 shows, many other institutions could have been tested against the ideal type of global experimentalist governance. Institutions highlighted in that chapter, such as the IUCN, UNEP, and UNESCO, could also form the basis of interesting and informative case studies. Additionally, there are organisations that were not discussed in detail in Chapter 5 that are highly relevant to the problem of OA, most notably the UNFCCC. While the climate change regime and, specifically, the UNFCCC and the Paris Agreement have been extensively discussed in the literature from a legal perspective, the instruments have received less attention from an OA governance viewpoint. Furthermore, it should be noted that the map in Chapter 3 is not exhaustive, as it only includes institutions identified as relevant to OA governance in the legal and scientific literature, as well as those found through Internet searches. The non-exhaustive nature of the map indicates that institutions which could serve as interesting case studies may not be included.

Second, this book does not engage with the potential significance of ammonia (especially regarding shipping) and methane hydrates for OA. Ammonia is mentioned alongside NO_x and SO_x as a possible contributor to changes in ocean chemistry, including OA.[961] Similarly, Billé et al. note the possible relevance of methane hydrates for OA.[962] The risk is that these methane hydrates, which represent

[961] Hunter and others (n 107) 1; Scott, 'Ocean Acidification' (n 29) 385.
[962] Billé and others (n 23) 764.

'a significant fraction of the amount of carbon globally stored',[963] may, with 'changes in sea level and/or deep oceanic warming (…) cause a transition from the hydrate into the gas phase, [and] therefore, would allow outgassing into the overlying ocean'.[964] This outgassing would then facilitate microbial aerobic oxidation. Through this process, the methane in the ocean water is, after the outgassing, converted with oxygen into CO_2.[965] This additional CO_2 would lead to further acidification. The significance of ammonia and methane hydrates for OA – including possible implications for governance issues – has not been explored in this book and would present an interesting and important topic for further research.

Apart from the limitations of the book, there are also some possible constraints regarding the theory of global experimentalist governance. The vision of global experimentalist governance merits critical scrutiny. Two particularly important issues emerged during the research for this book, highlighting potential constraints of global experimentalist governance in practice and warranting further investigation beyond this book.

First, there may be issues of communication and trust across governance levels. While communication consistently poses challenges in multilevel governance systems, it becomes particularly difficult in the context of global experimentalist governance due to the complexity and abstract nature of the problems it seeks to address. For instance, OA, with its various dimensions and Earth spheres it engages, is not easy to communicate. This not only creates barriers to communication between the scientific and policy communities but also between international institutions and domestic-level actors. In some linguistic contexts, there may not be adequate vocabulary to fully express or comprehend the concept of OA, which severely limits local engagement and the bottom-up feedback loops that global experimentalist governance relies on.

Second, there is the problem of comparison. A key tenet of global experimentalist governance is that actors can learn from one another through iterative experimentation and mutual assessment. However, in interviews conducted for this book – particularly with countries that have or intend to create NAPs – it became apparent that many stakeholders are skeptical about the transferability of solutions across borders. They often emphasise that their national contexts are too distinct for meaningful comparison and express doubt that experiments carried out elsewhere provide useful guidance for their own policy design. While the theory of global experimentalist governance assumes that localised experimentation can generate insights that diffuse across the governance system, this presumes a certain level of trust in the comparability of circumstances and the validity of peer learning, trust that may be lacking in practice.

These limitations do not invalidate the potential of global experimentalist governance, but they do suggest that its success depends on deeper contextual understanding and stronger communicative and epistemic infrastructures than are

[963] Ibid. [964] Ibid. [965] Ibid.

currently in place. Further empirical research is needed to understand how communication gaps, linguistic challenges, and doubts about comparability shape actors' willingness and ability to participate in experimentalist processes. Without addressing these issues, the promise of global experimentalist governance may remain more theoretical than practical.

This book has made it clear that OA is a complex problem posing a real threat to our environment, including people and ocean life. It has highlighted the necessity for a governance framework that not only understands this complexity but also synergises with the existing regime complex, finding global experimentalist governance to be a suitable match. Although the case studies reveal that only fragments of this approach are currently in place within the examined institutions, it remains a promising strategy for addressing OA. However, it is imperative to recognise that OA is merely one aspect of the myriad issues afflicting our oceans, particularly under the shadow of climate change. There is a need for more social science research that builds on natural science findings and transforms them into real world solutions to protect our oceans and ourselves. The path forward demands a proactive transdisciplinary approach, where scientific understanding is seamlessly integrated into governance strategies, ensuring the resilience of our oceans.

ANNEX A: DATA AND INFORMATION COLLECTION

Bodega Marine Laboratory (Ocean Climate Lab), UC Davis	
	Timeline March–April 2022 **Purpose of visit** Feedback on scientific information (chapter II) by Meghan Zulian, PhD candidate Answering outstanding questions with the help of scientists (chapter II)
Ocean Acidification Alliance	
	Timeline April 2022–October 2023, **Interviews** 4 in-depth interview, and shorter clarifying follow-up conversations with representative of the Alliance
International Maritime Organization (IMO)	
	Timeline December 2022–July 2023 **Meetings attended** ISWG – GHG 13: 5th–9th December 2022 MEPC79: 12th–16th December 2022 ISWG – GHG 15: 26th–30th June 2023 MEPC80: 3rd–7th July 2023 **Interviews** Eight interviews in total, six country delegates and two internal IMO experts

ANNEX B: OVERVIEW OF INTERNATIONAL OA ACTIVITIES (ORGANISED BY ACTOR IN ALPHABETICAL ORDER)

This annex is intended to provide a compact overview of the activities related to ocean acidification (OA) on the international plane. The material was gathered to enable the mapping activity in Chapter 3 and to assist with the identification of actors with significant potential to address OA in Chapter 5. Although the main findings of the material contained in this annex are summarised in Chapter 3, the information gathered has been included in the form of an annex in order to avoid interrupting the flow of the discussion of the main body of the book. Many readers will already be familiar with much of this information contained in this annex, and even those who are less familiar will find it easier to dip in and out of the material rather than confronting this quantity of information *en masse*.

This annex provides a snapshot of the international governance landscape relating to OA, some aspects of which have already been described in the book itself. The focus of the annex is on OA mitigation and adaptation and will not, for instance, include considerations regarding other ocean stressors such as other repercussions of climate change (for example, warming, sea-level rise) and plastic pollution. It examines all of the international actors analysed in this book and which are included on the 'map' in Chapter 3. It also includes three main sets of instruments: the Climate Change Regime, the Convention on Biological Diversity, and the Law of the Seas Regime. These sets of instruments will be discussed after the actor that they are associated with. Each institution discussed in the annex is analysed based on a set framework (as applicable), including general information about the institution, its founding documents/objective/mission, the measures they are empowered to adopt, and its explicit/implicit mandate, comprising also the latest OA relevant developments under the auspices of each institution. Much of the information included in this annex can be found in more detail in existing academic literature. This literature also provides discussions that were briefly highlighted in the literature review in Chapter 1 of this book. These discussions include issues such as the applicability of legal instruments to OA, due diligence obligations under UNCLOS, and dispute resolution under UNCLOS. Instead, this annex provides an overview of what is happening/has happened regarding OA in the international governance landscape.

Readers will notice that this annex does not include a discussion of all thirty-one actors identified in Chapter 3. It excludes five actors that focus exclusively on research activities in relation to OA. Also, because it is intended to give an overview of the international (or global) governance landscape, regional actors have not been included.

Table A.1 below offers a snapshot of the information included in this annex concerning the mandates/objectives/missions of international actors and relevant instruments to address OA, as well as identifying which institutions have taken action in relation to OA even without an explicit or implicit mandate to do so.

Table A.1 Overview of OA mandates/objectives/missions of international institutions

Actors/Instruments	*Explicit OA mandate/ objective/mission*	*Implicit OA mandate/ objective/mission*	*No explicit OA mandate/objective/ mission but steps taken to address OA*
ICAO		X	
IMO		X	X? *maybe Scrubber Guidelines
Law of the Seas Regime		X	X? *maybe High Seas Treaty, UNFSA
IUCN		X	X *recent actions
OAA	X		
Oceana		X	X *past actions
UNEP		X	
Climate change regime		X	X? *recent developments
CBD		X	X *recent developments
UNESCO		X	X *IOC–UNESCO
UNGA		X	X *recent developments
World Bank		X	
WOC		X	X *emerging issues
WWF		X	X *recent actions

Source: Compiled by author.

While actors have mandates, objectives, and sometimes missions, instruments often only have objectives. Usually, mandates are established by foundational treaties, objectives can be found in instruments, and missions or something equivalent are often used by actors who do not have a foundational treaty (see also Chapter 5). Sometimes, institutions have additional objectives or missions on their websites. The headings in the first line of the table are explained below, and an actor or instrument will receive an X in that column if they meet the criteria:

Explicit OA mandate/objective/mission:
: Explicit OA mandate/objective/mission indicates that the actor or instrument explicitly addresses OA through, for instance, its founding treaty, mission, or objective.

Implicit OA mandate:
: An implicit mandate/objective/mission indicates that the actor or instrument implicity addresses OA through, for instance, its mandate, mission, or objectives. An implicit OA mandate arises when the actor or instrument does not have an explicit mandate to tackle OA. However, it does have the mandate/objective/mission to deal with one of the other causes of OA or adaptation options in relation to OA. Therefore, these institutions have either a specific mandate to deal with, for example, CO_2, NO_x/SO_x, land-based pollution, or a broad mandate like 'protect the environment' that is relevant to OA. Thus, the actor or instrument in question is implicitly empowered to tackle OA through its mandate, mission, or objectives.

No explicit OA mandate but steps taken to address OA:
: This column indicates that the actor or instrument with an implicit OA mandate/objective/mission has taken steps to address OA in their work despite not having an explicit mandate to do so.

The International Civil Aviation Organization (ICAO)

The International Civil Aviation Organization (ICAO) is a specialised agency of the United Nations.[966] The Organization pursues five comprehensive strategic objectives, namely that global civil aviation should be safe, secure, efficient, economically viable, and environmentally responsible.[967] ICAO's founding document is the Convention on International Civil Aviation, also known as the Chicago Convention.[968] This convention was signed on 7 December 1944, by fifty-two states and entered into effect on 4 April 1947.[969] The Chicago Convention is an international treaty.

[966] ICAO, 'About ICAO' (2024) www.icao.int/about-icao/Pages/default.aspx accessed 4 May 2024.

[967] ICAO, 'Strategic Objectives' (2024) www.icao.int/about-icao/Council/Pages/Strategic-Objectives.aspx accessed 4 May 2024.

[968] Convention on International Civil Aviation 1944 (UNTS 15 (p295)) ch. VII.

[969] ICAO, 'The History of ICAO and the Chicago Convention' (2024) www.icao.int/about-icao/History/Pages/default.aspx accessed 4 May 2024.

ICAO is empowered to adopt standards and recommended practices (SARPs) as well as Procedures for Air Navigation (PANS). ICAO is in charge of over 12,000 SARPs across 19 Convention Annexes and six PANS to the Convention.[970] Article 44 of the Chicago Convention describes the objectives of ICAO. The article of the Chicago Convention tasks ICAO with '(…) developing the principles and techniques of international air navigation and to foster the planning and development of international air transport (…)'[971] Amongst other things, this involves ensuring that international aviation develops in a manner that is safe and orderly, but also that aviation '(…) can meet the needs of the peoples of the world for safe, regular, efficient and economical air transport'.

ICAO and OA

ICAO can only indirectly address OA as it primarily focuses on the principles and techniques of international air navigation and promotes the planning and development of international air transport to ensure safe and orderly growth, as seen above. However, ICAO's commitment to environmental protection is encapsulated in its strategic objectives, which include minimising the adverse environmental effects of civil aviation activities.[972] This commitment is defined on the website where it says that:

> ICAO serves as a multilateral platform for cooperation on international aviation environmental protection. Over the years, (…) 'ICAO Member States', have agreed to concentrate their aviation environmental collaboration on three core areas:
>
> - Climate change and aviation emissions
> - Aircraft noise
> - Local air quality[973]

As indicated by these categories and confirmed by the Organization's website, ICAO works on reducing CO_2 and NO_x, both drivers of OA. More precisely regarding CO_2, 'ICAO formulates policies, develops and updates Standards and Recommended Practices (SARPs) on aircraft emissions, and conducts outreach activities'.[974] At its 41st Session in 2022, the ICAO Assembly adopted Resolution A41-21, setting a long-term global aspirational goal for international aviation to achieve net zero carbon emissions by 2050, aligning with the Paris Agreement's temperature goal. This goal will be pursued through a combination of measures

[970] ICAO, 'How ICAO Develops Standards' (2024) www.icao.int/about-icao/AirNavigationCommission/Pages/how-icao-develops-standards.aspx accessed 4 May 2024; Convention on International Civil Aviation art 37.

[971] Convention on International Civil Aviation art 44.

[972] ICAO, 'Strategic Objectives' (n 967).

[973] ICAO, 'Environmental Protection' (2024) www.icao.int/environmental-protection/Pages/default.aspx accessed 4 May 2024.

[974] ICAO, 'Climate Change' (2024) www.icao.int/environmental-protection/pages/climate-change.aspx accessed 6 May 2024.

such as advancements in aircraft technology, operational improvements, the use of sustainable aviation fuels, and the implementation of market-based measures like CORSIA.[975] In addition, ICAO has been developing measures since the late 1970s to address aircraft engine emissions, including NO_x, which impact local air quality near airports, as detailed in Volume II of Annex 16 to the Convention on International Civil Aviation.[976]

Through these efforts, ICAO indirectly contributes to combating OA. By working to reduce CO_2 and NO_x emissions from aircraft, ICAO helps mitigate the drivers of OA. Therefore, ICAO's CO_2 and NO_x mitigation measures can be seen as part of a broader strategy that also benefits the marine environment, helping to address the challenges posed by OA indirectly.

The International Maritime Organization (IMO)

The International Maritime Organization (IMO) is a specialised agency of the United Nations responsible for regulating shipping to promote maritime safety, security, and environmental protection.[977] Established in 1948 under its original name, the Inter-Governmental Maritime Consultative Organization (IMCO), it was renamed the International Maritime Organization in 1982.[978] The IMO's foundational legal document, the Convention on the International Maritime Organization, outlines the IMO's structure, purpose, and functions. By its foundational document, the IMO is empowered to create binding international regulations pertaining to maritime safety and environmental protection.[979] Specifically, article 1(a) of the Convention charges the IMO with promoting 'the general adoption of the highest practicable standards in matters concerning (…) prevention and control of marine pollution from ships'.[980] The IMO is authorised to adopt a range of measures to achieve the purposes of the convention. The IMO should, pursuant to Part II, article 2(b) of the IMO Convention: 'provide for the drafting of conventions, agreements, or other suitable instruments, and to recommend these to Governments and to intergovernmental organizations, and to convene such conferences as may be necessary'.[981] Accordingly, the IMO has created several key maritime conventions, including the London Convention (LC) and Protocol

975 Ibid.

976 ICAO, 'Local Air Quality' (2024) www.icao.int/environmental-protection/Pages/local-air-quality.aspx accessed 6 May 2024.

977 Under: 'What Is the International Maritime Organization (IMO)?' IMO, 'Frequently Asked Questions' (n 769).

978 Under: 'What Is the International Maritime Organization (IMO)?' ibid.

979 IMO, 'Convention on the International Maritime Organization' (n 304); Amendments to the Convention on the International Maritime Organization Relating to the Institutionalization of the Committee on Technical Co-operation in the Convention; Convention on the International Maritime Organization.

980 Ibid; IMO, 'Strategic Plan for the Organization' (n 304).

981 Ibid.

(LP), and the International Convention for the Prevention of Pollution from Ships (MARPOL 73/78).[982]

IMO and OA

Although the IMO does not have an explicit mandate to tackle OA, the organisation's broad mandate enables it to address various sources of marine pollution, implicitly including those that contribute to ocean acidification.[983] Specifically, by means of the conventions that have been adopted under its auspices, the IMO addresses some of the causes of OA, such as CO_2 emissions (climate change), air pollution from ships through NO_x and SO_x, and geoengineering activities:

For example, MARPOL 73/78 is tailored to tackle pollution from ships, including air pollutants such as NO_x/SO_x that contribute to OA (see articles 1, 2(2), 2(3)(a)).[984] Specifically, Annex VI of the convention aims to prevent air pollution from ships, including NO_x and SO_x.[985] The direct control of these emissions under MARPOL 73/78 illustrates the IMO's mandate to tackle contributors to OA and, therefore, to implicitly address OA.

The IMO also tackles CO_2 emissions. In line with its pollution reduction purpose, the IMO's Marine Environment Protection Committee adopted a new chapter 4 to Annex VI of MARPOL 73/78 in 2011 named 'Regulations on energy efficiency for ships'.[986] Through its Marine Environmental Protection Committee, the organisation also adopted a (non-binding) resolution (MEPC.304(72)) in April 2018, setting up an initial IMO strategy on the reduction of GHG emissions from ships, which was then followed in October of the same year by the Programme of follow-up actions of the Initial Strategy up to 2023.[987] Then, in July 2023, the IMO adopted the Revised GHG Strategy (MEPC.377(80)).[988] *Building on the strategies, the MEPC's 83rd meeting in 2025 resulted in a landmark agreement on a 'net zero framework' which has to be formally adopted in October 2025.* This move affirms the organisation's goal to reduce CO_2 produced by the shipping industry.[989] The IMO has, therefore, started

[982] Convention on the Prevention of Marine Pollution by Dumping of Wastes and Other Matter; London Protocol to the Convention on the Prevention of Marine Pollution by Dumping and Other Matter; International Convention for the Prevention of Pollution from Ships, 1973, as modified by the Protocol of 1978 (MARPOL 73/78).

[983] Cf. Amendments to the Convention on the International Maritime Organization Relating to the Institutionalization of the Committee on Technical Co-operation in the Convention; IMO, 'Convention on the International Maritime Organization' (n 304); Convention on the International Maritime Organization; IMO, 'Strategic Plan for the Organization' (n 304).

[984] International Convention for the Prevention of Pollution from Ships, 1973, as modified by the Protocol of 1978 (MARPOL 73/78).

[985] IMO, 'Prevention of Air Pollution from Ships' (n 537).

[986] IMO, 'Greenhouse Gas Emissions' (n 568).

[987] Ibid; IMO, 'IMO's Work to Cut GHG Emissions from Ships' (n 569); International Maritime Organization (IMO), Marine Environmental Protection Committee (MEPC) (n 569).

[988] IMO, '2023 IMO Strategy on Reduction of GHG Emissions from Ships' (n 863); IMO, 'IMO's Work to Cut GHG Emissions from Ships' (n 569).

[989] IMO, 'Greenhouse Gas Emissions' (n 568).

to address CO_2 as part of its climate change programme. Since CO_2 emissions are a major contributor to OA, by reducing these emissions, the IMO indirectly contributes to mitigating the primary cause of OA.

Lastly, the LC/LP address geoengineering.[990] While carbon capture and storage (CCS) is allowed under the LC and the LP's 2006 and 2009 amendments, these instruments strictly regulate ocean fertilisation and other marine geoengineering activities.[991] More concretely, the 2013 amendment to the Protocol comprises a definition of geoengineering in that it adds paragraph 5*bis* to article 1 of the LP.[992] In addition, the 2013 amendment added article 6*bis* to the LP. Pursuant to the article's para 1, parties shall not permit the release of 'matter' into the ocean water for marine geoengineering activities included in the list in annex 4. The list in annex 4 mentioned in the paragraph entails 'ocean fertilization', defining it in para 1.1. as a geoengineering activity that accordingly forbids the placement of matter (albeit without defining what matter is) into the sea as part of this activity. As geoengineering, particularly ocean fertilisation, can trigger OA, the IMO indirectly tackles OA through the LC/LP. The IMO, in some resolutions regarding geoengineering and the LC/LP does indeed consider OA.[993] All these resolutions mention OA, albeit in the preambular clauses. However, they do express concern as they are '[r]eiterating the serious concern regarding the implications for the marine environment of climate change and ocean acidification, as a result of elevated levels of carbon dioxide in the atmosphere'.[994]

Therefore, the IMO's legal framework provides the authority for this organisation to regulate the aspects of shipping that contribute to OA, albeit indirectly through, for instance, air pollution controls. This authority is grounded in the international treaties which are concluded, implemented and enforced by IMO Members. However, it is important to note that while the IMO sets these standards, its direct mandate does not explicitly target OA. Instead, the IMO's legal commitment is to reducing maritime pollution and protecting the marine environment and this aligns with efforts to combat OA, even in the absence of a direct mandate. To date, the IMO has not taken any direct actions that specifically target OA.

The most specific action that the IMO has taken in relation to OA is its regulation of exhaust gas cleaning systems or so-called scrubbers of ships that can be found in guidelines formulated by the IMO, and that address certain parameters

[990] Convention on the Prevention of Marine Pollution by Dumping of Wastes and Other Matter; London Protocol to the Convention on the Prevention of Marine Pollution by Dumping and Other Matter.

[991] IMO, 'Resolution LP.1(1) – ON THE AMENDMENT TO INCLUDE CO2 SEQUESTRATION IN SUB-SEABED GEOLOGICAL FORMATIONS IN ANNEX 1 TO THE LONDON PROTOCOL.Pdf' (n 584); IMO, 'Resolution LP.3(4) – 2009 AMENDMENT TO ARTICLE 6 OF THE 1996 PROTOCOL TO THE CONVENTION ON THE PREVENTION OF MARINE POLLUTION BY DUMPING OF WASTES AND OTHER MATTER 1972' (n 584).

[992] IMO, 'LP.4(8)' (n 311).

[993] International Maritime Organization (IMO), 'LP.3(4)' (n 297); International Maritime Organization (IMO), 'LP.5(14)' (n 297); International Maritime Organization (IMO), 'LP.1(1)' (n 297).

[994] International Maritime Organization (IMO), 'LP.3(4)' (n 297) 1; see also: International Maritime Organization (IMO), 'LP.5(14)' (n 297).

such as pH in scrubber discharge water.[995] However, the voluntary nature of these guidelines, coupled with the initial absence of numerical criteria in 2005 and the modest enhancements made by 2008, suggests a lack of stringent oversight.[996]

The Law of the Seas Regime

Another set of treaties that governs the ocean is the broader Law of the Seas Regime. The regime includes the United Nations Convention on the Law of the Sea (UNCLOS), the Biodiversity Beyond National Jurisdiction (BBNJ) Agreement, and the Fish Stocks Agreement.[997] The IMO is explicitly mentioned in article 2 of Annex VIII of UNCLOS as the Organization is considered to be the expert body regarding 'navigation including pollution from vessels' but is also referenced as 'the competent international organization' by several articles.[998] In particular, the IMO is mentioned concerning the adoption of shipping rules addressing, among other things, the prevention and control of pollution from vessels.[999] In addition, the IMO includes UNCLOS on their website on several occasions, for example, under 'our work' in the 'legal affairs' section.[1000] Hence, even though UNCLOS is not an IMO instrument, the IMO is the competent organisation under UNCLOS for preventing and controlling pollution from vessels.[1001]

As part of the Law of the Seas Regime, UNCLOS provides a comprehensive legal framework laying out the rights and responsibilities of states in maritime zones, environmental regulations, scientific research, and the settlement of disputes.[1002] In

[995] MEPC, 'MEPC.130(53) – Guidelines for On-Board Exhaust Gas-SO_x Cleaning Systems' (n 297); MEPC, 'MEPC.170(57) – Guidelines for Exhaust Gas Cleaning Systems' (n 297); MEPC, 'MEPC.184(59) – 2009 Guidelines for Exhaust Gas Cleaning Systems' (n 297); MEPC, 'MEPC.259(68) – 2015 Guidelines for Exhaust Gas Cleaning Systems' (n 297); MEPC, 'MEPC.340(77) – 2021 Guidelines for Exhaust Gas Cleaning Systems' (n 297).

[996] MEPC, 'MEPC.170(57) – Guidelines for Exhaust Gas Cleaning Systems' (n 297); MEPC, 'MEPC.130(53) – Guidelines for On-Board Exhaust Gas-SO_x Cleaning Systems' (n 297); Comer, Georgeff and Osipova (n 555) 7, 8, 9.

[997] United Nations Convention on the Law of the Sea (UNCLOS); Agreement under the United Nations Convention on the Law of the Sea on the Conservation and Sustainable Use of Marine Biological Diversity of Areas beyond National Jurisdiction; Agreement for the Implementation of the Provisions of the United Nations Convention on the Law of the Sea of 10 December 1982 Relating to the Conservation and Management of Straddling Fish Stocks and Highly Migratory Fish Stocks (UN Fish Stocks Agreement).

[998] IMO, 'The United Nations Convention on the Law of the Sea (UNCLOS) and the International Maritime Organization' (n 539); United Nations Convention on the Law of the Sea (UNCLOS) arts. 211(1), 216(1), 217(4) etc.

[999] IMO, 'Convention on the International Maritime Organization' (n 304) preprint 211(1); IMO, 'The United Nations Convention on the Law of the Sea (UNCLOS) and the International Maritime Organization' (n 539).

[1000] IMO, 'The United Nations Convention on the Law of the Sea (UNCLOS) and the International Maritime Organization' (n 539); IMO, 'United Nations Convention on the Law of the Sea' (n 538).

[1001] For further discussion on the relationship between UNCLOS and IMO, see also Harrould-Kolieb and Stephens (n 52) 276.

[1002] United Nations Convention on the Law of the Sea (UNCLOS) Contents.

addition, UNCLOS is phrased openly, allowing further development in this area of law. Hence, the United Nations Fish Stocks Agreement and the BBNJ Agreement are implementing agreements under UNCLOS.[1003]

The Law of the Seas Regime and OA

The Law of the Seas Regime's relevance for OA is twofold, as it can tackle some of the causes of OA and contribute to adaptation to OA. UNCLOS, in particular, includes various regulations to protect and preserve the marine environment, addressing different types of activities, including pollution from land-based sources and vessel-source pollution.[1004] Even though UNCLOS does not have a direct objective to address OA, its objective is broad enough to include OA, similar to what has been seen above with regard to the mandate of the IMO. UNCLOS, for example, addresses different sources of pollution, including from the atmosphere and land, that lead to OA.[1005] Therefore, this legal instrument contributes indirectly to tackling the causes of OA.

With regard to adaptation, even without taking specific note of OA, UNCLOS and the UN Fish Stocks Agreement also address the management of fisheries, which can be used as an adaptation method in relation to OA.[1006] Lastly, the new BBNJ Agreement regulates marine protected areas (MPAs) and even mentions OA within this part of the agreement.[1007] Even though it is still not the primary concern of the agreement, it does highlight that MPAs can achieve (among other things) resilience to stressors, including those related to OA.[1008] These different ways in which the Law of the Seas Regime can address OA will be discussed in more detail in the following:

More specifically, in Part XII of UNCLOS, regulations can be found regarding the prevention and control of pollution of the marine environment. Article 192 UNCLOS establishes that '[s]tates have the obligation to protect and preserve the marine environment'. Articles 194 and 212 set rules for pollution through the atmosphere while article 211 includes rules for the pollution from vessels. Pursuant to these articles, states shall create measures, regulations, laws, rules, or standards necessary to 'prevent, reduce and control pollution of the marine environment from

[1003] United Nations Convention on the Law of the Sea (UNCLOS); Agreement for the Implementation of the Provisions of the United Nations Convention on the Law of the Sea of 10 December 1982 Relating to the Conservation and Management of Straddling Fish Stocks and Highly Migratory Fish Stocks (UN Fish Stocks Agreement); Agreement under the United Nations Convention on the Law of the Sea on the Conservation and Sustainable Use of Marine Biological Diversity of Areas beyond National Jurisdiction.

[1004] United Nations Convention on the Law of the Sea (UNCLOS) Part VII.

[1005] Ibid.

[1006] University of California, Santa Cruz and others (n 250) 122.

[1007] For example, Agreement under the United Nations Convention on the Law of the Sea on the Conservation and Sustainable Use of Marine Biological Diversity of Areas beyond National Jurisdiction art Part III; University of California, Santa Cruz and others (n 250) 118.

[1008] Agreement under the United Nations Convention on the Law of the Sea on the Conservation and Sustainable Use of Marine Biological Diversity of Areas beyond National Jurisdiction art 17(c).

any source',[1009] including from or through the atmosphere.[1010] As seen in these articles, UNCLOS provides that states are obliged to control and prevent these different types of pollution and shall create rules accordingly. However, from the articles, it also becomes evident that states need to create further instruments to achieve the goals set by UNCLOS. Nevertheless, the convention calls for states to deal with emissions causing OA and provides the basis for them to do so, including, for instance, NO_x/SO_x, and CO_2 emissions.

In addition, UNCLOS explicitly mentions pollution from land-based sources. Pollution from land-based sources is referred to in a general article for the prevention, reduction, and control of pollution (194(3)(a) UNCLOS) and article 207 UNCLOS, which is entirely dedicated to the problem. Pursuant to article 207, '[s]tates shall adopt laws and regulations to prevent, reduce, and control pollution of the marine environment from land-based sources'.[1011] As seen above, UNCLOS typically only calls for states to create laws and regulations instead of setting concrete targets itself. Nevertheless, UNCLOS provides the basis for these laws and regulations and encourages states to deal with this type of coastal activity. Again, even though there is no explicit recognition that land-based pollution needs to be tackled due to it triggering OA, by encouraging action in this field, UNCLOS does contribute indirectly to tackling this problem.

With regard to adaptation, particularly, UNCLOS and the UN Fish Stocks Agreement, address fishing. UNCLOS follows a zonal division of the world's oceans; notably, two of the zones are covered by specific articles regulating fishing, namely the exclusive economic zone (EEZ) and the high seas.[1012] While in the EEZ, the coastal state has a sovereign right to explore, exploit, conserve, and manage natural resources, including fish, on the high seas, the freedom of fishing prevails as states can exercise their sovereignty.[1013] Accordingly, the coastal state is in charge of conservation in the EEZ, which includes preventing overexploitation and regulating the utilisation of living resources, including fish.[1014] Furthermore, states shall coordinate and cooperate to realise conservation concerning stocks occurring within several EEZs or an EEZ and the high seas or in case of highly migratory species.[1015] In addition, the articles governing the EEZ include special rules concerning anadromous and catadromous stocks.[1016] On the high seas, states must take measures such as agreeing on an allowable catch limits to conserve living resources pursuant to article 119 UNCLOS. According to the article, to do so, states shall 'take measures (…) designed, on the best scientific evidence available to the States concerned, to maintain or restore populations of harvested species at levels which can produce the maximum sustainable yield'.[1017]

[1009] United Nations Convention on the Law of the Sea (UNCLOS) preprint 194(1).
[1010] Ibid arts. 194(3)(a), 212.
[1011] Ibid., 207(1).
[1012] Ibid., Parts V, VII.
[1013] Ibid arts. 56(1)(a), 87(1)(e).
[1014] Ibid arts. 61, 62.
[1015] Ibid arts. 63, 64.
[1016] Ibid arts. 66, 67.
[1017] Ibid., 119(1)(a).

It can be seen that UNCLOS provides guidelines to coordinate fishing, which could reduce the contribution of fishing to ocean stress and can be viewed as a measure to allow for adaptation of the ecosystem and species. However, as has been seen, UNCLOS often only calls for the further creation of regulations and measures.[1018] Consistent with this, the UN Fish Stocks Agreement was subsequently created. As its name suggests, it is an 'Agreement for the Implementation of the Provisions of the United Nations Convention on the Law of the Sea of 10 December 1982 Relating to the Conservation and Management of Straddling Fish Stocks and Highly Migratory Fish Stocks'. Its objective is – according to its article 2 – 'to ensure the long-term conservation and sustainable use of straddling fish stocks and highly migratory fish stocks' and to this end further defines what states ought to do to achieve this goal.[1019] Accordingly, both within UNCLOS and the UN Fish Stocks Agreement, there is an opportunity to manage fisheries in a manner that can help the adaptation of ecosystems and species to OA and ocean stress more generally.

In fact, the Review Conference on the Fish Stocks Agreement emphasised the importance of addressing environmental factors and explicitly references the problem of OA in this regard. Regional Fisheries Management Organizations[1020] were called upon to enhance efforts to research and mitigate the effects of climate change and ocean acidification on marine ecosystems.[1021] Subsequently, the Inter-American Tropical Tuna Commission, collaborating with the Secretariat of the Pacific Community, launched a study focused on the potential impacts of OA on yellowfin tuna. The results of this study are expected to inform conservation and management measures across various Regional Fisheries Management Organizations.[1022] Thus, on some occasions and despite not being the main concern of UNCLOS or the UNFSA, there is now some consideration given to OA.

In addition, as was noted above, the new BBNJ Agreement/High Seas Treaty allows for the creation of MPAs, which is a tool that can, similar to fisheries management, help species and ecosystems adapt to OA. In fact, one of the main themes of the newly drafted High Seas Treaty under UNCLOS is MPAs.[1023] The treaty's objective is: 'conservation and sustainable use of marine biological diversity of areas

[1018] For example, with regard to the conversation of straddling and highly migratory stocks UNCLOS demands States to cooperate directly or through an International Organization. ibid 63(2), 64.

[1019] Agreement for the Implementation of the Provisions of the United Nations Convention on the Law of the Sea of 10 December 1982 Relating to the Conservation and Management of Straddling Fish Stocks and Highly Migratory Fish Stocks (UN Fish Stocks Agreement).

[1020] For a full discussion of RFMOs and OA, see: Rayfuse (n 365).

[1021] President of the Conference, 'A/CONF.210/2010/7 – Report of the Resumed Review Conference on the Agreement for the Implementation of the Provisions of the United Nations Convention on the Law of the Sea of 10 December 1982 Relating to the Conservation and Management of Straddling Fish Stocks and Highly Migratory Fish Stocks' https://documents.un.org/doc/undoc/gen/n10/465/87/pdf/n1046587.pdf?token=L3KyZpZK326ovLo6ww&fe=true.

[1022] Kim (n 21) 249.

[1023] See IUCN, 'BBNJ Knowledge Series' (n 625); IUCN, 'Marine Biodiversity of Areas beyond National Jurisdiction (BBNJ)' (n 625); cf. Draft Agreement under the United Nations Convention on the Law of the Sea on the Conservation and Sustainable Use of Marine Biological Diversity of Areas beyond National Jurisdiction.

beyond national jurisdiction'.[1024] Article 1 of the draft defines the terms used in the treaty. MPAs, one of the tools to achieve this objective, has its own definition: 'Marine protected area' means a geographically defined marine area that is designated and managed to achieve specific long-term biodiversity conservation objectives and may allow, where appropriate, sustainable use provided it is consistent with the conservation objectives.[1025]

In addition, article 1(1) also clarifies that MPAs fall under the collective term 'Area-based management tool'. Part III of the High Seas Treaty is fully dedicated to these 'Area-based management tools, including marine protected areas'. Article 17, the first article of Part III, states the objectives regarding this part of the treaty. One of the objectives (article 17(a)) is to '[c]onserve and sustainably use areas (…) including through the establishment of a comprehensive system of area-based management tools, with (…) networks of marine protected areas'. It becomes apparent that the creation and functioning of MPAs are central to the new High Seas Convention. However, it is also crucial to recall again that the aforementioned Part III, which deals with MPAs, expressly mentions OA. Article 17(c) describes that one of the objectives of Part III is: '[p]rotect, preserve, restore and maintain biodiversity and ecosystems, including with a view to enhancing their productivity and health, and strengthen resilience to stressors, including those related to climate change [and] ocean acidification'.[1026]

Hence, the High Seas Treaty provides for the establishment of MPAs as a useful tool for adaptation to OA, even recognising that MPAs can enhance resilience to ocean stressors like OA despite not being the Agreement's main purpose.

In sum, OA can be considered under the Law of the Seas Regime, albeit indirectly, as, for instance, UNCLOS does not have provisions specifically designed to address OA. However, its broad objectives for the protection of the marine environment and the prevention of marine pollution are relevant, as has been seen above. For substantial actions to mitigate OA, parties under UNCLOS would need to adopt a separate implementing agreement, potentially integrating OA concerns into broader discussions on marine biodiversity or creating a standalone agreement for OA (unlike under the climate change regime, where parties regularly meet and adopt collective actions and measures (Article 7 UNFCCC)).[1027] In contrast to the UNFCCC COP, where parties can adopt decisions that interpret and elaborate upon provisions of the convention, the conference of the parties of UNCLOS (pursuant to article 319(2) UNCLOS) does not discuss substantive matters[1028] Significantly, parties to UNCLOS have generally deferred regarding the governance of OA to the framework of the UNFCCC, viewing it as the more appropriate forum for discussing

[1024] Agreement under the United Nations Convention on the Law of the Sea on the Conservation and Sustainable Use of Marine Biological Diversity of Areas beyond National Jurisdiction art 2.

[1025] Ibid., 1(9).

[1026] Draft Agreement under the United Nations Convention on the Law of the Sea on the Conservation and Sustainable Use of Marine Biological Diversity of Areas beyond National Jurisdiction Art 17(c).

[1027] Oral (n 47) 27.

[1028] Scott, 'Ocean Acidification' (n 29) 407.

and addressing the issue.[1029] This perspective was notably supported during discussions at the United Nations Open-ended Informal Consultative Process on Oceans and the Law of the Sea.[1030] More specifically: '(…) several delegations raised concerns over the impacts of climate change on oceans including sea level rise and ocean acidification. Many delegations agreed on the need to address climate change in the context of the principles set out in the United Nations Framework for the Convention on Climate Change'.[1031]

According to Kim, this can be understood in the sense that some states suggested convening a debate regarding the adverse effects of climate change, including OA, but left their governance to the Climate Change Regime.[1032] Nevertheless, recent developments under the Law of the Seas Regime and, in particular, under the new BBNJ Agreement increasingly show recognition of the relevance of OA.

The International Union for Conservation of Nature (IUCN)

The International Union for Conservation of Nature (IUCN) is a global environmental organisation that brings together governments, civil society organisations, and experts in partnership with over 1,400 member organisations and over 16,000 experts.[1033] Its mission is to influence, encourage, and assist societies throughout the world in conserving nature's integrity and diversity and ensuring that any use of natural resources is equitable and ecologically sustainable.[1034] IUCN was founded in 1948, initially as the International Union for the Protection of Nature (IUPN), before it changed to its current name in 1956.[1035] The founding document of IUCN is its Statute, which has been amended several times to reflect the evolving scope and structure of the Organization.[1036] The IUCN Statute serves as the Organization's constitution, providing for its institutional framework and

[1029] UN Ad Hoc Open-Ended Informal Working Group to Study Issues Relating to the Conservation and Sustainable Use of Marine Biological Diversity beyond Areas of National Jurisdiction Co-Chairs, 'A/65/164 – Report on the Work of the United Nations Open-Ended Informal Consultative Process on Oceans and the Law of the Sea at Its 11th Meeting' (UN, 2010) para 90 https://digitallibrary.un.org/record/688502 accessed 30 April 2024; Kim (n 21) 252.

[1030] Co-Chairs, 'Report on the Work of the United Nations Open-Ended Informal Consultative Process on Oceans and the Law of the Sea at Its 11th Meeting' (n 1029) para 90; Kim (n 21) 252.

[1031] Co-Chairs, 'A/66/186 – Report on the Work of the United Nations Open-Ended Informal Consultative Process on Oceans and the Law of the Sea at Its Twelfth Meeting' (2011) para 58 https://documents.un.org/doc/undoc/gen/n11/431/39/pdf/n1143139.pdf?token=aK7q3hlWEdebSqYVHx&fe=true.

[1032] Ibid; Kim (n 21) 253.

[1033] IUCN, 'About IUCN | IUCN' (2024) www.iucn.org/about-iucn accessed 6 May 2024.

[1034] Ibid.

[1035] IUCN, 'Seventy Five Years of Experience | IUCN' (2024) www.iucn.org/about-iucn/history accessed 6 May 2024.

[1036] IUCN, *Statutes of 5 October 1948… (Including Rules of Procedure…) and Regulations…Last Amended on 13 December 2023* (n 586); see also: IUCN, *Statutes (Including Rules of Procedure) and Regulations (Last Amended on 31 March 2019)* (IUCN, International Union for Conservation of Nature 2019) https://portals.iucn.org/library/node/48398 accessed 20 January 2022.

objectives.[1037] The IUCN is registered as a legal entity in accordance with article 60 of the Swiss Civil Code, and it is allowed to operate internationally.[1038] The Union's objectives can be found in Part II of the IUCN Statute, and its article 2 stipulates that '[t]he objectives of IUCN shall be to influence, encourage and assist societies (…) to conserve the integrity and diversity of nature'.[1039] Hence, IUCN does not have an explicit mandate to deal with OA directly in its founding documents. However, it addresses OA implicitly through its broader conservation and environmental protection efforts. IUCN is empowered, pursuant to article 3 of Part II to, in order to achieve the objectives of the Organization, for example, build alliances, influence policy, disseminate research, and 'contribute to the preparation of international agreements (…) and encourages states to adhere to these agreements'.[1040]

IUCN and OA

The conservation of nature is a broad and general mandate, but the actor provides more details regarding its work on its website. Many of the Organization's actions and programmes are directly and indirectly relevant to tackling OA, so only a few examples will be provided here. For example, under the website's 'our work' and, more specifically, 'themes' section, IUCN explains the Union is working on 'climate change', 'ocean and coasts', 'protected areas and land use', 'nature-based solutions', which are all themes that are relevant to OA mitigation and adaptation.[1041] Within the 'ocean and coats' section, a webpage specifically deals with 'ocean and climate change'.[1042] As part of that section, OA is recognised as one of the issues caused by climate change in the ocean. 'IUCN's work on climate change in the ocean has been centred around furthering understanding the science of climate change threats to the ocean: ocean warming, acidification, (…)'.[1043] Under the 'our work' section of the 'ocean and climate change' website more information about OA can be found.[1044] IUCN hosts the OAiRUG, an expert group that distils the latest science on OA into policy advice and has advanced global understanding of OA. Following regional workshops supported by Foundation Prince Albert II, IAEA, and the Swedish Ministry of Environment, IUCN developed policy roadmaps for Latin America, the Caribbean, and the Western Indian Ocean, and is now focusing on raising awareness of multiple ocean climate stressors, including OA.[1045] Through

[1037] See: IUCN, *Statutes of 5 October 1948… (Including Rules of Procedure…) and Regulations…Last Amended on 13 December 2023* (n 586) Table of Contents.

[1038] Ibid I Legal Status, 1.

[1039] IUCN, *Statutes of 5 October 1948… (Including Rules of Procedure…) and Regulations…Last Amended on 13 December 2023* (n 586).

[1040] Ibid II, 3. (a), (d), (i), (j), (l).

[1041] IUCN, 'Our Work | IUCN' (2024) www.iucn.org/our-work accessed 6 May 2024.

[1042] IUCN, 'Ocean and Climate Change | IUCN' (2024) www.iucn.org/our-work/topic/ocean-and-climate-change accessed 6 May 2024.

[1043] Ibid. [1044] IUCN, 'Ocean Acidification | IUCN' (n 302). [1045] Ibid.

these efforts IUCN is therefore also directly working on OA and not just indirectly through its work on, for instance, climate change and nature-based solutions.

In addition, IUCN approaches blue carbon through one of the instruments linked to it (namely, RAMSAR). This linkage is based on the instrument's secretariat being located at the IUCN.[1046] The convention's mission can be found on its website and in articles of the text of the convention itself. The website says that Ramsar's mission is 'the conservation and wise use of all wetlands through local and national actions and international cooperation'.[1047] When referring to wetlands, the convention adopts a broad definition, including everything from coral reefs to marshes and mangroves.[1048] This mission is confirmed by articles 3.1, 4.1, and 5 RAMSAR.[1049] Thus, despite the convention not mentioning blue carbon protection, it does protect plants known for storing carbon, such as mangroves. RAMSAR can, in any case, protect the ocean from further acidification by protecting these wetlands.

The Ocean Acidification Alliance (OAA)

The Ocean Acidification Alliance (OAA), also known as the International Alliance to Combat Ocean Acidification or OA Alliance, is an international coalition of governments, organisations, and scientific entities aimed at combatting the global challenge posed by OA. More specifically, according to its mission, the OA Alliance is working together to '[t]ransform planning and response to climate-ocean change'.[1050] The OA Alliance was officially launched at the 2016 Our Ocean Conference in Washington, D.C., and operates under the guidance of foundational documents such as the 'Global Call to Action' which members endorse upon joining.[1051] The OA Alliance is a voluntary coalition with no authority to enact legally binding measures. It functions as a collaborative platform, encouraging its members to undertake specific actions and develop strategic plans to address OA. More specifically, members of the OA Alliance commit to creating and implementing OA Action Plans, which include measures such as reducing carbon dioxide emissions, enhancing scientific research, reducing local pollutants, developing adaptation and resilience strategies, and raising public awareness and understanding of OA. These measures are designed to guide members in their efforts to mitigate the impacts of OA.[1052]

The OA Alliance and OA

The OA Alliance's mission explicitly addresses OA. This is clear from its work to advance understanding, mitigation, and adaptation strategies to combat the effects

[1046] RAMSAR (n 613). [1047] RAMSAR (n 614). [1048] Ibid.

[1049] Convention on wetlands of international importance, especially as waterfowl habitat.

[1050] OA Alliance, 'About' (n 293).

[1051] Ibid; OA Alliance, 'Become a Member and Welcome Packet' (n 650).

[1052] OA Alliance, 'Action Plan Toolkit 2024' (n 294); OA Alliance, 'Our Impact' (n 294).

of increased ocean acidity, as evidenced by its primary focus and the specific goals outlined in the OA Action Plans. The Alliance explicitly seeks to elevate the issue of OA on public and policy agendas, ensuring that it is included in global, regional, and local climate action plans.[1053]

Oceana

Oceana is an international advocacy organisation solely dedicated to ocean conservation.[1054] Oceana was established in 2001 by a group of foundations, including The Pew Charitable Trusts, the Oak Foundation, the Marisla Foundation, and the Rockefeller Brothers Fund. The formation of Oceana resulted from a study commissioned by The Pew Charitable Trusts, which identified an opportunity to build an international organisation focused on oceans.[1055] Oceana is a registered non-profit organisation in the United States and operates as a non-governmental organisation (NGO) in other regions, including Europe, South America, and Central America.[1056] As an NGO, Oceana does not have any lawmaking powers. It campaigns for 'science-based policies that stop overfishing, protect habitat, increase transparency, protect our climate, curb plastic pollution, and increase biodiversity'.[1057] While Oceana does not have a founding document akin to a governmental organisation, it operates based on its organisational mission, which is to restore and preserve marine ecosystems.[1058] Oceana engages in advocacy and public policy work.[1059] They work to influence legislation and public policy decisions that relate to ocean conservation.[1060] However, the measures they advocate for are not adopted by Oceana itself but by governmental bodies. Thus, the legal status of the measures Oceana pushes for depends on their adoption by those legislative or governmental entities.

Oceana and OA

Oceana's mission is to advocate for the protection and restoration of the world's oceans. This mission includes efforts to combat OA, which is implicitly covered under its broader goals of reducing pollution and promoting sustainable marine policies. In fact, some of Oceana's current campaigns work on issues relevant to OA.

[1053] OA Alliance, 'Our Impact' (n 294).

[1054] Oceana, 'What Does Oceana Do' (*Oceana*, 2024) https://oceana.org/about/ accessed 2 May 2024.

[1055] Ibid.

[1056] 'Oceana International Offices' (*Oceana*, 2024) https://oceana.org/oceana-international-offices/ accessed 2 May 2024; Oceana, 'What Does Oceana Do' (n 1054).

[1057] Oceana, 'Oceana Campaigns' (*Oceana*, 2024) https://oceana.org/campaigns/ accessed 2 May 2024.

[1058] Oceana, 'What Does Oceana Do' (n 1054).

[1059] Oceana, 'Victories Archive' (*Oceana USA*, 2024) https://usa.oceana.org/victories/ accessed 2 May 2024; Oceana, 'What Does Oceana Do' (n 1054).

[1060] Oceana, 'Victories Archive' (n 1059); Oceana, 'What Does Oceana Do' (n 1054).

For example, the Organization is working to stop the expansion of offshore drilling, which has the potential to reduce greenhouse gas emissions, including CO_2.[1061] Oceana also works on MPAs and sustainable fisheries;[1062] with both being important tools in adapting to OA. Currently, there are no campaigns that directly address the problem of OA. However, Oceana has been more involved in work surrounding OA in the past. For instance, Oceana presented the OA message at COP-15, emphasising the global impacts of OA and proposing solutions to this growing problem.[1063]

The United Nations Environment Programme (UNEP)

The United Nations Environment Programme (UNEP) is the leading global environmental authority that sets the global environmental agenda. The founding document of UNEP is the resolution 2997 (XXVII) of the United Nations General Assembly, which established UNEP as a result of the Stockholm Conference on the Human Environment in 1972.[1064] This resolution not only initiated UNEP but also outlined its core functions and responsibilities. These functions and responsibilities include, for example, promoting international cooperation in the field of the environment and recommending policies to support such cooperation (see Section I.2.(a)).[1065] In the same vein, UNEP is entitled to provide general policy guidance for directing and coordinating environmental programmes across the United Nations system (Section I.2(b)).[1066] In addition, UNEP reviews the global environmental situation (Section I.2(d)) and promotes the contribution of international scientific and professional communities in acquiring, assessing, and exchanging environmental knowledge (Section I.2(e)).[1067] While UNEP has a very broad mandate, they significantly impact the formation and adoption of international environmental treaties and agreements, as will be seen below.

Key legal instruments and panels for the environment have been facilitated or influenced by UNEP. Panels include, for instance, the Intergovernmental Panel

[1061] Oceana, 'Stop Offshore Drilling' (*Oceana*, 2024) https://oceana.org/campaign-page/protecting-our-climate-by-stopping-offshore-drilling/ accessed 2 May 2024.

[1062] Oceana, 'Protecting Ocean Habitats' (*Oceana*, 2024) https://oceana.org/campaign-page/protecting-important-ocean-habitat/ accessed 2 May 2024; Oceana, 'Save the Oceans, Feed the World' (*Oceana*, 2024) https://oceana.org/our-campaigns/feedtheworld/ accessed 2 May 2024; Oceana, 'Stop Overfishing' (*Oceana*, 2024) https://oceana.org/campaign-page/overfishing/ accessed 2 May 2024.

[1063] Oceana, 'Oceana Presents Ocean Acidification Message at COP-15' (*Oceana*, 2024) https://oceana.org/press-releases/oceana-presents-ocean-acidification-message-cop-15/ accessed 2 May 2024.

[1064] UNEP, 'About the United Nations Environment Programme' (*UNEP – UN Environment Programme*, 2024) www.unep.org/who-we-are/about-us accessed 30 April 2024; UNEP, 'UNEP: 50 Years of Environmental Milestones' (*UNEP – UN Environment Programme*, 13 September 2021) www.unep.org/environmental-moments-unep50-timeline accessed 30 April 2024; UN General Assembly (27th Sess.: 1972), 'A_RES_2997(XXVII) – Institutional and Financial Arrangements for International Environmental Co-operation'. https://digitallibrary.un.org/record/191561 accessed 30 April 2024.

[1065] (Sess. 1972) (n 1064).

[1066] Ibid. [1067] Ibid.

on Climate Change (IPCC) and the Intergovernmental Science-Policy Platform on Biodiversity and Ecosystem Services, and instruments include the United Nations Framework Convention on Climate Change (UNFCCC), the Global Programme of Action for the Protection of the Marine Environment from Land-based Activities (GPA), and the Convention on Biological Diversity (CBD). However, these are just a few examples of the many outlets through which UNEP indirectly tackles OA.[1068]

UNEP and OA

UNEP's mandate to address OA is implicit, derived from its broader objectives to mitigate environmental degradation and promote sustainability. While UNEP does not have an explicit legal mandate to tackle OA directly, it influences actions against OA through its environmental programmes and its role in fostering the development of science-based policies and international agreements.

The UNEP website provides extensive information about its work, including a dedicated page called 'what we do' that describes its work. A few examples of how UNEP indirectly tackles OA will be described below.

The website shows that one of the topics under the 'what we do' section on the website is 'climate action'. Under climate action, different topics are explained further, including 'adaptation & resilience', 'mitigation', or 'loss & damage'.[1069] Under each of these topics, the website explains actions that UNEP has been taking in this area. For instance, with regard to climate change mitigation, it says that 'UNEP promotes cost-effective and available solutions to reduce emissions from the energy systems, industry, buildings, transport and AFOLU sectors to help close the emissions gap'.[1070] Without going into too much detail, it can be seen that UNEP clearly uses its broad mandate to also take actions against climate change. Reducing emissions of CO_2 indirectly also reduces OA.

Taking another example, UNEP highlights emissions of NO_x/SO_x on its website under '[w]hat we do'. When looking through the 'Air' section of the website, it can be seen that UNEP is, for example, working on air pollution.[1071] Accordingly, as suggested by the UN Environment Assembly, UNEP regularly undertakes assessments of member states' progress regarding improving air quality. Hence, UNEP produced and updated the 2016 Actions on Air Quality report, creating a picture of national efforts towards better air quality. The update will also be accompanied

[1068] See, for example, UN Environment, 'Secretariats and Conventions' (*UNEP – UN Environment Programme*, 30 October 2017) www.unep.org/about-un-environment/why-does-un-environment-matter/secretariats-and-conventions accessed 30 April 2024.

[1069] UN Environment, 'Climate Action' (*UNEP – UN Environment Programme*, 5 October 2023) www.unep.org/topics/climate-action accessed 30 April 2024.

[1070] UN Environment, 'Mitigation' (*UNEP – UN Environment Programme*, 18 October 2023) www.unep.org/topics/climate-action/mitigation accessed 30 April 2024.

[1071] UN Environment, 'Air' (*UNEP – UN Environment Programme*, 17 October 2023) www.unep.org/topics/air accessed 30 April 2024.

by, for instance, country-specific case studies.[1072] The Actions on Air Quality report considers NO_x and SO_x to be part of the air pollution problem.[1073] This example shows that UNEP is working on the reduction of the emissions of NO_x and SO_x, which also contribute to OA.

With regard to reducing relevant coastal activities. On UNEP's website (under 'Oceans and Seas'), the actor, for instance, explains that it hosts the GPA to address land-based pollution.[1074] Land-based pollution, as a form of coastal activity is one of the activities carrying nutrients into the water, which then results in OA. After having initially tackled nine different 'source categories' of pollution, the GPA, since the 2012 Manila Declaration, has started to focus only on three source categories: marine litter, nutrient management, and wastewater.[1075] Thus, this example shows that UNEP (and the GPA specifically) considers the tackling of damaging coastal activities to be one of its goals.

Regarding adaptation, UNEP is particularly active when it comes to MPAs and the protection and restoration of blue carbon ecosystems. Again, the Programme's website, under 'oceans, seas, and coasts', provides a large amount of information about the variety of work that UNEP conducts in these areas.[1076] For instance, under the section 'Blue Ecosystems' and more specifically, 'Mangrove Forests', the website explains that 'UNEP is one of the world leaders in supporting climate change mitigation (e.g., blue carbon) and adaptation in the marine & coastal environment, through a wide range of partnerships (...)'[1077] Thus, even though UNEP is not specifically working on these adaptation techniques to ameliorate acidification, it nevertheless facilitates adaptation to OA.

Despite being aware of OA, UNEP does not have a section dedicated to OA under 'what we do' on the website.[1078] Instead, OA is mentioned within other parts; for instance, under ocean-climate nexus, the website merely states that OA is the '[i]ncreasing acidification is limiting the ocean's capacity to moderate climate change by diminishing its capacity to absorb CO_2'.[1079] Thus, UNEP does not give OA any specific consideration. In essence, UNEP's role in combating OA is characterised by its capacity to integrate environmental objectives into global agreements and policies, driving international efforts that indirectly mitigate and adapt to the impacts of acidification.

[1072] UNEP, 'Actions on Air Quality Report Update' (n 547).

[1073] Environment, 'Actions on Air Quality' (n 548).

[1074] UNEP, 'Addressing Land-Based Pollution' (n 576).

[1075] Ibid; UNEP, 'Governing the Global Programme of Action' (n 577).

[1076] UN Environment, 'Ocean, Seas and Coasts' (*UNEP – UN Environment Programme*, 5 October 2023) www.unep.org/topics/ocean-seas-and-coasts accessed 30 April 2024.

[1077] UN Environment, 'Mangrove Forests' (*UNEP – UN Environment Programme*, 23 November 2023) www.unep.org/topics/ocean-seas-and-coasts/blue-ecosystems/mangrove-forests accessed 30 April 2024.

[1078] Environment, 'Ocean, Seas and Coasts' (n 1076).

[1079] UN Environment, 'Nexus of the Ocean and Climate' (*UNEP – UN Environment Programme*, 18 December 2023) www.unep.org/topics/ocean-seas-and-coasts/nexus-ocean-and-climate accessed 30 April 2024.

The International Climate Change Regime (UNFCCC, Kyoto Protocol, Paris Agreement)

Before turning to examine the UNFCCC under this heading, it is important to recall the relevance of UNEP also in this context. Since its inception, UNEP has played a pivotal role in the coordination of efforts to combat climate change. A key milestone facilitated by UNEP in addressing climate change was the establishment of the IPCC in 1988 in collaboration with the World Meteorological Organization (WMO). The IPCC was created to provide a clear scientific view of the current state of knowledge with regard to climate change.[1080] The formation of the UNFCCC, which was opened for signature at the Earth Summit in Rio de Janeiro in 1992, was another significant achievement influenced by UNEP's early and ongoing efforts.[1081] The UNFCCC emerged as a result of international discussions about climate change, where UNEP had been instrumental, as indicated above.[1082] Furthermore, the Paris Agreement, adopted in 2015 under the UNFCCC framework, enhances the implementation of the UNFCCC through commitments by all countries to limit global temperature increases and strengthen societies' ability to deal with the impacts of climate change.[1083] The agreement (UNFCCC) is legally binding and aims for a carbon-neutral world by mid-century, marking a significant step forward in global climate efforts.[1084] As the main cause of OA is the increase and absorption of anthropogenic CO_2 emissions from the atmosphere, the climate change regime dedicated to the reduction of greenhouse gases, including CO_2, can indirectly contribute to tackling OA.

For the purpose of the discussion here, the Climate Change Regime consists of the UNFCCC, (previously) the Kyoto Protocol, and the Paris Agreement. The Paris Agreement is the third major international treaty aimed at addressing climate change, following the establishment of the UNFCCC and the Kyoto Protocol. The UNFCCC establishes overarching goals and principles such as common but differentiated responsibilities. The Kyoto Protocol introduced legally binding emissions reductions for developed countries with flexible market mechanisms. The Paris Agreement expanded this framework to include all countries, emphasising nationally determined contributions (NDCs) to limit global warming to well below 2°C and pursuing 1.5°C.[1085]

[1080] IPCC, 'IPCC Factsheet – What Is the IPCC' (2021) www.ipcc.ch/site/assets/uploads/2021/07/AR6_FS_What_is_IPCC.pdf accessed 7 May 2024.

[1081] United Nations, 'From Stockholm to Kyoto: A Brief History of Climate Change' (*United Nations*, 2024) www.un.org/en/chronicle/article/stockholm-kyoto-brief-history-climate-change accessed 7 May 2024.

[1082] Ibid.

[1083] Paris Agreement art 2.1(a).

[1084] 'The Paris Agreement | UNFCCC' (2024) https://unfccc.int/process-and-meetings/the-paris-agreement accessed 8 May 2024.

[1085] Daniel Bodansky, 'PARIS AGREEMENT' https://legal.un.org/avl/pdf/ha/pa/pa_e.pdf accessed 8 May 2024.

The Climate Change Regime and OA

Within the climate change regime, the UNFCCC is a framework convention outlining the general rules and defining the regime's ultimate objective.[1086] The overall objective can be found in article 2 of this agreement.[1087] Pursuant to article 2, as is already indicated by the name the '(…) stabilization of greenhouse gas concentrations in the atmosphere (…)' is to be achieved.[1088] The Paris Agreement, adopted under the UNFCCC (as explained above) in 2015 as an implementing Agreement,[1089] further clarifies this ultimate objective and pursuant to article 2(1)(a), aims to limit the increase of the global temperature to well below 2°C above pre-industrial levels and to pursue efforts to limit the increase to 1.5°C.[1090] According to article 4(1) Paris Agreement, the parties agree to '(…) undertake rapid reductions (…), so as to achieve a balance between anthropogenic emissions by sources and removals by sinks of greenhouse gases (…)'.[1091] In accordance with article 4, these rapid reductions shall be accomplished through NDCs.[1092] Such rapid reductions in greenhouse gas emissions, including CO_2, would also have a positive effect on the oceans, as CO_2 emissions are the primary driver of OA. Thus, the climate change regime can indirectly tackle OA.

Nevertheless, despite addressing OA's primary cause, namely emissions of CO_2 (one of the greenhouse gases tackled by the regime), the Climate Change Regime also more indirectly targets OA. It should, for example, be noted that even where targets for reducing greenhouse gas emissions exist, be it under Kyoto or within NDCs, these tend to aggregate major greenhouse gases without specifying bespoke targets for CO_2. That is to say, specific targets for individual greenhouse gases, and in particular, specific targets for CO_2 emissions, the main driver of OA, are lacking.[1093]

Also, as noted, states decide at the national level about their mitigation and adaptation commitments, which then take the form of 'nationally determined contributions' to achieve the global temperature goals of the Paris Agreement.[1094] This setup gives states the liberty to decide which gases they prioritise and to what extent.[1095] Thus, emissions reductions to achieve the Paris Agreement's long-term temperature goal, even on a 1.5-degree pathway (article 2 (a)), might be secured in many different ways. Impacts on the ocean would, however, be different depending on which route is chosen to contribute to the attainment of the temperature goal. More specifically, the impact on the ocean will depend on which GHGs are reduced, to what extent and how fast.[1096] As a result, even though OA can be reduced through the CCR, the setup of the regime is not guaranteed to lead to the reduction of CO_2

1086 UNFCCC. 1087 Ibid. 1088 Ibid. 1089 Paris Agreement art 2(1).
1090 Paris Agreement. 1091 Ibid. 1092 Ibid.
1093 Many authors are making this point, see, for example, Harrould-Kolieb and Stephens (n 52) 273.
1094 Cf. Scott, 'Ocean Acidification' (n 29) 395; Paris Agreement art 2.
1095 See, for example, Gordon (n 31) 41.
1096 Cf. Harrould-Kolieb, 'Implications of the Paris Agreement for Action on Ocean Acidification within the UNFCCC' (n 57) 30.

needed to tackle OA. This is a shortcoming in the climate change regime from the point of view of OA.

Yet, OA has progressively gained attention within the climate change regime. The issue first surfaced in formal UNFCCC discussions in 2005 when the United Kingdom, representing the European Community (Union), addressed it during the 23rd session of the Subsidiary Body for Scientific and Technological Advice (SBSTA). The potentially significant impacts of acidification on marine biota were highlighted, and this, for the first time, established discussions around ocean health within the climate change negotiations.[1097]

In 2010, during COP 16, OA was embedded in the Cancun Agreements, where it was noted as an example of a 'slow onset event' in the COP's formal documentation.[1098] This inclusion marked a foundational recognition of the issue within international climate negotiations. However, OA was named alongside several other slow-onset events and did not receive any attention beyond that.[1099]

OA has received some attention within the scientific body of the Convention on a few occasions. More specifically, the SBSTA has highlighted the importance of OA during its sessions, emphasising the necessity of robust scientific research and observation to fully understand its implications.[1100] This scientific backing can inform and shape the policy frameworks developed under the UNFCCC. The scientific focus on OA culminated in its more detailed consideration in different IPCC reports. For example, the Fifth Assessment Report in 2014 underscored the potential disruptions to marine ecosystems due to increased ocean acidity.[1101] Another example is the IPCC Special Report on Global Warming of 1.5°C, which suggests that ocean acidification impacts would be less severe if global temperatures were stabilised at 1.5°C through effective emissions reductions, demonstrating an indirect yet vital link between temperature targets and oceanic pH levels.[1102] This attention to OA is further evolving, as indicated by the IPCC's Special Report on The Ocean and Cryosphere in a Changing Climate.[1103] In addition to research

[1097] SUBSIDIARY BODY FOR SCIENTIFIC AND TECHNOLOGICAL ADVICE, 'Paper No. 4 FCCC/SBSTA/2005/MISC.15 – Views on the Report on Progress Made towards Implementing the Initial Ocean Climate Observing System, and on the Final Report on the Analysis of Data Exchange Issues in Global Atmospheric and Hydrological Networks' (n 308) 8; Harrould-Kolieb, 'Ocean Acidification and the UNFCCC: Finding Legal Clarity in the Twilight Zone' (n 57) 616–617.

[1098] United Nations, 'FCCC/CP/2010/7/Add.1' (n 41) 6.

[1099] Ibid.

[1100] SUBSIDIARY BODY FOR SCIENTIFIC AND TECHNOLOGICAL ADVICE, 'FCCC/SBSTA/2007/7 – Report on the Workshop on Climate-Related Risks and Extreme Events' 6; SUBSIDIARY BODY FOR SCIENTIFIC AND TECHNOLOGICAL ADVICE, 'FCCC/SBSTA/2008/MISC.8 – Information Provided by Regional and International Climate Change Research Programmes and Organizations on Developments in Research Activities Relevant to the Needs of the Convention' 3 https://unfccc.int/resource/docs/2008/sbsta/eng/misc08a01.pdf; Subsidiary Body for Scientific and Technological Advice, 'FCCC/SBSTA/2011/L.4 – Research and Systematic Observation' 2.

[1101] Pachauri, Mayer, and Intergovernmental Panel on Climate Change (n 308) 69.

[1102] IPCC (n 308) 209, 222.

[1103] Cf. for example, IPCC, 2019, 'Summary for Policymakers' in HO Pörtner and others (eds), *IPCC Special Report on the Ocean and Cryosphere in a Changing Climate: Special Report of the Intergovernmental Panel on*

under already existing scientific bodies, a collaborative network of institutions was established (GOA-ON) to produce research on OA and inform policies during COP 22.[1104]

Recent updates to the NDCs reveal that over 70 per cent now include ocean-based climate measures, signifying a stronger recognition of the ocean's role in climate strategies.[1105] This significant shift reflects a broader consensus on integrating marine environments into national climate action plans, emphasising mitigation and adaptation efforts focused on blue carbon and coastal ecosystems.[1106] Previous studies by Harrould-Kolieb and Stephens, as well as Gallo, Victor, and Levin, found that OA was mentioned specifically in some of the NDCs.[1107] However, an analysis by the Secretariat of the gap between the current NDCs committed by parties as of February 2021 and the actions needed to meet the goals of the Paris Agreement indicates that the existing commitments are insufficient to maintain global temperatures below 2°C.[1108]

The Ocean and Climate Change Dialogue under the UNFCCC was formally established during COP 25 in Madrid in 2019, recognising the crucial role of oceans in the global climate system and the urgent need to address ocean-related issues within climate policies.[1109] This decision led to the first session of the Dialogue in December 2020. The ocean-climate dialogue, along with the voluntary submissions it receives, marks the first occasion under the UNFCCC for party and non-party stakeholders to contribute their views regarding the inclusion of ocean-related topics in climate negotiations.[1110]

COP 26 in Glasgow marked an important moment regarding ocean-climate action. The Glasgow Climate Pact invites the chair of the SBSTA to further ocean-based action by holding annual dialogues starting in 2022.[1111] More importantly, the Glasgow pact not only reinforces the commitment to cap temperature rises at 1.5°C, but also established a new target to cut CO_2 emissions by 45 per cent by 2030 from 2010 levels, aiming for net zero by mid-century.[1112]

Climate Change (1st ed., Cambridge University Press 2022) 9, 12, 13, 18, 19, 22, 24, 27 www.cambridge.org/core/product/identifier/9781009157964/type/book accessed 20 July 2023.

1104 Scott, 'Ocean Acidification' (n 29) 396; GOA-ON, 'GOA-ON : Approach & Goals' (n 366).

1105 Rodriguez (n 309). 1106 Ibid.

1107 Natalya D. Gallo, David G. Victor and Lisa A. Levin, 'Ocean Commitments under the Paris Agreement' (2017) 7 *Nature Climate Change* 833, 834; Harrould-Kolieb and Stephens (n 52) 274.

1108 UNFCCC. Secretariat, 'FCCC/PA/CMA/2021/8 – Nationally Determined Contributions under the Paris Agreement' 5; Gordon (n 31) 41; Karen N Scott, 'The BBNJ Agreement: Strengthening the Oceans-Climate Nexus?', *Peaceful Maritime Engagement in East Asia and the Pacific Region* (Brill Nijhoff 2022) 408 https://brill.com/display/book/9789004518629/BP000032.xml accessed 8 May 2024.

1109 United Nations, 'FCCC/CP/2019/13/Add.1 – Report of the Conference of the Parties on Its Twenty-Fifth Session, Held in Madrid from 2 to 15 December 2019' (n 309) s Decision 1/CP.25, para 31, p. 4.

1110 Bobbi-Jo Dobush and others, 'A New Way Forward for Ocean-Climate Policy as Reflected in the UNFCCC Ocean and Climate Change Dialogue Submissions' (2022) 22 *Climate Policy* 254, 256.

1111 The Conference of the Parties, 'Decision -/CP.26 – Glasgow Climate Pact' para 61 https://unfccc.int/sites/default/files/resource/cop26_auv_2f_cover_decision.pdf accessed 8 May 2024.

1112 Ibid., 16, 17.

Recently, COPs started to include the so-called Ocean Pavilions at COP events. The Pavilion was established during COP 27 in Sharm El-Sheikh, Egypt, in November 2022.[1113] The pavilion marked a significant development in integrating ocean-related issues within the main discussions of the UN Climate Change Conferences.[1114] Organised by leading institutions like the Woods Hole Oceanographic Institution and Scripps Institution of Oceanography, the pavilion serves as a central hub for discussions, bringing together experts from various fields to emphasise the crucial role of the ocean in climate change mitigation and adaptation strategies.[1115] The Ocean Pavilion hosts a range of sessions and events that highlight the ocean's significant impact on the global climate and the various science-based solutions to leverage ocean processes for climate goals.[1116]

Convention on Biological Diversity (CBD)

The Convention on Biological Diversity (CBD) was established under the auspices of UNEP, which collaborates with biodiversity-related conventions and scientific bodies, including hosting the CBD Secretariat.[1117] The CBD itself is an international, legally binding treaty that comprehensively covers biodiversity at all levels – ecosystems, species, and genetic resources. Similar to the climate change regime, the CBD also has a COP.[1118]

CBD and OA

Article 1 of the CBD explicitly states the objective of the convention as 'the conservation of biological diversity'.[1119] The scope of biological diversity is further defined in article 2 of the CBD as 'the variability among living organisms from all sources including, marine and other aquatic ecosystems and the ecological complexes of which they are part: this includes diversity within species, between species and of ecosystems'.[1120]

This broad definition explicitly includes marine ecosystems and their ecological complexes. Given OA directly threatens these marine ecosystems by altering the chemical environment necessary for the survival of many marine organisms, it is

[1113] Pogo, 'Ocean Pavilion at COP-27' (*Partnership for Observation of the Global Ocean*, 29 April 2024) https://pogo-ocean.org/news/ocean-pavilion-at-cop-27/ accessed 29 April 2024; Polina Savina, 'Ocean Pavilion Partners Unveil COP28 Dubai Ocean Declaration in Advance of UN Climate Conference' (*Ocean Decade*, 20 November 2023) https://oceandecade.org/news/ocean-pavilion-partners-unveil-cop28-dubai-ocean-declaration/ accessed 29 April 2024.

[1114] Woods Hole Oceanographic Institutions (n 300).

[1115] UNESCO, 'The Ocean Pavilion Announces Schedule of Events for COP27 | UNESCO' (n 300); Pogo (n 1113); Woods Hole Oceanographic Institutions (n 300).

[1116] UNESCO, 'World Heritage Marine Programme' (n 632).

[1117] Environment, 'Secretariats and Conventions' (n 1068).

[1118] Convention on Biological Diversity.

[1119] Ibid., 23.

[1120] Convention on Biological Diversity.

indirectly addressed as an issue under the CBD's mandate. With regard to OA, the Convention offers provisions that are useful for adaptation, more precisely, for establishing MPAs through articles 6, 8, and 10 CBD.[1121] In addition, there are two sets of targets the CBD COP decided on, namely the Aichi Biodiversity Targets (2010–2020) and the Montreal Post-2020 Global Biodiversity Framework under the Convention on Biological Diversity (CBD), aimed at conserving biodiversity.[1122] Many of these targets are relevant for OA. The Aichi Targets, established in 2010, outlined specific goals for biodiversity preservation by 2020.[1123] The Montreal Post-2020 framework, discussed at COP15 in Montreal, seeks to build on and expand these goals post-2020, setting new, more ambitious targets for global biodiversity efforts into the future.[1124] These frameworks guide actions and policies to meet the overarching objectives of the CBD.[1125] Many of the old and new targets are relevant to OA. Some examples regarding the causes of OA, Aichi target 8 (reducing pollution) and Montreal Post-2020 target 7 (reducing pollution) indirectly reduce nutrient pollution, one of the causes of OA. Aichi targets 11 (protected areas) and 6 (fishing), and Montreal Post-2020 target 3 (conserved areas) and 5/9 (overexploitation/sustainable species management) are all relevant to adaptation and, if pursued, can indirectly contribute to it. In addition, Target 10 of the Aichi targets[1126] and Target 8, 'Minimize the Impacts of Climate Change on Biodiversity and Build Resilience' of the Montreal Post-2020 Framework specifically mention OA. The new Montreal Post-2020 Framework target calls to '[m]inimize the impact of climate change and ocean acidification on biodiversity and increase its resilience through mitigation, adaptation, (…), including through nature-based solution and/or ecosystem-based approaches (…)'.[1127] Thus, the CBD clearly recognises OA as an important environmental problem relevant to the convention, which can also be seen when looking at how OA has been referred to over time.

The CBD has been progressively addressing OA over the years through a series of decisions and actions that reflect its growing recognition of this issue's importance. Below, some examples will be pointed out.

[1121] Ibid.

[1122] CONFERENCE OF THE PARTIES TO THE CONVENTION ON BIOLOGICAL DIVERSITY, 'X/2 – The Strategic Plan for Biodiversity 2011–2020 and the Aichi Biodiversity Targets' para 13, see Annex for Target 11 www.cbd.int/doc/decisions/cop-10/cop-10-dec-02-en.pdf accessed 1 May 2024; Unit (n 300); Biosafety Unit, 'Aichi Biodiversity Targets' (18 September 2020) www.cbd.int/sp/targets?fbclid=IwZXh0bgNhZW0CMTAAAR0Ev7UyYKorQV7EQTn6PWLYaRJ9JbdOQBuX3_6vrdNE1E7CNGpMOPo1NW4_aem_AXP1mrxHD_o8fyjhSTm2cNrjtR6ftxpbNS8ONYIrq7pvydLMhMKv5_xWDkJvXoTQHdm3SwvPIK7JYrwrc3Kd3Ehh accessed 3 May 2024; CONFERENCE OF THE PARTIES TO THE CONVENTION ON BIOLOGICAL DIVERSITY, 'CBD/COP/DEC/15/4 – Kunming-Montreal Global Biodiversity Framework'.

[1123] Unit (n 1122). [1124] Unit (n 300).

[1125] Cf. CONFERENCE OF THE PARTIES TO THE CONVENTION ON BIOLOGICAL DIVERSITY (n 1122) Section B; CONFERENCE OF THE PARTIES TO THE CONVENTION ON BIOLOGICAL DIVERSITY, 'X/2 – The Strategic Plan for Biodiversity 2011–2020 and the Aichi Biodiversity Targets' (n 1122) Annex.

[1126] Unit (n 1122). [1127] Unit (n 300).

OA was formally recognised by the CBD at the 9th Conference of the Parties (COP 9) in Bonn in 2008. During this conference, two critical decisions were made:[1128] (1) The first decision involved a request for the Executive Secretary to gather and analyse information on the interactions between OA, climate change, and nutrient loading as threats to biodiversity. This action recognised OA as a significant threat to the Convention's goals.[1129] (2) The second decision called for the compilation and synthesis of existing scientific data on the impacts of OA on marine biodiversity, which was to be reviewed at a future meeting of the Subsidiary Body on Scientific, Technical, and Technological Advice (SBSTTA) before the next COP.[1130] These decisions marked the beginning of integrating OA into the CBD's agenda, setting a foundation for future actions and discussions within the Convention's framework.

Following the 2008 acknowledgement, the CBD Secretariat released a 'Scientific Synthesis on the Impacts of Ocean Acidification on Marine Biodiversity' in 2009, which summarised the state of scientific knowledge on the impacts.[1131]

This effort was enhanced during COP 10 in Nagoya, 2010, where the parties were urged to address '(…) climate change-related aspects of marine and coastal biodiversity, including the potential adverse impacts on marine and coastal biodiversity of ocean acidification as a direct consequence of the increased concentration of carbon dioxide (…)'.[1132] This conference also set the Strategic Plan for Biodiversity 2011–2020 and the Aichi Biodiversity Targets in which OA is mentioned.[1133] At the Tenth Meeting of the Conference of Parties to the CBD in 2010, another significant decision was made regarding OA. The Executive Secretary was tasked to work with major international bodies, including the Intergovernmental Oceanographic Commission of UNESCO, the Food and Agriculture Organization, the UNFCCC Secretariat, and others. This collaboration aimed to create joint expert review processes to monitor and evaluate the impacts of OA on marine and coastal biodiversity, underscoring the urgency and importance of this issue to global parties and organisations.[1134]

[1128] See also: Simons and Stephens (n 17) 17; Gordon (n 31) 45; Kim (n 21) 248; Downing (n 19) 265; Baird, Simons and Stephens (n 18) 469.

[1129] CONFERENCE OF THE PARTIES TO THE CONVENTION ON BIOLOGICAL DIVERSITY, 'IX/16 – Biodiversity and Climate Change' www.cbd.int/doc/decisions/cop-09/cop-09-dec-16-en.pdf accessed 1 May 2024.

[1130] CONFERENCE OF THE PARTIES TO THE CONVENTION ON BIOLOGICAL DIVERSITY, 'IX/20 – Marine and Coastal Biodiversity' www.cbd.int/doc/decisions/cop-09/cop-09-dec-20-en.pdf.

[1131] Secretariat of the Convention on Biological Diversity, 'Scientific Synthesis of the Impacts of Ocean Acidification on Marine Biodiversity' (2009) Technical Series No. 46 www.cbd.int/doc/publications/cbd-ts-46-en.pdf accessed 1 May 2024.

[1132] CONFERENCE OF THE PARTIES TO THE AND CONVENTION ON BIOLOGICAL DIVERSITY, 'X/29 – Marine and Coastal Biodiversity' para 13.dwww.cbd.int/doc/decisions/cop-10/cop-10-dec-29-en.pdf accessed 1 May 2024.

[1133] CONFERENCE OF THE PARTIES TO THE CONVENTION ON BIOLOGICAL DIVERSITY, 'X/2 – The Strategic Plan for Biodiversity 2011–2020 and the Aichi Biodiversity Targets' (n 1122) para 13, see annex for Target 10.

[1134] CONFERENCE OF THE PARTIES TO THE AND CONVENTION ON BIOLOGICAL DIVERSITY (n 1132) paras 66, 67.

In 2012, guidance was noted for practical responses to the impacts of OA during a meeting of the CBD's SBSTTA. Parties and organisations were encouraged to use this guidance to address various threats from OA effectively.[1135]

By 2014, an updated synthesis of the impacts of OA on marine biodiversity was released, which further highlighted the ongoing efforts and the need for a continued focus on this issue.[1136]

These examples show that, in recent years, the CBD has continued to make efforts to emphasise the importance of OA. In addition, the CBD started to integrate OA into broader environmental governance frameworks. This includes enhancing cooperation with other international agreements like the UNFCCC and UNCLOS.[1137] In Kim's words, the CBD has been most proactive and proven effective as an in-house coordinator facilitating mutually reinforcing relationships between the UNFCCC and UNCLOS.[1138]

Overall, the CBD is very active in the area of OA. Through its work, it contributes to raising awareness and enhancing mitigation and adaptation efforts regarding the problem despite its limited mandate mentioned above.[1139] According to Downing, the efforts of the CBD parties in addressing OA are commendable. However, the effectiveness of any decisions related to mitigating this issue depends on the voluntary cooperation of member states. The CBD lacks the authority to enforce these decisions, as it does not possess the legal power to compel the contracting parties to comply with the obligations set out at the Conferences of the Parties (COP).[1140] The nature of the obligations under the CBD is generally non-coercive. This is evident from the language used in the Convention, which often encourages parties to take actions 'as far as possible and as appropriate', reflecting a degree of flexibility and voluntary commitment rather than binding enforcement.[1141] These limitations highlight the ongoing need for the CBD to refine its strategies and strengthen its collaborations to improve its impact on mitigating ocean acidification and protecting marine biodiversity.

[1135] SUBSIDIARY BODY ON SCIENTIFIC, AND TECHNICAL AND TECHNOLOGICAL ADVICE, 'UNEP/CBD/SBSTTA/16/6 – ADDRESSING ADVERSE IMPACTS OF HUMAN ACTIVITIES ON MARINE AND COASTAL BIODIVERSITY, INCLUDING CORAL BLEACHING, OCEAN ACIDIFICATION, FISHERIES AND UNDERWATER NOISE' para 20 www.cbd.int/doc/meetings/sbstta/sbstta-16/official/sbstta-16-06-en.pdf accessed 1 May 2024.

[1136] Secretariat of the Convention on Biological Diversity and others (n 9).

[1137] EXPERT MEETING TO DEVELOP A SERIES OF JOINT EXPERT REVIEW PROCESSES TO MONITOR AND ASSESS THE IMPACTS OF OCEAN ACIDIFICATION ON MARINE AND COASTAL BIODIVERSITY, 'UNEP/CBD/EM-IOAMCB/1/2 – BACKGROUND DOCUMENT TO AN EXPERT MEETING TO DEVELOP A SERIES OF JOINT EXPERT REVIEW PROCESSES TO MONITOR AND ASSESS THE IMPACTS OF OCEAN ACIDIFICATION ON MARINE AND COASTAL BIODIVERSITY' 31 www.cbd.int/doc/meetings/mar/emioamcb-01/official/emioamcb-01-02-en.pdf accessed 3 May 2024; 'Kim – 2012 – Is a New Multilateral Environmental Agreement on O.Pdf' 252 www.researchgate.net/profile/Rakhyun_Kim/publication/256043173_Is_a_New_Multilateral_Environmental_Agreement_on_Ocean_Acidification_Necessary/links/59ee81fbaca272029ddf71f8/Is-a-New-Multilateral-Environmental-Agreement-on-Ocean-Acidification-Necessary.pdf accessed 20 January 2020; Gordon (n 31) 45.

[1138] Kim (n 21) 252.

[1139] See also: Harrould-Kolieb and Stephens (n 52) 279.

[1140] Downing (n 19) 265.

[1141] Convention on Biological Diversity art see, for example, 5, 6(b).

Fennel and VanderZwaag found a way of explaining the key ways in which the CBD has engaged with the issue of OA: The CBD has tackled OA by synthesising scientific data to understand its impact on marine biodiversity, evidenced by significant reports in 2009 and 2014. It has also promoted adaptation measures through its Strategic Action Plan for Biodiversity 2011–2020 and the Aichi Biodiversity Targets. Additionally, the CBD has addressed broader mitigation strategies and the regulation of geoengineering practices, advocating for a precautionary approach to ensure these interventions are scientifically justified and globally regulated.[1142]

The United Nations Educational, Scientific, and Cultural Organization (UNESCO)

UNESCO is a specialised agency of the United Nations that promotes world peace and security through international cooperation in education, the sciences, and culture.[1143] UNESCO pursues its objectives through major programmes in education, natural sciences, social/human sciences, culture, communication and information, and the ocean.[1144] UNESCO's founding document is its Constitution, adopted on 16 November 1945, and formally came into force on 4 November 1946.[1145] The legal character of UNESCO's Constitution is that of an international treaty. Pursuant to article I(1) of its constitution, the original purpose of UNESCO is 'to contribute to peace and security by promoting collaboration among the nations through education, science and culture'.[1146] To achieve this goal, the organisation has a whole catalogue of tools. For example, the constitution states, 'the Organization will: (a) Collaborate in the work (…) through all means of mass communication and to that end recommend such international agreements as may be necessary'.[1147] UNESCO has a very broad remit, but it becomes clear that its work's foundation is education, science, and culture. To reach its goals, the organisation can, under certain circumstances, recommend international agreements. Through this broad mandate the organisation can indirectly also address OA.

UNESCO and OA

In practice, many of the Organization's actions and programmes are indirectly and directly relevant to tackling OA, so only a few examples will be provided here.

[1142] Fennel and VanderZwaag (n 47) 353, 354.
[1143] UNESCO, 'UNESCO in Brief | UNESCO' (2024) www.unesco.org/en/brief accessed 4 May 2024.
[1144] UNESCO, 'Our Expertise | UNESCO' (2024) www.unesco.org/en/our-expertise accessed 4 May 2024.
[1145] UNESCO, 'Constitution | UNESCO' (2024) www.unesco.org/en/legal-affairs/constitution accessed 4 May 2024; Constitution of the United Nations Educational, Scientific and Cultural Organization; UNESCO, 'History of UNESCO | UNESCO' (2024) www.unesco.org/en/history accessed 4 May 2024.
[1146] Constitution of the United Nations Educational, Scientific and Cultural Organization.
[1147] Ibid I(2)(a).

For example, UNESCO, as part of its rather broad mandate and based on its foundation's education and science branch, created the Intergovernmental Oceanographic Commission (IOC–UNESCO).[1148] IOC–UNESCO enhances international cooperation in marine sciences. It aims to improve ocean, coast, and marine resource management. According to the IOC website, '[t]he work of the IOC contributes to the mission of UNESCO to promote the advancement of science (…)'.[1149] In addition, the IOC is charged with coordinating the United Nations Decade of Ocean Science for Sustainable Development (2021–2030).[1150] The Ocean Decade has 7 Outcomes, and OA is relevant under many of them. However, two that stand out with regard to OA are 'a clean ocean' and 'a resilient ocean'.[1151] Both a clean ocean without pollution from land-based sources, which can cause OA, and a resilient, protected ocean through, for instance, MPAs are important milestones for OA. The Ocean Decade's Outcomes are also in line with the IOC's high-level objectives, such as 'Healthy ocean and sustained ocean ecosystem services' and 'Resilience to climate change and contribution to its mitigation'.[1152] Another example of OA-relevant work under IOC–UNESCO is that it is co-hosting the Blue Carbon Initiative.[1153] All of these examples can indirectly help tackle and adapt to OA. However, IOC–UNESCO also more directly supports the Global Ocean Acidification Observing Network (GOA-ON) and helps to enhance global collaboration and data sharing necessary to understand and tackle OA.[1154] UNESCO's very broad mandate founded on education, science, and culture does not directly order the Organization to work on OA. Nevertheless, UNESCO still contributes to OA mitigation and adaptation in many ways, indirectly and directly, especially within the scientific focus of its mandate.

In addition, UNESCO is connected to the World Heritage Convention as UNESCO's General Conference adopted the convention on 16 November 1972.[1155] The World Heritage Convention establishes the types of cultural or natural sites that qualify for inclusion on the World Heritage List.[1156] 'Natural heritage' is defined in article 2 of the World Heritage Convention. The third

[1148] UNESCO, 'Intergovernmental Oceanographic Commission | Intergovernmental Oceanographic Commission' (2024) www.ioc.unesco.org/en accessed 4 May 2024.

[1149] Ibid.

[1150] UNESCO, 'Ocean Decade – The Science We Need for the Ocean We Want' (*Ocean Decade*, 8 June 2023) https://oceandecade.org/ accessed 4 May 2024; UNESCO, 'Intergovernmental Oceanographic Commission | Intergovernmental Oceanographic Commission' (n 1148).

[1151] UNESCO, 'Vision & Mission' (*Ocean Decade*, 8 June 2023) https://oceandecade.org/vision-mission/ accessed 4 May 2024.

[1152] UNESCO, 'Mission & Objectives | Intergovernmental Oceanographic Commission' (2024) www.ioc.unesco.org/en/mission-and-objectives accessed 4 May 2024.

[1153] The Blue Carbon Initiative, 'The Blue Carbon Initiative' (*The Blue Carbon Initiative*, 2024) www.thebluecarboninitiative.org accessed 4 May 2024.

[1154] UNESCO, 'Ocean Acidification | Intergovernmental Oceanographic Commission' (n 298).

[1155] UNESCO, 'The World Heritage Convention' (n 622); Convention Concerning the Protection of the World Cultural and Natural Heritage.

[1156] Convention Concerning the Protection of the World Cultural and Natural Heritage art cf. article 11(1).

option included in the article defines natural heritage as 'natural sites or precisely delineated natural areas of outstanding universal value from the point of view of science, conservation or natural beauty'. This definition is broad and 'natural sites or precisely delineated natural areas' could potentially include blue carbon ecosystems such as mangrove forests. As outlined by the website set up by UNESCO for the convention, the instrument follows five strategic objectives regarding these sites. One of these strategic objectives is 'conservation', more specifically, the conservation of world heritage.[1157] This objective can be confirmed when looking at the World Heritage Convention itself. In fact, article 4 of the World Heritage Convention states, 'Each State Party (…) recognizes that the duty of ensuring (…) protection, conservation, (…) of the cultural and natural heritage (…) belongs primarily to that State. It will do all it can to this end'. Thus, with the help of this instrument, blue carbon ecosystems could be protected and conserved.

The United Nations General Assembly (UNGA)

The United Nations General Assembly (UNGA) is one of the six principal organs of the United Nations, composed of all member states.[1158] The founding document of the UNGA is the Charter of the United Nations.[1159] According to the Charter, the UNGA serves as a deliberative body where issues under the Charter of the United Nations or any issues within the scope of the Charter can be discussed.[1160] The UNGA '(…) may make recommendations to the Member States of the United Nations (…)'. The Charter of the United Nations is an international treaty establishing the UN and its organs, including the General Assembly. Due to its broad mandate, the UNGA does not have an explicit task to deal directly with OA. Nevertheless, in recent years, OA has gotten attention from the UNGA, and the organ has adopted various resolutions and decisions relevant to OA, some of which will be briefly mentioned below.

UNGA and OA

OA began appearing regularly within UNGA resolutions around 2008, signalling heightened awareness and concern about its impacts on marine

[1157] UNESCO, 'The World Heritage Convention' (n 622).

[1158] United Nations, 'UN Structure' (*United Nations*, 2024) www.un.org/en/model-united-nations/un-structure?fbclid=IwZXh0bgNhZW0CMTAAAR2XjSRHatS5r8p3MDjopEe1KN934SLzb0TpLbH0pIcOvJea-nh8LXVDEGs_aem_Ae417449by1uw1ov8XmrvWqOIDzK7twQfGprk7BhIWjCvJzIQM1XR8such71F5mLcr8pHhbOjzSJwhQKw5LfNXoM accessed 6 May 2024.

[1159] United Nations Charter 1945 ch. IV.

[1160] Ibid IV, preprint 10.

environments and biodiversity. This inclusion in substantive sections of resolutions marked a shift towards more concrete discussions and calls for action regarding the ocean's health.[1161] The UNGA has progressively integrated OA into its resolutions and actions, focusing on mitigation and adaptation strategies. For instance, the UN Open-ended Informal Consultative Process on Oceans and Law of the Sea dedicated its 14th meeting in June 2013 to OA, highlighting the need to address OA mitigation and adaptation.[1162] The 2017 UN Secretary-General's report on Oceans and the Law of the Sea partly focused on OA.[1163] Apart from that, OA is addressed under Sustainable Development Goal 14. The Sustainable Development Goals (SDGs) are a global framework of 17 goals adopted by the UNGA to address major global challenges by 2030, with the UNGA overseeing progress, setting policies, and hosting forums to promote and review global and national efforts towards these goals.[1164] Goal 14 aims to conserve and sustainably use the oceans, seas, and marine resources. SDG 14.3 specifically targets minimising and addressing the impacts of OA, enhancing scientific cooperation, improving ocean health, and implementing sustainable management practices.[1165] In 2017, during the UN-Oceans conference, a register for voluntary commitments in the implementation of SDG 14 was created.[1166] As of mid 2024 over 300 commitments by states and other entities are registered when filtering for OA and SDG goal 14[1167] In addition, proclaimed for 2021–2030, the UN Decade of Ocean Science aims to generate scientific research solutions to support the sustainable development of the oceans and better understand the

[1161] UNGA, 'A/RES/62/215 – Resolution Adopted by the General Assembly on 22 December 2007' para 81 www.un.org/en/development/desa/population/migration/generalassembly/docs/globalcompact/A_RES_62_215.pdf accessed 6 May 2024; UNGA, 'A/RES/63/111 – Resolution Adopted by the General Assembly on 5 December 2008' para preamble, 99 www.un.org/en/development/desa/population/migration/generalassembly/docs/globalcompact/A_RES_63_111.pdf accessed 6 May 2024.

[1162] Co-Chairs, 'A/68/159 – Report on the Work of the United Nations Open-Ended Informal Consultative Process on Oceans and the Law of the Sea at Its Fourteenth Meeting' (2013) https://documents.un.org/doc/undoc/gen/n13/398/71/pdf/n1339871.pdf?token=HJgLerD27v1e4tpvX0&fe=true.

[1163] UNGA, 'A/72/70 – Oceans and the Law of the Sea' https://documents.un.org/doc/undoc/gen/n17/059/35/pdf/n1705935.pdf?token=QJk1JUCbxZ5zX00jP4&fe=true accessed 8 May 2024.

[1164] United Nations, 'THE 17 GOALS | Sustainable Development' (2024) https://sdgs.un.org/goals?fbclid=IwZXh0bgNhZW0CMTAAAR13PsXSXLin2EbvnQSLI2WF9wPAjtAMQ2L9IgNLXNUeYQc6gD67eoE0E5E_aem_Ae5chcGSmkAyBgCaVe46x08TAD9RETt7u4hIHpCxFA0VrKkkJtBv9-uRXq0MKl3Io0GFbHp5x_xtlyp39Un92PNC accessed 7 May 2024.

[1165] UNGA, 'A/RES/66/288 – The Future We Want' para 166 www.un.org/en/development/desa/population/migration/generalassembly/docs/globalcompact/A_RES_66_288.pdf accessed 6 May 2024; UNGA, 'A/68/970 – Open Working Group of the General Assembly on Sustainable Development Goals' para 14.3 https://sustainabledevelopment.un.org/content/documents/1579SDGs%20Proposal.pdf accessed 6 May 2024.

[1166] United Nations, 'Voluntary Commitments for the Implementation of Sustainable Development Goal 14 | Department of Economic and Social Affairs' (2024) https://sdgs.un.org/topics/oceans-and-seas/vcs#undefined accessed 8 May 2024.

[1167] United Nations, 'Ocean Commitments | Sustainable Development' https://sdgs.un.org/partnerships/action-networks/ocean-commitments?_gl=1*tlkgaz*_ga*Njg1NTAyNDkuMTcxNDQ3NjQxNA.*_ga_TK9BQL5X7Z*MTcxNTE1MjQ1Ny41LjEuMTcxNTE1MjkyNC4wLjAuMA. accessed 8 May 2024.

impacts of issues like OA.[1168] The United Nations Decade of Ocean Science was announced by the General Assembly and led by UNESCO.[1169] However, despite these progressing discussions of OA under the UNGA umbrella, States recognise that the governance of adverse effects of climate change needs to be left to the UNFCCC.[1170]

World Bank

The World Bank is an international financial institution composed of two key components: the International Bank for Reconstruction and Development (IBRD) and the International Development Association (IDA).[1171] The founding documents are the Articles of Agreement for the IBRD, signed in 1944 at the Bretton Woods Conference, and for the IDA, established in 1960.[1172] The World Bank is committed to ending extreme poverty and fostering shared prosperity on a liveable planet, emphasising the urgent need to address environmental crises such as climate change, biodiversity loss, and resource depletion. Through integrated strategies that focus on sustainable growth, job creation, and resilience to environmental shocks, the Group collaborates with a broad network of partners, including multilateral institutions, the private sector, and civil society, to promote sustainable development and environmental stewardship.[1173] The World Bank is an international organisation with its own legal personality. It can, for example, provide loans, grants, and technical assistance to its member countries, as well as make investments.[1174]

1168 UNESCO, 'Vision & Mission' (n 1151).

1169 UNGA, 'A/RES/72/73 – Oceans and the Law of the Sea' para 292 https://documents.un.org/doc/undoc/gen/n17/421/90/pdf/n1742190.pdf?token=uCq5igZ77kYwLxpn9E&fe=true.

1170 Co-Chairs, 'A/66/186 – Report on the Work of the United Nations Open-Ended Informal Consultative Process on Oceans and the Law of the Sea at Its Twelfth Meeting' (n 1031) 58; UNGA, 'A/RES/62/215 – Resolution Adopted by the General Assembly on 22 December 2007' (n 1161) para 83.

1171 The World Bank, 'Home – Timeline' (*World Bank*, 2024) https://timeline.worldbank.org/en/timeline/home accessed 8 May 2024.

1172 World Bank, 'International Development Association – Press Release No. 1' https://timeline.worldbank.org/content/dam/sites/timeline/docs/migrated/event26-ida-pressrelease-30205492.pdf accessed 8 May 2024; International Bank for Reconstruction and Development, 'United Nations Monetary and Financial Conference – Bretton Woods' https://timeline.worldbank.org/content/dam/sites/timeline/docs/migrated/event01-brettonwoods-finalact-1849790.pdf; 'Who We Are' (*World Bank*) www.worldbank.org/en/who-we-are accessed 8 May 2024; World Bank, 'INTERNATIONAL BANK FOR RECONSTRUCTION AND DEVELOPMENT – Articles of Agreement' https://thedocs.worldbank.org/en/doc/722361541184234501-0330022018/original/IBRDArticlesOfAgreementEnglish.pdf accessed 8 May 2024; World Bank, 'INTERNATIONAL DEVELOPMENT ASSOCIATION – Articles of Agreement' https://thedocs.worldbank.org/en/doc/341581541440486864-0330022018/original/IDAArticlesofAgreementEnglish.pdf accessed 8 May 2024.

1173 'Who We Are' (n 1172).

1174 World Bank, 'INTERNATIONAL BANK FOR RECONSTRUCTION AND DEVELOPMENT – Articles of Agreement' (n 1172) art I; World Bank, 'INTERNATIONAL DEVELOPMENT ASSOCIATION – Articles of Agreement' (n 1172) art I.

World Bank and OA

The World Bank does not have an explicit mandate to address OA. However, its broad mission to support sustainable development and its work on climate change implicitly include addressing environmental issues such as OA through its environmental policies and funding of relevant projects. For example, according to the filter on their website, the World Bank currently has forty-six projects concerned with the oceans.[1175] One example of OA relevant projects would be 5 (3 active) ones regarding blue carbon, under titles such as 'unleashing the blue economy in the Caribbean'.[1176] While the World Bank shows awareness of the problem of OA as a problem, as it is mentioned on their website, they are not directly addressing it.[1177]

World Ocean Council (WOC)

The World Ocean Council (WOC) is an international non-profit organisation that brings together the multi-sector ocean business community with the mission to address '(...) cross-cutting oceans sustainable development challenge'.[1178] The WOC was established through collaborative efforts among various stakeholders in the private sector.[1179] Specific foundational documents such as a charter or a constitution may exist but are not publicly specified like traditional treaties for intergovernmental organisations. The WOC operates as a non-governmental organisation and does not have the same legal status as a body created by an international treaty.

WOC and OA

The mandate of the WOC to address OA is implicit. Its broader objective is to promote the health of the marine environment and sustainable business practices. This clearly encompasses issues such as OA. Nevertheless, WOC also actively engages with emerging marine issues that impact 'ocean industry operations', including

[1175] The World Bank, 'Projects' (*World Bank*, 2024) https://projects.worldbank.org/en/projects-operations/projects-list accessed 11 May 2024.

[1176] The World Bank, 'Development Projects: Unleashing the Blue Economy of the Caribbean (UBEC) – P171833' (*World Bank*, 2024) https://projects.worldbank.org/en/projects-operations/project-detail/P171833 accessed 11 May 2024.

[1177] World Bank, 'Climate Explainer: Oceans and Climate Change' (*World Bank*, 2024) www.worldbank.org/en/news/feature/2022/02/08/what-you-need-to-know-about-oceans-and-climate-change accessed 8 May 2024; World Bank, 'Oceans, Fisheries and Coastal Economies' (*World Bank*, 2024) www.worldbank.org/en/topic/oceans-fisheries-and-coastal-economies accessed 8 May 2024.

[1178] World Ocean Council, 'Mission' (*World Ocean Council*, 2024) www.oceancouncil.org/about-us/mission/ accessed 8 May 2024; ibid.

[1179] World Ocean Council, 'The Organization' (*World Ocean Council*, 2024) www.oceancouncil.org/about-us/the-organization/ accessed 8 May 2024.

blue carbon and OA.[1180] Through monitoring, analysis, and fostering cross-sectoral collaboration, the WOC develops industry-driven solutions to enhance sustainable ocean use and addresses environmental challenges linked to increased ocean exploration.[1181]

The World Wildlife Fund (WWF)

The World Wildlife Fund (WWF) is a conservation organisation that operates globally to sustain the natural world.[1182] It is a global network, with the WWF office in Gland, Switzerland. It functions through a network of affiliate offices around the world, each operating under the same WWF brand but focusing on conservation issues relevant to their specific regions.[1183] The mission of WWF is to stop the degradation of the planet's natural environment and to build a future in which humans live harmonically with nature. This is achieved by conserving the world's biodiversity, ensuring the sustainable use of renewable natural resources, and promoting the reduction of pollution and wasteful consumption.[1184] This broad mission of stopping degradation can also include OA, at least indirectly. WWF International was established in 1961 by a group of individuals, not through a traditional founding treaty but as a foundation registered under Swiss law.[1185] The WWF International is governed by a board of trustees and adheres to statutes that provide a structured governance framework in coherence with Swiss law.[1186] These statutes define WWF's legal and operational structure, including its institutional set-up and purposes.[1187] The purpose set out by the statutes is '[t]o conserve the natural environment and ecological processes worldwide'.[1188] According to the statutes, part of the environment and processes that need to be conserved are fauna and flora, and water, which also includes the ocean and its ecosystems.[1189] Hence, WWF can indirectly address OA as a problem in line with the mission statement and the statute. WWF can take action such as collecting, managing, and disbursing funds, promoting awareness, and developing moral and financial support.[1190]

[1180] World Ocean Council, 'Emerging Issues' (*World Ocean Council*, 2024) www.oceancouncil.org/global-issues-platforms/program-focus/emerging-issues/ accessed 8 May 2024.

[1181] Ibid.

[1182] WWF, 'About WWF | WWF' (2024) https://wwf.panda.org/discover/about_wwf/ accessed 3 May 2024.

[1183] WWF, 'How Is WWF Run?' (2024) https://wwf.panda.org/discover/about_wwf/how_were_run/ accessed 3 May 2024.

[1184] WWF, 'About WWF | WWF' (n 1182).

[1185] WWF, 'History | WWF' (*World Wildlife Fund*, 2024) www.worldwildlife.org/about/history accessed 3 May 2024.

[1186] WWF, 'How Is WWF Run?' (n 1183); WWF, 'WWF Statutes' (2024) https://wwf.panda.org/discover/about_wwf/how_were_run/statutes/ accessed 3 May 2024.

[1187] WWF, 'WWF Statutes' (n 1186).

[1188] Ibid.

[1189] Ibid.

[1190] See: ibid (a), (b), (e).

WWF and OA

On its website, the WWF provides more information about how it achieves the goals set out in the Organization's mission statement and statute. The website clarifies that its work is focused on 'safeguarding the natural world' and 'challenging the two most urgent threats to nature'.[1191] Under the first category, the WWF considers, for instance, oceans; under the second, it considers climate change.[1192] On the oceans page itself, it is explained that the Organization is 'protecting the ocean's natural treasures' and, more precisely, that it, for example, supports initiatives to restore and secure environments, including reefs and mangroves.[1193] More concrete information is available on the specific 'ocean and climate' website linked under the more general oceans webpage. The 'ocean and climate' page immediately mentions OA as a threat to the oceans.[1194] WWF has published four principles for ocean-climate action to guide efforts by countries to incorporate ocean-based actions into their climate action plans.[1195] WWF's effort is meant to provide more practical guidance on using, for example, global commitments to unfold the potential of ocean-climate solutions.[1196] The four principles include raising ambition for mitigation and adaptation and making nature part of the solution. The latter principle refers, for instance, to blue carbon.[1197] Thus, it can be seen that the WWF not only indirectly works on tackling CO_2 and conserving blue carbon ecosystems, for instance, but that the Organization is aware of OA and targets the problem as part of their actions in the ocean-climate nexus. Hence, despite its broad mission statement and statute, it indirectly and directly tackles OA.

[1191] WWF, 'About WWF | WWF' (n 1182). [1192] Ibid.
[1193] WWF, 'Ocean | WWF' (2024) https://explore.panda.org/oceans accessed 4 May 2024.
[1194] WWF, 'Ocean and Climate' (2024) https://wwf.panda.org/discover/our_focus/oceans_practice/ocean_and_climate/ accessed 4 May 2024.
[1195] Ibid. [1196] Ibid. [1197] Ibid.

BIBLIOGRAPHY

AALCO, 'Member States | Asian African Legal Consultative Organization' (2024) <www.aalco.int/Members> accessed 13 January 2024

Abbott K, 'Strengthening the Transnational Regime Complex for Climate Change' (2013) 3 *Transnational Environmental Law* 57

Abbott KW, 'The Transnational Regime Complex for Climate Change' (2012) 30 *Environment and Planning C: Government and Policy* 571

Alter KJ and Meunier S, 'The Politics of International Regime Complexity' (2009) 7 *Perspectives on Politics* 13

Altieri AH and Gedan KB, 'Climate Change and Dead Zones' (2015) 21 *Global Change Biology* 1395

Anthony KRN, 'Coral Reefs under Climate Change and Ocean Acidification: Challenges and Opportunities for Management and Policy' (2016) 41 *Annual Review of Environment and Resources* 59

Arctic Council, 'Wastewater Discharges from Vessels in the Arctic' (*Arctic Council*, 2022) <https://arctic-council.org/projects/wastewater-discharges-from-vessels-in-the-arctic-a-survey-of-current-practices/> accessed 17 January 2022

Arctic Monitoring and Assessment Programme (AMAP) and others, *AMAP Assessment 2013: Arctic Ocean Acidification* (2013) <https://oaarchive.arctic-council.org/items/b92fb2d9-578a-4fd0-b2d2-b9e64de664db>

Arctic Monitoring and Assessment Programme (AMAP), *AMAP Arctic Ocean Acidification Assessment: Summary for Policy-Makers* (2013) <www.amap.no/documents/download/1126/inline>

AMAP Assessment 2018: Arctic Ocean Acidification. (2018) <www.amap.no/documents/doc/amap-assessment-2018-arctic-ocean-acidification/1659>

Armeni C, 'Global Experimentalist Governance, International Law and Climate Change Technologies' (2015) 64 *International and Comparative Law Quarterly* 875

Ayres I and Gertner R, 'Filling Gaps in Incomplete Contracts: An Economic Theory of Default Rules' (1989) 99 *The Yale Law Journal* 87

Babila TL and others, 'Capturing the Global Signature of Surface Ocean Acidification during the Palaeocene–Eocene Thermal Maximum' (2018) 376 *Philosophical Transactions of the Royal Society A: Mathematical, Physical and Engineering Sciences* 1

Baird R, Simons M and Stephens T, 'Ocean Acidification: A Litmus Test for International Law' (2009) 3 *Carbon & Climate Law Review* 459

Benedick RE, *Ozone Diplomacy: New Directions in Safeguarding the Planet* (Enl ed., Harvard University Press 1998)

Biermann F and others, 'The Fragmentation of Global Governance Architectures: A Framework for Analysis' (2009) 9 *Global Environmental Politics* 14

Bijma J and others, 'Climate Change and the Oceans – What Does the Future Hold?' (2013) 74 *Marine Pollution Bulletin* 495

Billé R and others, 'Taking Action against Ocean Acidification: A Review of Management and Policy Options' (2013) *Environmental Management* 761

Billups FD, *Qualitative Data Collection Tools: Design, Development, and Applications* (SAGE Publications, Inc 2021) <https://methods.sagepub.com/book/qualitative-data-collection-tools> accessed 19 November 2023

Bodansky D, 'Paris Agreement' <https://legal.un.org/avl/pdf/ha/pa/pa_e.pdf> accessed 8 May 2024

Brinkmann S and Kvale S, *Doing Interviews* (SAGE Publications Ltd 2018) <https://methods.sagepub.com/book/doing-interviews-2e> accessed 19 November 2023

Broadgate W and others, *Ocean Acidification, Summary for Policymakers, Third Symposium on the Ocean in a High-CO_2 World* (2013) <www.igbp.net/download/18.30566fc6142425d6c91140a/1385975160621/OA_spm2-FULL-lorez.pdf>

Butnariu M, 'Consequences of Acid Rain' (2014) 04 *Journal of Ecosystem & Ecography* <www.omicsonline.org/open-access/consequences-of-acid-rain-2157-7625.1000e119.php?aid=32697> accessed 17 February 2021

Butz C and others, 'Towards Defining an Environmental Investment Universe within Planetary Boundaries' (2018) 13 *Sustainability Science* 1031

Cai W-J and others, 'Acidification of Subsurface Coastal Waters Enhanced by Eutrophication' (2011) 4 *Nature Geoscience* 766

Cao L and Caldeira K, 'Can Ocean Iron Fertilization Mitigate Ocean Acidification?' (2010) 99 *Climatic Change* 303

CARICOM, 'Home – Heads of Government Conference (HGC)' (2023) <https://hgc.caricom.org/> accessed 13 January 2024

Carilli JE and others, 'Century-Scale Records of Coral Growth Rates Indicate That Local Stressors Reduce Coral Thermal Tolerance Threshold' (2010) 16 *Global Change Biology* 1247

Cazenave A and Cozannet GL, 'Sea Level Rise and Its Coastal Impacts' (2014) 2 *Earth's Future* 15

Chikamoto MO, DiNezio P and Lovenduski N, 'Long-Term Slowdown of Ocean Carbon Uptake by Alkalinity Dynamics' (2023) 50 *Geophysical Research Letters* 1

Christiansen B, Denda A and Christiansen S, 'Potential Effects of Deep Seabed Mining on Pelagic and Benthopelagic Biota' (2020) 114 *Marine Policy* 103442

Christianson AB and others, 'The Promise of Blue Carbon Climate Solutions: Where the Science Supports Ocean-Climate Policy' (2022) 9 *Frontiers in Marine Science* 851448

Co-Chairs, 'A/66/186 – Report on the Work of the United Nations Open-Ended Informal Consultative Process on Oceans and the Law of the Sea at Its Twelfth Meeting' (2011) <https://documents.un.org/doc/undoc/gen/n11/431/39/pdf/n1143139.pdf?token=aK7q3hlWEdebSqYVHx&fe=true>

'A/68/159 – Report on the Work of the United Nations Open-Ended Informal Consultative Process on Oceans and the Law of the Sea at Its Fourteenth Meeting' (2013) <https://documents.un.org/doc/undoc/gen/n13/398/71/pdf/n1339871.pdf?token=HJgLerD27v1e4tpvX0&fe=true>

Co-Chairs UAHOIWG to SI relating to the C and SU of MBD beyond A of NJ, 'A/65/164 – Report on the Work of the United Nations Open-Ended Informal Consultative Process on Oceans and the Law of the Sea at Its 11th Meeting' (UN, 2010) <https://digitallibrary.un.org/record/688502> accessed 30 April 2024

Cohen J and Sabel C, 'Directly-Deliberative Polyarchy' (1997) 3 *European Law Journal* 313

Cohen-Shacham E and others (eds), *Nature-Based Solutions to Address Global Societal Challenges* (IUCN International Union for Conservation of Nature 2016) <https://portals.iucn.org/library/node/46191> accessed 2 June 2023

Comeau S and others, 'Pacific-Wide Contrast Highlights Resistance of Reef Calcifiers to Ocean Acidification' (2014) 281 *Proceedings. Biological sciences / The Royal Society* 1

Comer B, Georgeff E and Osipova L, 'Air Emissions and Water Pollution Discharges from Ships with Scrubbers' (International Council on Clean Transportation (ICCT) 2020) <https://theicct.org/wp-content/uploads/2021/06/Air-water-pollution-scrubbers-dec2020.pdf>

Conference of the Parties to the Convention on Biological Diversity, 'X/29 – Marine and Coastal Biodiversity' <www.cbd.int/doc/decisions/cop-10/cop-10-dec-29-en.pdf> accessed 1 May 2024

'IX/16 – Biodiversity and Climate Change' <www.cbd.int/doc/decisions/cop-09/cop-09-dec-16-en.pdf> accessed 1 May 2024

'IX/20 – Marine and Coastal Biodiversity' <www.cbd.int/doc/decisions/cop-09/cop-09-dec-20-en.pdf>

'X/2 – The Strategic Plan for Biodiversity 2011–2020 and the Aichi Biodiversity Targets' <www.cbd.int/doc/decisions/cop-10/cop-10-dec-02-en.pdf> accessed 1 May 2024

'CBD/COP/DEC/15/4 – Kunming-Montreal Global Biodiversity Framework'

Cooke SL and Kim SC, 'Exploring the "Evil Twin of Global Warming": Public Understanding of Ocean Acidification in the United States' (2019) 41 *Science Communication* 66

Côté IM, Darling ES and Brown CJ, 'Interactions among Ecosystem Stressors and Their Importance in Conservation' (2016) 283 *Proceedings of the Royal Society B: Biological Sciences* 20152592

Cyronak T and others, 'Enhanced Acidification of Global Coral Reefs Driven by Regional Biogeochemical Feedbacks' (2014) 41 *Geophysical Research Letters* 5538

de Burca G, 'New Governance and Experimentalism: An Introduction' (2010) 2010 *Wisconsin Law Review* 227

De Burca G, Keohane RO and Sabel C, 'New Modes of Pluralist Global Governance' (2012) 45 *New York University Journal of International Law and Politics* 723

'Global Experimentalist Governance' (2014) 44 *British Journal of Political Science* 477

De Burca G and Scott J, 'Introduction: New Governance, Law and Constitutionalism', *Law and New Governance in the EU and the US* (Hart Publishing 2006) <www.bloomsburycollections.com/book/law-and-new-governance-in-the-eu-and-the-us> accessed 31 July 2022

Delmas R, Serça D and Jambert C, 'Global Inventory of NOx Sources' (1997) 48 *Nutrient Cycling in Agroecosystems* 51

DeSombre ER and Kaufman J, 'The Montreal Protocol Multilateral Fund: Partial Success Story' in Robert O Keohane and Marc A Levy (eds), *Institutions for Environmental Aid: Pitfalls and Promise* (MIT Press 1996)

Dobush B-J and others, 'A New Way Forward for Ocean-Climate Policy as Reflected in the UNFCCC Ocean and Climate Change Dialogue Submissions' (2022) 22 *Climate Policy* 254

Doney SC and others, 'Ocean Acidification: The Other CO_2 Problem' (2009) 1 *Annual Review of Marine Science* 169

Downing Y, 'Ocean Acidification and Protection under International Law from Negative Effects: A Burning Issue amongst a Sea of Regimes?' (2013) 2 *Cambridge Journal of International and Comparative Law* 242

Draguljić G, 'The Climate Change Regime Complex: Path Dependence amidst Institutional Change' (2019) 25 *Global Governance: A Review of Multilateralism and International Organizations* 476

Dulière V, Baetens K and Lacroix G, *Potential Impact of Wash Water Effluents from Scrubbers on Water Acidification in the Southern North Sea* (2020)

Dupont S and Pörtner H-O, 'A Snapshot of Ocean Acidification Research' (2013) 160 *Marine Biology* 1765

Eilstrup-Sangiovanni M, 'Ordering Global Governance Complexes: The Evolution of the Governance Complex for International Civil Aviation' (2022) 17 *The Review of International Organizations* 293

Elver H and Oral N, 'Food Security, Fisheries and Ocean Acidification: A Human Rights Based Approach' in David L VanderZwaag, Nilufer Oral and Tim Stephens (eds), *Research Handbook on Ocean Acidification Law and Policy* (Edward Elgar Publishing 2021)

Endres S and others, 'A New Perspective at the Ship-Air-Sea-Interface: The Environmental Impacts of Exhaust Gas Scrubber Discharge' (2018) 5 *Frontiers in Marine Science* 139

Engler C, VanderZwaag DL and Fennel K, 'Ocean Acidification Post-Paris: Gauging Law and Policy Responses in Light of Evolving Scientific Knowledge' (2019) 33 *Ocean Yearbook Online* 207

Environment, 'Actions on Air Quality' (UNEP – UN Environment Programme, 2 July 2017) <www.unep.org/resources/assessment/actions-air-quality> accessed 18 March 2023

'Why Does Global Clean Ports Matter?' (UNEP – UN Environment Programme, 26 July 2017) <www.unep.org/explore-topics/transport/what-we-do/global-clean-ports/why-does-global-clean-ports-matter> accessed 18 March 2023

Environment UN, 'Regional Seas Programme – Why Does Working with Regional Seas Matter?' (*UNEP – UN Environment Programme*, 16 August 2017) <www.unenvironment.org/explore-topics/oceans-seas/what-we-do/working-regional-seas/why-does-working-regional-seas-matter> accessed 10 April 2020

'Secretariats and Conventions' (UNEP – UN Environment Programme, 30 October 2017) <www.unep.org/about-un-environment/why-does-un-environment-matter/secretariats-and-conventions> accessed 30 April 2024

'Climate Action' (UNEP – UN Environment Programme, 5 October 2023) <www.unep.org/topics/climate-action> accessed 30 April 2024

'Ocean, Seas and Coasts' (UNEP – UN Environment Programme, 5 October 2023) <www.unep.org/topics/ocean-seas-and-coasts> accessed 30 April 2024

'Air' (UNEP – UN Environment Programme, 17 October 2023) <www.unep.org/topics/air> accessed 30 April 2024

'Mitigation' (UNEP – UN Environment Programme, 18 October 2023) <www.unep.org/topics/climate-action/mitigation> accessed 30 April 2024

'Mangrove Forests' (UNEP – UN Environment Programme, 23 November 2023) <www.unep.org/topics/ocean-seas-and-coasts/blue-ecosystems/mangrove-forests> accessed 30 April 2024

'Nexus of the Ocean and Climate' (UNEP – UN Environment Programme, 18 December 2023) <www.unep.org/topics/ocean-seas-and-coasts/nexus-ocean-and-climate> accessed 30 April 2024

EU Commission, 'Stopping the clock of ETS and aviation emissions following last week's International Civil Aviation Organisation (ICAO) Council' (European Commission – European Commission, 2023) <https://ec.europa.eu/commission/presscorner/detail/fr/MEMO_12_854> accessed 16 July 2023

'Aviation and the EU ETS' (2023) <https://climate.ec.europa.eu/eu-action/european-green-deal/delivering-european-green-deal/aviation-and-eu-ets_en> accessed 16 July 2023

'Reducing Emissions from the Shipping Sector – European Commission' (2024) <https://climate.ec.europa.eu/eu-action/transport/reducing-emissions-shipping-sector_en> accessed 14 January 2024

European Project on Ocean Acidification (EPOCA), 'Ocean Acidification: The Facts – A Special Introductory Guide for Policy Advisers and Decision Makers'

European Project on Ocean Acidification (EPOCA), Laffoley D and Baxter JM, 'Ocean Acidification: Questions Answered' <https://portals.iucn.org/library/node/9721> accessed 15 November 2019

Expert Meeting to Develop a Series of Joint Expert Review Processes to Monitor and Assess the Impacts of Ocean Acidification on Marine and Coastal Biodiversity, 'UNEP/CBD/EM-IOAMCB/1/2 – Background Document to an Expert Meeting to Develop a Series of Joint Expert Review Processes to Monitor and Assess the Impacts of Ocean Acidification on Marine and Coastal Biodiversity' <www.cbd.int/doc/meetings/mar/emioamcb-01/official/emioamcb-01-02-en.pdf> accessed 3 May 2024

Faber J and others, 'Fourth IMO GHG Study 2020 – Full Report and Annexes' (International Maritime Organization (IMO) 2021) <wwwcdn.imo.org/localresources/en/OurWork/Environment/Documents/Fourth%20IMO%20GHG%20Study%202020%20-%20Full%20report%20and%20annexes.pdf> accessed 27 August 2023

Faude B and Gehring T, 'Chapter 7: Regime Complexes as Governance Systems', *Research Handbook on the Politics of International Law* (Edward Elgar Publishing 2017)

Fennel K and VanderZwaag DL, 'Ocean Acidification: Scientific Surges, Lagging Law and Policy Responses' in Robin Warner and Stuart B Kaye (eds), *Routledge Handbook of Maritime Regulation and Enforcement* (Routledge 2016)

Findlay HS and others, 'Ocean Acidification around the UK and Ireland' [2022] *MCCIP Rolling Evidence Updates* 1

Fisher B, Turner RK and Morling P, 'Defining and Classifying Ecosystem Services for Decision Making' (2009) 68 *Ecological Economics* 643

Friedrich T and others, 'Detecting Regional Anthropogenic Trends in Ocean Acidification against Natural Variability' (2012) 2 *Nature Climate Change* 1

Galdies C, Tiller R and Martinez Romera B, 'Global Ocean Governance and Ocean Acidification' in Walter Leal Filho and others (eds), *Life Below Water* (Springer International Publishing 2021) <http://link.springer.com/10.1007/978-3-319-71064-8_109-1> accessed 12 November 2023

Gallo ND, Victor DG and Levin LA, 'Ocean Commitments under the Paris Agreement' (2017) 7 *Nature Climate Change* 833

Garcia B, Foerster A and Lin J, 'Net Zero for the International Shipping Sector? An Analysis of the Implementation and Regulatory Challenges of the IMO Strategy on Reduction of GHG Emissions' (2021) 33 *Journal of Environmental Law* 85

Gaylord B and others, 'Ocean Acidification through the Lens of Ecological Theory' (2016) 6 *Washington Journal of Environmental Law and Policy* 253

GEF-UNDP-IMO GloMEEP and IMarEST, 'Ship Emissions Toolkit Guide No. 01 – Rapid Assessment of Ship Emissions in the National Context (GEF-UNDP-IMO GloMEEP and IMarEST)' <https://gmn.imo.org/wp-content/uploads/2018/10/ship_emissions_toolkit-g1-online.pdf> accessed 15 October 2023

'Ship Emissions Toolkit Guide No. 3: Development of a National Ship Emissions Reduction Strategy' <https://gmn.imo.org/wp-content/uploads/2018/10/ship_emissions_toolkit-g3-online.pdf> accessed 15 October 2023

Gerring J, *Case Study Research: Principles and Practices* (2nd ed., Cambridge University Press 2017)

GOA-ON, 'GOA-ON: Approach & Goals' (2023) <www.goa-on.org/about/goals.php> accessed 25 July 2023

'GOA-ON: OA Research for Sustainability (OARS)' (2023) <www.goa-on.org/oars/overview.php> accessed 29 July 2023

'GOA-ON: OARS – White Papers' <www.goa-on.org/oars/white_papers.php> accessed 29 July 2023

Goldstein G and Ansell C, 'Experimentalist Governance in Global Public Health: The Case of UNAIDS' (2018) 35 *Arizona Journal of International and Comparative Law* 219

Gordon J, 'The Legal Implications of Ocean Acidification' in Paul G Harris (ed), *Routledge Handbook of Marine Governance and Global Environmental Change* (Routledge 2022)

Green JF, 'Hierarchy in Regime Complexes: Understanding Authority in Antarctic Governance' (2022) 66 *International Studies Quarterly* 1

Greenpeace International, 'Who We Are' (Greenpeace International, 2024) <www.greenpeace.org/international/about/> accessed 13 January 2024

GreenVoyage2050, 'National Action Plan to Address GHG Emissions from Ships: GreenVoyage2050' (2023) <https://greenvoyage2050.imo.org/national-action-plan/> accessed 12 October 2023

'Partnering Countries: GreenVoyage2050' (2023) <https://greenvoyage2050.imo.org/partnering-countries/> accessed 14 October 2023

Haas B and others, 'Factors Influencing the Performance of Regional Fisheries Management Organizations' (2020) 113 *Marine Policy* 103787

Hale T, 'Transnational Actors and Transnational Governance in Global Environmental Politics' (2020) 23 *Annual Review of Political Science* 203

Harrould-Kolieb E and Herr D, 'Ocean Acidification and Climate Change: Synergies and Challenges of Addressing Both under the UNFCCC' (2012) 12 *Climate Policy* 378

Harrould-Kolieb E and Stephens T, 'Ocean Acidification' in Rosemary Rayfuse, Aline Jaeckel and Natalie Klein (eds), *Research Handbook on International Marine Environmental Law* (Edward Elgar Publishing 2023) <www.elgaronline.com/view/book/9781789909081/book-part-9781789909081-20.xml> accessed 12 November 2023

Harrould-Kolieb ER, 'Ocean Acidification and the UNFCCC: Finding Legal Clarity in the Twilight Zone' (2016) *Washington Journal of Environmental Law & Policy* 612

'(Re)Framing Ocean Acidification in the Context of the United Nations Framework Convention on Climate Change (UNFCCC) and Paris Agreement' (2019) 19 *Climate Policy* 1225

'Framing Ocean Acidification to Mobilise Action under Multilateral Environmental Agreements' (2020) 104 *Environmental Science & Policy* 129

'The UN Convention on the Law of the Sea: A Governing Framework for Ocean Acidification?' (2020) 29 *Review of European, Comparative & International Environmental Law* 257

'Implications of the Paris Agreement for Action on Ocean Acidification within the UNFCCC' in David L VanderZwaag, Nilufer Oral and Tim Stephens (eds), *Research Handbook on Ocean Acidification Law and Policy* (Edward Elgar Publishing 2021)

Harrould-Kolieb ER and Hoegh-Guldberg O, 'A Governing Framework for International Ocean Acidification Policy' (2019) 102 *Marine Policy* 10

Hassellöv I and others, 'Shipping Contributes to Ocean Acidification' (2013) 40 *Geophysical Research Letters* 2731

Hassoun AER and others, 'Ocean Acidification Research in the Mediterranean Sea: Status, Trends and Next Steps' (2022) 9 *Frontiers in Marine Science* 892670

Herr D and others, Ocean Acidification: International Policy and Governance Options. (2014) 'Pathways for Implementation of Blue Carbon Initiatives' (2017) 27 *Aquatic Conservation: Marine and Freshwater Ecosystems* 116

Hilborn R and others, 'Biocomplexity and Fisheries Sustainability' (2003) 100 *Proceedings of the National Academy of Sciences* 6564

Hoegh-Guldberg O and others, 'Impacts of 1.5°C of Global Warming on Natural and Human Systems' in V Masson-Delmotte and others (eds), *Global Warming of 1.5°C: IPCC Special Report on Impacts of Global Warming of 1.5°C above Pre-industrial Levels in Context of Strengthening Response to Climate Change, Sustainable Development, and Efforts to Eradicate Poverty* (Cambridge University Press 2018)

Hoffmann A, 'The Transnational and the International: From Critique of Statism to Transversal Lines' (2022) 35 *Cambridge Review of International Affairs* 796

Hoppit G and others, 'Are Marine Protected Areas an Adaptation Measure against Climate Change Impacts on Coastal Ecosystems? A UK Case Study' (2022) 2 *Nature-Based Solutions* 100030

Hunter KA and others, 'Impacts of Anthropogenic SO_x, NO_x and NH_3 on Acidification of Coastal Waters and Shipping Lanes: Acidification of Coastal Waters' (2011) 38 *Geophysical Research Letters* 54

IAEA, 'History' (8 June 2016) <www.iaea.org/about/overview/history> accessed 11 January 2022

IAEA, OA-ICC, 'Ocean Acidification International Coordination Centre (OA-ICC)' (5 February 2018) <www.iaea.org/services/oa-icc> accessed 11 January 2022

ICAO, 'Carbon Offsetting and Reduction Scheme for International Aviation (CORSIA)' (2023) <www.icao.int/environmental-protection/CORSIA/Pages/default.aspx> accessed 16 July 2023

'About ICAO' (2024) <www.icao.int/about-icao/Pages/default.aspx> accessed 4 May 2024

'Climate Change' (2024) <www.icao.int/environmental-protection/pages/climate-change.aspx> accessed 6 May 2024

'Environmental Protection' (2024) <www.icao.int/environmental-protection/Pages/default.aspx> accessed 4 May 2024

'How ICAO Develops Standards' (2024) <www.icao.int/about-icao/AirNavigationCommission/Pages/how-icao-develops-standards.aspx> accessed 4 May 2024

'Strategic Objectives' (2024) <www.icao.int/about-icao/Council/Pages/Strategic-Objectives.aspx> accessed 4 May 2024

'The History of ICAO and the Chicago Convention' (2024) <www.icao.int/about-icao/History/Pages/default.aspx> accessed 4 May 2024

'Local Air Quality' (2024) <www.icao.int/environmental-protection/Pages/local-air-quality.aspx> accessed 6 May 2024

ICC, 'ICC's Political Universe… | Inuit Circumpolar Council Canada' (2024) <www.inuitcircumpolar.com/about-icc/icc-political-universe/> accessed 13 January 2024

IMO, 'Resolution LP.1(1) – On the Amendment to Include CO_2 Sequestration in Sub-seabed Geological Formations in Annex 1 to the London Protocol.pdf' <wwwcdn.imo.org/localresources/en/KnowledgeCentre/IndexofIMOResolutions/LCLPDocuments/LP.1(1).pdf> accessed 14 May 2024

'Resolution LP.3(4) – 2009 Amendment to Article 6 of the 1996 Protocol to the Convention on the Prevention of Marine Pollution by Dumping of Wastes and Other Matter 1972' <https://cil.nus.edu.sg/wp-content/uploads/2019/02/2009-Amd-to-London-Prot.pdf> accessed 14 May 2024

'Resolution LP.4(8) On the Amendment to the London Protocol to Regulate the Placement of Matter for Ocean Fertilization and Other Marine Geoengineering Activities' <wwwcdn.imo.org/localresources/en/KnowledgeCentre/IndexofIMOResolutions/LCLPDocuments/LP.4(8).pdf>

'2023 IMO Strategy on Reduction of GHG Emissions from Ships' (2019) <www.imo.org/en/OurWork/Environment/Pages/2023-IMO-Strategy-on-Reduction-of-GHG-Emissions-from-Ships.aspx#:~:text=The%202023%20IMO%20GHG%20Strategy%20envisages%2C%20in%20particular%2C%20a%20reduction,at%20least%2040%25%20by%202030.> accessed 3 October 2023

'Brief History of IMO' (2019) <www.imo.org/en/About/HistoryOfIMO/Pages/Default.aspx> accessed 14 January 2022

'Convention on the International Maritime Organization' (2019) <www.imo.org/en/About/Conventions/Pages/Convention-on-the-International-Maritime-Organization.aspx> accessed 14 January 2022

'Convention on the Prevention of Marine Pollution by Dumping of Wastes and Other Matter' (2019) <www.imo.org/en/About/Conventions/Pages/Convention-on-the-Prevention-of-Marine-Pollution-by-Dumping-of-Wastes-and-Other-Matter.aspx> accessed 19 January 2022

'Equivalents (SOx Scrubber, Etc.) – Regulation 4' (2019) <www.imo.org/en/OurWork/Environment/Pages/Equivalents-(Sox-scrubber,-etc.)---Regulation-4.aspx> accessed 17 January 2022

'Frequently Asked Questions' (2019) <www.imo.org/en/About/Pages/FAQs.aspx> accessed 1 September 2023

'GESAMP' (2019) <www.imo.org/en/ourwork/environment/pages/gesamp.aspx> accessed 16 December 2023

'Greenhouse Gas Emissions' (2019) <www.imo.org/en/OurWork/Environment/Pages/GHG-Emissions.aspx> accessed 19 January 2022

'Historic Background' (2019) <www.imo.org/en/OurWork/Environment/Pages/Historic-Background.aspx> accessed 6 October 2023

'IMO 2020 – Cleaner Shipping for Cleaner Air' (2019) <www.imo.org/en/MediaCentre/PressBriefings/pages/34-IMO-2020-sulphur-limit-.aspx> accessed 15 December 2023

'IMO 2020 – Cutting Sulphur Oxide Emissions' (2019) <www.imo.org/en/MediaCentre/HotTopics/Pages/Sulphur-2020.aspx> accessed 17 January 2022

'IMO and Its Role in Protecting the World's Oceans' (2019) <www.imo.org/en/MediaCentre/HotTopics/Pages/oceans-default.aspx> accessed 30 August 2023

'IMO GHG Studies' (2019) <www.imo.org/en/OurWork/Environment/Pages/IMO-GHG-studies.aspx> accessed 7 October 2023

'IMO's Work to Cut GHG Emissions from Ships' (2019) <www.imo.org/en/MediaCentre/HotTopics/Pages/Cutting-GHG-emissions.aspx> accessed 24 August 2023

'Intergovernmental Organizations Which Have Concluded Agreements of Cooperation with IMO' (2019) <www.imo.org/en/OurWork/ERO/Pages/IGOsWithObserverStatus.aspx> accessed 11 October 2023

'International Maritime Organization' (2019) <www.imo.org/> accessed 17 March 2023

'Intersessional Working Group on Reduction of GHG Emissions from Ships (ISWG-GHG 15), 26-30 June' (2019) <www.imo.org/en/MediaCentre/MeetingSummaries/Pages/Intersessional-Working-Group-on-Reduction-of-GHG-Emissions-from-Ships-(ISWG-GHG-15),-.aspx> accessed 1 September 2023

'Marine Environment' (2019) <www.imo.org/en/OurWork/Environment/Pages/Default.aspx> accessed 1 September 2023

'Marine Environment Protection Committee (MEPC)' (2019) <www.imo.org/en/MediaCentre/MeetingSummaries/Pages/MEPC-default.aspx> accessed 1 September 2023

'Marine Environment Protection Committee (MEPC 70), 24-28 October (Closing Remarks)' (2019) <www.imo.org/en/MediaCentre/SecretaryGeneral/Pages/MEPC-70-closing.aspx> accessed 13 January 2024

'Marine Environment Protection Committee (MEPC) 75, 16-20 November (Virtual Session)' (2019) <www.imo.org/en/MediaCentre/MeetingSummaries/Pages/MEPC-75th-session.aspx> accessed 13 January 2024

'Member States' (2019) <www.imo.org/en/OurWork/ERO/Pages/MemberStates.aspx> accessed 1 September 2023

'Member States, IGOs and NGOs' (2019) <www.imo.org/en/About/Membership/Pages/Default.aspx> accessed 1 September 2023

'New Guidance for National Emissions Reduction' (2019) <www.imo.org/en/MediaCentre/Pages/WhatsNew-1697.aspx> accessed 15 October 2023

'Non-Governmental International Organizations Which Have Been Granted Consultative Status with IMO' (2019) <www.imo.org/en/OurWork/ERO/Pages/NGOsInConsultativeStatus.aspx> accessed 11 October 2023

'Prevention of Air Pollution from Ships' (2019) <www.imo.org/en/OurWork/Environment/Pages/Air-Pollution.aspx> accessed 15 January 2022

'Relations with Observer Organizations' (2019) <www.imo.org/en/OurWork/ERO/Pages/Relations-with-Observer-Organizations.aspx> accessed 4 October 2023

'Revised GHG Reduction Strategy for Global Shipping Adopted' (2019) <www.imo.org/en/MediaCentre/PressBriefings/pages/Revised-GHG-reduction-strategy-for-global-shipping-adopted-.aspx> accessed 24 August 2023

'Strategic Plan for the Organization' (2019) <www.imo.org/en/About/Strategy/Pages/Default.aspx> accessed 15 January 2022

'The United Nations Convention on the Law of the Sea (UNCLOS) and the International Maritime Organization' (2019) <www.imo.org/en/MediaCentre/SecretaryGeneral/Pages/itlos.aspx> accessed 17 January 2022

'United Nations Convention on the Law of the Sea' (2019) <www.imo.org/en/ourwork/legal/pages/unitednationsconventiononthelawofthesea.aspx> accessed 17 March 2023

'IMO Approves Net-Zero Regulations for Global Shipping' (2025) <www.imo.org/en/MediaCentre/PressBriefings/pages/IMO-approves-netzero-regulations.aspx> accessed 7 May 2025

'Circular Letter No. 5005 – Draft Revised Marpol Annex Vi (Secretariat)' <wwwcdn.imo.org/localresources/en/MediaCentre/HotTopics/Documents/Circular%20Letter%20No.5005%20-%20Draft%20Revised%20Marpol%20Annex%20Vi%20%28Secretariat%29.pdf> accessed 7 May 2025

IMO Assembly, 'Resolution A.963(23) – IMO Policies and Practices Related to the Reduction of Greenhouse Gas Emissions from Ships' <wwwcdn.imo.org/localresources/en/KnowledgeCentre/IndexofIMOResolutions/AssemblyDocuments/A.963(23).pdf> accessed 6 October 2023

Intergovernmental Oceanographic Commission (IOC) and others, 'Marine Climate Engineering "Ocean Fertilization: A Scientific Summary for Policy Makers"' (International Maritime Organization 2011) IMO Report LC/SG 34/INF.3

Intergovernmental Panel on Climate Change (IPCC), *The Ocean and Cryosphere in a Changing Climate: Special Report of the Intergovernmental Panel on Climate Change* (1st ed., Cambridge University Press 2022) <www.cambridge.org/core/product/identifier/9781009157964/type/book> accessed 29 April 2024

International Bank for Reconstruction and Development, 'United Nations Monetary and Financial Conference – Bretton Woods' <https://timeline.worldbank.org/content/dam/sites/timeline/docs/migrated/event01-brettonwoods-finalact-1849790.pdf>

International Conference of Parties to the MARPOL Convention, 'MP/CONF.3/35 Resolution 8 1997' <wwwcdn.imo.org/localresources/en/MediaCentre/PressBriefings/Documents/MP%20CONF.3%2035%20Resolution%208%201997%20CO2.pdf> accessed 6 October 2023

International Maritime Organization (IMO), 'Resolution LP.1(1) On the Amendment to Include CO_2 Sequestration in Sub-Seabed Geological Formations in Annex I to the London Protocol'

'Resolution LP.3(4) – On the Amendment to Article 6 of the London Protocol the Fourth Meeting of Contracting Parties to the 1996 Protocol to the Convention on the Prevention of Marine Pollution by Dumping of Wastes and Other Matter, 1972' <wwwcdn.imo.org/localresources/en/KnowledgeCentre/IndexofIMOResolutions/LCLPDocuments/LP.3(4).pdf>

'Resolution LP.5(14) – On The Provisional Application of the 2009 Amendment to Article 6 of the London Protocol – The Fourteenth Meeting of Contracting Parties to the 1996 Protocol to the Convention on the Prevention of Marine Pollution by Dumping of Waste and Other Matter, 1972' <wwwcdn.imo.org/localresources/en/KnowledgeCentre/IndexofIMOResolutions/LCLPDocuments/LP.5(14).pdf>

Marine Environmental Protection Committee (MEPC), 'Initial IMO Strategy on Reduction of GHG Emissions from Ships' <https://unfccc.int/sites/default/files/resource/250_IMO%20submission_Talanoa%20Dialogue_April%202018.pdf> accessed 24 August 2023

'2023 IMO Strategy on Reduction of GHG Emissions from Ships' <wwwcdn.imo.org/localresources/en/MediaCentre/PressBriefings/Documents/Clean%20version%20of%20Annex%201.pdf>

International Partnership for Blue Carbon, 'Our Partners | Blue Carbon Partnership' (8 April 2022) <https://bluecarbonpartnership.org/the-partnership/blue-carbon-partner-organisations/> accessed 13 May 2025

INTERTANKO, 'Membership – INTERTANKO' (2024) <www.intertanko.com/about-us/membership> accessed 13 January 2024

Interview with IMO Delegate #1, 'IMO Delegate Interview #1' (December 2022)

Interview with IMO Delegate #2, 'IMO Delegate Interview #2' (December 2022)

Interview with IMO Delegate #3, 'IMO Delegate Interview #3' (December 2022)

Interview with IMO Delegate #4, 'IMO Delegate Interview #4' (December 2022)

Interview with IMO Delegate #5, 'IMO Delegate Interview #5' (December 2022)

Interview with IMO Delegate #6, 'IMO Delegate Interview #6' (December 2022)

Interview with Internal IMO Expert #1, 'Internal IMO Expert Interview #1' (January 2023)

Interview with Internal IMO Expert #2, 'Internal IMO Expert Interview #2' (December 2022)

Interview with OAA Personnel #1, 'OAA Expert Information Exchange #1' (July 2023)

IPBES, 'About | IPBES Secretariat' (16 March 2017) <www.ipbes.net/node/40> accessed 30 July 2023

'History of the Establishment of IPBES' (IPBES secretariat, 17 January 2020) <https://ipbes.net/history-establishment> accessed 14 January 2022

IPCC, *Global Warming of 1.5°C: IPCC Special Report on Impacts of Global Warming of 1.5°C above Pre-Industrial Levels in Context of Strengthening Response to Climate Change, Sustainable Development, and Efforts to Eradicate Poverty* (1st ed., Cambridge University Press 2018) <www.cambridge.org/core/product/identifier/9781009157940/type/book> accessed 29 April 2024

'IPCC Factsheet – What Is the IPCC' (2021) <www.ipcc.ch/site/assets/uploads/2021/07/AR6_FS_What_is_IPCC.pdf> accessed 7 May 2024

'About – IPCC' (2023) <www.ipcc.ch/about/> accessed 30 July 2023

IPCC, 2019, 'Summary for Policymakers' in HO Pörtner and others (eds), *IPCC Special Report on the Ocean and Cryosphere in a Changing Climate: Special Report of the Intergovernmental Panel on Climate Change* (1st ed., Cambridge University Press 2022) <www.cambridge.org/core/product/identifier/9781009157964/type/book> accessed 20 July 2023

IUCN, 'Themes' (*IUCN*, 13 August 2015) <www.iucn.org/theme> accessed 20 January 2022

'Climate Change and the Ocean' (*IUCN*, 7 October 2015) <www.iucn.org/theme/marine-and-polar/our-work/climate-change-and-ocean> accessed 20 January 2022

'Marine Protected Areas' (*IUCN*, 7 October 2015) <www.iucn.org/theme/marine-and-polar/our-work/marine-protected-areas> accessed 24 January 2022

'Blue Carbon' (*IUCN*, 4 May 2017) <www.iucn.org/theme/marine-and-polar/our-work/climate-change-and-ocean/blue-carbon> accessed 23 January 2022

'IUCN – A Brief History' (*IUCN*, 6 October 2017) <www.iucn.org/about/iucn-a-brief-history> accessed 20 January 2022

'Marine Biodiversity of Areas Beyond National Jurisdiction (BBNJ)' (*IUCN*, 7 August 2018) <www.iucn.org/theme/environmental-law/our-work/oceans-and-coasts/marine-biodiversity-areas-beyond-national-jurisdiction-bbnj> accessed 23 January 2022

'About' (*IUCN*, 10 September 2018) <www.iucn.org/about> accessed 20 January 2022

Statutes (Including Rules of Procedure) and Regulations (Last Amended on 31 March 2019) (IUCN, International Union for Conservation of Nature 2019) <https://portals.iucn.org/library/node/48398> accessed 20 January 2022

'BBNJ Knowledge Series' (*IUCN*, 27 November 2020) <www.iucn.org/theme/marine-and-polar/our-work/international-ocean-governance/unclos/bbnj-knowledge-series> accessed 23 January 2022

'Fisheries and Aquaculture | IUCN' (15 June 2022) <https://iucn.org/our-work/topic/fisheries-and-aquaculture> accessed 13 May 2025

'Marine Ecosystems | IUCN' (15 June 2022) <https://iucn.org/our-work/topic/marine-ecosystems> accessed 13 May 2025

'Plastic and Other Pollution | IUCN' (15 June 2022) <https://iucn.org/our-work/topic/plastic-and-other-pollution> accessed 13 May 2025

Statutes of 5 October 1948… (Including Rules of Procedure…) and Regulations…Last Amended on 13 December 2023 (IUCN, International Union for Conservation of Nature 2023) <https://portals.iucn.org/library/node/51397> accessed 6 May 2024

'About IUCN | IUCN' (2024) <www.iucn.org/about-iucn> accessed 6 May 2024

'Government Partners | IUCN' (2024) <www.iucn.org/about-iucn/partners-and-donors/government-partners> accessed 20 February 2024

'Indigenous Peoples | IUCN' (2024) <www.iucn.org/our-work/topic/indigenous-peoples> accessed 20 February 2024

'Ocean Acidification | IUCN' (2024) <www.iucn.org/our-work/topic/oceans-and-climate-change/ocean-acidification> accessed 6 May 2024

'Ocean and Climate Change | IUCN' (2024) <www.iucn.org/our-work/topic/ocean-and-climate-change> accessed 6 May 2024

'Our Work | IUCN' (2024) <www.iucn.org/our-work> accessed 6 May 2024

'Seventy Five Years of Experience | IUCN' (2024) <www.iucn.org/about-iucn/history> accessed 6 May 2024

'Ocean and Climate Change | IUCN' (2025) <https://iucn.org/our-work/topic/ocean-and-climate-change> accessed 13 May 2025

'Our Work | IUCN' (2025) <https://iucn.org/our-work> accessed 13 May 2025

'Ecosystem-Based Mitigation | IUCN' (10 March 2025) <https://iucn.org/our-work/topic/ecosystem-based-mitigation> accessed 13 May 2025

Jagers SC and others, 'Societal Causes of, and Responses to, Ocean Acidification' (2019) 48 *Ambio* 816

Kapsenberg L and Cyronak T, 'Ocean Acidification Refugia in Variable Environments' (2019) 25 *Global Change Biology* 3201

Karrkainen BC, 'Information-Forcing Regulation and Environmental Governance', *Law and New Governance in the EU and the US* (Hart Publishing 2006) <www.bloomsburycollections.com/book/law-and-new-governance-in-the-eu-and-the-us> accessed 30 November 2022

Kelly M, 'Adaptation to Climate Change through Genetic Accommodation and Assimilation of Plastic Phenotypes' (2019) 374 *Philosophical Transactions of the Royal Society B: Biological Sciences* 20180176

Kelly R and others, 'Mitigating Local Causes of Ocean Acidification with Existing Laws' (2011) 332 *Science* (New York, N.Y.) 1036

Keohane RO and Victor DG, 'The Regime Complex for Climate Change' (2011) 9 *Perspectives on Politics* 7

Keyzer L and others, 'The Potential of Coastal Ecosystems to Mitigate the Impact of Sea-Level Rise in Shallow Tropical Bays' (2020) 246 *Estuarine Coastal and Shelf Science* 1

'Kim – 2012 – Is a New Multilateral Environmental Agreement on O.Pdf' <www.researchgate.net/profile/Rakhyun_Kim/publication/256043173_Is_a_New_Multilateral_Environmental_Agreement_on_Ocean_Acidification_Necessary/links/59ee81fbaca272029ddf71f8/Is-a-New-Multilateral-Environmental-Agreement-on-Ocean-Acidification-Necessary.pdf> accessed 20 January 2020

Kim RE, 'Is a New Multilateral Environmental Agreement on Ocean Acidification Necessary?: Is a New Agreement on Ocean Acidification Necessary?' (2012) 21 *Review of European Community & International Environmental Law* 243

Kocs E, 'The Global Carbon Nation: Status of CO_2 Capture, Storage and Utilization' (2017) 148 *EPJ Web of Conferences* 1

Korpinen S and Bonsdorff E, 'Eutrophication and Hypoxia: Impacts of Nutrient and Organic Enrichment' (2015)

Krause-Jensen D and others, 'Sequestration of Macroalgal Carbon: The Elephant in the Blue Carbon Room' (2018) 14 *Biology Letters* 20180236

Kroeker K and others, 'Kroeker K. J., Kordas R. L., Crim R. N. & Singh G. G. – Meta-Analysis Reveals Negative yet Variable Effects of Ocean Acidification on Marine Organisms. Ecology Letters' (2010) 13 *Ecology letters* 1419

Kroeker KJ and others, 'Impacts of Ocean Acidification on Marine Organisms: Quantifying Sensitivities and Interaction with Warming' (2013) 19 *Global Change Biology* 1884

Krumhansl KA and others, 'Global Patterns of Kelp Forest Change over the Past Half-Century' (2016) 113 *Proceedings of the National Academy of Sciences* 13785

Kuffner I, 'Coral Reefs Could Drown as Sea Levels Rise' (2018) 558 *Nature*

Kumar B and Deepthi G, 'Trawling and By-Catch: Implications on Marine Ecosystem' (2006) 90(7) *Current Science* 992

Laffoley D and others, 'Ocean Acidification: Scientific Understanding and Challenges' in David L VanderZwaag, Nilufer Oral and Tim Stephens (eds), *Research Handbook on Ocean Acidification Law and Policy* (Edward Elgar Publishing 2021) <www.elgaronline.com/edcollchap/edcoll/9781789900132/9781789900132.00009.xml>

Laffoley ED and others (eds), *An Introduction to Ocean Acidification: What It Is, What We Know, and What May Happen* (International Union for Conservation of Nature and Natural Resources IUCN 2017)

Lamirande HR, 'From Sea to Carbon Cesspool: Preventing the World's Marine Ecosystems from Falling Victim to Ocean Acidification' (2011) 34 *Suffolk Transnational Law Review* 183

Lester S and others, 'Biological Effects within No-Take Marine Reserves: A Global Synthesis' (2009) 384 *Marine Ecology Progress Series* 33

Lin J and Scott J, 'Looking Beyond the International: Key Themes and Approaches of Transnational Environmental Law' (2012) 1 *Transnational Environmental Law* 23

Liu D and Chow D, 'China's Summer of Extremes Has Farmers Worried' (*NBC News*, 8 August 2023) <www.nbcnews.com/news/world/china-floods-drought-farming-wheat-climate-change-rcna96111> accessed 8 December 2023

Macreadie PI and others, 'Blue Carbon as a Natural Climate Solution' (2021) 2 *Nature Reviews Earth & Environment* 826

Makomere R and McDonald J, 'Responding to Ocean Acidification beyond Climate Governance' in Jan McDonald, Jeffrey McGee and Richard Barnes (eds), *Research Handbook on Climate Change, Oceans and Coasts* (Edward Elgar Publishing 2020) <https://china.elgaronline.com/view/edcoll/9781788112222/9781788112222.00026.xml> accessed 12 November 2023

'Marine Environment Protection Committee (MEPC) – 79th Session'

McKinley GA and others, 'External Forcing Explains Recent Decadal Variability of the Ocean Carbon Sink' (2020) 1 *AGU Advances* 1

MEPC, 'MEPC.67(37) – Guidelines on Incorporation of the Precautionary Approach in the Context of Specific IMO Activities (Annex 10)' <wwwcdn.imo.org/localresources/en/KnowledgeCentre/IndexofIMOResolutions/MEPCDocuments/MEPC.67(37).pdf> accessed 7 October 2023

'MEPC.130(53) – Guidelines for On-Board Exhaust Gas-SOx Cleaning Systems' <wwwcdn.imo.org/localresources/en/KnowledgeCentre/IndexofIMOResolutions/MEPCDocuments/MEPC.130(53).pdf> accessed 11 February 2024

'MEPC.170(57) – Guidelines for Exhaust Gas Cleaning Systems' <wwwcdn.imo.org/localresources/en/KnowledgeCentre/IndexofIMOResolutions/MEPCDocuments/MEPC.170(57).pdf> accessed 11 February 2024

'MEPC.184(59) – 2009 Guidelines for Exhaust Gas Cleaning Systems' <wwwcdn.imo.org/localresources/en/KnowledgeCentre/IndexofIMOResolutions/MEPCDocuments/MEPC.184(59).pdf> accessed 11 February 2024

'Resolution MEPC.203(62) – Amendments to the Annex of the Protocol of 1997 to Amend the International Convention for the Prevention of Pollution from Ships, 1973, as Modified by the Protocol of 1978 Relating Thereto (Annex 19)' <wwwcdn.imo.org/localresources/en/OurWork/Environment/Documents/Technical%20and%20Operational%20Measures/Resolution%20MEPC.203%2862%29.pdf> accessed 6 October 2023

'MEPC.259(68) – 2015 Guidelines for Exhaust Gas Cleaning Systems' <wwwcdn.imo.org/localresources/en/KnowledgeCentre/IndexofIMOResolutions/MEPCDocuments/MEPC.259(68).pdf> accessed 11 February 2024

'Resolution MEPC.327(75) – Encouragement of Member States to Develop and Submit Voluntary National Action Plans to Address GHG Emissions from Ships (Annex 4)' <wwwcdn.imo.org/localresources/en/OurWork/Environment/Documents/Air%20pollution/Resolution%20MEPC.327(75).pdf> accessed 12 October 2023

'MEPC.340(77) – 2021 Guidelines for Exhaust Gas Cleaning Systems' <wwwcdn.imo.org/localresources/en/OurWork/Environment/Documents/Air%20pollution/MEPC.340%2877%29.pdf> accessed 11 February 2024

'MEPC.1-Circ.899–2022 Guidelines for Risk and Impact Assessments of the Discharge Water from Exhaust Gas Cleaning Systems' <wwwcdn.imo.org/localresources/en/OurWork/Environment/Documents/Air%20pollution/MEPC.1-Circ.899.pdf> accessed 12 February 2024

'Resolution MEPC.367(79) – Encouragement of Member States to Develop and Submit Voluntary National Action Plans to Address GHG Emissions from Ships (Annex 12)' <wwwcdn.imo.org/localresources/en/KnowledgeCentre/IndexofIMOResolutions/MEPCDocuments/MEPC.367(79).pdf>

Millennium Ecosystem Assessment (Program) (ed), *Ecosystems and Human Well-Being: Synthesis* (Island Press 2005)

Mukherji A and others, 'Synthesis Report of the IPCC Sixth Assessment Report (AR6)' <https://report.ipcc.ch/ar6syr/pdf/IPCC_AR6_SYR_SPM.pdf>

'National Action Plans' (2019) <www.imo.org/en/ourwork/environment/pages/relevant-national-action-plans-and-strategies.aspx> accessed 12 October 2023

Nations U, 'From Stockholm to Kyoto: A Brief History of Climate Change' (*United Nations*, 2024) <www.un.org/en/chronicle/article/stockholm-kyoto-brief-history-climate-change> accessed 7 May 2024

'UN Structure' (*United Nations*, 2024) <www.un.org/en/model-united-nations/un-structure?fbclid=IwZXh0bgNhZW0CMTAAAR2XjSRHatS5r8p3MDjopEe1KN934SLzb0TpLbH0pIcOvJea-nh8LXVDEGs_aem_Ae417449by1uw1ov8XmrvWqOIDzK7twQfGprk7BhIWjCvJzIQM1XR8such71F5mLcr8pHhbOjzSJwhQKw5LfNXoM> accessed 6 May 2024

Nellemann C and GRID-Arendal (eds), *Blue Carbon: The Role of Healthy Oceans in Binding Carbon: A Rapid Response Assessment* (GRID-Arendal 2009)

NOAA, Global Monitoring Laboratory, 'Carbon Cycle Greenhouse Gases – Trends in CO_2' (2024) <https://gml.noaa.gov/ccgg/trends/weekly.html> accessed 15 January 2024

Nye JS and Keohane RO, 'Transnational Relations and World Politics: An Introduction' (1971) 25 *International Organization* 329

OA Alliance, 'International Alliance to Combat Ocean Acidification: A Global Call to Action' <https://static1.squarespace.com/static/6006d84247a6a51d636dd219/t/64d2bc821c15727478d960d9/1691532419019/OA_CALL+TO+ACTION_2016.pdf> accessed 18 April 2025

'Case Study: City of Vancouver, British Columbia, Canada' <https://static1.squarespace.com/static/6006d84247a6a51d636dd219/t/6481f79f94380172778dbfc8/1686239140858/OA_CaseStudy_VANCOUVER.pdf> accessed 18 April 2025

'OA Alliance Member Communications Survey 2020 (Internal Document Provided by OAA Personnel)'

'Supporting Member Messaging Comms Survey 2021 (Internal Document Provided by OAA Personnel)'

'About' (*OA Alliance*, 2021) <www.oaalliance.org/about> accessed 18 January 2022

'Action Plans' (*OA Alliance*, 2021) <www.oaalliance.org/action-plans> accessed 19 January 2022

'OA Alliance Strategic Planning Meeting December 2021 Summary and Outcomes (Internal Document Provided by OAA Personnel)'

'About Us' (*OA Alliance*, 2022) <www.oaalliance.org/about> accessed 14 September 2022

'Become a Member and Welcome Packet' (*OA Alliance*, 2022) <www.oaalliance.org/general-3> accessed 14 September 2022

'Current Members' (*OA Alliance*, 2022) <www.oaalliance.org/current-members> accessed 14 September 2022

'FAQs' (*OA Alliance*, 2022) <www.oaalliance.org/faqs> accessed 14 September 2022

'OA Getting Started' (2022) <https://static1.squarespace.com/static/6006d84247a6a51d636dd219/t/60196febec250f31a6dc64cd/1612279790011/OAGettingStarted_8.5x14.pdf> accessed 4 October 2022

'Our Impact' (*OA Alliance*, 2022) <www.oaalliance.org/ourimpact> accessed 4 October 2022

'Posters – OA Action Supports International Frameworks' (*OA Alliance*, 2022) <www.oaalliance.org/posters> accessed 4 October 2022

'What Can Local Governments Do to Address Ocean and Coastal Acidification?' (2022) <https://static1.squarespace.com/static/6006d84247a6a51d636dd219/t/6246cc9c062150292b3ac6de/1648807071761/OA_LocalGovernments_11x17.pdf> accessed 5 October 2022

'What Role Can Local and Regional Government Play?' (*OA Alliance*, 2022) <www.oaalliance.org/webinars/blog-post-title-four-6spzs> accessed 5 October 2022

'Advancing Ocean & Coastal Adaptation – Submission to the UNFCCC Ocean and Climate Change Dialogue, June 2022' <https://static1.squarespace.com/static/6006d84247a6a51d636dd219/t/6287d1b38414cb73a19d50c3/1653068212622/OAlliance_UNFCCCOceanDialogue2022_Submission.pdf> accessed 4 October 2022

'ACTION #3: Reduce Local Pollution That Exacerbates OA Action 3' (*OA Alliance*, 2023) <www.oaalliance.org/action-3> accessed 24 August 2023

'OA Alliance Initiative, Executive Committee, Articles of Governance 2023 (Internal Document Provided by OAA Personnel)'

'OA Alliance Webinar – Tribes and Indigenous Communities on the Front Lines' (*OA Alliance*, 2023) <www.oaalliance.org/webinars/tribes-and-indigenous-communities-on-the-front-lines> accessed 29 July 2023

'Perspective on Marine Carbon Dioxide Removal and Related Research' <https://static1.squarespace.com/static/6006d84247a6a51d636dd219/t/64d2b154b25a557b3828ac3e/1691529556581/OAA_Perspectives+on+mCDR_FINAL.pdf> accessed 15 August 2023

'Unveiling OA Action Plans' (*OA Alliance*, 2023) <www.oaalliance.org/webinars/qsks3gbjjcc9xwjsqwhk18laxldwxv> accessed 28 July 2023

'U.S. State-Led OA Action Planning in the Mid-Atlantic' (*OA Alliance*, 2023) <www.oaalliance.org/webinars/nmdyihmf9ge6hgq9742dhr7jd3xmis> accessed 28 July 2023

'Workshops and Webinars' (*OA Alliance*, 2023) <www.oaalliance.org/webinars> accessed 13 January 2023

'About' (*OA Alliance*, 2024) <www.oaalliance.org/about> accessed 7 May 2024

'About Us' (*OA Alliance*, 2024) <www.oaalliance.org/about> accessed 17 April 2025

'Action Plan Toolkit 2024' <https://static1.squarespace.com/static/6006d84247a6a51d636dd219/t/661f8d8189290b05c9a25e95/1713343878415/OAlliance_APToolkit2024_A.pdf> accessed 7 May 2024

'Become a Member' (*OA Alliance*, 2024) <www.oaalliance.org/becomeamember> accessed 18 April 2025

'Member Examples' (*OA Alliance*, 2024) <www.oaalliance.org/member-examples> accessed 18 April 2025

'OA Welcome Packet Government Members' <https://static1.squarespace.com/static/6006d84247a6a51d636dd219/t/65c39872ea60216b8dffd847/1707317370464/OA_WelcomePacket_GOVERNMENT_2024.pdf> accessed 18 April 2025

'Ocean Acidification Alliance Action Plan' (*OA Alliance*, 2024) <www.oaalliance.org/oaactionplan> accessed 18 April 2025

'Our Impact' (*OA Alliance*, 2024) <www.oaalliance.org/ourimpact> accessed 7 May 2024

'OA Alliance Action Plan Toolkit' <https://static1.squarespace.com/static/6006d84247a6a51d636dd219/t/661f8d8189290b05c9a25e95/1713343878415/OAlliance_APToolkit2024_A.pdf> accessed 18 April 2025

'Ocean Change Requires Solutions – UN Oceans Envoy' (2019) <www.imo.org/en/MediaCentre/PressBriefings/Pages/26-oceansenvoy.aspx> accessed 15 December 2023

Oceana, 'Financials' (*Oceana*, 2024) <https://oceana.org/financials/> accessed 20 February 2024

'Oceana Campaigns' (*Oceana*, 2024) <https://oceana.org/campaigns/> accessed 2 May 2024

'Oceana Presents Ocean Acidification Message at COP-15' (*Oceana*, 2024) <https://oceana.org/press-releases/oceana-presents-ocean-acidification-message-cop-15/> accessed 2 May 2024

'Protecting Ocean Habitats' (*Oceana*, 2024) <https://oceana.org/campaign-page/protecting-important-ocean-habitat/> accessed 2 May 2024

'Save the Oceans, Feed the World' (*Oceana*, 2024) <https://oceana.org/our-campaigns/feedtheworld/> accessed 2 May 2024

'Stop Offshore Drilling' (*Oceana*, 2024) <https://oceana.org/campaign-page/protecting-our-climate-by-stopping-offshore-drilling/> accessed 2 May 2024

'Stop Overfishing' (*Oceana*, 2024) <https://oceana.org/campaign-page/overfishing/> accessed 2 May 2024

'Victories Archive' (*Oceana USA*, 2024) <https://usa.oceana.org/victories/> accessed 2 May 2024

'What Does Oceana Do' (*Oceana*, 2024) <https://oceana.org/about/> accessed 2 May 2024

'Oceana International Offices' (*Oceana*, 2024) <https://oceana.org/oceana-international-offices/> accessed 2 May 2024

OECD, *Environment at a Glance 2020* (OECD 2020) <www.oecd-ilibrary.org/environment/environment-at-a-glance/volume-/issue-_4ea7d35f-en> accessed 4 March 2021

'Air and GHG Emissions' <www.oecd-ilibrary.org/environment/air-and-ghg-emissions/indicator/english_93d10cf7-en> accessed 9 February 2023

Oral N, 'Ocean Acidification: Falling Between the Legal Cracks of UNCLOS and the UNFCCC?' (2018) 45 *Ecology Law Quarterly* 9

Oregon State University and others, 'The Dynamics and Impact of Ocean Acidification and Hypoxia: Insights from Sustained Investigations in the Northern California Current Large Marine Ecosystem' (2019) 32 *Oceanography* 62

Orsini A, Morin J-F and Young O, 'Regime Complexes: A Buzz, a Boom, or a Boost for *Global Governance?*' (2013) 19 *Global Governance* 27

OSPAR Commission, 'OSPAR Has Become an Affiliate Member of the International Alliance to Combat Ocean Acidification' (*OSPAR Commission*, 14 December 2022) <www.ospar.org/news/oaalliance> accessed 28 February 2023

Our World in Data, 'CO_2 Emissions by Sector' (*Our World in Data*, 2022) <https://ourworldindata.org/grapher/co-emissions-by-sector> accessed 1 October 2023

Overdevest C and Zeitlin J, 'Assembling an Experimentalist Regime: Transnational Governance Interactions in the Forest Sector: Assembling an Experimentalist Regime' (2014) 8 *Regulation & Governance* 22

Oxford English Dictionary, 'Public Good, n.' <www.oed.com/dictionary/public-good_n?tab=meaning_and_use#9927762718> accessed 25 July 2023

Pachauri RK, Mayer L, and Intergovernmental Panel on Climate Change (eds), *Climate Change 2014: Synthesis Report* (Intergovernmental Panel on Climate Change 2015)

Parson E, *Protecting the Ozone Layer: Science and Strategy* (Oxford University Press 2003)

Pinheiro M and others, 'Stressors of Emerging Concern in Deep-Sea Environments: Microplastics, Pharmaceuticals, Personal Care Products and Deep-Sea Mining' (2023) 876 *Science of The Total Environment* 162557

Pinsky VC, Kruglianskas I and Victor DG, 'Experimentalist Governance in Climate Finance: The Case of REDD+ in Brazil' (2019) 19 *Climate Policy* 725

Pogo, 'Ocean Pavilion at COP-27' (*Partnership for Observation of the Global Ocean*, 29 April 2024) <https://pogo-ocean.org/news/ocean-pavilion-at-cop-27/> accessed 29 April 2024

Popattanachai N and Kirk EA, 'Ocean Acidification and Multilateral Environmental Agreements' in David L VanderZwaag, Nilufer Oral and Tim Stephens (eds), *Research Handbook on Ocean Acidification Law and Policy* (Edward Elgar Publishing 2021)

Port of Seattle, 'Port of Seattle Ocean Acidification Action Plan' <https://static1.squarespace.com/static/6006d84247a6a51d636dd219/t/6122fa91597e8b6a0dfa797b/1629682324883/Port_OA_Action_Plan.pdf> accessed 18 April 2025

Poynting M and Stallard E, 'How Climate Change Worsens Heatwaves, Droughts, Wildfires and Floods' *BBC News* (9 August 2021) <www.bbc.com/news/science-environment-58073295> accessed 8 December 2023

President of the Conference, 'A/CONF.210/2010/7 – Report of the Resumed Review Conference on the Agreement for the Implementation of the Provisions of the United Nations Convention on the Law of the Sea of 10 December 1982 Relating to the Conservation and Management of Straddling Fish Stocks and Highly Migratory Fish Stocks' <https://documents.un.org/doc/undoc/gen/n10/465/87/pdf/n1046587.pdf?token=L3KyZpZK326ovLo6ww&fe=true>

Qin D and others, 'Cryospheric Science: Research Framework and Disciplinary System' (2018) 5 *National Science Review* 255

Qin G and Yu H, 'Rescuing the Paris Agreement: Improving the Global Experimentalist Governance by Reclassifying Countries' (2023) 15 *Sustainability* 3207

Ramirez R, 'Without Climate Change, These Extreme Weather Events Would Not Have Happened' (*CNN*, 15 June 2023) <www.cnn.com/2023/06/15/world/extreme-weather-events-climate-change/index.html> accessed 8 December 2023

RAMSAR, 'The Convention on Wetlands and Its Mission | Ramsar' (2014) <www.ramsar.org/about/the-convention-on-wetlands-and-its-mission> accessed 24 January 2022

'The Secretariat | Ramsar' (2014) <www.ramsar.org/about/the-secretariat> accessed 24 January 2022

Raustiala K and Victor DG, 'The Regime Complex for Plant Genetic Resources' (2004) 58 *International Organization* 277

Rayfuse R, 'Regional Fisheries Bodies and Ocean Acidification' in David L VanderZwaag, Nilufer Oral and Tim Stephens (eds), *Research Handbook on Ocean Acidification Law and Policy* (Edward Elgar Publishing 2021)

Raza A and others, 'Significant Aspects of Carbon Capture and Storage – A Review' (2019) 5 *Petroleum* 335

Rennenberg H and Gessler A, '*Acid Rain*' (2001)

Richter I, Berking S and Müller-Schmid R (eds), 'Introduction', *Building a Transnational Civil Society: Global Issues and Global Actors* (Palgrave Macmillan 2006)

Riebesell U and Gattuso J-P, 'Lessons Learned from Ocean Acidification Research' (2015) 5 *Nature Climate Change* 12

Rockström J and others, 'A Safe Operating Space for Humanity' (2009) 461 *Nature* 472

Rodriguez K, 'A Breakthrough for Oceans: Scaling Nature-Based Solutions for Ocean-Based Climate Policy at COP28' (*Climate Champions*, 9 December 2023) <https://climatechampions.unfccc.int/a-breakthrough-for-oceans-scaling-nature-based-solutions-for-ocean-based-climate-policy-at-cop28/> accessed 29 April 2024

Royal Society (Great Britain), *Ocean Acidification Due to Increasing Atmospheric Carbon Dioxide.* (Royal Society 2005)

Sabel CF and Victor DG, *Fixing the Climate: Strategies for an Uncertain World* (Princeton University Press 2022)

Sabel CF and Zeitlin J (eds), 'Emerging Experimentalism in EU Environmental Governance', *Experimentalist Governance in the European Union: Towards a New Architecture* (Oxford University Press 2010)

(eds), 'Experimentalist Governance in the European Energy Sector', *Experimentalist Governance in the European Union: Towards a New Architecture* (Oxford University Press 2010)

'Learning from Difference: The New Architecture of Experimentalist Governance in the EU' in Charles F Sabel and Jonathan Zeitlin (eds), *Experimentalist Governance in the European Union: Towards a New Architecture* (Oxford University Press 2010)

'Experimentalist Governance', *Experimentalist Governance* (Oxford University Press 2012) <http://oxfordhandbooks.com/view/10.1093/oxfordhb/9780199560530.001.0001/oxfordhb-9780199560530-e-12> accessed 31 July 2022

Salisbury J and others, 'Coastal Acidification by Rivers: A Threat to Shellfish?' (2008) 89 *Eos, Transactions American Geophysical Union* 513

Savina P, 'Ocean Pavilion Partners Unveil COP28 Dubai Ocean Declaration in Advance of UN Climate Conference' (*Ocean Decade*, 20 November 2023) <https://oceandecade.org/news/ocean-pavilion-partners-unveil-cop28-dubai-ocean-declaration/> accessed 29 April 2024

Scott B, Shearing C and Kempa M, 'Changes in Governance: A Cross-Disciplinary Review of Current Scholarship' (2008) 41 *Akron Law Review* 1

Scott J and Rajamani L, 'EU Climate Change Unilateralism' (2012) 23 *European Journal of International Law* 469

Scott KN, 'Geoengineering and the Marine Environment' in Rosemary Rayfuse (ed), *Research Handbook on International Marine Environmental Law* (Edward Elgar Publishing 2015) <https://china.elgaronline.com/view/edcoll/9781781004760/9781781004760.00033.xml> accessed 14 May 2024

Scott KN, 'Ocean Acidification: A Due Diligence Obligation under the LOSC' (2020) 35 *The International Journal of Marine and Coastal Law* 382

'Ocean Acidification' in Elise Johansen, Signe Busch and Ingvild Ulrikke Jakobsen (eds), *The Law of the Sea and Climate Change* (1st ed., Cambridge University Press 2020) <www.cambridge.org/core/product/identifier/9781108907118%23CN-bp-5/type/book_part> accessed 10 April 2023

'The BBNJ Agreement: Strengthening the Oceans-Climate Nexus?', *Peaceful Maritime Engagement in East Asia and the Pacific Region* (Brill Nijhoff 2022) <https://brill.com/display/book/9789004518629/BP000032.xml> accessed 8 May 2024

Secretariat of the Convention on Biological Diversity, 'Scientific Synthesis of the Impacts of Ocean Acidification on Marine Biodiversity' (2009) Technical Series No. 46 <www.cbd.int/doc/publications/cbd-ts-46-en.pdf> accessed 1 May 2024

An Updated Synthesis of the Impacts of Ocean Acidification on Marine Biodiversity (2014)

Selman M and others, 'Eutrophication and Hypoxia in Coastal Areas: A Global Assessment of the State of Knowledge' [2008] WRI Policy Note 1

Sess.: 1972) UGA (27th, 'A_RES_2997(XXVII) – Institutional and Financial Arrangements for International Environmental Co-operation'. <https://digitallibrary.un.org/record/191561> accessed 30 April 2024

Silverstein T, 'Weak vs Strong Acids and Bases: The Football Analogy' (2000) 77 *Journal of Chemical Education – J CHEM EDUC* 849

Simons M and Stephens T, 'Ocean Acidification: Addressing the Other CO_2 Problem' (2009) 12 *Asia Pacific Journal of Environmental Law* 1

Singh A and Agrawal M, 'Acid Rain and Its Ecological Consequences' (2008) 29 *Journal of Environmental Biology / Academy of Environmental Biology, India* 15

Smith T and others, 'An Overview of the Discussions from IMO's 83rd Marine Environment Protection Committee' <www.shippingandoceans.com/post/phase-out-of-fossil-fuels-in-shipping-begins-in-earnest>

State of California, Province of British Columbia, State of Oregon, State of Washington, 'Letter Governors – Welcome Letter' (2016) <https://static1.squarespace.com/static/6006d84247a6a51d636dd219/t/604211fed050703aae69c45d/1614942721743/LetterGovernors.pdf> accessed 18 April 2025

Stephens T, 'Warming Waters and Souring Seas: Climate Change and Ocean Acidification' in Donald Rothwell and others (eds), *The Oxford Handbook of the Law of the Sea* (1st ed., Oxford University Press 2016) <https://academic.oup.com/edited-volume/42608/chapter/357548970> accessed 12 November 2023

Street J, 'Iron, Phytoplankton Growth, and the Carbon Cycle' (2005) 43 *Metal ions in biological systems* 153

Structured Expert Dialogue (SED), 'FCCC/SB/2015/INF.1' <https://unfccc.int/resource/docs/2015/sb/eng/inf01.pdf> accessed 22 October 2020

Subsidiary Body for Scientific and Technological Advice, 'Paper No. 4 FCCC/SBSTA/2005/MISC.15 – Views on the Report on Progress Made towards Implementing the Initial Ocean Climate Observing System, and on the Final Report on the Analysis of Data Exchange Issues in Global Atmospheric and Hydrological Networks' <https://unfccc.int/resource/docs/2005/sbsta/eng/misc15.pdf?fbclid=IwZXh0bgNhZW0CMTAAAR12G4aR6b-oApWNHx5TqD-_UG5i_wzclUaI7wSzWHaP3bzSglDwwo59tf8_aem_Aae5uLN9w4hdzdalgiWRQTjN8H2UN30k3hT5cm6duYHIZbWjGxAPw-mur0htPmM_drpupJOEz2YdS39J1YuUo7yG>

—— 'FCCC/SBSTA/2007/7 – Report on the Workshop on Climate-Related Risks and Extreme Events'

—— 'FCCC/SBSTA/2008/MISC.8 – Information Provided by Regional and International Climate Change Research Programmes and Organizations on Developments in Research Activities Relevant to the Needs of the Convention' <https://unfccc.int/resource/docs/2008/sbsta/eng/misc08a01.pdf>

Subsidiary Body for Scientific and Technological Advice, 'FCCC/SBSTA/2011/L.4 – Research and Systematic Observation'

Subsidiary Body on Scientific, and Technical and Technological Advice, 'UNEP/CBD/SBSTTA/16/6 – Addressing Adverse Impacts of Human Activities on Marine and Coastal Biodiversity, Including Coral Bleaching, Ocean Acidification, Fisheries and Underwater Noise' <www.cbd.int/doc/meetings/sbstta/sbstta-16/official/sbstta-16-06-en.pdf> accessed 1 May 2024

Sulyok K, *Science and Judicial Reasoning: The Legitimacy of International Environmental Adjudication* (Cambridge University Press 2021)

Swezey DS and others, 'Evolved Differences in Energy Metabolism and Growth Dictate the Impacts of Ocean Acidification on Abalone Aquaculture' (2020) 117 *Proceedings of the National Academy of Sciences* 26513

Teuchies J and others, 'The Impact of Scrubber Discharge on the Water Quality in Estuaries and Ports' (In Review 2020) preprint <www.researchsquare.com/article/rs-23441/v2> accessed 12 July 2023

The Blue Carbon Initiative, 'The Blue Carbon Initiative' (*The Blue Carbon Initiative*, 2024) <www.thebluecarboninitiative.org> accessed 4 May 2024

The Conference of the Parties, 'Decision -/CP.26 – Glasgow Climate Pact' <https://unfccc.int/sites/default/files/resource/cop26_auv_2f_cover_decision.pdf> accessed 8 May 2024

The Council of Europe, 'The Council of Europe at a Glance – Portal – Www.Coe.Int' (*Portal*, 2024) <www.coe.int/en/web/portal/the-council-of-europe-at-a-glance> accessed 13 January 2024

'The Paris Agreement | UNFCCC' (2024) <https://unfccc.int/process-and-meetings/the-paris-agreement> accessed 8 May 2024

'The Secretariat of the Convention | CMS' (2020) <www.cms.int/en/about/secretariat> accessed 20 January 2022

The World Bank, 'Environmental and Social Policies' (*World Bank*, 2022) <www.worldbank.org/en/projects-operations/environmental-and-social-policies> accessed 10 January 2022

'What We Do' (*World Bank*, 2022) <www.worldbank.org/en/what-we-do> accessed 10 January 2022

'Development Projects: Unleashing the Blue Economy of the Caribbean (UBEC) – P171833' (*World Bank*, 2024) <https://projects.worldbank.org/en/projects-operations/project-detail/P171833> accessed 11 May 2024

'Home – Timeline' (*World Bank*, 2024) <https://timeline.worldbank.org/en/timeline/home> accessed 8 May 2024

'Projects' (*World Bank*, 2024) <https://projects.worldbank.org/en/projects-operations/projects-list> accessed 11 May 2024

Thiel M and Maslanik J, 'Transnational Actors' in Markus Thiel and Jeffrey Maslanik (eds), *Oxford Research Encyclopedia of International Studies* (Oxford University Press 2010) <https://oxfordre.com/internationalstudies/view/10.1093/acrefore/9780190846626.001.0001/acrefore-9780190846626-e-105> accessed 26 July 2023

Traut M and others, 'CO_2 Abatement Goals for International Shipping' (2018) 18 *Climate Policy* 1066

Turner DR and others, 'The Potential Future Contribution of Shipping to Acidification of the Baltic Sea' (2018) 47 *Ambio* 368

Turner J and Bellerby R, 'Outcome #2: Identify Data and Evidence Needs for OA Mitigation and Adaptation Strategies, From Local to Global' <www.goa-on.org/oars/docs/oars-outcome_2-white_paper-2023.pdf> accessed 29 July 2023

UN, 'Intergovernmental Conference on Marine Biodiversity of Areas beyond National Jurisdiction' <www.un.org/bbnj/> accessed 21 January 2022

'UN Foundation Welcomes OA Alliance!' (*OA Alliance*, 2024) <www.oaalliance.org/news/ker0yxuif79nfwz7671tab5iryhacg> accessed 18 April 2025

UNEP, 'Addressing Land-Based Pollution' (*UNEP – UN Environment Programme*, 15 August 2017) <www.unep.org/explore-topics/oceans-seas/what-we-do/addressing-land-based-pollution> accessed 19 January 2022

'Governing the Global Programme of Action' (*UNEP – UN Environment Programme*, 16 August 2017) <www.unep.org/explore-topics/oceans-seas/what-we-do/addressing-land-based-pollution/governing-global-programme> accessed 19 January 2022

'Actions on Air Quality Report Update' (*UNEP – UN Environment Programme*, 25 March 2020) <www.unep.org/explore-topics/air/what-we-do/taking-stock-global-efforts/actions-air-quality-report-update> accessed 18 March 2023

'UNEP: 50 Years of Environmental Milestones' (*UNEP – UN Environment Programme*, 13 September 2021) <www.unep.org/environmental-moments-unep50-timeline> accessed 30 April 2024

'About the United Nations Environment Programme' (*UNEP – UN Environment Programme*, 2024) <www.unep.org/who-we-are/about-us> accessed 30 April 2024

UNESCO, 'One Planet, One Ocean' (UNESCO, 6 May 2013) <https://en.unesco.org/themes/one-planet-one-ocean> accessed 24 January 2022

'The Ocean We Need for the Future We Want | UNESCO' (2023) <www.unesco.org/en/ocean> accessed 20 March 2023

'The World Heritage Convention' (*UNESCO World Heritage Centre*, 2023) <https://whc.unesco.org/en/convention/> accessed 20 March 2023

'World Heritage Marine Programme' (*UNESCO World Heritage Centre*, 2023) <https://whc.unesco.org/en/marine-programme/> accessed 20 March 2023

'Ocean Decade – The Science We Need for the Ocean We Want' (Ocean Decade, 8 June 2023) <https://oceandecade.org/> accessed 4 May 2024

'Vision & Mission' (*Ocean Decade*, 8 June 2023) <https://oceandecade.org/vision-mission/> accessed 4 May 2024

'Constitution | UNESCO' (2024) <www.unesco.org/en/legal-affairs/constitution> accessed 4 May 2024

'History of UNESCO | UNESCO' (2024) <www.unesco.org/en/history> accessed 4 May 2024

'Intergovernmental Oceanographic Commission | Intergovernmental Oceanographic Commission' (2024) <www.ioc.unesco.org/en> accessed 4 May 2024

'Mission & Objectives | Intergovernmental Oceanographic Commission' (2024) <www.ioc.unesco.org/en/mission-and-objectives> accessed 4 May 2024

'Ocean Acidification | Intergovernmental Oceanographic Commission' (2024) <www.ioc.unesco.org/en/ocean-acidification> accessed 4 May 2024

'Our Expertise | UNESCO' (2024) <www.unesco.org/en/our-expertise> accessed 4 May 2024

'UNESCO in Brief | UNESCO' (2024) <www.unesco.org/en/brief> accessed 4 May 2024

'The Ocean Pavilion Announces Schedule of Events for COP27 | UNESCO' (29 April 2024) <www.unesco.org/en/articles/ocean-pavilion-announces-schedule-events-cop27> accessed 29 April 2024

'Blue Carbon | IOC UNESCO' <https://ioc.unesco.org/topics/blue-carbon> accessed 24 January 2022

UNFCCC. Secretariat, 'FCCC/PA/CMA/2021/8 – Nationally Determined Contributions under the Paris Agreement'

UNGA, 'A/RES/62/215 – Resolution Adopted by the General Assembly on 22 December 2007' <www.un.org/en/development/desa/population/migration/generalassembly/docs/globalcompact/A_RES_62_215.pdf> accessed 6 May 2024

'A/RES/63/111 – Resolution Adopted by the General Assembly on 5 December 2008' <www.un.org/en/development/desa/population/migration/generalassembly/docs/globalcompact/A_RES_63_111.pdf> accessed 6 May 2024

'A/RES/66/288 – The Future We Want' <www.un.org/en/development/desa/population/migration/generalassembly/docs/globalcompact/A_RES_66_288.pdf> accessed 6 May 2024

‘A/72/70 – Oceans and the Law of the Sea’ <https://documents.un.org/doc/undoc/gen/n17/059/35/pdf/n1705935.pdf?token=QJklJUCbxZ5zX00jP4&fe=true> accessed 8 May 2024

‘A/RES/72/73 – Oceans and the Law of the Sea’ <https://documents.un.org/doc/undoc/gen/n17/421/90/pdf/n1742190.pdf?token=uCq5igZ77kYwLxpn9E&fe=true>

‘A/68/970 – Open Working Group of the General Assembly on Sustainable Development Goals’ <https://sustainabledevelopment.un.org/content/documents/1579SDGs%20Proposal.pdf> accessed 6 May 2024

Unit B, ‘Aichi Biodiversity Targets’ (18 September 2020) <www.cbd.int/sp/targets?fbclid=IwZXh0bgNhZW0CMTAAAR0Ev7UyYKorQV7EQTn6PWLYaRJ9JbdOQBuX3_6vrdNE1E7CNGpMOPo1NW4_aem_AXP1mrxHD_o8fyjhSTm2cNrjtR6ftxpbNS8ONYIrq7pvydLMhMKv5_xWDkJvXoTQHdm3SwvPIK7JYrwrc3Kd3Ehh> accessed 3 May 2024

‘2030 Targets (with Guidance Notes)’ (2024) <www.cbd.int/gbf/targets?fbclid=IwZXh0bgNhZW0CMTAAAR1kVEpA8GTebjE0xr3ptX77yYEK3AlYwieL87FiI0N7YPAsvH4uGtZSUr4_aem_AXPK7NA2pnYXQ1DW2Pe2e0qF3MehsCBa8yuYKLbRWvIbm0s1dbv6MeiYF1cXwWtmQaLJ7XLyU3iVHcW-SYYfeveM> accessed 3 May 2024

United Nations, ‘FCCC/CP/2010/7/Add.1 – Report of the Conference of the Parties on Its Sixteenth Session, Held in Cancun from 29 November to 10 December 2010’ <https://unfccc.int/resource/docs/2010/cop16/eng/07a01.pdf> accessed 13 January 2024

‘FCCC/CP/2019/13/Add.1 – Report of the Conference of the Parties on Its Twenty-Fifth Session, Held in Madrid from 2 to 15 December 2019’ <https://unfccc.int/sites/default/files/resource/cp2019_13a01E.pdf?download> accessed 8 May 2024

‘THE 17 GOALS | Sustainable Development’ (2024) <https://sdgs.un.org/goals?fbclid=IwZXh0bgNhZW0CMTAAAR13PsXSXLin2EbvnQSLI2WF9wPAjtAMQ2L9IgNLXNUeYQc6gD67eoE0E5E_aem_Ae5chcGSmkAyBgCaVe46x08TAD9RETt7u4hIHpCxFA0VrKkkJtBv9-uRXq0MKl3Io0GFbHp5x_xtlyp39Un92PNC> accessed 7 May 2024

‘Voluntary Commitments for the Implementation of Sustainable Development Goal 14 | Department of Economic and Social Affairs’ (2024) <https://sdgs.un.org/topics/oceans-and-seas/vcs#undefined> accessed 8 May 2024

‘Ocean Commitments | Sustainable Development’ <https://sdgs.un.org/partnerships/action-networks/ocean-commitments?_gl=1*tlkgaz*_ga*Njg1NTAyNDkuMTcxNDQ3NjQxNA.*_ga_TK9BQL5X7Z*MTcxNTE1MjQ1Ny41LjEuMTcxNTE1MjkyNC4wLjAuMA.> accessed 8 May 2024

University of California, Santa Cruz and others, ‘Planning for Change: Assessing the Potential Role of Marine Protected Areas and Fisheries Management Approaches for Resilience Management in a Changing Ocean’ (2019) 32 *Oceanography* 116

Van Nes EH and others, ‘What Do You Mean, “Tipping Point”?’ (2016) 31 *Trends in Ecology & Evolution* 902

Vikas M and Dwarakish GS, ‘Coastal Pollution: A Review’ (2015) 4 *Aquatic Procedia* 381

‘Who We Are’ (*World Bank*) <www.worldbank.org/en/who-we-are> accessed 8 May 2024

Williams SJ, ‘Sea-Level Rise Implications for Coastal Regions’ (2013) 63 *Journal of Coastal Research* 184

Williamson P and Turley C, ‘Ocean Acidification in a Geoengineering Context’ (2012) 370 *Philosophical Transactions of the Royal Society A: Mathematical, Physical and Engineering Sciences* 4317

Woods Hole Oceanographic Institutions, 'First Ever Ocean-Focused Pavilion in the Blue Zone' (*www.whoi.edu/*, 29 April 2024) <www.whoi.edu/press-room/news-release/world-leaders-in-ocean-science-and-philanthropy-come-together-to-create-first-ever-ocean-pavilion-at-un-climate-conference/> accessed 29 April 2024

World Bank, 'International Development Association – Press Release No. 1' <https://timeline.worldbank.org/content/dam/sites/timeline/docs/migrated/event26-ida-pressrelease-30205492.pdf> accessed 8 May 2024

'International Development Association – Articles of Agreement' <https://thedocs.worldbank.org/en/doc/341581541440486864-0330022018/original/IDAArticlesofAgreementEnglish.pdf> accessed 8 May 2024

'International Bank for Reconstruction and Development – Articles of Agreement' <https://thedocs.worldbank.org/en/doc/722361541184234501-0330022018/original/IBRDArticlesOfAgreementEnglish.pdf> accessed 8 May 2024

World Ocean Council, 'About Us' (*World Ocean Council*, 2023) <www.oceancouncil.org/about-us/> accessed 16 March 2023

'Emerging Issues' (*World Ocean Council*, 2024) <www.oceancouncil.org/global-issues-platforms/program-focus/emerging-issues/> accessed 8 May 2024

'Mission' (*World Ocean Council*, 2024) <www.oceancouncil.org/about-us/mission/> accessed 8 May 2024

'The Organization' (*World Ocean Council*, 2024) <www.oceancouncil.org/about-us/the-organization/> accessed 8 May 2024

WWF, 'About WWF | WWF' (2024) <https://wwf.panda.org/discover/about_wwf/> accessed 3 May 2024

'Funding and Financial Overview | WWF' (*World Wildlife Fund*, 2024) <www.worldwildlife.org/about/financials> accessed 20 February 2024

'History | WWF' (*World Wildlife Fund*, 2024) <www.worldwildlife.org/about/history> accessed 3 May 2024

'How Is WWF Run?' (2024) <https://wwf.panda.org/discover/about_wwf/how_were_run/> accessed 3 May 2024

'Ocean | WWF' (2024) <https://explore.panda.org/oceans> accessed 4 May 2024

'Ocean and Climate' (2024) <https://wwf.panda.org/discover/our_focus/oceans_practice/ocean_and_climate/> accessed 4 May 2024

'WWF Statutes' (2024) <https://wwf.panda.org/discover/about_wwf/how_were_run/statutes/> accessed 3 May 2024

Yachi S and Loreau M, 'Biodiversity and Ecosystem Productivity in a Fluctuating Environment: The Insurance Hypothesis' (1999) 96 *Proceedings of the National Academy of Sciences* 1463

Yamamoto-Kawai M and others, 'Aragonite Undersaturation in the Arctic Ocean: Effects of Ocean Acidification and Sea Ice Melt' (2009) 326 *Science* (New York, N.Y.) 1098

Yuewen D and Adzigbli L, 'Assessing the Impact of Oil Spills on Marine Organisms' (2018) 06 Journal of Oceanography and Marine Research <www.omicsonline.org/open-access/assessing-the-impact-of-oil-spills-on-marine-organisms-2572-3103-1000179-102276.html> accessed 18 March 2021

Zachos JC and others, 'Rapid Acidification of the Ocean during the Paleocene-Eocene Thermal Maximum' (2005) 308 *Science* 1611

Zeitlin J (ed), *Extending Experimentalist Governance? The European Union and Transnational Regulation* (1st ed., Oxford University Press 2015)

Zulian M, PhD candidate in the Ocean Climate Lab at UC Davis & Bodega Marine Lab

Agreement for the Implementation of the Provisions of the United Nations Convention on the Law of the Sea of 10 December 1982 Relating to the Conservation and Management of Straddling Fish Stocks and Highly Migratory Fish Stocks (UN Fish Stocks Agreement) 1995 (UNTS vol. 2167, p 3)

Agreement under the United Nations Convention on the Law of the Sea on the Conservation and Sustainable Use of Marine Biological Diversity of Areas beyond National Jurisdiction 2023

Amendments to the Convention on the International Maritime Organization Relating to the Institutionalization of the Committee on Technical Co-operation in the Convention 1877 (UNTS 1380 (p268))

Biodiversity and Climate Change: C: Ocean Fertilization 2008 (UNEP/CBD/COP/DEC/9/16)

Constitution of the United Nations Educational, Scientific and Cultural Organization 1945 (UNTS 4 (p275))

Convention Concerning the Protection of the World Cultural and Natural Heritage 1972 (UNTS 1037 (p151))

Convention for the Protection of the Marine Environment of the North-East Atlantic 1992 (2354 UNTS 67)

Convention on Biological Diversity 1992 (1760 UNTS 79)

Convention on International Civil Aviation 1944 (UNTS 15 (p295))

Convention on the Conservation of Migratory Species of Wild Animals 1979 (UNTS 1651)

Convention on the International Maritime Organization 1948 (UNTS 289 (p3))

Convention on the Prevention of Marine Pollution by Dumping of Wastes and Other Matter 1972 (1046 UNTS120)

Convention on Wetlands of International Importance Especially as Waterfowl Habitat 1971 (UNTS 996 (p245))

Draft agreement under the United Nations Convention on the Law of the Sea on the conservation and Sustainable Use of Marine Biological Diversity of Areas beyond National Jurisdiction 2023

International Convention for the Prevention of Pollution from Ships, 1973, as modified by the Protocol of 1978 (MARPOL 73/78) 1973 (UNTS 1340 (p61), 1341 (p3))

Kyoto Protocol to the United Nations Framework Convention on Climate Change 1997 (2303 UNTS 3)

London Protocol to the Convention on the Prevention of Marine Pollution by Dumping and Other Matter 1996 (36 ILM 1 (1977))

Manado Ocean Declaration 2009

Montreal Protocol on Substances that Deplete the Ozone Layer (with annex) 1987 (UNTS vol. 1522)

OSPAR Decision 2007/1 to Prohibit the Storage of Carbon Dioxide Streams in the Water Column or on the Sea-bed 2007 (Decision 2007/1)

OSPAR Decision 2007/2 on the Storage of Carbon Dioxide Streams in Geological Formations 2007 (Decision 2007/2)

Paris Agreement 2015 (UNTS vol. 3156)

Statute of the International Atomic Energy Agency 1956 (UNTS 276 (p3))

United Nations Charter 1945

United Nations Convention on the Law of the Sea (UNCLOS) 1982

United Nations Framework Convention on Climate Change 1992 (1771 UNTS 107)

INDEX

Printed in the United Kingdom by TJ Clays Ltd.